THE

Cold War Romance

OF

Lillian Hellman

AND

John Melby

John Melby in the 1940s

Lillian Hellman in the 1940s

Lillian Hellman and John Melby at a conference on the McCarthy era spon-sored by the Committee of Concerned Asian Scholars at the Glide Memorial Church, San Francisco, California, April 1970. © Ilka Hartmann, 1970.

THE
Cold War Romance
O F
Lillian Hellman
A N D
John Melby

Robert P. Newman

The University of North Carolina Press / Chapel Hill & London

Library of Congress Cataloging-in-Publication Data

Newman, Robert P.
The Cold War romance of Lillian Hellman and John Melby / by Robert
P. Newman.
p.   cm.
Bibliography: p.
Includes index.
ISBN 0-8078-1815-1 (alk. paper)
1. Hellman, Lillian, 1906–1984. —Relations with men—John Melby.
2. Melby, John F. (John Fremont), 1913– . 3. Dramatists,
American—20th century—Biography. 4. Diplomats—United States—
Biography. 5. World politics—1945– . I. Title.
PS3515.E343Z8   1989
812'.52—dc19   88-22659
[B]   CIP

Excerpts from *An Unfinished Woman, Pentimento, Scoundrel Time, Three,* and the introduction to
The Big Knockover and from unpublished letters of Lillian Hellman are used with the permission
of the Literary Property Trustees under the Will of Lillian Hellman, the proprietor of the
copyright in such materials. No reproduction or quotation from such materials is permitted
without the written approval of the Trustees.

John Hersey's tribute to Lillian Hellman in a speech to the American Academy and Institute of
Arts and Letters was published in *Proceedings of the American Academy and Institute of Art and
Letters,* second series, no. 35 (1984), and excerpts are used here with permission of John
Hersey and the Academy.

After the publication of this book, letters from Lillian Hellman to John Melby will be deposited in
the Lillian Hellman Collection, Humanities Research Center, University of Texas, Austin, Texas,
and letters from John Melby's private papers will be deposited in the Harry S. Truman Library,
Independence, Missouri.

The paper in this book meets the guidelines for permanence and durability of the Committee on
Production Guidelines for Book Longevity of the Council on Library Resources.

Printed in the United States of America

93 92 91 90 89   5 4 3 2 1

To
John G. Adams, Esq.
Counselor, U.S. Army 1953–55,
who blew the whistle on Joe McCarthy

contents

Lillian Hellman's memoirs are notable not just for the entrancing stories she tells, but for what she does not tell. The friends and relatives she wrote about were all dead; there are no accounts of anyone still alive and close to her. Indeed, of the forty-four persons Hellman mentions in her will, which was opened in 1984, only four appear anywhere in her memoirs. Mostly she describes friends such as Dashiell Hammett, Henry Wallace, Dorothy Parker, Ernest Hemingway, Julia, Sergei Eisenstein, Arthur W. A. Cowan, and various relatives, none of whom were still around to read what she wrote about them. About her enemies, she is not so reticent; Richard Nixon receives a full measure of obloquy at her hands.

Of her many romantic affairs, only those with Arthur Kober (who was for five years her husband) and Dashiell Hammett receive any attention in her books. Her tempestuous affair with Ralph Ingersoll is never mentioned. She hints at others: in *An Unfinished Woman*, she notes that, although she kept an extensive diary of her Moscow trip in the winter of 1944–45, "Nowhere is there a record of how much I came to love, still love Raya, the remarkable young girl who was my translator-guide. Nor how close I felt then and now to a State Department career man whose future, seven or eight years later, went down the drain for no reason except the brutal cowardice of his colleagues under the hammering of Joe McCarthy."

The State Department career man is John Fremont Melby. Lillian's affair with John was one of her most intense romantic involvements. This book is the story of that affair, which began in November 1944 and never really ended. It is also the untold story of Lillian's involvement with arms of the inquisition other than the House Un-American Activities Committee (HUAC), such as the FBI, the Passport Office, the State Department Security Office, and various anonymous informers. Thirdly, this is the story of how John Melby was fired because of his association with Lillian. These stories intertwine.

I first met John Melby in 1976, when I was working on an analysis of the *China White Paper* of 1949; John was the principal author of that document. He told me then that he had been fired from the State Department by John Foster Dulles in 1953 because of a romantic affair with Lillian Hellman.

This did not connect with my major concerns at the time, and I did not pursue it.

My interest in the origins of the Cold War continued, however, and since John served in Moscow (1943 to 1945) and China (1945 to 1948), I kept in touch with him. Eventually I began to question him about the Hellman affair. It was fascinating.

As what follows will make clear, there were good reasons why John's firing never became public, and why Lillian did not mention it, or indeed her long affair with John, in her memoirs. However, it is a story that both John and I believed should be told—sometime. With the reinstatement of John's security clearance in 1980, one of the reasons for withholding this story disappeared. With Lillian's death in 1984, there seemed no longer to be cause for silence.

Despite the intensity and duration of their affair, John and Lillian were together very little: he was in Moscow, San Francisco, China, or Washington while she was in New York, Martha's Vineyard, or Europe. Consequently they wrote many letters, especially in the first five years of their relationship. When the inquisition descended in 1952, Lillian was afraid that someone would ask about and subpoena any letters she had from John. In order to be able to say truthfully that she had none, she insisted that they exchange the letters they had written each other. She subsequently destroyed her letters; fortunately John preserved his. Much of the story of the early years of their romance is reconstructed from the 588 pages of letters he wrote her between 1945 and 1949. Many of Lillian's letters to John between 1953 and 1978 survive, however, and the story of their later years depends heavily on Lillian's letters.

This is a tale of politics, personality, passion. As far as possible I have used the exact words of the participants. Readers who did not live through the Scoundrel Time of midcentury will find it difficult to believe that the United States was so gripped by hysteria. I invite serious skeptics to share the FBI files, transcripts of loyalty-security hearings, passport records, and other primary documents that provide the facts of the Hellman-Melby story. It is a classic case of "guilt" by association.

University of Pittsburgh
December 1987

❦ a c k n o w l e d g m e n t s ❦

My greatest debt is to John Melby. Over ten years, I have recorded dozens of hours of interviews with him, exchanged countless letters, and happily discussed the foibles of mankind many more hours when the tape recorder was not running. He and his wife, Roxana, have provided gracious hospitality many times at their home in Canada.

John has provided most of the material from which this book was written, primarily the 588 typewritten single-spaced pages he wrote Lillian, and the 669 pages of his loyalty-security hearings. He has also provided hundreds of letters to family and friends, his State Department security file, and his FBI file. The United States Government has provided (somewhat unwillingly) Lillian Hellman's FBI file, her passport file, and Louis Budenz's FBI file. Carl Rollyson, whose help has been monumental, has provided more information about Lillian than I could have gotten even if that *grande dame* had been able and willing to talk to me in her last irascible years.

Friends and students have given invaluable critiques of various drafts of the manuscript. I am indebted to all of them: John G. Adams, Barbara Biesecker, Mary Briscoe, John Paton Davies, Patricia Grady Davies, Kathleen Farrell, Richard M. Fried, Thomas Kane, Bill McLean, Trevor Melia, Richard Moreland, Star Muir, Eleanor Jackson Piel, Linda Tunnell, and Tom Wanko. My wife, Dale, has borne patiently the long preoccupation with this story.

No book about midcentury America could be written without the resources of a major library. The staff of Hillman Library of the University of Pittsburgh has cooperated in my research far beyond the call of duty: Jean Aiken, Ruth Carter, Pat Colbert, Mary Dimmick, Ingrid Glasco, Ann Gordon, Oxanna Kaufman, Mary Beth Miller, Marcella McGrogan, Norry Rossell, Adelaide Sukiennik, Phil Wilken, and Frank Zabrosky.

There are always gaps in the documents, and many of these were filled by busy people who consented to talk to me: Alan Barth, Michael J. Deutch, Samuel R. Gammon, Stephen Gillers, John Hersey, Ring Lardner, Jr., Robert A. Lovett, Kathleen Harriman Mortimer, James O'Sullivan, Linus Pauling, Jim Peck, Joseph Rauh, Jr., Albert Ravenholt, Dean Rusk, Orville Schell, Robert Silvers, Joseph Volpe, Jr., and Adam Watson.

Finally, I owe immense gratitude to friends who provided hospitality and sustenance while I was interviewing and using archival resources away from Pittsburgh: Bob and Sue Ainsworth, Bernard and Sue Duffy, Bruce and Wendy Gronbeck, Dan and Harriet Levitt, Alan and Alva Reeves, Tom and Mary Ann Rishel, Don Ritchie, Neil Smith, Paul and Elaine Tendler, Phil and Esther Wander, Jim and Chris Watkins. Equally helpful were Janet McCarthy, Sally Samuels, and Tracy Turner, who took my execrable scrawl and made it readable.

T H E

Cold War Romance

O F

Lillian Hellman

A N D

John Melby

Hellman's Road to Moscow

Lillian Hellman arrived in Moscow on 5 November 1944, on a "cultural mission" to our heroic wartime allies. She had come from Fairbanks in a frigid C-47, flown by a Russian crew that was ordered to take no chances with bad weather because of their important passenger. Since the weather was bad, they spent much time on the ground at primitive Siberian airports. This meant uncomfortable days and nights, inappropriate medicines for Lillian's various ills, and a bad case of pneumonia.

An Unfinished Woman describes this trip, and her ten weeks in Russia, extensively.[1] But she does not tell us much about why she went to the Soviet Union, why the Russians invited her, why the American government allowed her to go, or what resulted from the trip.

We know, from her passport file released in 1985, that twice before the Russian trip, Lillian was denied a passport because of alleged Communist activities.[2] On 28 April 1943, Passport Chief Ruth Shipley rejected her application for a passport to go to England with this notation: "Reason for refusal: Reported to be an active Communist. Refer any application to Fraud Section." Lillian was not told why the application was rejected.

Again, on 12 May 1944, Shipley rejected Lillian's request for a passport despite a supporting letter from Metro-Goldwyn-Mayer, who wanted her in England to work on a British Ministry of War Information production of Tolstoy's *War and Peace*. This time, her passport file included a lengthy report by "our friends"—meaning the FBI—to the effect that Lillian was "one of the key figures in the Communist Party," but Shipley did not tell her this. Shipley's letter to MGM attributes the refusal to "the present military situation."

But ten weeks later, when Lillian again asked for a passport, valid this time for travel to the Soviet Union, supporting her request with an invitation from Voks (the Soviet organization for cultural relations with foreign countries), Shipley speedily complied. Lillian's request was dated 31 July

1944; the passport was issued on 14 August. Clearly, where approval came so quickly, some superior authority was leaning on the Passport Office.

The Lillian Hellman who went to the Soviet Union in 1944 was many things: a passionate and emancipated woman with one marriage and many affairs behind her; a brilliant and witty conversationalist; a prickly, cantankerous adversary of anyone who crossed her; an esteemed playwright; a supporter of the Roosevelt New Deal; a Communist fellow traveler; but above all, an antifascist of burning intensity.

She was born in 1905 in New Orleans, of German-Jewish stock.[3] In 1912, her family moved to New York, and Lillian divided her time during the next ten years between New York and New Orleans, where she stayed with relatives. She was an only child, tempestuous, governable only by Sophronia, a black servant in New Orleans, whom she describes lovingly in her memoirs.

From 1922 to 1924 she enrolled at New York University, dropping out to work as a manuscript reader for the publisher Horace Liveright. Liveright's operation was prestigious and exciting; she met and mingled with many of the glamorous writers of the 1920s. She also met a not-so-glamorous but capable writer, Arthur Kober, by whom she became pregnant. She did not think pregnancy, nor the physical attraction which led to it, sufficient grounds for marriage; she had an abortion. But the attraction was strong, Kober was a likable fellow, and in 1925 they were married.

In 1927, Kober got an editing job in Paris. Lillian went with him, and acquired the taste for foreign travel that took her across the Atlantic so many times. She wrote some short stories while in Europe, and Kober published them, but neither he nor she thought them very good. Paris was not to her taste; she and Kober were not part of the intellectual ferment there, and Lillian journeyed off frequently by herself, enjoying Italy and the French Riviera and having occasional affairs which Kober did nothing to discourage. After six months, she left Kober and came back to New York.

She took various low-level literary jobs, but they did not energize her. Kober returned to New York, and they lived together for a while; but for four months during the winter of 1928–29, she left him again to work as a publicist for a stock company in Rochester. There she made enough money, allegedly playing cards, to finance a trip to Europe on her own. In the summer of 1929, intending to study in Bonn, she fell in with some young Nazis. At first, their brand of "socialism" appealed to her. When she learned of their controlling anti-Semitism, she recoiled. She says she left for home the next day. This was the beginning of her lifelong hatred of fascism.

Kober was glad to see her back in New York. They lived in "a beat-up old house on Long Island," which she liked, and they watched with growing concern the stock market crash, the tragedies of the depression, the burgeoning despair and poverty. But Kober was fortunate. In February 1930 he was offered $450 a week to write movie scripts in Hollywood. It was a magnificent sum in those days; he could not turn it down despite Lillian's objections to moving. He went to Hollywood alone; she followed him after several months, reluctantly.

It was in Hollywood that she met the most consequential man in her life: Dashiell Hammett. Hammett was, in November 1930, on the basis of his third novel, *The Maltese Falcon*, a literary light of major importance. How and when she met him are in dispute; what happened thereafter is not. They formed an attachment that lasted, in some form, until he died thirty-one years later. She left Kober, later divorcing him, for a new world of literary and political commitment. Hammett was a Marxist, and eventually joined the Communist party.

This is not to say that politics immediately became important to Lillian. Her relationship with Hammett was physical and spiritual. He was handsome, intelligent, worldly-wise, and when sober, kind and thoughtful. He became her mentor, goading and guiding her to the achievements of her playwriting career.[4] And he did gradually influence her politics. As a Pinkerton operative in Montana, he had been offered five thousand dollars to kill labor organizer Frank Little; this incident of capitalist cruelty conditioned his view of society for the rest of his life. Eventually, repelled by the suffering during the depression, Lillian came to share his concerns. But not his commitment.

Living with Hammett was not easy. While he clearly loved Lillian, he was incapable of being faithful, or even moderately discreet. Alcohol and prostitutes were addictions that no conceivable romantic attachment could rid him of. And when drunk, he was ugly. Their years together were tempestuous. Despite the casualness of her relations with Kober, Lillian now discovered that she became intensely jealous when Hammett went on one of his whoring escapades. She responded by having affairs of her own, some of them major, partly to pay him back.

Their affair was not entirely turbulent. They spent long periods in relative solitude, in Florida and on the Connecticut shore. During these periods of seclusion, both of them produced remarkable achievements. During their first four years together—by 1934—Hammett wrote *The Thin Man*, probably his best novel, and Lillian wrote *The Children's Hour*, which took Broadway by storm and made her a celebrity in her own right. It was the beginning for her, and the end for him. He never finished another book. She went on to a succession of triumphs and honors. Neither even suspected, at the time, that it would be that way.

In 1935, Lillian and Hammett were again in Hollywood; she was working on the screen play of *The Children's Hour*, produced as a movie called *These Three*. It went well, but living with Hammett in the Hollywood environment was nothing like living with him in some Florida hideaway. There was too much drinking, by both of them. Hammett's binges were always nasty, and she was constantly fighting with him and going off somewhere to recover her equilibrium. By summer 1935 she had finished *These Three*; feeling that she could no longer stand Hammett, she took a plane for New York. It was a fateful trip.

Ralph Ingersoll was on the same plane.[5] He had been in Hollywood on an assignment for Henry Luce, preparing a story for *Fortune*, where Ingersoll was a rising star. The plane was forced by a dust storm to stop overnight in Albuquerque; Ingersoll and Lillian met while disembarking. Their mutual attraction was immediate, and immediately gratified. Lillian fell in love with Ingersoll, and Hammett was forgotten for a while. Ingersoll, however, was married to a woman with tuberculosis. When he told his wife that he was in love with Lillian and wanted a divorce, her TB flared up. Ingersoll's conscience did not permit him to desert an ailing wife; so he went back to her. Her condition rapidly improved. Then he went back to Lillian. There were several such reunions and departures.

Had Ingersoll been free to marry Lillian, the Hellman story might have been quite different. But she learned from this affair that even an intense romantic involvement was no guarantee of a successful long-term relationship, and that marriage created for some men obligations that they could not cast aside. By the summer of 1936, when she rented a house on Tavern Island, Dash was back with her. The affair with Ingersoll was not entirely over. Ingersoll describes several visits to the Hellman-Hammett establishment. And Ingersoll threw a memorable cast party for *Days to Come* on 15 December 1936 at his bachelor quarters. The play was an utter failure; Lillian was drunk, sick, and disillusioned.[6] After the failure of *Days to Come*, Lillian went back to Hollywood, leaving Hammett alone in Princeton to wreck his rented house and scandalize his neighbors.[7]

Lillian's liaison with Ingersoll resulted in more than disenchantment with married men; it sharpened the political consciousness she had been developing by contact with Hammett and the increasingly left-wing Hollywood community. The fascism that she had first encountered in Germany was now ascendant, and Roosevelt's New Deal was solving neither the depression nor the threat of the Nazis. Francisco Franco had obtained the help of Hitler and Mussolini in his revolt against the legitimately elected government of Spain, and the anti-Franco sentiment of the American public was growing. Ingersoll and Lillian discussed these developments extensively.

Ingersoll's account of Lillian's political stance during this period is crucial to understanding her later activities. She was well aware of the shortcomings of both American capitalism and Soviet communism. She insisted that these were the only systems available; Ingersoll insisted that he would "invent" a new system that would avoid the ills of both. Two years after the notorious cast party for *Days to Come*, when Ingersoll was preparing for his innovative and crusading new newspaper *PM*, his prospectus clearly reflected these arguments with Lillian: "We do not believe all mankind's problems are solved in any existing social order, certainly not our own, and we propose to applaud those who seek constructively to improve the way men live."[8]

Lillian's own ambivalence about any panacea for mankind's ills is clearly reflected in *Days to Come*.[9] This, her second play, deals with labor strife in a small Ohio town. If she were to inject Marxist theory into any of her plays, this would have been the one. Her characters agonize over the dilemmas of adjusting legitimate owner interests to the equally legitimate needs of workers. If anything, she seems more attuned to the managers of the family-owned business. There is not a whiff of left-wing ideology in the play. Communist sources denounced it.

By 1937, Francisco Franco was getting an abundance of planes, tanks, and "volunteers" from the Axis powers: 17 thousand volunteers from Germany, including enough fliers to form the infamous Condor Legion; and approximately 75 thousand Italians, many of them veterans of Mussolini's conquest of Ethiopia.[10] Britain, France, and the United States remained neutral. Only the Soviet Union came to the aid of the Spanish Republic. Lillian now began her most intense series of Communist-front involvements in the many organizations favoring the Loyalists in the Spanish Civil War.

The Spanish Civil War was a seminal event for Americans. Not even the invasion of Ethiopia or the Japanese pillage of Manchuria seemed as prophetic of future conflict with the fascist powers. Allen Guttmann introduces *The Wound in the Heart*, his analysis of American reaction to the Spanish Civil War, with the claim that "no public event of the years between 1919 and 1939—excepting the Great Depression itself—moved Americans as did this Spanish conflict."[11] Americans felt the Spanish drama as a "personal tragedy," and it became "the last great cause." In *An Unfinished Woman*, Hellman offers a similar judgment: "Never before and never since in my lifetime were liberals, radicals, intellectuals, and the educated middle class to come together in single, forceful alliance."[12]

An opinion poll of December 1938 showed that 76 percent of the sample favored the Republican cause over that of Franco.[13] Despite this overwhelming preference, the United States government remained neutral. Not all American officials agreed with neutrality; Secretary of the Treasury Morgenthau tried to aid the Republic by buying its silver, in the teeth of opposition from John Foster Dulles and his partners at Sullivan and Cromwell, who were agents for Franco. Roosevelt was unyielding; isolationism was still strong in Congress, and the Catholic hierarchy, including Roosevelt's ally Cardinal Spellman, supported Franco.[14]

Government neutrality did not prevent the American Communist party from organizing volunteers to fight on the side of the Republic, nor from raising funds to provide those volunteers with transportation and minor equipment. Three thousand men, about 60 percent of them Communists, accepted the challenge to fight in Spain. They became part of the Abraham Lincoln Battalion or Brigade, which, with counterparts from Canada, Britain, France, the Balkans, and even Germany and Italy, formed the International Brigades.[15] Lillian gave the Lincolns her total support.

Item number two in the first FBI report on Lillian notes her participation in a fund raiser for the Friends of the Abraham Lincoln Brigade.[16] That, and other similar organizations are mentioned eighteen times in the nine-page summary report on Hellman in September 1941.[17] J. Edgar Hoover was a Franco supporter, and anyone who favored the Republic was on his list of subversives. It was, and still is, an article of faith of the American right wing that anybody who supported the Spanish Republic was at least a party member if not worse.[18]

This "subversive" cause enlisted some very conservative people. Sidney Hook, a confirmed anti-Communist, wanted to send a socialist volunteer group to fight against Franco, but the socialists were not well enough organized to bring this off. When the German Condor Legion bombed the Basque town of Guernica on 26 April 1937, Governor Alf Landon of Kansas, Colonel Theodore Roosevelt of Oyster Bay, Charles Taft II, and Senator William E. Borah all signed a letter condemning the atrocity.[19] When money was needed to bring wounded Abraham Lincoln Brigade veterans home from Spain in 1938, Mr. and Mrs. Henry Luce contributed $450; the financier Bernard Baruch put up $10,000.[20]

Communists spearheaded the effort to support the Spanish Republic, but vast numbers of non-Communists opposed Franco for their own reasons. Toward the end of the McCarthy madness, in 1955, even the Subversive Activities Control Board (SACB), charged by Congress with identifying disloyal organizations, concluded about those who fought against Franco: "The record shows that some Americans fought there on behalf of the Republic out of motivations alien to Communist purposes." Nonetheless, SACB cited Veterans of the Abraham Lincoln Brigade as subversive.[21] Not until October 1972 was the attorney general of the United States forced by a decision of the U.S. Court of Appeals in Washington to take Veterans of the Abraham Lincoln Brigade off his list of subversive organizations.[22]

Soviet influence in the Spanish Civil War was strong and ultimately iniquitous, as readers of George Orwell's *Homage to Catalonia* know. But the cause was viewed by most Americans, foremost among them Lillian Hellman, as just.

When Archibald MacLeish suggested to Lillian that she join him and other opponents of Franco in organizing to produce an anti-Franco film, she agreed, and they formed the organization Contemporary Historians to finance the film. Ernest Hemingway, Dorothy Parker, Hammett, and others put up the $13,000 needed. Hellman says that she went to Europe early in 1937 to help the Dutch film maker Joris Ivens produce *The Spanish Earth*, the only project of Contemporary Historians, but she got pneumonia and never reached Ivens.[23]

Lillian got to see *The Spanish Earth* on 10 July 1937, in the home of Fredric March. Hemingway was there, and made a speech soliciting contributions to the Republican cause. Lillian is derogatory about Hemingway's performance in her memoirs, and misdates the showing of the film to 1938. Others who were present thought Hemingway was very effective.[24]

In August 1937, Lillian again went to Europe, this time in the company of Dorothy Parker and her husband, Alan Campbell. Hellman was invited to a theater festival in Moscow; she suggested to Hammett that he might like to go along. He had never been to Europe, and his refusal to travel abroad was one of the enduring issues that led to friction between them. So she went without him, for the lengthy and controversial trip which she described in her memoirs.

Her 1937 visit to Europe began with several weeks in Paris. In contrast to her earlier stay in Paris with Kober, she was now a celebrity and kept company with celebrities, among them Hemingway and the Gerald Murphys. After about a month in Paris, she took the train to Moscow. Her memoirs give varying versions of this trip, one of which (the Julia story) seems largely invented.[25] In Russia, she was bored by the theater festival, had few contacts with Russians, acquired an active dislike for diplomats, and claims she was unaware of the purge trials then going on. After Moscow, she spent several weeks in Prague, about which visit we know nothing. She then went back to Paris.

In Paris she was persuaded that she had to visit Spain, to see the war first hand. Her accounts of this part of her trip, too, are highly controversial. Martha Gellhorn has gone to great lengths to show that the *Unfinished Woman* version could not have happened the way Lillian describes it; the travel logistics just don't add up.[26] Everyone agrees that Lillian was in Spain, that the experience deepened her antifascism, and that she subsequently supported the cause of the Lincolns even more vigorously than before. There the agreement stops.

After Spain, and an "unpleasant" few weeks in Paris, she went to London. There she dined with an old friend, met some snobbish and profascist aristocrats, and broke her ankle. She was immobilized for some time in a London hotel room. Her description of what happened then is significant.

> Nothing, of course, begins at the time you think it did, but for many years I have thought of those days in the lonely London hotel room as the root-time of my turn toward the radical movements of the late thirties. (I was late: by that period many intellectuals had made the turn. So many, in fact, that some were even turning another way.) It saddens me now to admit that my political convictions were never very radical, in the true, best, serious sense. Rebels seldom make good revolutionaries, perhaps because organized action, even union with other people, is not possible for them. But I did not know that then and so I sat down to confirm my feelings with the kind of reading I had never seriously done before. In the next few years, I put aside most other books for Marx and Engels, Lenin, Saint-Simon, Hegel, Feuerbach. Certainly I did not study with the attention of a good student, and Marx as a man and Engels and his Mary became, for a while, more real to me than my friends.[27]

What Lillian does not say in this passage is that part of her reading of Marxist works during those years was with an informal "study group," affiliated with the Communist party. During John Melby's interrogation by a State Department Loyalty-Security Board in 1952, the following dialogue took place:

Q: Mr. Melby, did you in 1952 ask Miss Hellman if she were a Communist?

A: Yes, in 1952.

Q: What did she say?

A: She said no.

Q: Had you ever asked her before?

A: I asked her in 1945.

Q: Where?

A: In the States, when I was back here.

Q: What was her reply?

A: She said no.

Q: Mr. Melby, did you ever ask Miss Hellman if she had ever been a member of the Communist Party?

A: Yes, and she said that—this was in 1945, well in 1952 she repeated it again, that in the period of 1938 and 1939 she had been interested in a small Marxist study group of intellectuals in New York, that she presumed that during that brief period that constituted membership, but that was her only connection with the Party, that she dropped out of this group sometime in 1939. And when she was writing *Watch on the Rhine* she had never had anything to do with the group since then or with any other group that she knew to be a Communist group, nor had she ever again been approached by them on those grounds. . . .

Q: She told you both in 1945 and 1952 that since the termination of the 1939 experience she had had no further affiliation or contact with groups, did I understand you to say, of that sort?

A: Groups she knew to be Communist groups. She said obviously some of them had Communists in them.[28]

What led Lillian to the reading of Marxist literature, and participation in a study group, was her exposure to the Spanish Civil War.

She wrote, in *Pentimento*, that she spent two weeks in Helsinki in 1937, where she was outraged at pro-Hitler signs and sentiment; but she does not mention this journey in *Unfinished Woman*, and her enemies deny that she could have been there at all. Lacking her diaries, we cannot know. Nor do we know when she returned to New York from the 1937 trip; her passport file is surprisingly blank on the whole matter.

Lillian's new political consciousness caused her to sign a manifesto in 1938 which later led to the charges of Stalinism against her. In 1936, Stalin began accusing both party and military leaders in his regime of cooperating with Leon Trotsky and the Nazis to destroy Bolshevism. Trotsky, exiled and living in first Norway, then Mexico, was not the root cause of Stalin's purges; Stalin was basically eliminating potential rivals for power, and Trotsky was a convenient focal point for his purges. In the early trials, prominent Bolsheviks abjectly confessed to anti-Stalin plots and sabotage; they were all found guilty and executed. In later purges, there were no show trials; the accused were simply shot.

Early American reactions to the trials were generally favorable to Stalin. Even the *New York Times* seemed to accept the verdicts.[29] A gigantic frame-up, with all the confessions procured by torture and brainwashing, as Khrushchev later revealed, was hard to believe. The newspaper correspondents who originally accepted the trials at face value were not entirely naive. Trotsky, the anti-Stalinist leader, was hardly a hero to liberal democrats. His main quarrel with Stalin was over the emphasis to be put on worldwide revolution: Trotsky thought that the Soviet Union should actively promote it, while Stalin preferred to first build socialism in Russia. Trotsky was a revolutionary firebrand, Stalin a Great Russian nationalist.

Most American liberals supported Stalin; so did some rock-ribbed conservatives. One of the latter was Newton D. Baker, who, as American secretary of war in 1918, had ordered United States troops into Siberia to fight the Bolsheviks.[30]

In the Communist *New Masses* of 3 May 1938, 138 Americans put their signatures to "The Moscow Trials: A Statement by American Progressives." The signers of this statement included many Communists: Louis Francis Budenz signed it, and Dashiell Hammett. But some, including Lillian, were not Communists. The text of the statement makes clear that the signers' pro-Soviet attitude was conditioned by Soviet resistance to Hitler, by Soviet attempts to improve the living conditions of Russians, and by Soviet efforts to strengthen the League of Nations as a force for peace. Lillian's signature on this document is neither surprising nor damning; it is precisely what one would expect of a person whose prime motivation was antifascism.

Lillian's 1938 political activities also included active participation in all the efforts to support Loyalist Spain. But these efforts did not dominate her life that year. She was hurting badly from the failure of *Days to Come*, determined to write another serious play, and indefatigable in her efforts. Hammett helped her; she credits him with a major role in the success of her next play, *The Little Foxes*.[31] This drama also addresses social issues that were important to Lillian: human greed and avarice. These were not, at the moment, themes emphasized by her left-wing friends, nor does *The Little Foxes* have a socialist slant to it. Hammett possibly could have steered her toward a general repudiation of capitalism in the play, but there is no evidence that he tried. What he helped her to write was a drama about predatory southerners who resemble her New Orleans family. The play was a smash hit. She bought her beloved Hardscrabble Farm in Pleasantville, New York, with the profits.

She also, despite Hammett's selfless contribution to her writing, had an affair with Herman Shumlin, director of *The Little Foxes*, during the run of the play. This is surprising; her bond with Hammett seemed strong enough at the time to preclude such a liaison.

Shortly before *The Little Foxes* opened in Baltimore on 2 February 1939, Hammett and Lillian worked with Ingersoll on his plans for *PM*, which had a long gestation period and did not finally appear until June 1940. Hammett screened most of the applicants for writing positions and read all the copy for the early issues.[32] Hellman's FBI file records an unknown informant's claim that she was to write a series of articles for *PM* attacking the FBI; the Bureau checked this out thoroughly and found no truth to it.[33] Hammett continued working for Ingersoll for a month after the newspaper appeared. He quit in a huff when Ingersoll published a naive piece acknowledging charges that *PM* had a Communist cell among its staff.[34]

With *The Little Foxes* running smoothly, Lillian turned to a theme which, despite her protestations that she had no use for political drama, emerged as one of her most anti-Soviet acts: *Watch on the Rhine* was, and still is, a powerful encomium to those who opposed Hitler. She began *Watch* in early 1939, when the Soviet Union was still desperately trying to persuade the Western democracies to join in an anti-Hitler campaign. But on 23 August 1939, Stalin did an about-face, signing a nonaggression pact with Hitler, which pact led on 1 September to the joint German-Soviet invasion of Poland, and to World War II. This reversal of Soviet policy threw the American Communist party into turmoil. Members resigned in droves. Those who remained were obliged to show their loyalty to Stalin by abruptly dropping their pleas for antifascist solidarity, and by taking up a new line opposing American involvement in the European war. The Party now formed the American Peace Mobilization, picketing the White House because of Roosevelt's rearmament policies and his efforts to support Britain.

Lillian's position on the Hitler-Stalin pact is puzzling. The testimony of some of her friends is that she supported the pact.[35] She signed the call to the Fourth National Congress of the League of American Writers in June 1941; an antiwar statement accompanied this call. One informant (name denied) told the FBI that she had helped pay for American Peace Mobilization pickets at the White House; this the Bureau checked out and found to be false.[36]

How could she have followed the Communist party line in this fashion while she was writing *Watch on the Rhine*? Possibly she supported the pact, and the League of American Writers, out of loyalty to Hammett and other left-wing friends.

She wrote *Watch* in 1940, mostly at the Pleasantville farm, after conducting extensive research into the European antifascist movement from which she draws the hero of the play. Hammett apparently played no role in this script. He was beginning to sense that his own writing career was finished, and was visiting Manhattan bars and brothels more frequently, which visits a year later led to the end of his sexual relations with Lillian.

Watch opened on 1 April 1941; it was a great success. The Communist press panned it. After Hitler attacked the Soviet Union on 21 June 1941, the Party reversed itself again: *Watch* became acceptable.[37] Lillian was unmoved. She was nobody's girl: she wrote what she felt and thought, and not even Hammett attempted to get her to pull her punches.

Lillian began psychoanalysis with Dr. Gregory Zilboorg in 1940. She was disturbed by her own heavy drinking, appalled by Hammett's, and uneasy because of her frequent flashes of anger. She became a close friend of Zilboorg; he was privy to all her affairs, disappointments, triumphs, and rages for the next decade.

Pearl Harbor seemed to Lillian to validate all her antifascist sentiments. When Hitler and Mussolini declared war on the United States, she joined vigorously in mobilization activities. So did Hammett; to Lillian's surprise, he joined the army in September 1942, at the age of forty-eight, and with weakened lungs due to an earlier bout of tuberculosis. He told Lillian the day of his induction that it was the happiest day of his life. He did not see combat, spending most of his enlistment in Alaska. He missed Lillian, and also the fleshpots of New York.

With Hammett gone, Lillian threw herself into writing and speaking in support of the war. One of her appearances, a prowar rally on 16 October 1942, got into her FBI files.[38] She called for the opening of a second front in Europe, a cause dear to the heart of the Kremlin. That many highly patriotic Americans also pushed a second front did not make that cause acceptable to the FBI. If the Soviets wanted it, J. Edgar Hoover was against it. It had to be a subversive cause.

Similar notice was taken of her next writing effort. Lillian describes in *Unfinished Woman* the genesis of her first script written exclusively for a movie: *North Star*. Samuel Goldwyn suggested that she and William Wyler do a movie about the impact of the war on Soviet citizens. Surprisingly, the Russians gave permission for her and Wyler to go to Russia to do the filming. Lillian's passport file has a letter she wrote to Ruth Shipley, head of the Passport Office, on 22 June 1942, asking for help in getting a passport from the New York branch of that office. Shipley stalled. She was a bitter anti-Communist, uneasy at the American alliance with godless Communists and unpersuaded that there was legitimate reason for the likes of Hellman and Wyler to do a movie in Russia. Shipley did not have to make a decision in 1942. Wyler was given an air force assignment elsewhere, and the project fell through.[39]

Lillian's account of how *North Star* emerged from the aborted Russian trip is in *An Unfinished Woman*:

> But Goldwyn and I—and Washington, behind the scene—went on talking about a Russian picture and finally came to what seemed like, and could have been, a sensible solution: we would do a simple, carefully researched, semi-documentary movie to be shot in Hollywood. I have, during the last year, read again my script for *North Star*. It could have been a good picture instead of the big-time, sentimental, badly-acted mess it turned out to be. Halfway through the shooting, Mr. Goldwyn and I parted company.[40]

Lillian violently objected to director Lewis Milestone's many changes in her script, and bought out her interest in it. *North Star* later surfaced as one of the subversive charges against her, but even a casual reading of the script as she wrote it makes this charge look ridiculous. There are no politics in *North Star*, not even a hint at the achievements of communism. There are only heroic Ukrainian villagers.[41]

In the summer of 1942, Lillian began another play with an antifascist theme, this one set partially in the 1920s when Mussolini was coming to power. It is not only antifascist, it is anti–Foreign Service. Her distaste for diplomats is given free rein, and cookie-pushers in striped pants are pilloried. In *The Searching Wind*, produced in April 1944, an indecisive and unprincipled American Foreign Service officer called Alex Hazen epitomizes her opinion of diplomats. Hazen is made to appear a wimp, refusing to take a stand against fascism, distorting the truth about Mussolini in his early years, refusing to report that Nazi planes are bombing Madrid during the Spanish Civil War, and finally toning down an analysis of the damage done to the democracies by Neville Chamberlain's compromises with Hitler at Munich. One can hardly find a more unflattering portrait of a diplomat than Hellman's depiction of Hazen in *Searching Wind*.

Searching Wind was yet another play for which the Communist flacks took her to task.[42] She may have joined all the right fronts, but she wrote the wrong plays. This time even the conservative press took notice. The *New York World-Telegram* review of *Searching Wind*, by Burton Rascoe, marveled that one could find no "Communist propaganda" in it at all; Rascoe noted that the "Communist letter-writing factory" had bombarded him for praising the play. And a *Washington Times-Herald* editorial said that one of her characters sounded, glory be, like an America-firster.[43]

All was not work for Lillian during the first two years of the war. As the FBI compiled her record in September 1943, she was one of the hosts at a Hollywood reception for a Soviet film director, and in December she was the honoree at a luncheon in New York at which Paul Robeson spoke. And she tried once again to get abroad. As noted earlier, MGM prodded the Passport Office to let her go to England in April 1944 to work on the production of Tolstoy's *War and Peace*. Shipley again refused. But in the summer of 1944 it was different.

If the Lillian Hellman who accepted an invitation to wartime Russia was a complex and ambiguous character, she at least was a believer in the international politics of culture. Her plays were by then being produced in New York, London, Paris; this was theater bringing the peoples of the world closer together. The arts served as a bridge between peoples; what politicians tore asunder, artists and writers should attempt to repair. Even the vast rupture between the Soviet Union and the West might be amenable to improvement via the arts. Thus when the Russians reversed their attitude toward *Watch on the Rhine* after Hitler attacked Russia, and invited Hellman to consult on its production in Moscow in 1944, she was willing to go. *The Little Foxes* was also scheduled for rehearsal by a Russian company. And the Russians gave her some credit for *North Star*, since it portrayed the determination of Russian peasants to defend their homeland.

Adam Watson, a British diplomat who first met Hellman in Moscow, says that in the atmosphere of 1944, she was not alone in hoping for future improvements in Western relations with the Russians: "Insofar as we thought of the post-war world, that kind of rapprochement seemed possible."[44] If cultural exchanges could contribute to such a rapprochement, Lillian seemed clearly to be an appropriate emissary.

This seemed plausible also to Franklin Roosevelt, who met Lillian on 25 January 1942 at a special showing of *Watch on the Rhine*, and to his most trusted advisor, Harry Hopkins. Hellman, in her Foreword to Lev Kopelev's bitter anti-Stalinist memoir, *To Be Remembered Forever*, says that her cultural mission "was approved by President Roosevelt and arranged by Harry Hopkins, neither of whom wished to appear in the negotiations." Perhaps

Hopkins did initiate the trip; he was instrumental in arranging the earlier goodwill mission of Eric Johnston, who toured Soviet factories and film studios at the height of the Nazi invasion.

It is also possible that Archibald MacLeish, a close friend of Hellman who in 1944 was associate director of the Office of War Information, had a part in suggesting to Hopkins the idea for such a mission. A year later, when MacLeish was assistant secretary of state for public and cultural affairs, he tried hard to recruit Lillian as cultural affairs attaché in the Moscow embassy. She turned him down. She could not imagine enduring the repressive Soviet atmosphere for any length of time.[45] A three-month cultural mission in 1944, however, she could tolerate.

Roosevelt's motives in approving a goodwill mission such as Lillian's are not hard to uncover. When the United States entered World War II at the time of Pearl Harbor and thus became an ally of the Soviet Union, Hitler's legions were smashing deep into Soviet territory. Most American military experts gave the Russians little chance of repelling the German invasion; their expectations were that Hitler would soon control the whole of Europe. Hitler would then turn to an invasion of England; England and the United States would stand alone against a manic and victorious Germany.

Roosevelt did not accept this pessimistic outlook; he believed the Russians could hold out, occupying 240 Nazi and satellite divisions on the eastern front while the United States and Britain established a second front in France. To Stalin, a second front was all-important; obtaining American war matériel for Soviet armies was also a high priority. On both these matters, American performance was far short of promises and expectations. Roosevelt promised a second front in 1942; for many reasons he could not keep the promise, nor could he bring it off in 1943. British and American forces engaged the Germans in Africa, a tertiary theater, instead of attacking toward the heart of Germany. Roosevelt was forced to cancel the Murmansk supply convoys due to heavy losses. As James MacGregor Burns describes Stalin's mood in the spring of 1943,

> By now he was seething at his allies. His grievances were many and painful. They had broken off the convoys. They had got bogged down in Africa and let the Red Army take the brunt of the winter fighting. They had never accepted the Polish-Soviet frontier of 1939. They had not broken with Finland. The Soviet government, he felt, had made concession after concession, gesture after gesture. Had he not responded to Anglo-American wishes in dissolving the Comintern, even though he had sworn on Lenin's tomb never to abandon the cause—

Lenin's cause—of world revolution? And still no second front. To Stalin this was not a question of strategy alone. The blood of his people was at stake. Hundreds of thousands of Russians would perish because the Anglo-Americans would invade Europe in 1944 instead of 1943 or 1942. . . . The second-front delay far more than any other factor aroused Soviet anger and cynicism. . . . was this not evidence that the West, whatever its protestations, was following a strategy of letting Russia and Germany bleed each other to death? By mid-1943 the grand coalition was floundering in a welter of broken promises and crushed expectations.[46]

Roosevelt sought every possible strategem to mollify Stalin. One of his tactics was sending a series of goodwill emissaries to the Soviet Union, sometimes with personal messages for Stalin, sometimes not. Wendell Willkie, Joseph E. Davies, Eric Johnston, Patrick Hurley, and Henry Wallace were among those whom Roosevelt dispatched largely for goodwill reasons. Lillian Hellman's trip was part of this effort.

It was not only Lillian's plays that made her an ideal candidate for such a mission; she was one of the few people who bridged the gap between the left-wing theater-movie world and upstage American society. Her ties with the left were well established, not only through her early Bohemian years in the movie colony and her on-and-off liaison with Dashiell Hammett, but also by her willingness to sign petitions and join pro-Soviet organizations.

Less well known is the extent to which her friendships encompassed the other end of the political spectrum. Loy Henderson, conservative chief of the State Department Division of Eastern European Affairs, was not only her friend but an ardent admirer. Christian Herter, later secretary of state under Eisenhower (succeeding Dulles) and Mrs. Herter were friends of long standing. Adele Lovett, wife of Robert Lovett, assistant secretary of war in 1944 and later secretary of defense, was a lifelong friend and frequent companion. Both Averell Harriman and his daughter Kathleen were friends. Harriman regarded Lillian as a "fellow wanderer," but he knew there was not a disloyal bone in her body, and he was very fond of her. Lillian was, as New York society knew, an adornment at any dinner table.[47]

Despite this establishment imprimatur, opposition to Hellman in the Passport Office, in other anti-Soviet recesses of the State Department, and in the FBI caused bitter arguments over the proposed cultural mission. Hopkins, Roosevelt, and like-minded supporters of Lillian may have won. But the official Department of State cable to the Moscow embassy, dispatched on 18 October 1944, shows Secretary Hull (or the conservative Eastern European desk, which probably wrote the cable) distancing himself from any responsibility for her trip: "AMEMBASSY MOSCOW: The Department has issued a passport for travel to the Soviet Union to Miss Lillian Hellman, playwright and authoress who is going to the Soviet Union at the invitation of Voks. She is proceeding via Siberia and should arrive sometime the latter part of October. Miss Hellman is proceeding to the Soviet Union as a private individual and has no connection with any branch of this Government. HULL."[48] An information copy of this telegram was sent to the ever-suspicious FBI.

The FBI seemed to watch Lillian in spurts. In 1941, when the unknown informant told them that she was paying for the American Peace Mobilization pickets then parading in front of the White House, the Bureau produced a five-page rundown of her "Communist" activities: memberships in the Friends of the Abraham Lincoln Brigade, Spanish Refugee Relief Campaign, American Council on Soviet Relations, Women's Conference to Aid the *Jewish Day*, and so on.[49]

The next activity in her Bureau file was recorded in October 1943, when J. Edgar Hoover ordered the New York office to update the data on Lillian. Presumably this was to justify her inclusion in the Security Index, Hoover's list of people to be detained in the event of a national emergency. The New York Office scurried around and produced a twenty-two-page report listing all her previous memberships, plus every mention they could find of her in such eminent periodicals as the *Daily Worker*, and the accretion of new memberships and causes. New York held that she was a "key figure" in Communist activities, and she was placed on the Security Index.[50]

In July 1944, New York again updated Lillian's file. She had recently "addressed a meeting of the 135th Street Branch of the New York Public Library. Miss HELLMAN discussed negro-white relations and in response to a question, said that American fascists would be punished in due time." There were several other incriminating acts: she worked on a code of the Committee for Democratic Culture, spoke to the Women's Division of the Joint Anti-Fascist Refugee Committee (where she was lauded by Raymond Massey, Margaret Webster, Paul Robeson, and Herman Shumlin), spoke at a Carnegie Hall rally in honor of Georgi Dimitroff on the tenth anniversary of the Reichstag Fire Trial, and arranged a special preview of her play *The Searching Wind* to benefit the American-Soviet Medical Society. The Bureau included a kind word for Lillian in this report; the *Daily Worker* did not like

The Searching Wind. But just so government agents would be able to appre-
hend her when the time came, New York sent FBI headquarters two photos
of her.[51]

A month later, in August 1944, the Bureau swung into high gear. Rumor
of her approaching trip to the Soviet Union was about. It is not clear
whether Hoover volunteered a report on Lillian to the State Department, or
whether Assistant Secretary of State Adolf Berle requested it; in any case,
a two-page letter went to Berle by special messenger with a brief summary
of her activities and a listing of sixteen suspect organizations with which
she was affiliated. Surprisingly, there was no mention of Dashiell Hammett
in any of these reports. She did have unwholesome friends, however; the
letter to Berle noted, "Miss Hellman has been closely associated with a
number of individuals who have been identified as members of the Communist Political Association and has frequently appeared on programs
sponsored by Communist controlled or infiltrated groups."[52] If Berle tried
to use this information to block Lillian's trip to Moscow, he failed.

Hoover did more than write Berle. He also instructed the Los Angeles
FBI office to keep tabs on Lillian when she arrived there en route to
Moscow. When Hoover learned that she was also stopping over in Seattle,
he instructed the office there to report on her too.

R. B. Hood, the special agent in charge (SAC) in Los Angeles, cabled
Hoover (and Seattle) on 7 October that Lillian had arrived on the fourth,
was staying with her ex-husband's parents, had a conference with Hal
Wallis, and would leave for Seattle on the tenth. In a later report, Hood
supplied all the details. When it came to trivia, the FBI could gather them:

> [Deleted] advised the writer on October 10, 1944, that a reservation
> for the subject in Bedroom M, Car 72 of the "Lark" leaving Los
> Angeles at 9 P.M. on October 10th had been obtained by SID STREET
> of the Paramount Studios in Hollywood. . . . On the evening of Octo-
> ber 10, 1944, Special Agents [deleted] observed subject arriving at the
> Glendale station in a 1937 Cadillac bearing California license 57-V-
> 356 registered to CYRUS DAGGETT, 725 Westlake Avenue. This auto-
> mobile was driven by a liveried chauffeur and subject was accompa-
> nied by a man and a woman. The man was described as 40, 5'10", 180
> pounds, black receding hair, dark eyes, glasses. The woman was
> described as 30, 5'5", 120 pounds, dark brown hair, dark eyes, attrac-
> tive face. Subject was described as wearing a dark brown sheared
> beaver coat, a dark blue chalk striped suit and brown pumps.[53]

The Los Angeles agents, however, were pikers compared to those in Seattle. Seattle knew not only how she spent every minute of her two days there, but also the backgrounds of the people who met her, what books she purchased at the Frederick and Nelson Department Store, how much cash she had in her pocketbook, her passport number, and the contents of her luggage. Presumably this last item might have been of use to the Bureau. The luggage search revealed that she had a copy of *Colliers* with Wendell Willkie's article "Citizens of Negro Blood" in it; a copy of *The Kings English* by Fowler; a power of attorney issued to Herman Shumlin; a contract with *Colliers* for several articles, each of which was to bring her two thousand dollars; and blank typing paper, among other things.[54] The Bureau, no doubt, concluded that she was not carrying state secrets to the Russians.

But did it? Her next stop was Fairbanks, Alaska. The report from SAC H. L. McConnell in Anchorage, whose jurisdiction included Ladd Field in Fairbanks where Lillian waited for Russian transportation, had four lengthy paragraphs deleted for "national security" reasons. One other sentence partially deleted read "Although Miss HELLMAN did not engage in any Communistic activities while in Fairbanks [deleted]." So we do not know what her quasi- or non-Communist activities were. However, we do know that she harbored evil thoughts: "HELLMAN expressed an attitude of sympathy to Russian Institutions and stated that she desired to build up goodwill in the United States towards Russia. She felt that the Russians were right in destroying Nazism."[55]

Fairbanks did not, apparently, search Lillian's luggage. Nor was there the detailed surveillance Seattle had conducted. But there was surveillance of another kind: of the Russians at Ladd Field.

The Russians were our allies during World War II, and American opinion of the Soviet Union was then more favorable than it had been before or has been since. However alliance did not mean trust; the U.S. military monitored Soviet communications throughout.

Thus on 16 and 18 October 1944, the U.S. Army Military Intelligence Service recorded conversations concerning Lillian between the commander of Soviet forces at Ladd Field and his superior in Washington. The Russians appeared disorganized. Army Intelligence gave a transcript of the conversation about Lillian to the FBI:

S-E-C-R-E-T

EXCERPT FROM

GENERAL SUMMARY OF MONITORING ACTIVITIES

16 October 1944

1050 AWT

Colonel KISILEV, LADD FIELD, and

General RUDENKO, WASHINGTON, D.C.

KISILEV: Comrade General, I have called you today because this writer, LILLIAN HELLMAN arrived here today. She is going to USSR but I don't have any information or any orders about it.

RUDENKO: HELLMAN?

KISILEV: Yes, HELLMAN.

RUDENKO: I don't know anything either so you better wait before you send her over. I will call you about it.

KISILEV: Okay, she is going from New York. The counsel out there sent her through. She was showing me the telegram of who had invited her. It was POUDOVKIN and MOSKVIN and some other of our artists.

RUDENKO: Well, I don't know anything about it yet, so don't send her through.

KISILEV: All right, I won't.

18 October, 1944

0925 AWT

Colonel KISILEV, LADD FIELD, and FEDOSEEV.

Russian Embassy, WASHINGTON, D.C.

KISILEV: LILLIAN HELLMAN—I don't have any information about her. You sent her here. Better find out right away. It is very hard to call you. I don't understand anything of what you say.

FEDOSEEV: Colonel KISILEV, she is an American citizen?

KISILEV: Yes, she is an American citizen.

FEDOSEEV: She's got a passport?

KISILEV: Yes, she has a passport.

FEDOSEEV: And on the passport there should be our visa. If she's got a visa, you should let her through.

KISILEV: Listen, next time I would like you to give me advance notice.

FEDOSEEV: She might have received that visa from the consulate at San Francisco.

KISILEV: Well, this one she received in New York. It is received from KISILEV.* Why didn't he notify me?

FEDOSEEV: KISILEV has signed it?

KISILEV: Yes.

---

*This is not an error. The Soviet visa official in New York was also named Kisilev.

FEDOSEEV: Well, so it's we that have issued the visa. We are going to have to let her through. One should notify you next time.[56]

So Lillian got off to the Soviet Union on 19 October 1944, by a Russian plane en route to Moscow. J. Edgar Hoover, sure that something subversive was going on, instructed the FBI agents in Seattle, San Francisco, Los Angeles, Butte, St. Paul, and New York to watch for her return. The first two paragraphs of his letter to them dated 21 December are deleted because they affect "national security." The third paragraph says, "The Bureau desires that appropriate arrangements be made by each of the field divisions receiving copies of this letter to examine the baggage and personal effects of Lillian Hellman at the time she reenters the United States."[57] The Bureau then neglected Lillian for a while, and we can turn to her doings in Moscow.

Lillian's reception in Moscow on 5 November was appropriately led by Sergei Eisenstein, Russia's spectacle-producing equivalent of Cecil B. DeMille. Since she was the guest of Voks, and no official responsibility of the U.S. Embassy, she was booked into the National Hotel, Room 219. Averell Harriman, American ambassador to the USSR, was in Washington. George Kennan, chargé in Harriman's absence, heard of her traumatic journey from Alaska and of her illness; he suggested that she move to Spaso House, the massive ambassadorial residence, where she could receive American medical attention and probably be more comfortable. This she did. When she recovered from her pneumonia, she moved back to the National.[58] She was living there, on 11 November, when her life took a strange new turn.

Melby's Road to Moscow

John Fremont Melby was born on 1 July 1913, in Portland, Oregon. His father was a YMCA official who moved several times during John's childhood. Five years of his youth were spent in Brazil, where he acquired fluent Portuguese from his school and French from a governess. Most of his adolescence was spent in Bloomington, Illinois; he graduated from Bloomington High School and attended Illinois Wesleyan University, majoring in French literature with a minor in classical Greek. He edited the student newspaper and was active in theater.

Nineteen thirty-four, when John graduated from Illinois Wesleyan, was the depth of the depression; fascinated as he was by the arts and humanities, the perilous times seemed to demand some changes in the way American society functioned. Many of his contemporaries moved into left-wing politics; John read law in Bloomington for a year. This did not seem to be an avenue for social change; so he went to graduate school at the University of Chicago in 1935 to see what the new social sciences had to offer a floundering world.

They offered a lot. John was lucky enough to study with Quincy Wright and Frederick Schuman. He passed his Ph.D. comprehensive exams with two years of study. By 1937, he had to earn some money. The Foreign Service seemed an appropriate job, and his Chicago mentors thought him a good candidate. He passed the exams easily. In August 1937, he was sent to Ciudad Juárez as vice-consul.

Juárez was not one of the State Department's glamor posts. For John, however, it had a big advantage. Foreign Service officers assigned to Juárez could live just across the river in El Paso. In London, Paris, Rome, or Berlin, a brilliant performance by a fledgling diplomat would have no home audience. In El Paso, there was a very attentive American audience.

John blossomed in El Paso. Despite his youth (he was twenty-four at the time) he was in much demand as a speaker. Unlike most cautious diplomats, he took on cosmic themes and poured his own views into them. His 21 June 1938 speech to the Women's Circle of the First Presbyterian Church dealt with "The Peace Movement in America Today." Two weeks later he addressed the El Paso Kiwanis on "The Trade Agreements Program," incorporating a healthy chunk of Keynesian economics. He spoke ceremonially at events such as the El Paso Boy Scout Field Day and Rally, and wrote regular book reviews for the *El Paso Herald Post*.[1]

El Paso also offered an opportunity to continue his interest in theater. The Little Theater group gave him the role of Marchbanks in George Bernard Shaw's *Candida*, and according to his boss, Consul George P. Shaw, John was a "decided success."[2] Katherine Cornell was touring with a road show of *Candida* at the time, and Cornell asked John to join the road show; he declined. Theater was attractive, but he saw his future in international relations.

Consul Shaw seems to have encouraged John's rapid prominence; Shaw regularly forwarded texts of his speeches to the State Department Division of Research and Publications with favorable comments. A Mr. Wynne of Research and Publications was startled by John's brashness, expressing some concern at his presumption in interpreting John Maynard Keynes and at his hostile reference to "one of Chicago's more notorious newspapers." *The Chicago Tribune*, Wynne wrote to Consul Shaw, was not only isolationist, it was looking for opportunities to savage American diplomats. Melby should be more discreet.[3]

This cautionary note did not appear in the evaluations by Melby's immediate superiors. Ambassador Daniels in Mexico City warmly commended John's extensive report on "Mormon Colonies in the State of Chihuahua," and the Treasury Department went out of its way to praise his "untiring efforts" in helping them suppress a counterfeiting ring operating near Juárez.[4] It was an auspicious record for a young diplomat in his first post.

During his participation in the Little Theater group, John met Florence Cathcart, the daughter of a prominent El Paso physician. They began keeping company, and in early 1938, Consul Shaw sensed that marriage might be imminent. This did not please him. In one of his lengthy reports on John to the chief of Foreign Service Personnel, Shaw noted that while Florence Cathcart was of "good family and position . . . unfortunately she is a divorcee, is 11 or 12 years older than John Melby, and . . . I can not look with favor on this match."[5] John did not know of Shaw's reservations. He and Florence were married in the spring of 1938.

Consul Shaw did not make note of what became the major irritant in Melby's relations with his in-laws: politics. John was raised in, and accepted the values of, a religious family to whom Roosevelt's New Deal was a sincere and needed effort to remedy the plight of that third of the nation which was ill-fed, ill-housed, and ill-clothed. His wife's family, as befitted the status of a prominent physician, looked with disfavor on the New Deal and all its works. John was not aggressive in stating his political beliefs, and the Foreign Service was not a profession where political activism could properly be displayed in any case. It was not until the Cold War broke out that the potential conflict between YMCA liberalism and Texas conservatism became significant.

El Paso was followed by six months of Foreign Service School in Washington; John got uniformly high ratings. He was then posted to Venezuela in the summer of 1939. Venezuela provided no opportunities to lecture on Keynes or international trade to appreciative American audiences, but it offered a different kind of opportunity. World War II had broken out, and many German ships caught in the Western Hemisphere sought asylum in neutral ports. One of them, the SS *Sesostris*, took refuge in Puerto Cabello, Venezuela. The Department of State believed that every German ship in the hemisphere should be kept under surveillance. There was no United States official permanently stationed in Puerto Cabello, and as low man on the totem pole in Caracas, John drew the assignment of going to Puerto Cabello with no official duties other than watching the *Sesostris*. He had plenty of time, while monitoring his ship, to write a Ph.D. dissertation on rubber production in the Amazon basin. This was accepted by the University of Chicago shortly thereafter, and John became one of only three Foreign Service officers of that time to have a doctorate. After four months in Puerto Cabello, he was brought back to Caracas.

His superior in Caracas, Ambassador Frank Corrigan, was as impressed with John's performance as Consul Shaw in El Paso had been. Venezuela held its first free election in many years while he was there, and John was one of several officers assigned to appraise the candidates and issues. Corrigan noted: "Although the junior officer of the Embassy, his political reporting was superior to that of the other officers."[6]

In May 1941, John was brought back to Washington and assigned to the Peru-Ecuador desk. Here he worked for Under Secretary Sumner Welles, whose artful promotion of the Good Neighbor Policy toward Latin America influenced John greatly. Under Welles's tutelage, John played a major role during 1942 in settling a bitter Peru-Ecuador boundary dispute.[7] John still regards Welles as the giant among American diplomats; it was an exciting apprenticeship, far more attractive than the work of a consul in Juárez.

John became wholly committed to diplomacy as a profession. He was well on his way to becoming a skilled Hispanic language officer.

But the war was requiring large numbers of officers for the military, and John realized that a military record would be helpful in his chosen career later on. In the spring of 1943, when he had finished work on the boundary dispute, he applied for military leave. This was refused. He was ordered to Portugal.

John had no objection to an assignment in Lisbon. It was a cauldron of international intrigue where young diplomats could be expected to sharpen negotiating and conspiratorial talents. But there was a post he preferred to Lisbon. In 1943, the focus of the Western world was on the Soviet Union, where a nation most Westerners assumed was little more than one giant gulag was shattering Hitler's legions. Melby wanted Moscow.

There was small chance that an officer only six years in the service could engineer a change of orders such as Melby asked for. He was never sure how it went through, but on 20 March 1943, Cordell Hull ordered John to Moscow as Third Secretary and Vice-Consul of the Embassy. Thus began the odyssey that was his undoing.

Moscow was a hardship post, one to which the wives of lower-ranking officials could not accompany their husbands. John's wife and his two sons went back to Texas.

Soviet inefficiency, or bloody-mindedness, or both, stalled John's visa for two months. Transportation was also hard to come by. It was 15 June 1943 when he finally reached Moscow, to join the cloistered, frustrated, tightly knit colony of Western officials who were trying to coordinate the Allied war effort.

Wartime Moscow was an environment such as few Westerners have experienced. Despite John's relatively cosmopolitan background, nothing had prepared him for this. For all the excitement of the war, Soviet secretiveness built a wall around foreigners like none the Americans had seen elsewhere. They were thrown in upon themselves for the kinds of everyday conversation people in other cultures found at work, in pubs and restaurants, and in normal social contacts. George Kennan's description of the atmosphere as he found it when he joined the Embassy staff in July 1944 is classic:

> Outside the little oasis of the diplomatic colony there stretched still, fascinating and inviting, the great land and life of Russia, more interesting to me than any other in the world. I could not enter into this life

as a participant. The wartime association between Russia and the United States had changed nothing, I soon learned, in the isolation of American diplomats from the population. It was obvious that in the eyes of the secret police we, though nominally allies, were still dangerous enemies, to be viewed with suspicion and held at arm's length from Soviet citizens—lest we corrupt them, I suppose, with insidious tales of another life, or pry from them secrets on the preservation of which, even from ostensibly allied powers, Russia's security was somehow seen to depend. We were sincerely moved by the sufferings of the Russian people as well as by the heroism and patience they were showing in the face of wartime adversity. We wished them nothing but well. It was doubly hard, in these circumstances, to find ourselves treated as though we were the bearers of some species of the plague.[8]

At the end of a year in Moscow, John wrote his parents in a similar vein:

Despite all superficial appearances to the contrary and the fine words which are mouthed for the record, things are distinctly not going well here. We kid ourselves now and then that we can break down the diplomatic ghetto in which we are jailed and bring in outside influences, but it ain't so. These birds [the Russians] invented the system and they intend to keep the place exclusive. The result is that beyond official and formal contacts the only Russians we can know are whores and that gets stupid after a while. The great honeymoon of the Moscow Conference came to an end about July 1 [1944] and the kosher laws are in full force.

Under these conditions, Spaso dinner table conversation was mostly carping about the Russians. This negative attitude permeated Embassy cable traffic to Washington. Before John left for Moscow, Assistant Secretary Adolf Berle warned him, "We have to get along with the Russians. All I hear from those guys in the Embassy is bitching. I don't want to hear it from you; if I do, I'll haul you back." But after two years, the strains of Moscow life got to John as to the others. Their isolation from ordinary Russians and their pervasive negativism made such visitors as Eric Johnston, James Reston, Edgar Snow, Ed Flynn, C. L. Sulzberger, and later Hellman and other world travelers extremely welcome.

Admiral William H. Standley was ambassador when John arrived in Moscow. Standley assigned John, as junior officer, to oversee the Embassy mess. This was hardly what he had foreseen for himself, but, as with the unglamorous detail he had drawn at Puerto Cabello, he made the most of it. Spaso House, the ambassadorial residence, was a huge three-story, thirty-room monster, with a reception room measuring thirty by a hundred feet and a chandelier that John said "would look better in the Chicago Opera House." As overseer of the mess, John fed forty people a day, including twenty-three servants, and ran a laundry operation even more demanding. He wrote to his parents: "Very broadening business is the foreign service."

His first diplomatic assignment was as acting director of the Office of War Information (OWI). The Soviets, far more cut off from events abroad than any other Allied people, were to be provided a glossy magazine titled *America*, as an attempt to penetrate the Russian shell and develop some understanding of the far-off and mysterious ally from which came much of the war materiel the Russians used to push back Hitler's armies. Shortly after John arrived in Moscow, Averell Harriman replaced Admiral Standley as Ambassador. John worked on the OWI tasks with Harriman's daughter, Kathleen.

The Harriman Embassy was quite different in style from that of Admiral Standley. In a letter of 22 October 1943, John wrote:

This new regime here is distinctly more on the big-shot side of life. The conversation is all Winston this, Tony [Eden] that, and Franklin the other. In one sense it rather means that the White House has moved into the Embassy and the Department of State has moved out. And of course in all these changes it is also apparent that the fine Italian hand of one Harry Hopkins and his lend-lease boys has taken over. Strange that the New Deal which began with a dream should finally end up under the control of the old gang from Wall Street of whom Harriman and Stettinius are exceedingly able components. Let us see how they will operate.

John's admiration for Harriman clearly shows in his letters during those years. A comment of 12 September 1944 on the ambassador and his daughter is typical: "I suppose one does not build great railroads for nothing. His Excellency can dish it out, but he can also take it—which makes it all ok. In my experience his daughter is the only woman I have ever known who could also do it and slug it out, a quality I wholeheartedly approve of in females, but seldom find."

One of the assignments Melby drew developed out of an unusual invitation by the Soviet government in February 1944 to Western journalists.

The journalists were to visit Katyn Forest, where the Russians hoped to convince them that the Nazis had murdered 10,000 Polish officers and dumped them in mass graves. Kathleen, who had been a journalist before joining her father in Moscow, wanted to go to Katyn. Ambassador Harriman, uneasy at the prospect of his daughter's making such a trip on her own, told the Soviet Foreign Office that he would like Kathleen to go if accompanied by Third Secretary Melby. This was approved, and the two "official" American representatives joined the two dozen reporters on the inspection of Katyn. Neither Melby nor Miss Harriman was overwhelmed by the Russian "evidence"; ultimate judgment was that the Russians had carried out the massacre.

One outcome of the Katyn trip was unexpected. Bill Downs, an American correspondent, filed a dispatch for his U.S. clients stating that Melby had gone to Katyn as chaperone for Miss Harriman. This report reached El Paso, where Melby's wife took much kidding over it. Letters from El Paso cooled perceptibly.

There were, in fact, very few letters from El Paso, and John found them uniformly frustrating and unsatisfactory. He was most anxious to hear about his two sons, particularly since one letter from his wife noted that the elder one had an ear infection, but John did not learn the outcome for months, and then in a confusing fashion. He regretted missing their childhood. When a Mexican contingent whose members he had known in Juárez arrived in Moscow, having seen his boys in El Paso just before leaving Mexico, they reported in extenso; John was "startled at the height and size they attribute to the youngsters." Concern about and interest in the boys permeates his letters to his folks in Bloomington, whom he constantly urged to visit El Paso and send him an extensive report.

As to his wife, there were nothing but complaints. She had a joint banking account with him; he never knew how much money was in it. When the family house was sold, she did not give him her new address for months. There was no reaction to his descriptions of life in wartime Moscow. He began to envy George Kennan, whose rank enabled him to bring his Norwegian wife and two daughters with him to Moscow; Melby was enchanted with the daughters, and wrote his father, "Having been around the Kennan's two girls here I now for the first time want a daughter. But that I guess I cannot have unless I can make some arrangement for a second family."

Among the topsy-turvy features of Moscow life were the weird hours kept by the Kremlin. Government offices (at least those of the Foreign

Ministry) opened at 4:00 P.M. and conducted business until 3:00 A.M. The ballet and theater were in the afternoon, film showings at night; John was required to go to many of the latter, which lasted until midnight.

And there were other eccentricities:

It is rather typically Russian that the electricity has gone off in this section of town. Obviously it would affect Spaso, but weirdly enough it affects only the southern rooms in the place. Just why is something no one can answer. I guess it is just the slavic way. . . . This is Saturday night and my room is one of the few with light, hence something of a community center at the moment. The Ambassador is pacing up and down, fidgeting as to whether to go to bed with a toothache or play bezique or settle the problems of the world. Kathleen is sitting upside down somewhere trying to read, three colonels are around, two shooting craps in a corner and a third improving his mind by sleeping, and Mr. Harriman's personal secretary is wondering what to do with himself. And I am making a frightful noise on a battered typewriter. [1 April 1944]

John's room in Spaso was large and relatively comfortable; he prided himself on the accumulation of furniture he dragooned from Moscow stores. Frequently he would be dispossessed by visiting firemen. One of those from whom he learned an alarming lesson in government security was Wild Bill Donovan, head of the Office of Strategic Services (OSS)—the forerunner of CIA. Donovan was in Moscow for a week, presumably to see what he could set up by way of cooperative intelligence with the Soviets. Donovan quickly learned that this was not much; so, according to John, Donovan decided to take Russian lessons. He spent most of his time in John's room, struggling with the language and reading the stream of telegrams that came for him. After Donovan left, John learned, to his astonishment, that Donovan had read these telegrams, scribbled notes on some of them, and then secreted them somewhere around the room. John discovered them under the mattress, behind the cushions of chairs, under the rug, everywhere they could be stuffed out of sight. John gave them to the ambassador as he discovered them, and resolved never to trust OSS with anything confidential.

Attached to his job as director of the Office of War Information, John had responsibilities which in a fully staffed embassy would be assigned to a cultural affairs officer. This included film. He ran the movie program for the Embassy and wrote his father in March 1944 that "in the last few months I have seen more movies than all the rest of my life put together. I am also rather amazed to find myself beginning to get interested in them as a technique. It is mildly amusing to know the movie people, some of them rather interesting. I suppose you have seen *North Star*. It stinks but the Russians for some weird reason love it."

There is much political comment in his letters home, displaying the varying moods of the ambassador and of the foreign colony. Although the war was going well, postwar probabilities continually intruded on the diplomatic consciousness. Could peace be achieved on a lasting basis? Melby felt that there was little basis for continued cooperation between the West and Russia; for one thing, the Russians had "absolutely no conception of our idea of political democracy," and no desire to learn. They were fighting for Russian soil, and in order to establish for the first time a cordon of buffer states that would absorb the first blows were the Germans to again go on a rampage. But the blame was far from unilateral. Writing to his father on 22 October of the Foreign Ministers Conference of 1943, John noted:

> The whole process has been characterized by a systematic, if not deliberate, ignoring of Russia by the States and England in all matters that pertain to the course and unfolding of the war. Roosevelt and Churchill have preferred to make their own decisions and then later inform the Kremlin of what has been done. The reaction here has been what you might have expected, though I should add that by no means all virtue resides on this side of the line. The Russians have relentlessly and cynically pushed us by all means at their disposal into military ventures which would help them, but be unduly costly to us. This of course is the notorious front which the Russians in rather callous fashion now define as the first million American casualties. In other words, they will not be satisfied until we have lost as much as they have. And they resent it now because they realize we can win without anywhere near that number of casualties.

Despite the ravages of war, the Russians did not draft their artists, and the cultural life of Moscow continued only slightly diminished. The Russians were determined to keep their actors and musicians at full proficiency; the ballet, the theater, the symphonies, the museums were kept going. The Embassy had a box at the Bolshoi. In winter months, Melby was less inclined to attend concerts and plays; most of the theaters were unheated. He did, however, attend the premiere of Shostakovich's Eighth

Symphony in November 1943 and wrote to his father: "No good. He is still trying to write a party line and that does not mix well with music, no matter what the line. I met the man the other day at a party. He is an insignificant little person, but amiable."

There are no raves in John's Moscow efficiency reports comparable to those he received in Juárez and Caracas. In August 1944, Harriman noted that John had managed Spaso House "smoothly and with good taste," had developed "useful contacts in Russian press and other official circles," but needed a "somewhat more systematic approach to his work."[9] Nonetheless in October he was promoted to second secretary.

George Kennan produced the final efficiency report on John in August 1945. It is a study in ambivalence. Kennan thought him lazy: John "had no real feeling for the intense ideological issues of Russian life and Soviet policy, and always remained a disinterested amateur with respect to Russian matters." On the other hand, John was good at handling callers, succeeded in getting other people to do a surprising amount of work, and would be a very good officer for intelligence gathering. Kennan suggested a Latin assignment for him.[10]

Melby did not see this assessment until 1985. By then, he had proved in spades that he was anything but lazy and had caught on to the importance of ideology sufficiently to satisfy even a theoretician like Kennan. Since Harriman's was the opinion that counted in his next assignment, Melby got a distinct promotion, and went up the career ladder exceptionally fast.

And while Kennan did not think that John fitted well in Moscow, John thought a Soviet assignment was just what he wanted. As he wrote to his parents on 15 June 1944, he admired the Russian people tremendously for their bravery and determination to rebuild after the German devastation: "They are an amazing people, these Russians. You cannot break people like these, you can conquer them, overwhelm them perhaps, but you cannot break them. . . . For this reason alone, if for nothing else, Moscow is probably the single most important job in the world today. In so many ways the end of the war, which we can now begin to see, will be but the beginning of the hardest job which faces the world."

On about 3 November 1944, John was invited by L. J. Michael, an official of the U.S. Department of Agriculture who came to Russia periodically to do a survey of the prospective wheat crop, to go to Murmansk. Nothing big was happening at the Embassy, Michael was a fascinating individual who produced uncannily accurate reports, and this was a chance to see a different part of the Soviet Union. Murmansk was above the Arctic Circle, a thirty-six-hour train ride from Moscow. Melby went. He and

Michael were in Murmansk for the celebration of 7 November; they were amused to see "fat old generals" dancing with each other, and delighted to have far better food than was available in Moscow. They left to return to the Embassy on the morning of the eighth. The evening of John's arrival back at Spaso, on 11 November 1944, there was a new face at the Embassy table.

The Beginning of the Affair

Lillian did not like John that first night at the dinner table. He was, after all, just another Foreign Service officer, probably like Alex Hazen. She no doubt assumed he would be as anti-Russian as the rest of the Spaso crowd, carping about living conditions and Russian ingratitude, waiting only for word that he could return to God's country. He was handsome, though.

She was not ripe for romance as she had been when she met Ralph Ingersoll getting off the plane at Albuquerque. At that time, she had given up on Hammett and didn't care if she ever saw him again. In Moscow in 1944, she was carrying a torch for Hammett, looking forward to his return from Alaska to share her apartment in New York and her farm at Pleasantville.

And while she and John were at the same dinner table, they had no significant personal contact. Lillian was not interested in his reports of Murmansk, or of the probable wheat crop, or of Russian generals dancing together. So they did not take to each other that first night.

To John, Hellman was just another visiting big shot; he had barely heard of her, and he did not put her in the same category as the previous goodwill ambassadors like Eric Johnston. Falling in love was not on his agenda, either. His wife was neglecting him, but there were two sons back in El Paso for whom he cared a lot.

So nothing happened that first night, and they hardly saw each other the two following weeks. John got the flu the next day and was in bed for a week. Then on the twentieth, Lillian got the flu; she moved back to Spaso to be tended by the Embassy doctor.

But Lillian was not a compliant patient. On 23 November, George Kennan, still in charge of the Embassy in Harriman's absence, gave a big Thanksgiving party at Spaso. Despite her illness, Lillian was up and celebrating. There was dancing in the elegant Spaso ballroom. John and Lillian found themselves together, and the chemistry was right. It was love at second sight.

After a while on the dance floor, they joined a group in the bar upstairs for drinks. John no longer remembers what they talked about, but whatever it was, Lillian decided that he was no Alex Hazen, that his interest in the humanities, theater, music, and world affairs was genuine and extensive. John found that the wit and wisdom of this very feminine playwright captivated him as no other woman ever had.

Whatever might have happened that first night was postponed. Annelise Kennan decided that John should go back to the ballroom and dance with her. By the time he returned to the bar, Lillian had gone to bed. There was nothing left for him but to do likewise. But next morning, at breakfast, they found the magic still held. From then on, discreetly but frequently, they were a pair.

Moscow proved to be the ideal incubator for an affair between two such high-spirited people. It was a never-never land, full of the tension of the greatest war in history, with imminent victory over Germany giving both Russians and foreigners a sense of momentous events. Almost every night the big guns in the Kremlin boomed out to celebrate a battlefield triumph.

The week following Kennan's Thanksgiving party saw their relationship ripen and intensify. They took long walks through the wintry Moscow streets. One such occasion is described in *An Unfinished Woman*, the only time Lillian mentions John by name in her memoirs. They went into a state-owned antique store. She writes:

> John Melby and I had found two nineteenth-century children's picture books and were on our way out to the street. Then he touched my arm and pointed to a high shelf. On the shelf was a large photograph of the real faces of Garbo and the director Rouben Mamoulian, with crudely faked bodies arranged in one of the poses of love. Both Melby and I advanced toward the picture in movements evidently so furtive that the two ladies who attended at the store came toward us. I put out my hand to take the picture but John shook his head and pulled me to the door. When we were on the street, I turned to go back, but he held my arm and said that of course some joker had put it there, but as foreigners we would never be forgiven for buying it. He only got me back to Spasso by promising that he would get one of the Russian employees at the embassy to go around and buy it for me. But two days later, the Russian messenger said the picture was gone. Maybe, maybe not.[1]

On 29 November, Eddie Gilmore, Associated Press correspondent in Moscow, gave a party they attended. Marjorie Shaw, one of the guests, observed that Melby looked especially happy. Lillian replied: "He'd better."

Happiness was interrupted from 30 November to 8 December by Lillian's visit to Leningrad. The siege of that city had only recently been lifted, and few foreigners had been allowed to go there. Surprisingly, Lillian says nothing about it in *Unfinished Woman* except that having been there, she was, on her return to Moscow, "more interesting than I had been to foreign embassies. Dinner invitations came thick and fast. . . ."[2] John recalls that Archibald Clark-Kerr, British ambassador, invited her often to his embassy, as did Dana Wilgress, the Canadian minister. Luis Quintanilla, flamboyant Mexican envoy whose path crossed theirs in future years was also fond of Lillian. While she was in Leningrad, Ambassador Harriman and Kathleen returned to Moscow.

Shortly after Lillian got back from Leningrad, Eddie Gilmore held what John describes as a "really bolshoi brawl, which lasted forever." They were both hung over from it. Hangovers to the contrary, the next day, Sunday, 10 December, found them back together for dinner, for drinks around the Franklin stove in Kathleen Harriman's room, and then for the walk back through the deserted streets to the National Hotel. Though neither this night nor the rest of her nights with John are described in Lillian's memoirs, it was on this night that they first slept together. During the years that followed, especially during John's long absence in China, the tenth of each month was the occasion for a commemorative telegram each sent the other.

One would hardly suspect, given the flood of events described in *An Unfinished Woman*, that Lillian Hellman had time left over for a romantic affair during her days in Moscow. But the inhabitants of Spaso House knew: the ambassador and his daughter-hostess, Kathleen; and Eddie Page, Elbridge Durbrow, and Robert Meiklejohn of the Embassy staff. Outside the Embassy, even in the diplomatic colony, few were privy to such goings-on. As Kathleen Harriman Mortimer told me in 1985, "We were very discreet."

John accompanied Lillian to many of the activities she describes in *Unfinished Woman*. He was often with her for tea at Sergei Eisenstein's apartment, and during her visits to the Metropole Hotel. They saw *Ivan Grozny*, *Swan Lake*, and *Don Quixote* at the Bolshoi, and attended a Prokofiev premier together. But most often, they were together at Spaso.

Unconventional, witty, and caustic, Lillian had considerable impact on Spaso House. Robert Meiklejohn, Harriman's aide-de-camp, acknowledged that she was "very entertaining to talk to," but recorded in his diary reservations about her unconventionality: "Our meals have been enlivened since

Kathleen and Melby found that they could make toast on the electric floor heater. For a while we were coy and passed the finished product around the table hand-to-hand, but yesterday Miss Hellman let herself go and started tossing it about like feeding the fish."[3]

Christmas Eve was particularly notable for such a cloistered group. John's letter to Lillian a year later recalls how he remembered it:

Do you remember what we did last year at this time? It was a Sunday then and we spent the afternoon at the National where together we were warm and easy and comfortable and very Christmasy. Then we came back to Spaso and somehow got involved in eating those foul sandwiches Chin used to make . . . And then the party at which you proceeded to get drunk as fast as possible and I was sore because Deane was making passes at you. It was quite a brawl, with more than the usual amount of rowdyism and gypsies where you got slugged with two full glasses of scotch . . . It is just about midnight, which means that at this time last year we were going into the movie room where the gypsies had moved and they were singing *Los Cuatro Generales* [a Spanish Civil War song]. They did not know what it was, and neither did Quintanilla. But they sang it and you knew what it was, and that is all that counts. [24 December 1945]

Lillian stayed in Spaso that night, sleeping in her own room. Early Christmas morning, as John later reminded her, she "came padding down the hall in those oversize pajamas and made a dive into bed. I think you really needed me that morning and I am glad that you came to me. We talked a while and had each other and slept as long as time seemed to permit and I said that unless I could wake up each morning with you I did not want any more mornings" (letter, 27 December 1945).

Two days after Christmas, Lillian left for the war front near Warsaw. From John's point of view, this adventure was just a void in the brief time they could be together. He recalled her departure in a letter a year later:

It was a year ago tonight that you set off for Lublin and I was jealous because I could not go with you and unhappy because some of your all too few days in Moscow were going to be away from me. We had quite a job packing, especially when it came to the goings on about the coat, and getting books and cigarettes. You looked very fetching bundled up and wearing valenki. I wanted very much to be alone with you that evening before you went; only Frank Roberts did not seem to get the point. (We always did have trouble being alone in Spaso. Considering that and other difficulties from the very beginning, I think it speaks well for what we are to each other that we came through. But that sort of difficulty MUST stop and stop pronto.) And after I kissed you good bye Frank and I went up to my room and got very drunk, the only time I have seen him that way. He too I think must have been feeling low and lonely that night. [letter, 4 January 1946]

Lillian wrote several accounts of this trip to the front, one published in *Colliers*, March 1945, and another in *Unfinished Woman*.[4] Critics note that these accounts are somewhat different. In her later memoir, she mentions things that were absent from the *Colliers* article, such as visiting the German concentration camp at Maidaneck. She also leaves out interesting events related by her translator-guide, Raisa (Raya) Orlova, who published her own memoirs in 1983.

According to Orlova, they attended the first session of the Soviet-sponsored State Peoples Council in Lublin, and after the formal meeting, the Poles held a New Year's Reception. Bierut and Gomulka, the leaders of the Lublin Government, spoke at the reception. Lillian may not have understood Polish, but she sized up the speakers. Orlova writes, "We went out on the street and Lillian said to me, 'Raya, there was no Lenin among those people there, am I right?'"[5]

Both Hellman and Orlova disliked the Russian major from the Ministry of Defense who accompanied them on the trip to the front. Neither names him, both found him stupid and offensive. Both talk about him in their memoirs, but Orlova has the better narrative:

Lillian created a story about him: "Look, Raya, like all military types, he was at the front at the beginning of the war. Let's say that he was in a platoon. There they immediately saw what kind of bird he was. But how to get rid of him? So they decided to advance him, to 'promote' him to a regiment. Then to a division. Then to the Political Department at the front. And, finally, to the Chief Political Department. What to do with him, what kind of job to give him so that he would cause the least amount of harm? They decided to send him off to the front with this eccentric American woman."

This was perceptive. This major, armed, came running into our room when the shooting started in Lublin and screamed at me hysterically: "Why aren't you getting up, why are you in bed?"

No doubt about it. Hellman was more comprehensible to me, closer to me, more my own kind of person than this fool, boor, and coward.[6]

When Lillian got back to Moscow on 9 January, she and John gave up the pretense of maintaining separate bedrooms, and "set up housekeeping" together. Privacy was not notable; the ambassador would "pop in and out at weird hours" and other residents were constantly going to the bathroom next door. But they were together, with little time remaining before Lillian was to leave.

For John, this was the first great rapture of his life. Whatever affection he had felt for Florence when he married her in El Paso, it was as nothing compared with his passion for Lillian. He was devastated at the prospect of her departure. He felt, in fact, that she had "made a man" out of him in a way that neither marriage nor fatherhood nor diplomatic service had done. "She knew how to make a man feel like a man." Her wit, her vigor, her straightforwardness were enchanting.

Lillian, too, was in love, as she had once been with Hammett and then with Ingersoll. Her past had taught her to be wary of physical attraction, even more so of married men. She also knew well the probable professional complications were John to divorce his wife to be with her, and the difficulties she and John would have making a new life under those circumstances. Furthermore, she knew well her own adventurous and independent nature. But the officer-gentleman *had* captivated her; he deepened her insight into the global politics of the midtwentieth century, and he meshed well with her literary and artistic background. She spent every available remaining minute of her Moscow stay in the company of Second Secretary of Embassy John Melby.

Not only the second secretary was affected by her presence. The other inhabitants of Spaso, and the Russian intelligentsia, knew she was a personality to be reckoned with. Years later, John described her interaction with the Embassy people to a Department of State Loyalty-Security Board:

> Most of us had been in the confinement of Moscow a long time, too long, without much to do, seeing too few people, often for months even without mail from home, and subject to the infinite number of petty harassments which the Russian bureaucracy had developed into a fine art. The net result was that as far as those stationed in Moscow were concerned after awhile, there was literally nothing which was right. Even when it was right it was wrong. Miss Hellman came fresh from the outside world into war devastation and she reacted strongly against the carping criticism of the American community against absolutely everything Russian. That community was not slow in picking her up on the most insignificant details, partly because

here was a welcome relief from the local boredom. Seldom was there much real substance to the argument and the baiting at times became rather extreme, particularly when it tended to become Miss Hellman vs. the field; and I know she was often personally and deeply offended. It made her in reaction defend some things more strongly than she might have otherwise. Shortly before she left she did say to me once that she seriously doubted she could live in Moscow for any length of time without becoming soured herself on the place. Perhaps what she really needed was the full treatment of exposure to the place to learn what it really meant.

It was paradoxical that she always, to me anyway, passionately defended the United States and everything American. On several occasions I heard her in arguments with Russian literary and artistic people strongly support anything American which cropped up in the conversation, even when it meant attacking something Russian I had previously heard her defend to us.[7]

As for the Soviets, they appreciated her bluntness, particularly in contrast to the sycophancy of Edward C. Carter, secretary general of the Institute of Pacific Relations, who was also in Moscow at this time. John observed to me in 1980 that "Carter spent half his time intoxicated, the other half kissing ass. It was too obvious." Certainly the Russian intellectual community enjoyed Lillian. Despite uneasy moments when she was critiquing rehearsals of *Watch on the Rhine* or *The Little Foxes*, they found her candor refreshing. When she invited her Soviet acquaintances to a farewell party, they all came. Meiklejohn's diary entry for 12 January 1945 gives a jaundiced view of this event:

> Lillian Hellman, the playwright staying with us, gave a party at Spaso House for the Moscow "cultural elite" with whom she has been doing her business. As mangy a gang of literati as I have ever seen—untidy, unclean, hungry, awkward and badly dressed. The only party we've ever had where everything was eaten up, and they drank their weight in champagne. The only one of the whole crowd that looked as if she might be allowed in a first class restaurant in the United States was a dignified grey haired lady sculptress.

But the Russians loved Lillian. Harriman thought hers was the most effective goodwill mission in his experience.

Lillian was to go to England before the end of January 1945 to work on a movie. The precise time of her departure would be determined by the weather. On 17 January, according to *An Unfinished Woman*, she was contacted by the Kremlin: Stalin was willing to see her on February second or third. She did not include this story in her *Colliers* article, saying instead that she had wanted to see Stalin but that he was too busy. John remembers the first version: she told him that Stalin had invited her but she did not want to go. John was sorry she turned the invitation down; it would have kept her in Moscow longer.

On the morning of 18 January, weather was suitable for flying. She was to depart at daybreak. John's letter to her of 18 January 1946 captures the mood of that somber parting:

> Sweetheart, it was a year ago this morning, and a dreary one, that I took you out to that airport, listened to a lot of silly sleepy chatter, kissed you goodbye, and watched the plane disappear into the snow flurries. That was the bleakest ride of my life as I went back to the house, not knowing what lay ahead or whether I even dared to hope. That house which you had made so warm and lovely had become cold and hateful and too full of shadows without you. The night before had been confused and mixed and in too much of a hurry; but toward morning you said: "I was bad tired; now I am good tired." And that made it all right. That strange, strange house has been so strong an influence in my life, and the *ambiente* of so many emotions, that some day I must go back to see it again. Only, I must do it with you. [18 January 1946]

First Separation, January 1945

The first leg of Lillian's journey, in Ambassador Harriman's plane, was to Baku, where the plane stopped overnight. Lillian sent John a cable and a letter. The cable never arrived; the letter reached him three weeks later, on 7 February.

On 19 January Lillian reached Teheran after a very rough flight. Facilities for travelers there were not outstanding; Lillian was fortunate to be known to the British minister, who invited her to stay at the British embassy until she could get passage to Cairo. She was in Teheran for ten days. It was not a pleasant time. She wrote John at least once from Teheran, complaining about the rough flight, about her inability to sleep, and about the "open sewers, open narcotics trade, and open corruption." He received this letter on 12 February, and immediately responded with his own commentary on Iran; he was "pleased to know that you share my views on that country which shock most people who are bedazzled with the love of the Persian Garden and the Golden Domes of Isfahan." John confessed to a more heretical judgment; Russian occupation might clean up Iran significantly.

Then she went on to Cairo in an American military plane. We know nothing of her stay in Cairo, or of her trip from there to London, except that sometime on this journey she cracked a tooth. She arrived in London on 31 January and immediately cabled John. This cable, the only message to him during their first separation which arrived in reasonable time, he received on 2 February.

Lillian's stay in London was in many ways a great relief from her long journey. She was at the Savoy, even in wartime a superb hostelry, and infinitely more comfortable than her accommodations en route. To her relief, she found on 3 February that she was not pregnant. She was no stranger to abortions, but another one at this time would not have been welcome.

Lillian was in love with John, but hers was not the overwhelming emotion that possessed him. She had made him no promises and given little encouragement that they could have any kind of life together. Nevertheless she was affected; her second telegram from London said, "I miss you too much." To this he responded, "That is impossible." In letters from London, she asked him for a "calendar of significant events" of their time together in Moscow; this he supplied on 21 February. She also asked for a photograph. He responded, "That is a problem, for I really have no idea where such exist. But you can do this. As you know, Harris and Ewing in Washington have a habit of taking photographs of us prominent citizens which appropriately can be dragged out of the files and run in the local hometown newspapers when we die of dysentery in someone's banana port. That was done with me before I came out, and though I myself never went to look at the results, rumor said some were good. You can write them for one."

Lillian was in London to work on a long-postponed movie for the British Ministry of Information. By the time she arrived, however, the war was coming to an end so swiftly that her hosts no longer felt the need for this production. The picture was called off by mutual agreement. Lillian recuperated in London for a month, with several visits to a dentist, and flew home on 26 February. This brought her back into the jurisdiction of the FBI.

When she had left Alaska on this suspicious trip the previous October, Hoover had instructed the FBI offices in six cities to "examine the baggage and personal effects of Lillian Hellman when she reenters the United States." In early February 1945, he sent a reminder to the six offices. Unfortunately for the Bureau, the only East Coast port of entry Hoover contacted was New York. Lillian's plane took her to Baltimore. When she arrived there the morning of 27 February, no Bureau agent was present to give her the works.

On 23 March, the New York FBI office routinely reported to headquarters on Lillian's latest activities, which included an interview that appeared in the *New York Herald Tribune* on 2 March.[1] This routine report did not penetrate to the top level of the FBI. Four days later Hoover sent an exasperated letter to New York complaining that their office had not reported Hellman's return, of which he had heard rumors, despite his reminder in early February.[2] New York responded with admirable restraint: the special agent in charge told Hoover that she had not arrived in New York but in Baltimore, and that New York had faithfully reported her doings since then.[3]

So the Bureau wrote Baltimore. SAC Fred Hallford replied immediately, but it was already two months after her arrival. Hoover was not comforted by the outcome:

> For your information the subject arrived at Baltimore, Maryland, on February 27, 1945, as a passenger on the BOAC Clipper *Bangor* from the United Kingdom. She was not interviewed at great length but advised that she was a playwright, having residence at 63 East 82nd Street, New York City, and was returning from a tour which she began October 1, 1944, and during which she traveled in Alaska, Russia, Iran, Egypt, North Africa, France, and England. She stated that during the trip she was a guest of the Soviet and British Governments. She described her tour as a cultural tour.
>
> For your confidential information Miss HELLMAN displayed at the time of the interview some indignation that a person of her prominence should be subjected to any questioning upon entrance into the United States. . . . It is to be noted further that no baggage or body search of the subject was conducted upon her entry at the Port of Baltimore.[4]

So much for the best laid plans.

In Moscow, John was suffering the pangs of unrequited love. The eighty-five pages, single-spaced, that he wrote Lillian from Moscow are a powerful tribute to the depth of his affection. Despite Lillian's doubts and discouragement, he poured out his love in letter after letter. He wanted to marry her, he wanted to have children by her, he wanted to get back to the States as soon as possible so that she could learn that the closeness they had experienced in Moscow was not a fluke and would sustain them the rest of their lives. He acknowledged her skepticism ("certainly you never gave any encouragement in words") but insisted that her actions meant more than she was willing to admit.

The mementos John had of Lillian's visit helped him live with the anguish of her absence. Most precious was a charming love note she had penned at the airport in Moscow just before departure. He had memorized it before the end of the day she left. Unfortunately, it too perished during the witch hunt with the rest of her pre-1952 letters. As he wrote her on 21 January,

> The first shock of your going is wearing off very fast and is being replaced by a growing emptiness and sense of loss. I know that I must get home before very long, for the time we had was altogether too

short to start out with. And one way or another I will. In one sense you seem very far away and very long ago, and yet I keep continually turning and expecting to see you come in the door or hear your voice only to find it is all in my head. It is strange—and wonderful—how deep a relationship can grow in a short period, how many of the details you miss and how much you can learn of the things that really count. And when I get too gloomy about things I take the note you wrote me at the airport and read it. For it is the nicest letter I have ever received. If that is the way you say good-bye badly, then a good one is something to look forward to—if you like good-byes, which I don't.

John also derived great satisfaction from a copy she gave him of the famous picture of her printed in *Vogue*. He found a frame that fit it perfectly in an antique store, and put the picture on his mantel: "the first thing that strikes your eye when you come into my room. So there you sit for all the world to see, a regal picture in a regal setting."

The Embassy staff were not pessimistic about the future of the Melby-Hellman relationship. Joe Phillips's wife Treacy displayed her affection for her husband openly and frequently. John was jealous that the object of his affections was not there too. But he did get advice, as he told Lillian on 12 March: "Last night Treacy took occasion to give me a long lecture about you. 'You really love Lillian? Yes. To be with Lillian is the most important thing in your life, isn't it? Yes. Well, then, blankety blank blank do something about it. Since you know she feels the same way about you, be with her no matter what else happens.' Do you really feel that way? I wish I could be as sure about it as she is. What I do know darling is that the emptiness gets worse each day and the longing to be with you."

Lillian does not report in her memoirs her extensive purchases of china and books while in Moscow. She was, from the first flush of affluence, a lover of fine things. She made major acquisitions in Moscow. John spent endless hours attempting to get her purchases shipped to New York; at least ten pages of his letters describe his hilarious negotiations with the Soviet bureaucracy. His first report, on 25 January: "This afternoon I went over to Voks for a plenary session involving the shipment of your boodle to the States. The results were mildly inconclusive, but that is not the important part. I was greeted with this wide-eyed interest. AND what did you hear in your last telegram from Lillian? This begins the raised eyebrow department: Being completely taken unaware, 'Ah, nothing.' 'Oh? Ah, well. Oh!' Then followed a quick change of subject. You may think this funny, but I don't."

By 8 February Russian obstructionism was beginning to show:

The real dolly, my dear, concerns your china which is getting to be quite a career. I think I will decide that I go with it too. Without too much trouble I got it packed. Then came labelling and now I have a much greater respect for sign painters than I ever had before. I tried free-wheeling as you will see on one box and with disastrous results. So there was nothing to do but stencil. Try it sometime. Anyway I am kind of proud of the results. There are five boxes of which only two come within the eight kilo limit and one is almost forty kilos. That threw them for a loss. But in time they decided it could be done someway. Ten days ago Morozova called me to say if I would get the two small ones to her in an hour they would go out. I did. And yesterday I saw them still sitting in the vestibule of VOKS. At the same time I learned that one of our men goes north tomorrow and could take them with him if they could be cleared by customs today. So I put it up and this afternoon the real blow fell. Before customs will touch it, an export permit must be obtained from Foreign Trade and for that a complete list must be made. I'll try to bluff on my memory on that one. Then the censorship must see and examine each of the books and stamp it. Now it just happens that by various dishonest means I obtained oil paper to wrap each one to protect against damage from moisture. But I guess there is nothing to do except unpack and repack. After that customs will insist on seeing each piece of china. That is where I will stand and give battle, for I will be goddamed if I will allow that, for you will never get it intact that way. Well, it is anybody's guess when it will move. Anyhow it is getting to be a sort of crusade and a game. But be patient, darling, you will get it if I have to carry the stuff. Only remember that I go with it. What I really feel sorry about it all is that Voks is so embarrassed by the monkey shines. I think I could ram it through diplomatic channels with the use of pressure and avoid most of this, but it seems to have become a matter of pride with them that they will get through if it takes ten years. And I don't feel that I can just override them—or that you would want it—and arbitrarily take it out of their hands which would only add humiliation to their embarrassment. They get kicked around enough in their own Govt. without me to add to it.

On 21 March, he was still at it:

As for your boxes, woe is me. Voks sent two of them by air several weeks ago, so you should have had them. The Red Army of course took them in hand, but they refuse to give Voks any information as to whereabouts or when or why. So there is nothing to do there but wait. As for the three large ones, Voks has continued to maintain they would handle them and I was to do nothing. Then the day before your last cable Orlova called me and said she could do nothing. Regretfully she would have to leave that to me. So now there is nothing for me to do but get them through customs, get an export license and censorship clearance and ship them via the north.

On 25 March:

To continue the blow by blow account of the celebrated case of the People vs The Hellman China: I had a little session with Voks on it yesterday afternoon. As the matter now stands the State Historical Commission, or some such organization, is shortly to come around to unpack and inspect it and decide whether it can be permitted to leave the country. The application states that it is all composed of gifts to you. Remember that. Kemenev was quite cheerful in his opinion that permission will be denied! I asked what then and he said that had not occurred to him. But I do not take quite so pessimistic a view. I daresay they may well turn it down in the first instance, but then we go on from there. There can be many a turn.

John inherited not only the task of shipping Lillian's purchases, but also the responsibility of continuing some of her arguments with various Muscovites. One of these was with Ilya Ehrenburg. When John wrote Lillian about the Ehrenburg colloquy, he also moved into a discussion of philosophical and political matters of great import to their personal relationship. It was the compatibility of their basic approaches to people and ideas which, during the long months of their affair, undergirded the physical passion. It was the later weakening of the philosophical bond, when John edged into a Cold War position and Lillian supported Henry Wallace, that kept them apart at the crucial moment when John was able to obtain a divorce.

John wrote her on 15 March about a banquet held by Voks for visiting American editors:

Next to me at the table was Marshak who as you know is a lot of fun. Across the table was Ehrenburg who is not a lot of fun and with whom I found myself involved in the same idiotic argument you had with him about Hemingway. He also indulged in the nasty trick of getting two of the American editors into an argument with each other about the future possibilities of fascism in America and then turning it on both of them since no two of the three were talking with the same definition. He is really an evil man. And a charlatan.

March 18. Sweetheart: I forgot to tell you what was really the important point in the wrangle the other day with Ehrenburg. What started the chatter on fascism was discussion as to the difficulty of eradicating it in its psychological and therefore more dangerous forms and manifestations. He said it would take two generations in Europe and asked me what I thought of America. I said, to the horror of my colleagues here who of course deny there was ever any suggestion of fascism in America that I thought it would take one generation if we were lucky. (This really did put the brand on me in certain quarters). Then I asked him what about Russia. He said ten years. I wanted to ask him how it could be done so quickly in the areas that had been occupied, but thought better in the given company. I think he is too optimistic and probably did not mean it anyway. Which brings up another point. It is possible to get awfully fed-up with endless hoopla in the Russian press about the need to cleanse this and that of fascism. It is of course fashionable to say that it is the cover plan for ulterior and dastardly plans. The fact of course is that the Russians understand the nature, the sources, the methods, and the objectives of fascism infinitely better than do we. Nor does a Marxist make the mistake of identifying it solely with German Nazis. He can see it potentially in any individual, group of individuals, or society, and I think correctly, which has as its primary objective the sanctity of property or the glorification of the physical State (which is after all just another form of property). Property, rather than labor or human life, is the criterion used. And this becomes all entangled and covered up with the hoary shibboleths of free enterprise etc. etc. There is of course only one answer which is given by property to this—and I have had it thrown in my face a thousand times by my dear El Paso family—and that is that property etc is what has made America a great country. This obviously is wrong. We were made great by a concept of free men, of the worth of the individual, in short of democracy, and we were the fools of luck to happen to have with it and us an almost inexhaustible store of untouched wealth which we were able to exploit and use. The weakness in our system—which did not become particularly perti- nent until we reached the limit of our physical expansive power—was and IS that the vested interests in property, whether it be great wealth or merely a supposed security in a clerical job, in its insecurity comes to place property above the values of personality. This influence is opposed to and at least unconsciously tends to undermine and eventually to destroy the true sources of our strength. I believe that this accounts for much of what Jefferson did and believed, even though the words he used were different and some of the actions did not secure the desired objective inasmuch as they failed to take into account and utilize the coming industrialization. Fascism, then, I would define as the corruption of things. And the problem: Can an individual once corrupted by things be made honest again?

The argument with Ehrenburg became a reference point for many later discussions between John and Lillian. They were agreed: fascism did have deep roots in the United States, and it threatened the creation of the kind of world they both wanted to see.

Many of John's letters contained a running commentary on world events. These letters kept up until his correspondence with Lillian tapered off in 1948, and they offer a fascinating history of the end of World War II and the beginning of the Cold War. John participated in these events as an insider, observing the breakdown of Soviet-American relations first from the cockpit of the Embassy in Moscow, then as a member of the United States delegation to the United Nations founding conference in San Francisco, and finally as a staff member of the American embassy in China.

Much of what John wrote Lillian during this period found its way into his classic account of the Chinese Civil War, *Mandate of Heaven*, finally published in 1968. But the letters are infinitely richer than *Mandate*, spiced as they are with uninhibited judgments of people and events intended for Lillian's eyes only.

John's first commentaries were on the Yalta Conference of 4 to 11 February 1945. Yalta probably represented the high point of Soviet-American good will: Roosevelt got Stalin's promise to enter the war against Japan in the Pacific, and Stalin got assurances that, with cosmetic "elections" in Poland, he could largely have his way in Eastern Europe.

Ambassador Harriman and several other staffers of the American Embassy in Moscow attended the Yalta Conference; John began hearing their stories about it when Harriman returned to Moscow on 13 February, bringing with him Secretary of State Edward Stettinius and other officials from Washington. John's first comments to Lillian had to be guarded, as Yalta was top secret: "The big show went wondrously, far better than anyone had dared to hope." Stettinius was received with great cordiality in Moscow: "All is well, very very well" (13 February 1945).

The night before Stettinius left Moscow, the Russians put their very best foot forward. As John reported it to Lillian: "Then last night the best performance of *Swan Lake* I have ever seen and an atmosphere of greater genuine cordiality than I have known. It would be difficult to over-estimate the importance of the success of the last two weeks. I am only sorry that you have not been here during this period" (14 February 1945).

One unexpected visitor who came to Moscow with Stettinius and stayed for a while John could write about. That visitor was Ed Flynn, Democratic boss of the Bronx, whose unexplained presence at Yalta had startled the Russians and presumably the British and Americans as well. Only Roosevelt knew what Flynn was doing. Flynn was an old political associate of Roosevelt's credited with helping persuade Roosevelt to run for governor of New York in 1928.

Flynn had had an alcohol problem. By now he was on the wagon, but Harriman was determined that he be kept sober during his time in Moscow. Melby was given this detail. According to John, Flynn knew very well why John accompanied him everywhere, and was somewhat amused by it. John wrote Lillian:

> A good part of my business now consists of one Ed Flynn whom I seem to have inherited to squire through Voks. In many ways he is an interesting man, of great charm and without pretensions. Despite his close Roman affiliations, he has a rather refreshing attitude toward this country which he puts something like this: I suppose I should oppose it. But I can see what it has accomplished. I don't understand the system or why it works. But it does and in many respects better than ours. So who am I to say it is wrong?—That is either great candor or great Jesuitry. This much I can say, that he is genuinely interested to learn. Well, we shall see what he develops. This proposition has more ramifications than meet the eye, as I will tell you one day. [14 February 1945]

During three weeks of squiring Flynn around, John became good friends with the mysterious politico. He also learned the reason for Flynn's presence. Roosevelt had brought Flynn to Yalta, then sent him on to Moscow and later to Rome, to further one of Roosevelt's pet ideas: mediating a Vatican-Kremlin détente. As a prominent Catholic layman, and a canny politician, Flynn was as likely as anyone to bring off such a startling rapprochement.

In the temporary glow of good feeling immediately after Yalta, prospects for Flynn's mission seemed promising. Molotov was interested. Flynn reported Molotov's reaction to John: "Why not? Time doesn't mean anything to us, Kremlin or Vatican. Why shouldn't we begin conversations?" And as the friendship between Flynn and Melby grew, Flynn made a proposal: when he was officially assigned as the American-sponsored mediator in this fantastic enterprise, he would take Melby along as his assistant.

The Flynn mission intrigued Melby. As he reported to Lillian in the long letter of 13 February, he was not inclined to stick with his Latino specialty; the corridors of influence seemed now to lead to Soviet-American relations. Flynn's mission fit this prospectus neatly.

But the Flynn mission was still very tentative, and very much in the future. John's more immediate prospects were presented to him by Harriman on 21 February:

> Sweetheart, here it comes. The shadow of the axe became very distinct this morning. Harriman hauled me into his boudoir this morning after breakfast. It seems Dept. and White House have become gravely concerned at the paltry number of available officers who have any Russian experience, there being practically no post which does not need one. To remedy this the officer staff in the chancery is to be increased to 45 by the end of this year. But the Balkans, Central Europe, the periphery of Germany cannot wait that long so within the next three or four months every officer who has been here longer than six months is being transferred. He offered me what I gathered to be first choice. I squirmed and I wiggled but I don't think it did much good. We all go! Of course there is many a slip between the talk and the move, but it looks to me as though the cards had been stacked. I gather that what they have in mind for me is to be the political officer in the American section of the Allied Control Commission for Hungary. Will you go to Budapest with me? I suppose that professionally it is the best of the jobs for Hungary is the undefined area, and east and west of it is pretty well laid out. Many of the indications of what can be expected will show up there. Interestingly enough Voroshilov is the head of the Russian section. And it is in Hungary that the three spheres of influence and the east and the west will meet. Obviously this is important, except that damn it I would prefer to come back here. Unfortunately this is war and preferences do not always count. In any event it seems I will be going to the States for leave and consultation in April or May and after that . . . well . . .

Harriman then went on to some interesting comments. He said he was disturbed by the reports coming from our people in the Balkans now because they always take the gloomy and negative reaction to everything the Russians do and he does not like it for this reason: if the pessimistic is right, then we are going to lose everything anyway. But if the optimistic is right then we have everything to gain by taking that attitude from the beginning, and nothing to lose in any event. So he wishes to spot open Russian minds hither and yon. And says he to me: Since Hungary is the hardest and most uncertain of the problems and you of all the people here are the most disposed to give the Russians the benefit of any doubt (though I do not always agree with you) I would like you to go there . . . Well, so what? I am not completely sure that I know what my reaction to all this is. [22 February 1945]

Then, for several days, John's concerns shifted to the imminent opening of the Russian version of *Watch on the Rhine*. This finally came off on 24 February, and John's letter to Lillian the next day concerned little else.

Feb 25—My Dearest: Last night the *Watch* made its appearance. What to say about it? There are two approaches. The first would be yours and the general American. In this sense it was really pretty bad on the whole. Your work on Sara was a success in that she only once had to resist a temptation to do a spread-eagle act on the table and gave a quiet dignified performance. Ulrich I thought very good and impressive who only occasionally acted as though he were thrashing through the underbrush. David, Teck, and Martha were good. But, my dearest darling, that unlovely-looking Birman woman! Such goings on I have never seen. She clowned the part from beginning to end, she whooped and she howled, she grinned and smirked, she danced, she tried to climb the wall, she draped herself against the bookcases, every time a speech would start she stalked from right to left and left to right. I think she was under the impression that Fanny was first cousin to Ivan Grozny. It was a good counterpart to the mad scene of Gloucester in Lear. And the Russians loved it, for one said to me: She really is an eccentric character isn't she? The idea of just another silly American woman was not there at all. In fact there was a tendency to put in a touch of burlesque every now and then by all characters. This went best with the children who were very good.

Staging was good and costumes excellent. Liberties were taken with a few lines. For example, in the last scene Ulrich says: "He who wishes to live has the best chance to live. I wish to live. I wish to live my life with you." This came out: "He who wishes to live will live. I wish to live." I don't quite understand why the change. It hardens the character certainly, which I suppose would be approved, thought that seemed hardly necessary to me. The point to me in the way you wrote it is that it makes him also a human being.

The other approach—and I think this more important here—is the Russian. It was definitely a hit with the audience which laughed and applauded and in the farewell scene wept to the last man, including Mme Molotov and Lozovski and the bodyguards. They loved the portrayal of an American scene and it was a pretty good picture of that. They were reaffirmed in their views of Rumanians. I think they got the point about Americans prior to the war and their opinion of us did not go up. Birman said: "Lillian has courage, for it takes courage to tell the truth." So I think it will be a success here. I think it will even be the right kind of success. . . . From your view as author, I don't know whether the above tells you what you want to know. I hope it is not too bad. So let me have it. And yes, at the party afterwards, there were many toasts to you, nice things said, and genuine regrets that you could not be present. So I continue to be very proud of you, darling.

In the month following the Yalta Conference, John's letters began to include hints about things going wrong—about renewed difficulties with the Russian hierarchy, and about American soldiers freed by the Russians from Nazi prison camps making hostile remarks about their Soviet liberators. The most serious problems had to do with Stalin's treatment of the Eastern European areas liberated from Germany. As John told Lillian in his letter of 21 February, Harriman had at that time been cautiously optimistic about what would happen in the areas then coming under Soviet control; it had then seemed that those areas would be allowed to establish relatively independent governments with only minimal Soviet control—and that for purposes of preventing another invasion of the Soviet Union from the west. Now, in March, this hope was vanishing.

The euphoria of the Yalta Conference was dissipating; in one month the Embassy in Moscow was swept by a wave of pessimism and hostility. John duly reported this to Lillian:

> Harriman is in the grimmest and most rebellious frame of mind I have ever seen him in. I do know the whole Balkan and Eastern European business is a complete bust and stalemate. Personally, I think bad handling over the last two years has jockeyed us into a position which is nobody's fault but our own and which we should

have kept out of in the first place. Now we should sit up and take our medicine like little men. Or perhaps that is politically impossible at home. After two years away I would not know about that. There are other things which cannot go in writing, but I will tell you—and this obviously like the rest not for repetition—that this Embassy considers Yalta as pretty completely washed up. If you think the atmosphere when you were here bad, you should see it now. Under pressure of endless needling from Bob, Eddy, and George life is almost intolerable for everyone. [21 March 1945]

John was equally disturbed about the attitudes of the freed American soldiers.

I will say this much. If the remarks our prisoners are making as they come out ever get in the press at home, it is going to do no one any good. Most of the kids are sick and unhappy and have forgotten how all armies behave. I don't know what they expected, or if they thought that an army in motion provides hot running water each morning, or if they have forgotten that an area fought over is messy and rather gruesome things happen at times. Maybe they have even forgotten how the American army is reported to have looted in Sicily. Or maybe that is different. Their comments on front line troops are favorable, and anything but that on the rear. [21 March 1945]

Toward the end of March, the ambassador and Kathleen both got letters from Lillian. John never saw them, but whatever they said, he was elevated to new status in the Embassy. He asked Lillian: "Just what did you say? Whatever it was, it has made me the object of a certain amount of affection and a considerable amount of awe" (30 March 1945).

Also at the end of March, John Paton Davies and his wife Patricia arrived in Moscow, where Davies was to serve for two years. In the weeks remaining of Melby's Moscow assignment, they became fast friends. Melby's description of Davies in his letters to Lillian was prophetic: Davies accurately predicted the triumph in China of Mao's Communists, which triumph Melby later witnessed. This prophecy, wrote Melby, would very rapidly "get Davies in the doghouse here" (30 March 1945). Neither man knew that the gathering forces of the inquisition would gun them both down before a decade had passed.

In New York, Lillian began to unburden herself of the impressions she had received during her stay in Russia. She held a press conference at her house on East 82nd Street on 1 March. The *New York Times* covered this conference. Unfortunately, the edition of the *Times* that was microfilmed, and hence has entered the "official" record, contains an abbreviated version of the conference. The full record, carried in an earlier edition, was clipped by the FBI, and resides still in their files. It contains significant material not in the microfilm.

The lead of the *Times* story is, appropriately, Lillian's comments on fascism. She was asked by the Soviet officers she met on her trip to the front, "What would the United States do about Argentina?" Lillian countered "What will Russia do about Franco?" They responded, "We'll take care of fascism on the European continent, and hope that you'll take care of it on the American."

From fascism she went to observations about the Russian people. They were, she said, "polite, Puritan, romantic, terrific" people about whom too little is known, too much misunderstood. But she specifically declined the role of "expert" on Russia, except about Russian intellectuals. "Artists are treated like kings in Russia in the respect and remuneration accorded them," she said. She considered contemporary Russian music better, but literature worse, than American. She found the Russians quite willing to acknowledge lend-lease aid; everywhere, they proudly showed her American-made goods—from trucks, jeeps, and planes to sheets and sweaters.

Then there was politics, and a remarkable statement for one who was considered so left-wing. "I wouldn't want to see Communism here," she said. "We're never going to have it. It is no problem with us. I see no signs of it here."[5] This part of her statement was omitted from summaries of her FBI file as they were later passed out to right-wing columnists, congressional committees, and the Passport Office.

Three weeks later, when Lillian spoke at a dinner sponsored by the Spanish Refugee Appeal, remarks she made were pounced on avidly by the FBI, and repeated in subsequent versions of her file to show her true pro-Communism. Spain's tragedy, she said, was followed by the tragedy of millions everywhere, and the Soviet people suffered more than others. This was, of course, heretical. And worse, she attacked a recent bitter anti-Soviet book by William L. White: *Report on the Russians*. White's book, she said, "is the first of many that will follow by other reactionaries like him. It is not a question of whether we approve of the Soviet system. They like it and fight for it remarkably."[6]

In the 31 March 1945 issue of *Colliers*, Lillian's article "I Meet the Front-Line Russians" appeared. It is a lengthy, journalistic style piece, with versions of her trip that conflict with the account in *Unfinished Woman*. There is no satisfactory explanation for the discrepancies. Presumably when she wrote the memoir years later she still had her diary to draw on; if not, she could have relied on the *Colliers* article. Why she did not do so is a mystery; it would have saved her much obloquy.

But the *Colliers* piece as published was damning enough. It was friendly toward the Russians: not the government but the people. This was sufficient to attract the attention of the hate-right, in the person of Westbrook Pegler. His column of 24 April, in the *Washington Times-Herald* and elsewhere, excoriated *Colliers* for carrying articles by Lillian Hellman and Ella Winter without warning readers that these writers were Communists. Says Pegler:

> Hellman has 42 citations in the index of the Dies Committee and as you flip the pages of the committee report to see what they refer to you find the usual run of committees, rallies, causes, and little, no-account sheets that hardly anybody ever heard of.
>
> Now, of course, this index contains the names of many individuals who are no more Communist than Mussolini is a Chinaman, so it doesn't necessarily follow that these two old babes are Commy or pro-Commy merely because they run such a high score.
>
> As to that, you have to draw your conclusions from the consistency of their activity and the character of the outfits and movements with which they associated themselves and I have drawn mine. Moreover, it is okay with me for anyone to be a Communist or pro-Communist, which is a degree of tolerance that I have never encountered among those people, but I just sort of think that *Colliers*, in presenting their stuff and blowing kisses at Winter and Hellman, would have served the public interest if it had indicated their sympathies and politics as suggested by their records.[7]

This was the first trickle of what became a flood.

John was on a week's visit to Leningrad with Ed Flynn during the early part of March. It was, he told Lillian, a friendly, responsive, lovely city; and the mayor gave, in Flynn's honor: "A whopping brawl which was the easiest and most cordial Russian affair I have ever been to. But I missed you the whole time. The same Intourist gal who picked out your china was our interpreter. She rather startled me before the end of the first half hour by asking if I were in love with you. When I gave her the obvious answer she said she would have known I would have good taste. Perhaps I am beginning to wear that Lillian Hellman look on my face. I hope you won't object too strenuously" (6 March 1945).

On 1 April, John got orders to proceed in a hurry to the United Nations founding conference in San Francisco, where he was to be liaison officer to the Soviet delegations. This, to him, was a "fantastic break"; the premier statesmen of the entire nonfascist world would be there. But there was an additional assignment included in his orders: after San Francisco, he was to go to Buenos Aires. Both he and Harriman were outraged at this—John because he despised Perón, Argentina's profascist dictator, and Harriman because he wanted John's Russian experience utilized in one of the countries bordering the Soviet Union.

Accordingly, the cable Harriman sent Secretary of State Stettinius on 1 April said in the strongest terms that it would make sense to send John to San Francisco, but no sense at all to send him to Buenos Aires afterward. John wrote Lillian: "We shall know shortly how well and convincingly we draft cables around here." They were not to know for five and a half months.

At noon on Tuesday 3 April, Voks called John to say that *The Little Foxes* would open *that night*. Everyone at the Embassy was to come. How many tickets would they need? John of course did not know; he was anguished at the peremptory opening. He himself was scheduled to attend a reception at the Dutch embassy, but he could skip that. The Harrimans, however, were committed to a private party for Mrs. Winston Churchill, who had just arrived in Moscow; this they could not cancel. Few other Americans were available that evening. John requested several tickets and was assured they would be delivered to Spaso. When he went to pick the tickets up at the receptionist's that evening on his way to the theater, there were no tickets. He wound up going to the Dutch party after all.

On 8 April, John wrote Lillian: "Yesterday at the brittle point of a frightful hangover a lot of mail came from you just in time to save my life. It included three letters from New York and one from London which must have had quite a journey." In the London letter, she mentioned having sent cables from Teheran and Baku, which he never got, and several from New York, also missing. There were other foul-ups: he had asked his father to send flowers to Lillian in New York; the cable his father received said something about a baby elephant. Nancy Bragdon, Lillian's secretary, had written to friends in Bloomington "to inquire as to just who the Melbys were." John was encouraged by this. If Nancy took the affair seriously, she had some significant clues from her employer.

That same day, 8 April, *The Little Foxes* was produced again in Moscow, with a full American contingent in the theater.

April 9—My Darling: The Foxes turned out to be a hell of a good job last night, one which you can be proud of and for which I am proud of you. The most extraordinary thing about it was the success in capturing a pretty good reproduction of an American, and a southern, atmosphere. Almost without exception the cast was good and effective. Best I thought was Birdie, and in them all the influence of the movie version was obvious, especially Regina trying to look and act like Bette Davis—which she did. They all could not resist the temptation occasionally to overact—as in most Russian theatre—but this did not change it much, except in the case of Ben who had hysterical lapses. I suspect this tendency to overact was a good thing in that subtler forms would probably have been lost on an audience which is not particularly well-informed about the details of American society, particularly some of its more exotic manifestations.

Costumes were excellent, the set authentic except for a cactus backdrop and some sort of funny-business involving breakfast on a second-story balcony, and incidental music tended to be Dixie, Old Folks at Home, and Drink to Me Only. One interesting and rather original touch was that over the stage in huge block letters was a sign reading HUBBARDS. I suppose it was intended to fix in the Russian audience mind the identity between family and business. The attitude of the cast was radically different from that of the *Watch*, the former being sure of what it was doing and having no qualms about it, which was hardly true of the latter. Between acts the conventional eating and drinking, for some reason this time it was cordial, but never really unbent and got drunk. Okhlopkov made his toast to you, his pleasure not only in putting on your play but also that it could be the play of an American woman whom he regretted could not be here to see it, especially since she understood Russians and Russians understood her. He did this really very nicely and graciously.

This was the last letter John mailed from Moscow. On 10 April he sent a restrained but exultant cable: "LEAVING THIS WEEK FOR SAN FRANCISCO CONFERENCE WILL SEE YOU SOON DARLING DO SEND ONE WORD BEFORE I LEAVE MUCH LOVE."

But the end was not yet. On 12 April, the night before Melby and General John Deane were to leave Moscow, Harriman gave a farewell party. About 1:00 A.M., the Embassy duty officer called. Kathleen Harriman took the call and passed the news to her father: Roosevelt was dead. That ended the party. Harriman phoned Molotov, told him the news, and asked for an appointment. Molotov insisted on coming over to Spaso immediately. According to John's recollection in 1980, Molotov was a wild man, pacing the corridors of Spaso: "What are we going to do? Who is this man Truman? We could get along with Roosevelt, he understood us and we understood him. Now he is dead. Who is this man? What can we do?"

"Harriman picked the last question right up," John recalls, "because at that point the Russians had not indicated they would send a high-level delegation to the United Nations founding conference at San Francisco. Harriman said, 'The first thing you can do is go to San Francisco.' Molotov responded 'I will do it. I will leave tomorrow.'" The next day, Stalin gave his approval, and Molotov left soon thereafter for the United States. Molotov's visit with Truman en route to San Francisco, however, did little to assuage Soviet fears about the loss of Roosevelt.

John left the next morning for Kiev, Naples, Algiers, the Cape Verde Islands, Newfoundland, and New York. Army planes, hard bucket seats, and no sleep.

New York and San Francisco

John landed at LaGuardia late in the afternoon on 15 April 1945. Military planes not following rigorous schedules, he was unable to notify Lillian in advance of his time of arrival. An army general he met on the plane provided him transportation to Manhattan and got him a room at a Lexington Avenue hotel not far from Lillian's 82nd Street house. John phoned: she was not in. He had dinner, drank in a bar, and kept phoning. At about nine o'clock, she answered. They met on 82nd Street under a streetlight; he remembers that she was wearing a tan coat.

They were both nervous, meeting for the first time on American soil, in surroundings familiar to her but strange to him—and so different from Moscow. She ran to his arms, and this, he wrote her later, "seemed the most natural thing in the world." They stayed, that night, at her place on East 82nd. It was as if they had never parted.

Lillian's play *The Searching Wind* was opening the next day at the National Theater in Washington; she had invited Robert Lovett, assistant secretary of war, and his wife Adele to be her guests for the first performance. Transportation on the Eastern seaboard that spring was terrible. She had no reservations for travel to Washington. They bought train tickets, boarded a day coach at Penn Station, and started looking for seats. Luck was with them. Mary Pickford and Charles 'Buddy' Rogers were on the train, holding two extra seat reservations for friends who did not show. Lillian and John were ensconced in the extra seats.

In Washington, Lillian had reserved a room at the Statler. It seemed unwise for John to stay with her, and he finally found a place at the Everett. After his exhausting trip from Moscow, and the excitement of their reunion in New York, he was in no shape to join an upstage theater party. When Lillian went to meet the Lovetts, John phoned Llewellyn 'Tommy' Thompson, a friend and Russian expert in the Foreign Service, went over to

Thompson's place for dinner, and promptly fell asleep. Twelve hours later he was fit to join Lillian for breakfast.

The few days they had together in Washington flew by mercilessly. They did see *The Searching Wind* together; they met Ruth Gordon and Garson Kanin while leaving the theater and joined them for a drink. Other than that, John does not remember whom they met nor what they did. The six days together, he says, went by in quadruple time. It was paradise, but on the edge of a knife.

They were on borrowed time. John was already overdue in San Francisco, but the State Department could not provide a flight west until 21 April. Lillian gave him two of her books while they were in Washington. Her inscription in *The Searching Wind* reads "For John, with love, with respect. Lillian April 1945." In the Random House edition of *Four Plays* she wrote, "For John, with much love and much else. Lillian April 1945." John's plane left on time the morning of the twenty-first. The parting, this time, was less traumatic than in Moscow.

During a layover in Chicago he saw his parents briefly; they came up from Bloomington. It was not until his plane was over the Arizona desert that he took pen in hand to begin the next series of letters.

April 22, 1945.

It was a wonderful time that we have had this past week & I resent it like hell that there must be interruptions. The more time we have together the more convinced I am that it is right—right for me I know & if you will pardon the impertinence for you too. To me you are a fine, lovely, saucy person. You are also a lusty wench, as I said, & thank God. My love for you is such that I would take it on any terms. And when you ask if I would spend my life being unhappy with you, the answer is that that even would be infinitely preferable to spending it being unhappy without you. That is the way it is. After this last week anything else is inconceivable. And last night was a hard one. Half dozing on a fairly rough trip my mind kept going over things said & done—the words that say no & the actions which so unconsciously say yes and finally you standing at the airport looking almost as forlorn as I felt. Darling—love me—I want you.

The United Nations founding conference in San Francisco was a madhouse. There were too many high-ranking guests and too few first-class hotel rooms, too few interpreters and too many bruised egos. To John, the whole thing seemed disorganized. His own part, keeping the Soviet delegates happy, was easy enough. But only sixty-seven automobiles were assigned to the conference, hardly enough for the American delegation alone; and the Department of State was already out of money.

The enjoyable times for John were the lunches and dinners with old friends, and with some new ones. Every paragraph he wrote Lillian reporting on breakfast with the flashy Quintanilla, or dinner with Alaska governor Ernest Gruening, or lunch with James Reston and Raymond Gram Swing plaintively concluded by telling her how much more enjoyable it would have been were she there.

The battles with the Russians over Poland (Russia wanted the Communist Poles centered in Lublin admitted to the United Nations) and Argentina (Russia wanted Perón excluded) were heating up; John's sedulous descriptions of how the United Nations was beaten into shape are as stellar a participant-observer account as exists. Despite the fact that he and Lillian were now both on the same continent, with frequent phone calls possible, he still wrote: fifty-nine crowded pages during the two-month conference.

The difference in time zones caused them some trouble. The best times for him to phone her were in the morning before any official breakfasts, and late at night when the parties were over. But she was frequently at work and out of the house when it was breakfast time in San Francisco, and if he called her when his day was over, it was 3:00 or 4:00 A.M. in New York. One of them was always apologizing for shorting the other's sleep. They did manage to talk, but always there was an immense agenda left over, undiscussed, as his letter of 28 April indicated:

Sweetheart: As always it was nice to hear your voice this morning. The only trouble with these calls is that they can't last long enough. It is wonderful to be able to talk with you, even briefly, but it makes me miss you all the more. And if I start missing you much more than I do I shall probably have to say to hell with this business and come back east.

Yesterday was a rough day in which some things were settled and during which Molotov almost literally got the shit kicked out of him, if you will pardon the expression. By the compromise he lost on the conference chairmanship and did not like it. He then won hands down on the Ukraine and White Russia. Then he made one of the greatest mistakes of his career. He whanged into the Polish question. Before he had even finished his statement the entire gang of foreign ministers rose to their feet and shouted NO! After that there followed a series of violent denunciations of Russia and Russian policy that were appallingly outspoken. I don't know whether this represents a spontaneous development or whether someone organized it, but Russian prestige here has taken a frightful beating overnight. It was a bad mistake in judgment on his part. He should have known that in any event he could not win here on Poland and he was doing all right on other counts, even his acceptance of the chairmanship compromise having in a sort of way helped his position. Now he has lost the initiative he wanted and had for a while and will find it extremely difficult to recover it. There are altogether too many people here who want to kick him around. It will not help that he is probably leaving the middle of next week. There may be a sort of pale utility to it in that this is the first large-scale conference in which he has participated and there are some things about how such shindigs operate that he does not know. If I know anything about Russians they will learn fast. It is too early to know what the eventual results will be, but we shall see.

As for me, I continue to mosey around. It seems that the function of the liaison officers is to do all the nasty jobs no one else wants to do, and to keep hands off on what someone else does want. A combination of nursemaid, office boy, and messenger. So I hold their hands, get them tickets, smooth out their squabbles, get them hotel rooms, typewriters and God only knows what else. But the Russians are a lot less trouble than most in this respect since they do most things for themselves and only holler when they get into trouble which is not often. Some of the others have not been so fortunate, the French being far and away the worst. Then there was the incident of the Ecuadoran who ended up in jail and the Arabian with no knowledge of English who tried to make an elevator girl in the elevator by whispering "pussy, pussy, pussy." Also the Jugoslavs who had been forgotten for hotel rooms and spent their first night here sitting with their luggage out on a curbstone.

On 30 April, he reminisced about the first night they talked in New York:

The papers tonight also announce that we refuse to recognize the government set up in Soviet-held Vienna. And another agreement is gone. You remember the background on the prisoners of war business. The papers also print a blast from General Golikov charging American atrocities against Soviet prisoners and our failure to live up to the Yalta agreement. Sweetheart, where does all this come out? I remember that we sat in your lovely living room and you wondered whether there actually could be any basis for a genuine understanding. Perhaps you are right, perhaps you are right. Obviously the speculative possibilities and explanations are legion. . . . Certainly it is one way to wreck a peace conference. And tonight I am dreadfully tired and in low spirits. And as never before I want to see you tonight and to hold you close to me.

From John's letters, we know only snippets of what Lillian was doing in New York. She complained to him about her new birthday dress and sent him a photograph; he said it was "quite becoming." She complained that she had to spend an evening alone; John, who was fed up with the forced socializing of the conference, told her the only thing wrong with such an evening was that he was not there. She apologized for not writing more often; he responded, "I think I know how you feel about writing, and the real answer is that I am piggish about you and no matter how much I had, would always want more" (Letter, 7 May 1945). When she mentioned attending a cocktail party at Kathleen Harriman's, he wanted to know who was there and what was discussed. She noted one favorable omen: her shipment of china had arrived from Moscow.

On 8 May, John got notice of what was in store for him:

Yesterday morning Harriman asked me to come up to see him. It was the first real talk I had with him since I have been here. (He leaves later today for Washington and will be there only two or three days. He did not indicate that he planned to go to New York.) The point of it was that the most important job as political advisor in the world today for the US is the job in Chungking. (Everybody knows that anyway.) The Department wants me to take it on. But, says Harriman, he wants to be satisfied in his own mind that I will be a good boy. This comes from the fact that almost everybody in Chungking has misbehaved, questioning that the Kuomintang [the political party headed by Chiang Kai-shek] is the greatest outfit since Boss Tweed. They have so expressed themselves even though the Washington line is to support the Kuomintang. Obviously it has been necessary to transfer them. We must realize what Communists are, we must know how to protect future American interests. We must reinforce the case against the Soviets because that is the only possible answer. I must report according to the line, not according to what I believe.

Sweetheart, suddenly I felt very sick and very cold inside. And then I became so angry I could not speak. Magazines like *Cosmopolitan* used to write articles about the Russians priming their boys that way. And there I was looking down the same barrel in the United States of America. In the background Grandpa Chip [Ambassador Charles

Bohlen] nodded wisely, his contribution being that his party was not the anti-Soviet party but the non-Communist Russian party—whatever that one means. It was obviously a choice of playing ball or getting out, though Harriman finally destroyed his own argument in the end by saying that he did not mean this to sound as it did. He really meant that the United States would be in no danger as long as we had a policy, any kind of a policy; that we have no policy, that he must find one, that we must change no line until we are sure of the facts on which we base a new one, and I am a fine boy and he recommends me unqualifiedly for the assignment. This spiel is all obvious and muddled and nonsense. Basically the line indicates a frightening confusion as to what we do want in the face of a determined policy on the other side and our fear that we cannot uphold our own. Consequently in our panic we drop into opposition.

As I say, it made me very angry. It made me goddamed if I was going to quit. It made me very certain that I was going to get the job and play it out my way, even if they crucify me for it in a year. I don't intimidate easily. It is probably the most dangerous game I have ever played and I play it on the chance that the next year is going to see enough upheavals at home to reorient us and create a new and constructive foreign policy. If I am right I come out on top. And if I am wrong I look for something else to do. I have no illusions of my chances, but it will be fun anyway. And if I go down, there will be a good many of us who go down together. Won't you come along, darling? That is a hell of an offer, but it seems to be the best I can do. This of course may not go through and in any event I take the Russian language course this summer and will not go abroad until October. And between now and then a lot of things can happen. This I know, that we shall not see peace in our time. Hitler used to brag that he was making history for a thousand years. I doubt if we are doing any such thing, but perhaps we can help guide its direction. [9 May 1945]

Lillian apparently took this in stride. Telephone conversations in the following days found her asking him for a photograph, providing him with the latest New York rumors about Harriman's next assignment, and agreeing with his position on the necessity for avoiding an all-out breach with the Russians.

John had trouble getting a photograph for her. He found most photo shops out of paper but finally located a high class studio that would do the job in a week. The "piece of art work" which he sent her on 19 May "makes my flesh creep. Something really should be done about me, but the question is what." She wrote him that she had had dinner with her father, who brought his girlfriend along; this, John responded, struck him as funny. "Somehow I got the impression that he is as old as Noah and that he should have a girl friend is amusing." One time when he called, she was out of breath from running up the stairs; he remarked, "Sometime please get out of breath over me instead of from running up stairs" (letter, 19 May 1945).

It was 13 May when John got the first clear signal that Lillian's feelings for him were strong enough to cause a first-class attack of jealousy. By most standards, she was relatively free from such negative emotions. She had endured Hammett's whoring and drunkenness with only occasional shows of anger. Now, on a Saturday night, she phoned John from New York, at least twice and probably oftener, getting no answer from what the hotel clerk claimed was his room as late as 1:00 A.M. San Francisco time. She tried again at 6:45 A.M. California time—no answer. When he talked to her later that day, she was boiling and abrupt.

His letter of 14 May tried to get things back on an even keel. He had, he claimed, been in bed and alone when she called at 1:00 A.M. The hotel help was notoriously incompetent and had rung some other room. At 6:45 A.M. he was indeed out—there was an ugly squabble about the disposition of the conference motor pool, and the liaison personnel were called to an early meeting to settle it: "The Russians, Ukrainians, and Argentines got their lines fouled in a conference style tong war over who was to get what car at what time." In the end, he said, they all took a bus.

John, too, was upset. He wrote her: "I have never lied to you, nor will I." She should have more faith in him than that, he said. If she didn't know by now how much he loved her, she was a wretch, and he would have to knock some sense into her. His conclusion was upbeat: "The only cheerful thing I see in this is that possibly you care more than you have so far been willing to admit, or perhaps even want. Please do, darling. You make all the difference in the world to me."

John's letter of 14 May, in addition to dealing with their relationship, contained an extensive essay on the international situation. His perspective coincided with Lillian's completely. He bemoaned the loss of Roosevelt's leadership, the compromise of the ideals that had been articulated in the Atlantic Charter and that had presumably guided the United States in its prosecution of the war, and the conspiracy theory increasingly being applied to the Soviet Union:

Things move along rather dispiritedly and with too much compromise. Very badly the moral genius and personality of Roosevelt are missed. And for lack of them in the direction, the feeling of a cause, the crusading spirit which have always been so completely American are not to be found and the little men push special interests and quibble over words. Coincidentally the moral leadership is drifting by default into Russian hands. It is precisely what has happened in so many countries in Europe. We have gone in, destroyed the existing forms, and offered nothing in their place claiming to leave that to the local populace. Inevitably the Russians are sucked into the resultant vacuum. Of course we are hurt and bewildered and see the wily hand of the devil at work. The conspiratorial theory becomes an obsession. And it never occurs to anyone to look at our own hands and ask the obvious question. So, here we are merrily betraying almost every ideal we are supposed to believe in. It is a strange, depressing, frightening spectacle. And the more it becomes so the greater the volume of parties.

Nostalgia cropped up regularly in their correspondence. One manifestation of Lillian's irrepressible personality brought forth this comment from John on 25 May:

Sweetheart, I don't think it is silly to make strange noises and gurgles in the springtime. In fact I think it is rather wonderful to be able to do so and I love you for it. There are times when your inarticulate sounds are quite as wonderful and meaningful as the articulate ones—no cracks, please—sometimes more so, and always exciting. I would give a great deal to hear some of them right now, instead of having to remember them. I can get very lonesome for them and for you and miss you both terribly. It is odd how lonely it is possible to be in the midst of so many people. Darling, I am very much in love with you.

And for once, John enjoyed a diplomatic party, this one given by Lord Halifax to celebrate the third anniversary of the Anglo-Soviet alliance.

The Halifax party turned out to be very small and very pleasant, with not over twenty people there and most of them agreeable. I had a long talk with Manuilsky. I think that guy is a honey, shrewd, witty, and just plain damned good company, even if some of our proper colleagues are wary of being contaminated by his long Comintern background. He is quite apparently the real man of the three delegations. He promised me that when we recognize the Ukraine he will see that I am the only person who will be persona grata as ambassador. He said he thought young men made the best diplomats anyway. How would you like to live in Kiev?

By the end of May, Lillian acknowledged an affection that she had not previously admitted. They talked on the phone May 30; she told him that their love had grown, that it was stronger each day, that this had been going on from the beginning and would unquestionably go on until they died. John was ecstatic.

The next day, ecstasy gave way to pessimism about the competence of the State Department, especially Secretary Edward Stettinius, Jr.:

> There are a couple of stories about Junior [Stettinius] which indi-
> cate pretty well the low level to which the American delegation has
> sunk and which help to explain why we don't look any better here
> than we do. At the height of the regionalism fight one of the principal
> members of the American delegation said to the Sec: "You have been a
> good general manager for the State Department. Now it is about time
> that you started being Secretary of State in fact as well as in name." On
> another occasion during a very small big four meeting on trusteeship
> the big boys were airing their views. Finally Jr. pulled a card out of his
> pocket and read a sentence from it. Later he again read another
> sentence, and again a third time. At no time did he say a word that had
> not been written down on his scrap of paper and when the conversa-
> tion veered from that he was completely lost, not having the faintest
> idea of what it was all about. This same fuzziness had led him to make
> commitments to some of the delegations which underlings have later
> had to go around and disavow because they made no sense. How long
> can this sort of thing go on? And it is too bad because he is really a nice
> guy personally who is entirely beyond his depth. . . . And again the
> man who grows here is Stassen. Colonialism has been made his
> particular baby, something on which he did not know too much when
> he arrived. But he has mastered it so well that even the Russians and
> the old British colonial hands come around to him even for factual
> data. And they all listen when he has something to say. Too bad it is
> politically impossible for him to be Secretary of State now. Even the
> reporters are impressed with him. Otherwise things continue muddy.
> [31 May 1945]

John was equally disturbed about the breaking *Amerasia* case, in which six people were arrested on 6 June 1945 in New York and Washington for giving classified documents to that left-wing magazine owned and edited by Philip Jaffe.[1] One of the persons arrested was John Stewart Service, China language Foreign Service officer who had worked for General Stilwell, and who, like all other firsthand observers of the Chinese Communist areas, found Mao and cohorts far ahead of Chiang Kai-shek's Kuomintang in capturing the allegiance of the Chinese peasantry. Patrick Hurley, then Ambassador to China, attacked Service publicly, accusing him of praising the Communists, thus sabotaging efforts to make peace in China.[2]

Service had given eight or so documents to Jaffe. They were reports that Service had written about conditions in the Communist areas of China and that he had himself classified at a low level, as was normal diplomatic practice for nonsensitive intelligence. But as was also common practice, not only in China but elsewhere, he had given these copies to Jaffe as he would, and as other diplomats did, to any journalist for background use. What Service did not know was that Jaffe was then under FBI surveillance and was a fellow traveler, if not even farther to the left.

When the six persons arrested in the *Amerasia* case went before the Washington grand jury, three were indicted for unauthorized possession and transmittal of government documents. The only State Department officer arrested, John Stewart Service, was not indicted; the grand jury voted unanimously against indicting him. Truman ordered the three indictees prosecuted, and the Justice Department speedily went to court. Unfortunately, the Office of Strategic Services and the FBI had used illegal methods in collecting evidence against the *Amerasia* defendants, and the Justice Department had very little admissable evidence to present. As a result, Jaffe got off with a modest fine.

This outcome did not please the anti-Roosevelt forces, who were convinced that Truman had squelched prosecution in the *Amerasia* case. To them, all six who had been arrested were traitors and spies. It was the opening round in the hunt for subversives. *Amerasia* joined Yalta, and later the Hiss case, as a key symbol of what Joe McCarthy called twenty years of treason.

John accurately commented to Lillian in a letter of 7 June on the probable significance of the *Amerasia* case, though he did not know the facts that exonerated Service:

The Department scandal continues to develop as I anticipated. The relatively minor charges of espionage against Jack Service are being broadened into the basic issue of Far Eastern policy and the Kuomintang-Chinese fight. Hurley has obviously bitched it so badly he was facing disgrace and needing someone to hang it on has of course picked the other side. This would not excuse Service if he did what he is accused of, for that is treason in any terms, but it is also true that he did no more than many others, including his boss, that this is partially a frame-up, and that we shall all pay for it. Certainly it will ruin the China service which was excellent. If anti-Russian elements wish to make enough of it, and if there are further similar exposés, I see no reason why the Dept will not find itself with more on its hands than it bargained for and find the cross-currents of public reaction pulling down the whole structure. As for that, we shall have to wait and see how it develops, but I think it cause for extreme concern. I don't know how far the FBI intends to go at this time, but I do know that certain parts of the press are going to drag in everything and everyone they can.

John had begun, in fact, to wonder if he wanted the assignment to China, or even the Ed Flynn project, which was still lurking in the wings. It was not just the complications of the *Amerasia* case, or the intractable problems for the United States of dealing with a probable Chinese Civil War. It was again the question of the basic competence and integrity of the United States government that worried him. These qualms he expressed to Lillian in a letter on 11 June:

Saturday evening I had dinner with an assortment of people and sat next to a girl I have known many years who was Sumner Welles' secretary during those years. It made me rather sad and really for once in my life very old. Since he left she has been bounced into some obscure corner of the Department doing nothing much. I really think I saw perfection too young in my career. The ten years of the Good Neighbor policy were the sort of thing this Government has never seen before. The Latin American division was young and alive and capable and full of ideas that worked. And we all worked like hell and loved it because we believed in it. Very few people know how close we came to catastrophe during this war, except for the margin that policy gave us and had it not been for that it is unpleasant to think where we might be now. And this is literally no exaggeration. That policy was the conception and vision of Welles and the Division had whatever it is that could make it work. It was the Golden Age of American foreign policy. Even Harriman who held no brief for such nonsense once admitted that the policy would go down in history as the most brilliant stroke of foreign policy of any country during the last 150 years. That I think is what sometimes makes me feel old—to have started out with something that good and then still at my age to have to go on with muddling and confusion and indirection. The Welles sure touch with latinos is sorely missed now, as the President's is in the larger field. Maybe the answer, sweetheart, is to go off some place where no one has ever heard of anything.

On 14 June sad news came from New York. Lillian had suffered from bad problems with her teeth. Several of them had to come out. John was doubly distressed, both because of her agony and because of his inability to be with and comfort her. His letter that day showed an extra effort to lift her spirits.

It is a pity some one is not writing an anecdotal history of this shindig. Some of the stories are priceless. My favorite so far concerns Paul Boncour and that sterling citizen Sol Bloom, both being about the same age. Boncour is very deaf. He and Sol were congratulating each other on how young the other looked. Boncour asked Bloom how he accounted for it: Says Sol, "No liquor and no women." Says Boncour who had not heard the "no," "Ah, you too. Well, I am glad to see you." Boncour has quite a reputation with women, even having acquired a girl friend here to minister to whatever a man his age needs.

Separately I have sent you a picture of me taken here. It could be labelled as the portrait of a liaison officer in a busy moment. Some day when our children ask with that plaintively inquiring tone, "Just what did Daddy do at the San Franciso Conference?" you will have the evidence to prove it.

I finally managed to corral Archibald MacLeish for a few minutes yesterday. I had missed him all around previously because he shuttled back and forth aimlessly between here and Washington. Restless no doubt. Or I would be busy. When I did see him he came bustling in and opened up: "Lillian told me the one person I must talk to is you. So let me tell you what I have in mind." And he proceeded to do it. We did not get very far because he had a report to finish, but we are going to have dinner sometime next week. He seemed worried about what we do with Russia and how we do it and equally important what we do about the American public. The big hurdle at the moment, and this is not for repetition, is that you know who has vetoed any cultural program for Russia as susceptible of being misunderstood. Balls. He also said he would like to have you as cultural attaché, but did not think he could get away with it. I almost told him I would lay down some conditions there myself. He would take it himself, only he couldn't get away with it either. Only, darling, don't you try going without me or I'll make a fuss.

But the dinner with MacLeish was not to be. Events were rushing to a conclusion. John spent his last week in San Francisco working on the Russian translation of the final text of the UN charter, which had to be in five languages. They were gruelling eighteen-hour days.

The final event of the conference was the signing of the charter by the various heads of state with a reception afterward hosted by President Truman. John was selected to do homework on all the visiting chiefs and to introduce them to Truman in the receiving line with some comment about each one. Truman told John that he had done a great job.

When John finally boarded the train for New York on 30 June, his relief at getting away from the intensity of that last week was exceeded only by his anticipation of seeing Lillian again.

Fulfillment: The Summer of 1945

By July 1945, John had been on continuous service, most of it at a "hard-ship post," since March 1943; he had accumulated substantial leave time. He spent most of it in New York with Lillian. It was the summer of their fulfillment. Periodically he needed to check in with the Department, on "consultation" as State Department jargon puts it, but he was there only long enough to satisfy formal reporting requirements. It was no secret that the famous playwright and the handsome diplomat were keeping company, but despite Lillian's prominence, no gossip columnist spread the word of her new lover.

John got to know many of Lillian's friends. She had for years been seeing the prominent psychoanalyst, Dr. Gregory Zilboorg, both as a client and as a friend. She and John had dinner with the Zilboorgs three or four times during the summer. When John left for China in October, Zilboorg gave him a beautiful leather attaché case, which he still has, and a bottle of vintage Scotch, which John and John's brother Everett were to consume at a reunion in Rome while John was en route to Chungking. John, in return, sent the Zilboorg's daughter, who collected liquor bottle labels, several prize specimens from his travels.

Arthur Kober, to whom Lillian had once been married, and Kober's second wife, were also on Lillian's dinner party list; the Kobers lived near her Manhattan place, and they often exchanged visits. John was enamored of Kober's daughter, Cathy; later from China he sent her a peddler's drum. This is an instrument on a long handle with a hammer attached by a string, and it makes, according to John, a "wondrous penetrating, musical staccato note you can hear for miles." Cathy loved it.

John and Lillian went to a large party at Herman Shumlin's on the west side; Shumlin produced several of Lillian's plays. There were weekends at the Pleasantville farm, with the Kobers, Dorothy Parker, Archibald Mac-Leish, and other guests John does not now remember.

One July Sunday John and Lillian drove to a luncheon at the Westchester estate of Eustace Seligman, taking with them Vera Micheles Dean, then editor of the Foreign Policy Association. Paul Robeson and Ruth Gordon had dinner with them at Lillian's. They also dined with Mrs. James Warburg, and visited Mr. and Mrs. Gerald Murphy.

Louis Kronenberger came by the house on business one day. Lillian lived on the second floor. As Kronenberger was leaving, he turned at the bottom of the stairs, looked up at John and Lillian on the second floor landing, and observed, "You two look as though you belong together."

They also lunched with Ed Flynn. Flynn was still expecting, in July, that when Truman got settled into the presidency, he would take up the Vatican-Kremlin détente idea.[1] Flynn still wanted John to go with him. John's assignment to Buenos Aires was still officially in force, though the prospects for China, as Harriman had indicated, were likely; the Irishman believed that either of these could be canceled, or John recalled from China, for the European mission.

Flynn, to John's surprise and approval, still felt that the United States had to get along with the Soviet Union, that Russia had a right to establish its own Monroe Doctrine. Flynn claimed to have sold this line to Jimmy Byrnes, just appointed secretary of state, and this may have been a major influence on Byrnes's early "soft" position on relations with the Communist bloc.

Lillian was uneasy during the lunch with Flynn. The talk reinforced her discomfiture at the ease with which Foreign Service officers could be summarily uprooted and sent halfway around the world.

John did not stay in New York all of July. He had not visited his parents in Bloomington, nor his two sons living with his estranged wife in El Paso, since he had gone to Moscow. On 22 July he took a train for Texas. His penchant for writing went with him, and his letters back to Lillian again provide a contemporary record of their affair:

> July 23, 1945. Sweetheart: The swaying of this train may make my handwriting even more illegible than usual, but the objective is still to say that I love you very, very much and that I want you to marry me. While looking out at this beautiful countryside I have found myself speculating and ruminating on what you said last night about getting a place near Washington. I like that. Then, too, since I know that countryside pretty well, I have been thinking of possibilities. I know a couple of very nice ones up the river with lovely water frontage, good stands of trees and bluegrass fields. I'm even figuring on the house &

what it would be like, Darling, don't ever doubt for a second that we can & will do it.

Two days later, in Kansas: "A good deal of the time I can convince myself that you do love me and then again it takes prodding. While on this subject, if you told Arthur that any lack of public display of my feeling for you is my fault, I shall see that you regret it. And no cracks about that warm Mediterranean nature of yours!"

His six days in El Paso were painful. He enjoyed his sons, now grown to mischevious age, but everything else was agonizing. His establishment in-laws expressed their hostility toward Roosevelt, the federal government, and the Soviet Union freely. John did not, as some of the in-laws expected, return looking and speaking like a 1920s Bolshevik; but anyone who had spent two years in Moscow had to be tainted.

Then there were the medical and dental rounds. Eye tests, and new glasses. A sinus infection which, if treated over a long period, might clear up. Wisdom teeth out, "by a dentist who missed great opportunities as a riveter," as he told Lillian during one of their frequent phone calls, apologizing as he did so for complaining about his teeth to her, who had just lost so many of hers.

He left Texas with relief, and spent a week with his parents, which was more pleasant but still tense and frustrating. By 6 August he was back in New York.

John was by now convinced that there was no chance whatever of maintaining the formality of his first marriage, even for the sake of the children. He fully expected his wife, who had the necessary residence, to file for divorce. He and Lillian talked seriously of marrying.

Then came the letter from the Secretary of State. Harriman had won out. The assignment to Argentina was canceled as of 14 August, and he was to go to Chungking. For several days he and Lillian talked of little else. His friends in the Department assured him that transportation was so tight that he could expect a long delay in getting travel orders; the war in the Pacific was over, but chaos still reigned. Who could know what would happen in the confusion and euphoria of victory?

John phoned Ed Flynn. "Yes," said Flynn, "I still expect the Vatican-Kremlin mission to go, and I still want you as deputy. Have you ever been to China?" John said no. Flynn then said, "Go take a look at it and see what it's like; as soon as I can, I'll send for you." The prospect of John's "waiting in China for Ed Flynn's call" was hardly encouraging to Lillian. The Moscow separation had been bad enough, with lost letters, endless delays of telegrams, and a psychic distance that seemed unbearable. Now it was to be China, twice as far, infinitely more mysterious, totally out of reach. He might as well be on the moon.

She was very much in love with John, but he knew from her letters that she suspected his commitment to his career to be so great that he would follow it wherever it led. For all his protestations about wanting her more than anything in the world, she felt that if duty called him to Xanadu, he would go. Being a Foreign Service officer did not mean spending most of one's time in Washington. They had no further talk of buying a place on the Potomac.

Then the summer was interrupted by a serious accident. John and Lillian were dining alone in her apartment, on roast duck. Probably because of her new dentures, Lillian got a duck bone stuck in her throat. Her doctor met her at the hospital and ordered surgery. She was there for several days; John first met her father while visiting at the hospital.

The throat incision caused Lillian some embarrassment, and she was hesitant to continue her normal social and professional schedule. It had been a long time since she had stayed at the shore; this seemed to be a good time to look for a beachfront cottage. Lillian read the *Times* "classified" section and found a promising listing in East Hampton. John endorsed the idea.

When Lillian phoned the listing agency, she detected a certain coolness in its response. Probing brought the admission that the house was in a restricted neighborhood—no Jews. John now saw the famous Hellman temper in full display. Many of the prominent members of the New York Jewish community were friends of Lillian's, and she mobilized a powerful and indignant task force. Whether it was their influence or the agency's fear of unfavorable publicity from denying rental to a famous playwright, the restriction was lifted. John and Lillian moved to East Hampton sometime in July.

The pace there was more leisurely. They took long walks on the beach, went on fishing expeditions and picnics—sometimes with Lillian's friends but more often by themselves. John remembers one picnic at Mrs. Averell Harriman's, a fishing trip with Marya Mannes, and a garden party at which Mrs. Christian Herter greeted him with "So you're the mysterious young man from Moscow."

In September Lillian and John moved back to Manhattan and faced an awkward situation. Hammett was discharged from the army and got back to New York on 6 September. The Hammett phase of Lillian's life had receded into a somewhat murky past. When she fell in love with John,

Hammett was still in Alaska—not on Adak anymore, but terrorizing the bars on the mainland and complaining that her letters were cool and infrequent. What she wrote him about John we do not know; Hammett did know that something had changed.

Hammett's possessions were stored at Lillian's Manhattan apartment. She told John that it would take a day or two for Hammett to retrieve them and find a place of his own. Would John move out for a few days? John took a room at the Plaza for two nights, and Hammett was gone. John and Hammett met for the only time in the hallway the day of Hammett's arrival.

Lillian later wrote of her relations with Hammett that "the years after the war, from 1945 to 1948, were not good years; the drinking grew wilder and there was a lost, thoughtless quality I had never seen before."[2] Hammett had, indeed, lost something of value—the devotion which Lillian now reserved for John. She did not see Hammett again until after John left for China.

John checked with the Department weekly. In early October he got a hint that transportation to China was opening up. It came with crushing suddenness. On 16 October he was to be in Washington packed and ready to go. This parting was as painful as earlier ones. John and Lillian had survived earlier separations with their love intact, and they were secure in their mutual affection. But China was a long way from Manhattan.

John's Air Transport Command C-47, with hard bucket seats, took off from New York on 18 October bound for Newfoundland, carrying him to what he thought would be a brief interlude before he could take up a normal life with the woman he loved.

China, 1945 to 1946

Newfoundland, the Azores, Casablanca. The powers of observation and description which had already earned John a handful of professional commendations, and which had been honed by his letters to Lillian from Moscow and San Francisco, were now turned with unparalleled energy to provide her with a colorful account of his trip, and a tragicomic history of the death throes of the Chinese Nationalist government.

But before the world scene came the personal anguish. Flying over the eastern Atlantic, he told her: "After your comments on departure you took it a lot better than I. The last few minutes I was sure I was going to break down and bawl. And somehow the words got all mixed up with that. However much I bumbled it you must know & believe that I love you, that I want you to marry me, & that I will come back for you soon" (19 October 1945).

Over the Mediterranean approaching Naples he began to speculate on how Lillian was spending her time: "Dozing on the plane earlier this morning I found myself wondering what you were doing and being very jealous about it. Not that there was anything wrong with what you do, but simply that I know so little of what takes up your time. I guess it is that the immediacy of you & me this past summer was so compelling and engrossing there never seemed to be occasion to find out what you do with yourself. Doubtless you feel the same about me" (21 October 1945).

Four days in Rome. John met his brother, Everett, a State Department employee who had married a Dutch girl and spent the war years in Switzerland. They downed Zilboorg's Scotch, saw some of the sights, and took in embassy parties. John's language in letters to Lillian describing reactionary types he and Everett had met at a party given by Alexander 'Buffy' Kirk was scatological; he was incensed at the fascist sympathies of several air force officers and of Angelo Giannini of the Bank of America. As for the Italians, he saw them as straining to convince the United States to treat them well so they would become "a great mainstay against the Russians" (23 October 1945).

Karachi, October 28—a cable to Lillian: "FURTHER I GET THE MORE I MISS YOU HOPE ARRIVE CHUNGKING MONDAY ALL MY LOVE DARLING."

Calcutta: "Baby, do you suppose I can get any more homesick for you than I have already? I don't think I could take it. I keep seeing you and the lovely way you looked at the airport, very elegant in black and brown with your new hat, & me a goddamned fool on the other side of the world" (29 October 1945). He was delayed in Calcutta and sent another cable.

India was not to John's liking; British imperialism usually set off a torrent of obloquy that he indulged freely in Calcutta. His letter of 30 October specified graphically what he would do with the "next Englishman with his [expletive deleted] gin." He acknowledged, though, that "in a place like Calcutta you see them at their shit-ass worst."

On 2 November 1945, John landed at Kunming, China, beginning a stay in the tinderbox whose consumption by the fires of Communism was to inflame not only all of Asia, but American politics as well. John's mission to China, as Averell Harriman had conceived it, and as his State Department superiors had approved it, was to keep tabs on what chicanery the Russians were up to there. John was to be the Soviet watcher at the Embassy in China. He soon discovered that there was not much of a story in this. The Russians had by then denuded Manchuria of its Japanese plants and equipment, claiming them as reparations, and had settled down to a correct relationship with Chiang Kai-shek and his Nationalist government.

The possibility most feared by American officials was a Soviet effort to supply and support the Chinese Communists led by Mao Tse-tung and Chou En-lai, who ruled a large area of northwestern China centered in Yenan, and who claimed the allegiance of the Chinese peasantry and all patriotic Chinese. Mao held sway in the North China territory because of the Communists' superior organizing ability and the integrity of their rule. Americans could hardly believe that any Communist regime could really command the loyalty of its subjects; the right wing in the United States was convinced that Mao remained in power only because of Russian support. The United States was committed to the Nationalist government as the legal government of China; when Mao won the civil war and founded the People's Republic of China in 1949, the American position was that the Soviet Union had gained control and created a satellite in North China.

Avoiding civil war in China was the foremost American aim; the vacuum created by the defeat of Japan, which had controlled much of China until the end of the war, had to be filled with a strong, united, and "democratic" regime friendly to the United States. The wish was father to the thought; a series of myths grew up about China that ultimately corrupted American policy abroad and domestic policy as well.

The China myths of midcentury include a large cluster of beliefs, probably none of which were held by all of the Amerian electorate, but most of which had general acceptance during the forties and fifties, and many of which still command rocklike allegiance among the 20 percent of the electorate that remains opposed to our recent détente with China. The central myth, deployed with devastating effect by the China bloc in Congress, holds that Chiang was China's true and popular leader, and that he lost the civil war because of inadequate moral and material support from the United States, which support was withheld because of treason in the White House and the State Department. Like Vietnam two decades later, we "lost" China in Washington, not on the field of battle.[1]

But the lode of fantasy goes much deeper than this core myth. It reaches well back into the nineteenth century. We have generally believed, since the Open Door notes of 1899, that the United States has been good to China, has been her protector against the rapine of the European powers, that our relations with China lacked the venality shown by Britain, France, Russia, and Japan. A corollary myth holds that, at least until 1949, China was friendly toward the United States, that we had some kind of hold on China which would justify the assertion that we "lost" China to the Communists.

We also believed that Generalissimo Chiang was a Western-style democrat, that since he had been converted to Christianity his government had to be humane and enlightened, that he was popular with the Chinese— "China's real symbol," as many of his American followers put it. Hence his defeat was largely our fault.

Regarding the other side in the Chinese conflict, perhaps the most pernicious and long-lived myth was that the Chinese Communists were aggressive just like their masters the Russians; when the Chinese intervened in Korea in 1950 this myth became gospel truth.

These myths came about for several reasons. One important factor was the historic volatility of American perceptions of the Chinese. In American opinion of China there are all the wild swings of a love-hate relationship, all the excesses of a frustrated courtship. We have never been able to make up our minds about the mysterious, aloof, precocious Chinese. In our perceptual ambiguity, the sinister and repulsive Fu Manchu turns overnight into the smiling and canny Charlie Chan. The endearing peasant created by

Pearl Buck metamorphoses into the Communist devil painted by Joe Mc-
Carthy and Pat McCarran, and even in the 1980s by the Heritage Foundation and the remnant of the old China lobby.

A second factor in our relations with China had nothing to do with
China intrinsically, but arose because China went Communist. Our friend
Chiang, the savior of the Orient, he whom Roosevelt had defined (to
Churchill's and Stalin's consternation) as the leader of a great power, was
not just displaced; he was displaced by a Communist. When Communists
came to power in China, ousting a Methodist secular saint and his Joan of
Arc wife, ancient fears of proletarian revolt boiled to the surface. This fear
of Communism was reinforced by the commitment of American missions
to China: China was the largest single theater of the American Christian
missionary enterprise. In the mid-1930s, before Japan invaded China,
there were at least 6,059 Protestant missionaries in China, each with a
built-in constituency in the United States. As Sherwood Eddy, one of the
prominent chroniclers of China missions, noted of his youth, "China was
the goal, the lodestar, the great magnet that drew us all in those days."[2] It
was not just Eddy for whom China was the lodestar; Henry Luce, born in
China of Christian missionaries, developed a lifelong attachment to the
cause served by his father, to the country where his father served, and to
the great Methodist captain (Chiang) who ruled that country. In the Luce
theology, which all of his publishing empire promulgated until his death,
missions and righteousness, Republican politics, Chiang and Americanism
were all bound together inseparably.

When, in 1949, the American missionary enterprise suffered a defeat,
Luce and similar Sinophiles were outraged. The heathen Communists had
beaten them at their own game. Mao had won the theological battle, the
battle for China's soul. Mao, with his rigid codes of self-abnegation and
service to the people, had captured the spirit of the Protestant ethic and
turned it against us. John Leighton Stuart, fifty years a missionary in China
and then ambassador during part of John's service in China, was one of
many who loathed Communism, but found Mao's triumph understandable. As Stuart put it in his memoirs, *our* China, the Nationalist government
of Chiang, was riddled with "graft and greed, idleness and inefficiency,
nepotism and factional rivalries." The Communists, on the other hand,
were disciplined and abstemious: "This was no mean achievement, especially in the perspective of Kuomintang shortcomings."[3] For Stuart, Luce,
and the witch-hunters of the 1950s, Armageddon was fought in China, *and
the devil won*. It was into this developing inferno that John Melby stepped
on 2 November 1945.

John's first stop was in Kunming, just over the hump from India. Phil Sprouse, whom John had met at San Francisco, was consul there; Sprouse gave John his first briefing on what was happening in China. It was chilling and prophetic: American marines had already been killed in northern China while supporting Chiang's efforts to regain territory from the Communists. Kunming was a center of opposition to the Nationalists; as John wrote Lillian, "[Sprouse] says that even Kuomintang Chinese are laughing at us for a bunch of saps. He feels it is already too late to prevent catastrophe here & that the civil war has lined up with us on the wrong and eventually losing side" (2 November 1945).

From Kunming John flew to Chungking, then the capital of Nationalist China. He expected to be there no longer than six months. By then Ed Flynn's operation would be underway, John would be whisked back to Western Europe with Lillian at his side, and the universe would restore itself to proper order.

In the next three years, John sent 390 pages of letters and cablegrams to Lillian from China. It was a time of great anguish for both of them, yet neither Lillian's memoirs, nor John's *Mandate of Heaven*, hint at the personal trauma they both endured.

The difficulties of communication with postwar China were worse than with wartime Moscow. It was 7 November, twenty days after he left Washington, when John received his first cable from Lillian. She had sent him many; they lodged at American embassies in Rome, Cairo, Calcutta, or wherever, a few of them reaching him weeks later. Letters were equally irregular and misrouted. The absence of news from New York heightened John's initial repugnance for what he now faced.

Chungking inevitably suffered by comparison with Moscow. Three days after John's arrival, he wrote: "After the intense personal vigor of the Russians, I find the Chinese a rather depressing gang. This would really not make too much difference were it not for the poisonous attitude around the Embassy itself. In turn every officer here has taken me aside and given me advice on what I can say to whom and who should be trusted and who spies for whom. It is a real gestapo atmosphere. Consequently no one seems to do much of anything except eavesdrop and duck around corners" (2 November 1945).

Part of the reason for the demoralization of the Embassy was the conduct of the ambassador, Patrick J. Hurley, an oil tycoon whom Franklin Roosevelt had sent on various missions during the war. Hurley's last mission was to China, and the objective was to patch things up between Chiang's Kuomintang (Nationalist) party and Mao's Communists. Hurley at first thought he had accomplished this, and he told Albert Ravenholt, an American journalist, that he hoped for a Nobel Peace Prize for such a major accomplishment. When his inept negotiations went sour, Hurley sought a scapegoat: the China Foreign Service officers were conveniently at hand. At the time John arrived in Chungking, Hurley was in Washington demanding that Jack Service, John Paton Davies, George Atcheson, and others who belittled his efforts be kept out of Asian affairs. The Embassy John Melby entered was split between those who thought, with Hurley, that the United States should go all out to support Chiang when war came, and the China specialists who thought the Communists already too strong for any outside intervention to stop them.[4]

As John wrote Lillian, "The Hurley boys want me to go to work and pump the Russian Embassy here to find out what devious schemes they are pushing" (2 November 1945). John had already done this; he was convinced that Soviet relations with Mao's Communists were minimal; there was, in fact, bad blood between them. Kung Peng, one of Chou En-lai's assistants, told John that the Communists felt betrayed by Soviet plundering in Manchuria.

In addition to a poisonous Embassy atmosphere, Chungking was an uncomfortable place to live. Spaso had been luxurious by comparison. Coming by air with limited luggage, John was even short of clothes. This to Lillian on 11 November: "Darling, I have another pair or two of pajamas either at Pleasantville or the gladstone in town. Since I can't sleep with you, would you please send me out a pair. I find I have only one with me. I could use some of the books too. But I don't want any of the other clothes. They would just be ruined in this mud and it is better just to ruin what I have here."

Even though physical discomfort and professional discontent generated a steady mood of pessimism, the erratic arrival of mail from Lillian, when it came, produced temporary joy:

> November 16, 1945. Darling: This has suddenly become a very beautiful day. The mail just arrived with three wonderful letters from you. I see you have been having your troubles and annoyances. But, my Lily darling, I am coming to the conclusion that some of the world might have a better chance at our hands if we were together. When I am with you I can't really be very annoyed with anything or anyone and when I am away from you I can't really be pleased about anything. I suppose it is hard on the world, but I don't give a damn because that is the way I feel and that is the way I love you and always will. . . . I

like your acting as though I were your first beau. That is the way it should be. It must come out right, sweetheart, and it will.

On 12 November, John had lunch with Chou En-lai, who was in Chungking as Communist representative for the negotiations. Chou was, as John told Lillian, "a very handsome and intelligent man who talked quite freely," and who was to become in the eyes of John and many Americans (including General George Marshall) the outstanding leader of the Chinese Communists. Had Chou, rather than Mao, been top man in the Communist hierarchy, John believed the later bitter hostility between the Peking regime and the United States might have been avoided. By most accounts, Chou was a statesman of towering stature; John ranked him with Sumner Welles.

By the end of November, John discovered that Lillian's fame as a playwright extended even to China:

I see by the Chinese press that you have been making more speeches. They misspell your name too. Which reminds me: I vaguely remember hearing you splutter shortly before I left New York about a Chinese translation of *Watch* and something about blaming it on *OWI*. It is all very vague in my mind. Anyway, I have found out that it was translated by some little Chinese in Kunming who did it on his own for his friends as an example of American anti-Fascist literature. As far as I can find out OWI had nothing to do with it. An amateur group is giving it in Kunming now. The little guy, who appears to be all right, is very much hurt that he has not had an acknowledgement of the manuscript of it he sent you. He is now working on a translation of *The Little Foxes*. If you haven't done so already, do write the guy a note and thank him or give him hell, depending on your reaction to it. Some of these poor bastards here without strong friends get pushed around by everyone under the sun. The idea of translating *The Little Foxes*, incidentally, is to show what modern America drama is like.

Last night I saw a kind of foolish movie called The Clock. Its one advantage was that part of it was laid in Central Park and I found myself trying to get off the Park and down 82nd street. Suddenly I saw the curtains billowing out in the living room, the green walls, the low light and the red chairs with you sitting in one of them. It was almost too much. It was all I could do to go on sitting there. It was just six weeks ago tonight that I left NY. Time for me has usually been fast, but these six weeks have been interminable. It seems sometimes as though I had been here all my life and would never leave. Baby, I want to be back with you where my only regret is that time moves too fast. Sweetheart, I love you, I miss you, I want you always. [28 November 1945]

Hurley's explosive resignation as ambassador on 26 November, when he blasted various Foreign Service officers as pro-Communist, plunged John once more into despair. Hurley's targets were his friends. News accounts reaching China indicated that Hurley was getting strong public support, and that an investigation of Hurley's charges would seriously hurt the State Department. John wrote Lillian, "Unless the Department takes a stronger stand in support of the service than it has so far there simply will be no service left because we will be so completely discredited. And there will be no future left to staying in it. Reactionary, communist, imperialist—what the hell are we? It must be a great gang that can be all three. The hell of it is that once you get this kind of dirty business started there is no telling where it goes, usually the wrong way" (30 November 1945).

But again, two good letters from Lillian revived his spirits. One of the hesitations Lillian had in projecting a life with John was her lingering relationship with Hammett. This seemed, in late 1945, to be all but over; as she wrote in her introduction to *The Big Knockover*, "By 1945, the drinking was no longer gay, the drinking bouts were longer and the moods darker."[5] Hammett was reacting to Lillian's new devotion to John. Her letters to John that arrived in early December said as much. He responded:

Chungking, December 2, 1945. My Lovely Darling: I think I can understand what Dash means when he says you two no longer have points of contact. I would not know really what they were before since I did not know you then. Somehow now you move in different worlds, different lines, different objectives, or at least different methods of approach. But you are right that if you want to keep anything from it, you cannot live in the same house much longer. . . . I am glad, sweetheart, that you are writing again and particularly that you are thinking about *The Little Foxes*. The trilogy should be done. I was thinking that last night when I was reading the first act of it over again. . . .

One of the Coburn pictures of you I have has your fingers in a V. It reminds me of a story going the rounds here about two sharks, one lean and one fat, who met at the end of the war. The fat one was amazed by the skinny one and could not understand his condition. He said: "During the war I followed an American submarine and every so often when a Jap ship was sunk I would pick up a couple of Japs. Mighty tasty eating. But what is the matter with you?" The other said:

"Well, I followed a Jap submarine after British ships. Every so often it would sink one. And as the Englishmen would go down they would make the V sign and shout 'There will always be an England' and I just simply could not swallow that crap." Darling, the 'I just simply could not swallow that crap' look on your face in the picture is wonderful and makes me want to break furniture for wanting to be with you again and for always.

I got word a few days ago from Moscow that my trunk and the boxes of books have been or are about to be shipped to the States. Just what that means in terms of arrival I don't know, but sometime. Fyfe knows about them and will notify you. Please do with the stuff whatever you please, storage or use them yourself. It would make me feel warmer if you would use the red quilt we used so nicely in Moscow. [John still has the quilt.]

Lillian by now was acknowledging the desire for and possibility of a permanent life with John. One of her November letters talked about her previous romantic entanglements, not only with Arthur Kober and Hammett, but also with Herman Shumlin, and about her need to wipe the slate clean. John responded on 4 December:

I have been thinking much of what you wrote about your troubles with Herman, about me putting up with things, about the price for being wrong and unrealistic. Darling, I think we both need to clean a lot of debris out of our backyards, we need it clean so we can live there together at peace with each other and with the past. When something is finished it is over and trying to hang on to some part, except in distant fashion, is only to befuddle and cause new trouble. I think I have always known that, though I have not always been consistent about it. Lily darling, I want us to clean out our lives soon so we can start out together and be happy. That is the only thing that matters and with that nothing else can seem very difficult. You and I have so far had a physical, mental and spiritual companionship that straightens out the rest. Darling, I need you and all my love is for you always.

On 6 December 1945 a cultural program in Chungking brought John in contact with Lillian's foremost Chinese admirer:

Last night OWI had in a native troop of some kind that put on Tibetan and Yenan folk dances which were fascinating, especially the Yenan ones, filled with charm, and real artistry. The music is full of strange half-monotones, but very haunting and not unlike music you find in the Ecuadoran highlands. The director of the troupe is a Chinese who was born and raised in Trinidad, studied ballet in London, and now is here and married to one of the leading cartoonists. Some combination.

Also present for the occasion was a young gentleman named Feng, who told me several interesting things before he knew who I was. He is the one who has translated *The Watch*. It was the first time I had had an opportunity to get his story firsthand. You are quite the queen in his young life—mine too, you not he. *Watch* is to be given in Kunming after the first of the year. He translated it, one, as anti-fascist propaganda; and, two, because he and his colleagues consider you the greatest technician in the modern theatre. For that reason he is now working on *The Little Foxes*. *Watch* has apparently been published in Chinese in the Shanghai *Vanguard*, some kind of literary magazine. His wife has translated your *Colliers* piece on Russia and it will appear in the same magazine. And, Christ, how he wants a letter from you. When I finally told him I knew you he almost fell into the fireplace, and then please, please wouldn't I ask you to send him a copy of *The Searching Wind* and *North Star*. I suggested he might ask permission from you for all this. Yes, he thought so too, but mail takes so long (the one script he sent you apparently took eight months) and he does not belong to any faction which exactly permits him to get KMT [Kuomintang] Govt. help. We are having trouble in general now on that score.

The tenth of December was the anniversary of their first night together. John was positively maudlin.

It was a year ago today that you and I started out together. And so it has been a hard day since we are so far apart now and tonight. All day I have been living that time over so completely that I am only occasionally conscious of being here and not in Moscow. I am even mildly surprised that there is no snow on the ground and deeply depressed that I do not see you when I look around, and profoundly indifferent to anything here. There is only one place I want to be and that is with you. Today I even have the same kind of physical reaction I had then of anxiety and anticipation, a sort of fever. And all sorts of emotions keep churning over inside me. All the ones of that day on which are superimposed those added since, until sometimes I think it will choke me. It is so damned hard to be so far away and to hear so little, for it has now been over a week since I have heard anything from you.

The next morning brought some relief: "When I woke up this morning your nice cable had arrived which puzzled me for a minute because I could have sworn you were in bed beside me. Bless you, darling, I love you."

But four days later her letter of 25 November arrived; it was angry and accusatory. She had met Luis Quintanilla at a party, and he told her that on the basis of talking to John at San Francisco, he did not think John wanted a divorce, and he claimed not to know that John was in love with her. John's response was apoplectic: "I swear I will kill that bastard Quintanilla when I see him. The bastard must know about us because the first thing he asked me when I saw him was where you were and hadn't you come with me" (14 December 1945). John's letters for several days after were bitter about Luis, and even more than normally reassuring of his affection. Lillian apparently got over her pique; her letters of 26 November and 1 December John described as "good." She wrote of wanting to share a home with him, as contrasted with just sharing a house. This he loved.

He did not, however, love his diplomatic associates.

Dec. 20. My Darling: It was a rarified company that foregathered last night with the counsellor for one of those exclusive little dinners which are supposed to be the reason men become diplomats. I used to think the counsellor was just eccentric; now I think he is nuts since I learned a few years ago while crossing the Pacific someone dropped a trunk on his head and shattered some vertebra. His wife is one of those dopey Smith belles from old Virginia who plays the accent, eats on her elbows, and wears evening dresses striped pale green and magenta. We don't like each other. Petrov was there, and his wife was lovely in something rose. Also the Agent General for India, a smooth cooky with an Oxford accent who when I asked him what he thought of Indian troops killing Indonesians said "Quaint, eh?" For a moment I thought he was joking, but he wasn't. His wife had a diamond the size of a peanut in her nose and a fur coat that did not come for free anywhere. The Chinese were the Vice Minister for Foreign Affairs who tried to act as though he were at a fraternity reunion and the Secretary General of the Kuomintang, who was just simply noisy without reference to anything. I sat next to his wife at dinner and could not take my eyes off her hands because they were so much like yours. . . .

What interested me most about it was the Chinese. These men, and others in their position, were at one time the flaming revolutionaries of the Orient, and a real gang of wild men who cut their way right and left, passionately devoted to Dr. Sun and what he stood for, intimate friends of Borodin. The Northern Expedition of 1927 was one of the sagas of our time. Now they are sleek, polished, well-fed, worldly, cynical, reactionary. Interested now only in maintaining their own positions and prerogatives. Their women are the same, and some of these women once marched barefoot with them out of Canton to the north. Their hands are soft now, and so are their heads. What is it that happens to men to make this change? Is there a point at which ideas begin to atrophy along with arteries? Cannot a man keep his spirit young? To see what happened to these men here is the saddest and most depressing thing in Chungking. My father once said that when the day came that he could no longer adjust his thinking to the attitudes of men in their twenties he would not wish to live.

Following Hurley's resignation as ambassador, Truman asked General George Marshall to go to China as personal representative of the presidency to negotiate between the warring Chinese. John was commissioned to prepare several briefing papers for Marshall, which he was both pleased and sad to do. Pleased, because he admired Marshall and thought him a great military leader; sad, because he knew Marshall was walking into a hopeless situation, could not succeed, and would suffer personally because of the inevitable failure. A dozen times in the December 1945 to June 1946 period John wrote Lillian explanations of how Marshall was doing his level best only to be stymied by the hatreds and suspicions of the contending Chinese parties.

John was also disturbed at the treatment China was getting in the American media. On 28 December he wrote:

> Yesterday Till Durdin came to see me. Several weeks ago I had insulted him by suggesting that his NY Times was increasingly given to altering news stories for its own ends. Yesterday he was mad, he was good and mad. He had just received a several months batch of his article clippings and to his dismay he found that almost every article had been changed, paragraphs rearranged, words dropped out, whole sections omitted, all done to throw a bad light on Yenan. Every word of human interest on them was out. His wife also told him that very little of John Roderick's stuff for AP is appearing. That is too bad, for he is living there and his articles which I see in the communist press here are excellent.

In late December John caught the flu and was ordered to bed. This did not interfere with his writing Lillian, nor did it keep visitors away:

Dec. 29, Sweetheart: There is one thing about this illness of mine which is interesting to watch. During it a lot of people have been in my room who have never been here before. One of the first things they all notice is your *Vogue* picture which is on the wall over the bed. Many don't say anything, but keep glancing at it. The reactions of those who are vocal about it vary from one lad who rushed out to send his wife a cable demanding that she have one taken of herself just like yours, to our lop-eared counsellor who could not figure out whether the life-raft you are sitting on is floating on black water or resting on a table. I should add also that the story of your being married to Herman is certainly widespread and has been assumed to me as a fact by a couple of people here who have no reason or interest in knowing or not knowing.

Always there was the question of how long he would be away from her. Her letter of 18 December was insistent and melancholy. He answered on 3 January 1946: "I am sorry that you are depressed, though I would not have you too happy without me. That would make me sad, for I love you very dearly, and am increasingly restless away from you. Sometimes it seems so long since I have held you that I wonder how I can bear it any longer. I should be hearing something from Flynn before long and on the basis of that propose to start things moving."

On 4 January, he asked her to send him one of the jugs of pipe tobacco he had left at Pleasantville. On 7 January, in a bitter mood, he acknowledged that he "was a goddamned fool, no matter what was involved, to leave you and come out here." His cable of 8 January read: "WILL MISS YOU THIS TENTH AS ALWAYS BUT SUGGEST WE DREAM OF ALL TENTHS ALL MY LOVE." On 10 January, he declined her offer to have some shirts made for him:

> I don't believe I left any shirts anywhere and a goodly number of what I have here have already been pilfered, or at least borrowed by the servants' cousins. You are sweet to think of having some made, but I would hesitate to have anything good sent out here. Already everything I have looks as though it had been put through a cement mixer. Maybe now you would like to send that sky blue coat—hopefully. All my white shirts are baby shit brown, linen handkerchiefs have the hems ripped, and the woman who does pressing burned a hole the size of a silver dollar in the middle of the coat of my new gray suit. To be sure, she had it rewoven before she told me, but unfortunately the color of the new material is not exactly what you would call gray. It

passes for a gravy spot. What the servants don't do the flying mud of Chungking does, flying because all transport is open jeeps. When I get back I will look as though I had been working in your chicken coop, which is what I would prefer to do anyway.

The mails continued to give them problems. Mail to China was faster than mail to New York; John got his tobacco and a shirt he forgot in Pleasantville on 17 January, but Lillian had not yet received the Christmas present he had sent her in November. John repeated several times his *mea culpa*: "It was stupid, stupid and wrong of me to come out here and to leave you." He was beginning to worry about the Flynn mission, and was making inquiries at the Department as to how he might get transferred to Washington. Zilboorg wrote him, saying that Lillian was working hard on her new play, that it was good for her to be busy, and that she and John "were happy together and would be" in the future. About world politics, Zilboorg was gloomy. So was John:

What scholars call internal evidence has been piling up the last few days that the anti-Russian line in the Dept. is far deeper and stronger than I had thought, though there is some reason to believe that Byrnes does not share it. Army and Navy are even worse. I wish I knew more about that. There was a long stinking telegram in from George [Kennan] today on Soviet Chinese ambitions. Even if you wished to grant his original premise the way it was developed could hardly have been more vicious in the hands of those who want to use it. Certainly all agencies out here start on the thesis of the [Soviet] menace and then proceed to collect the desired evidence. I fight the communist battle so interminably and on such a low level that sometimes, tonight being one of them, I have an almost irresistible desire to run away from it all. Darling, even if it is hot let's go to the Amazon and study the rubber boom. When it gets too hot we can always go to the Guiana highlands where not much of anybody lives and life is pleasant and easy. All I ever really want to do anyway is make love to you. [21 January 1946]

The Embassy in Chungking expected a visit from Ambassador Harriman and his staff sometime during early 1946. There were several target dates and as many postponements. Suddenly on 28 January they arrived:

My Dear Darling: Well, I was deep in bed last night with a copy of Guadalcanal Diary when I was called to the phone and from the other end at the Gimo's [Generalissimo] country place the entire clan was on my neck. They had unexpectedly arrived a day early. There was the conventional banter and the information that they had picked you up in New Delhi and brought you on here. This morning they came into town and had lunch with me. It seemed to brighten up the place and there was much to talk about. It started right out with more cracks about how you had decided you really did not want to come into town to see me after all and preferred the country. When I did not rise to any of this, it suddenly stopped and we lapsed into the old easy way of so long ago. For a time it was fine and we gossiped about people and things and places and got caught up on the last year.

Moscow seems to have changed little. They had a number of letters for me from assorted Russians which was nice. The Spaso line also has changed little, except I think it is sharper. It all caused great waves of nostalgia for a time and a place that seem dreadfully remote, and with it such bright pictures of you there, walking in the snow around St. Basil, the hotel, banging on a typewriter in our corner at Spaso, getting into the bathtub, sitting in my room when I came back at noon, fights at the table, a purple suit and gold beads, lying very close and loving next to me in bed, a deep peace inside me even though I could not know if I would ever have it again, and then suddenly you gone and it was winter again. It made everything here seem so silly and useless.

February was relatively quiet in Chungking. Marshall had rammed through a settlement between the Nationalists and Communists on paper. John had no faith in its durability, but at least it decreased tensions. From Lillian came word that she had been elected to the American Academy of Arts and Letters, for which John duly congratulated her. Her letters were now upbeat and loving enough even for him. She suggested sending him a sun lamp, since he complained so much about the damp and cloudy Chungking winter. This he declined; it wouldn't operate there. The current "is so feeble you can't even read at night without punishing your eyes."

On 12 February John rejoiced:

A little squib from the Dept. this morning says that the Vatican has indicated its willingness to reconsider its relations with Moscow, if the Kremlin will make the first advance. I would say this is a good sign, very good. As a result I annoyed the counsellor no end by being absent-minded in making mental plans when he thought I should be listening to his ignorant remarks, and forgot to tell General Marshall he had an appointment with General Feng Yu-hsiang which did little to endear me to either general. To hell with it, all I want is to be with you and spend all the rest of my life with you.

He also rejoiced over her inscription in the Modern Library Edition of *Four Plays*, which reached him in February: "For John Darling, on a sad night which waits on happy nights, forever. My love, Lillian."

As a political officer, John had frequent contacts with the Chinese Communist delegation in Chungking for peace talks. He continued to be much impressed with the skill and candor of Chou En-lai. John accepted the testimony of all observers who came back from Chinese Communist headquarters in Yenan to the effect that the Communists had remarkable support from the people living under their rule. The most convincing evidence of Communist strength came from Ivan Yeaton, an American colonel who had previously served in Moscow; though loudly anti-Soviet, he concluded after spending several months in Yenan that *these* Communists, unlike the Russians, really had popular support.

John had always been skeptical of the belief expressed by some journalists (not by Foreign Service officers) that Mao was not an ideological Communist and would refuse to align his movement with the Kremlin. Chou had several times emphasized to John that his movement *was* Communist with all that implied. During his first months in China, John was not especially disturbed at the prospect that the Chinese Communists would eventually win out over the venal Kuomintang; he read Chiang's book, *China's Destiny*, in the unexpurgated edition, and knew it to be a fascist tract. He shared with Lillian a conviction that almost anything would be preferable to unconstrained Kuomintang rule.

The first hint John showed of hostility toward the Chinese Communists was in a letter he wrote Lillian on 5 March 1946. He noted that Yenan had changed its lexicon. Previous blasts at the Nationalists had called Chiang's government "reactionary elements or destroyers of Chinese unity or some such thing." Now the Yenan propagandists were using the word "fascists" in the same way Moscow used it. This John thought ominous. It was not that he thought the label inappropriate; the disturbing aspect was timing. From here on, his suspicion and distrust of the Chinese Communists grew steadily, eventually encompassed the Russians, and led to changes in his orientation that Lillian found distressing.

The same letter to Lillian that reported his unease with Yenan also noted "I have the key to your front door in my pocket where it is a source of irritation at not being used. It should be bright and shiny, not tarnished from disuse. However, it keeps company with your silver dollar. Both want to get back to you as fast as I do."

A steady stream of packages arrived in China from Lillian: three "very elegant pairs of pajamas and four cartons of welcome and Christmasy

Camels"; Fred Schuman's latest book; a book of Zilboorg's; packages from Saks Fifth Avenue and other elite stores; and a book of blank checks on his Bloomington account, which he had left with her. Lillian was assiduous in providing her absent lover with tokens of esteem.

His letter of 16 March reflected his appreciation of her efforts:

> I received a couple of very welcome letters from you last night—the first in two weeks—one from NY and the other from New Orleans. The one from the Roosevelt made me nostalgic because that is where I have stayed the two or three times I have been in New Orleans, the first time having been back in 1933 when I went to a foolish fraternity conference mostly to get a free trip.
>
> One thing I want to make clear from the beginning: That concerns you and children. I would be sorry if we did not have children, mostly for your sake, darling. If there were the slightest question that having any might harm you I would never agree to having any. You must believe me, sweetheart, that I love you rather than your breeding potentialities. With or without children, it is you I want now and always. It is you I love. All right?
>
> As for the boxes and trunk [John's belongings shipped to her from Moscow] I have no particular choice as to what you do with them. The boxes have books, mostly, I think. The trunk has odds and ends of what I had in Moscow, some clothes, the ornaments from my room, the paintings, the red quilt we used etc. If there is any of the stuff you want to use, by all means open them up and do so. Some place there are manila folders of papers which I would like to have put away untouched if you do open them because while there is nothing very secret in any of them, they are also nobody's business either. I would like to have the ikons in the hall closet in town opened to see what condition they are in since they have now been packed for almost a year, and anyway I think you said you wanted to use some of them which you can of course do anytime with me or anything of mine. It is all yours to begin with.

Then the mood changed again. Two days later, he had to respond to her letter of 28 February. She reported hearing from Harriman that John could expect to be in China two more years. He responded with an expletive. It was the beginning of a crisis in their affair, as time went by and he was first unable, and then ultimately unwilling, to pull out of an Embassy that depended on him increasingly. In a letter of 6 April, he tried to convince her that he really "will be back within the year of leaving; if all goes well, before then." A week later, responding to her complaint that even if Flynn did call him back from China it would only be to take him off again to Europe, he acknowledged that disadvantage. He was now, he said, pretty well stuck with the Latin American field; he wanted a Washington desk for one of those countries. He did not directly confront her complaint that as a Foreign Service officer he would have to spend much of his life abroad.

In April, the Embassy moved to Nanking, and he sent Lillian an extensive description of his new setting.

From here on, the question of his desire and opportunity to return to the United States was a constant theme in their correspondence. On 3 May, he responded to a challenge from her with "It is not true, darling, that I have no plans for coming back to the States this year." On 4 July, again in response to a complaint from her, he said he heard from a contact in the Office of the Under Secretary for Latin American Affairs that the head of that office, Spruille Braden, had approved a request for his services—but it would take some time to arrange.

In New York, Lillian was beginning the intense involvement with the peace movement that led to partisan politics and culminated in her work for Henry Wallace's Progressive party in the presidential election of 1948. The FBI kept close watch on these activities.

On 18 November 1945, the First Conference on American-Soviet Cultural Cooperation was held in New York. It was not yet treasonable to favor such an activity, and the conferees were an all-star cast: Leonard Bernstein, Olin Downes, Serge Koussevitsky, Aaron Copland, Margaret Webster, Cheryl Crawford, Harold Clurman, John Hersey, Helen Gahagan Douglas—and Lillian Hellman. The FBI comment on this conference is blacked out, for reasons of national security. Certainly the call to the Conference was enough to raise Hoover's hackles: "The future of all of us depends to a very large extent upon whether or not there can be successful cooperation and understanding between the United States and the Soviet Union."[6]

In December 1945, a group of intellectuals who believed that Truman was not carrying out Rooseveltian principles formed the Independent Citizens Committee of the Arts, Sciences, and Professions (ICCASP). There were antecedents of ICCASP both in New York and Hollywood; Ronald Reagan belonged to the Hollywood group (Hollywood Democratic Committee). Lillian was on the board of directors of the new ICCASP; Harold Ickes, one of Roosevelt's chief lieutenants, agreed to be executive chairman.[7]

In February 1946, the notorious attack on Communist party perfidy by

Albert Maltz appeared in *New Masses*.[8] Maltz argued that the Party should not impose a doctrinaire standard on literary works, demanding that it adhere to the Soviet line of the moment or else face condemnation. His main illustration was the Party's about face on Lillian's *Watch on the Rhine*, which the Party condemned in 1940 because Stalin was allied with Hitler, then praised in 1942 after Hitler attacked Russia. Lillian was thrust unwillingly into the middle of Party polemics. When Maltz, who was himself a Party member, was forced to recant, she kept silent—until 1947, when she unleashed some prime invective on Hollywood, the Communists, HUAC, and the intellectuals who were falling all over themselves in their eagerness to prove they were Cold Warriors.

March 1946 saw Lillian at the Soviet Consulate in New York to speak at a tea commemorating International Women's Day; it was sponsored by the National Council of American-Soviet Friendship. Major newspapers ignored this event; the FBI got word of it only through the pages of the *Daily Worker*.[9]

But plenty of notice was taken a week later, on 15 March, when Ickes's appointment as chairman of ICCASP was celebrated at a banquet in the Commodore. A thousand people attended. Churchill had just made his "Iron Curtain" speech, and the ICCASP banquet featured vigorous attacks on him and his "war-mongering." Lillian's speech, according to the FBI, claimed: "The stage is being set for future wars. Let us not be asked to arrange crusades against socialist Britain, Communist Russia, or radical France."[10]

At the time, John heartily approved of her activities. He wrote on 20 March:

My Dearest Darling: Some of the best news in a long time came through today in the form of the announcement that Ickes is going to be executive secretary of the ICC[ASP]. It sounds like a natural and whoever thought of it had a stroke of genius. The story also said something about the ICC getting to work to drum up votes for Wallace for President. That too, if true, pleases me and I am glad your committee is seriously trying to perpetuate itself and makes me sad that I am so damned far away from such goings on and from you in them and in everything else. The comical little end of this particular story was a final sentence saying the Wisconsin Progressives had disbanded to join the Republicans. . . . Anyway I think you will enjoy working with Ickes. I wish I knew him better. Probably with all he has had to do he will not remember me, but if you run across his son Raymond he will.

About China, however, John had only pessimism. From his letter of 8 April:

All parties now admit that things are a mess, but when the General [Marshall] gets back he will straighten them out. Which he will for a time. But that is the problem. Left to themselves there can be only civil war. . . . But the only way to prevent civil war is continued and endless American intervention. It means intervention on the most colossal scale of any country in modern times; it means assumption of responsibility for the Far East to an extent for which we are unprepared and probably incapable. We literally cannot afford to become involved and we dare not get out. . . . For us there is no good answer any longer. The only answer that would work would be a frank and complete understanding with Moscow and you are just as capable as I of guessing the chances of that.

For long generations the old Chinese policy has been to win by setting barbarian against barbarian. That they are doing now and every sniveling little Chinaman is very busy snuggling up and saying that the enemy is Russia and the spearhead of the defense must be KMT China and so the US should build it up fast. I understand the Japs are using the same technique. When one pulls that on me I have an answer that usually sets him back. I tell him he is absolutely right; there will be war between Russia and the States and the sad part for China is that it will be fought on Chinese soil, and with new weapons China will be completely annihilated within the first two days; then everyone will see how foolish it is and call it off; but won't it be nice not to have to worry about China anymore. That gets them. It also has a good deal of truth to it.

Sweetheart, what would you think if I got us transferred to Ecuador? It would not affect the world in the least. Quito is one of the wonderful places of the world to live in; there is a great job of cultural relations to be done there; and we could say to hell with it all and be happy and cultivate our own garden patch. I want to live with you, preferably in peace and quiet, but with you in any event. Darling, I miss you so terribly, I adore you, I am in love with you always.

John had followed the course of Lillian's psychoanalysis closely. He was friendly with Zilboorg, and believed Lillian's mental state to be improving, at least partially because of Zilboorg's influence. On 10 May, he wrote:

I am enjoying the Zilboorg [book] you sent me. The man really writes well and convincingly. This emboldens me to stick my neck into a bucket of water: I have been interested in and thinking about what you wrote me about getting your pa to get married again. You once suggested that the root of your neurosis you thought would turn out to be the relationship between you and him. I have also noticed that you have from time to time spoken of wishing that he would marry. It would be nice for a lonely old man; but is there something of the other in it too? It may be coincidence, and probably is caused by something else, but all your letters since you told me of the contract [her father's marriage contract] have a different tone to them, somehow a feeling of an inner peace that is not usually there. Or am I just being clever-ignorant?

Politics took center stage for the rest of May. On 11 May 1946, three liberal political groups met in New York to form an alliance. Sidney Hillman of the CIO Political Action Committee spearheaded the conference; joining him were the ICCASP, with Ickes as spokesman, and the National Citizens Political Action Committee headed by Frank Kingdon. Lillian participated as a representative of the ICCASP.[11]

The statement of goals to which this alliance-forming conclave subscribed fitted her beliefs perfectly. Foremost among the policy planks was "increased unity and cooperation among the United States, Great Britain and the Soviet Union; an uncompromising program to destroy the roots of fascism in Germany and Japan, and to quarantine the sources of fascist infection in Spain and Argentina." Domestically, the coalition supported a Fair Employment Practices Commission and elimination of poll taxes. This was a Hellman agenda. There were no Hollywood lefties at this clambake; joining Lillian as ICCASP delegates were Mrs. Edward Warburg, Mrs. Marshall Field, and Mrs. J. Borden Harriman.

John did not comment on this meeting; perhaps Lillian did not write about it. There is no doubt that he would have heartily approved. Two weeks later, in his letter to her of 29 May, he expressed sentiments that were shortly to be echoed by Henry Wallace, as well as continuing unhappiness with developments in China:

There is an interesting trial going on in Nanking of the puppet Minister of Information under the Wang Ching-wei Govt. A few of the puppets have been tried and shot; but most of them are forgiven and taken back into the Natl. Govt. Lin's defense was a most interesting one in which he admitted that all the charges against him were true and he had no regrets; he had done what he thought best for China; that he knew he would be shot; that some day history would prove him right to work with the Japs against the white man, but that some sacrifice had to be made now to placate him—and the audience cheered. I sometimes wonder what I would have done had I been Chinese. We hate the Japs for their cruelty, but it is no worse than Chinese daily practice on each other—so that leaves no resentment here. Furthermore, the west has never done anything which would create any great love for itself here. The treaty port mentality is still at the base of all thinking. Why shouldn't the little yellow boys band together and free themselves. For us the implications are serious and we don't seem to realize them. We are quite happily working to build up the Orient as a buffer against Russia; but is there any good reason to suppose they won't play along with that idea until they are strong and then turn around and slug us? If the Russians continue to be suspicious of us, there is no reason to suppose they too would not be happy to play along with the same idea. I will go even farther and suggest the possibility that since we are the most powerful nation in the world today and therefore disliked we may one day wake up to find the entire world against us. Power is fine and necessary, but it isn't always enough. A little more reading of history would not hurt us.

No letter from you for over a week now, darling, and I am getting fidgetty. I try to console myself that it means good progress on the play. Maybe some mail tomorrow. I love you.

John's fear that we would wake up to find the whole world against us was also one of Wallace's worries; there were many points of agreement between the two in early 1946.

John was nonetheless moving away from a position of willingness to grant the Soviet Union a modicum of reasonableness and consistency. On 8 June, he told Lillian: "That was quite a load of crap the Russians put out in Izvestiya about why it is good to renew relations with Argentina. It was reprinted in their bulletin here. They should be ashamed of themselves for that sort of double-talk. If they want to have relations well and good and that is their business; but it looks kind of foolish to cover it with fancy talk, especially coming right on the heels of their stand on Spain. The world is full of lunatics."

June and July found the two exchanging presents. John sent Lillian some rare crochet work from the hinterlands, and a set of wooden bowls used by the peasants of Szechuan to ladle water. He also investigated the possibility of buying her a panda; the creature's eating habits put a quick stop to that, as bamboo was not among the flora at Pleasantville.

He reported to her that his transfer to Washington was in the mill. He responded to her suggestion that he not put such derisive comments about public figures in his letters; this "cramped his style," but perhaps she was right. In his letter of 3 June 1946, he says: "My Dearest: The week got off to a good start this morning with your May 21. It seems you have been having a time with various characters. Much of it sounded funny, though I am sure it was not that to have to go through it. Maybe there is consolation that so many people come to you for solace. Me too, I need it from you. Anyway I am glad Dash was nice, especially since I was included in it."

John no longer remembers in what way Dash was being nice. In one respect he was being obnoxious. Diane Johnson, in her biography of Hammett, notes: "That summer of 1946, Lillian's play *Another Part of the Forest* went into production. The cast included beautiful Patricia Neal, whom Hammett couldn't keep his eyes off. The cast got used to seeing him at the theater day after day, usually dead drunk. He was funny and could make helpful remarks, but it often seemed to anger Lillian, who knew he just hung around to see Pat."[12]

Another Part of the Forest angered one of the FBI's anonymous informants. The play was not really about a greedy southern family, as it seemed; its main purpose was to show "the Communist technique to play up the weak spots of American life. According to the informant, this play tended to revive the hatred of the North and South in a villainous form."[13]

The biggest development in China that summer was the appointment of a new ambassador. John reacted skeptically at first:

> The first news was that Leighton Stuart has been named ambassador to China, which has produced an atmosphere of unmitigated gloom around the Embassy. The gent is seventy, a professional missionary, has been in China forty years, is a close friend of the Gimo [Generalissimo], very pro-KMT, and will probably run his own show his own way. I assume it means Marshall will soon give up and go home and we will continue to dilly-dally along, without taking any very definite line of policy on anything. Most disturbing is that he apparently is sold on the line that the KMT lipservice to democracy means something. [10 July 1946]

Increasingly, John found fault with Communist tactics. When he returned from a trip to Manchuria in August, he read a Communist blast at Marshall that he considered stupid, uncalled for, and ill-advised. Marshall was not a completely free agent: "And furthermore, as they well know, or should know, he may well be about the best and most genuine friend they have in this world. He has taken from them what he has taken from no one else, and been understanding when he has raised bloody hell with others" (17 August 1946). By this time Marshall loomed in John's estimation as one of the genuine heroes of an otherwise sick world. Communist attacks on the general probably did more to turn John against them than anything else.

On 18 August, he took several hours to describe to Lillian, in three dense single-spaced pages, his reaction to Manchuria:

The trip to Manchuria came off and it was wonderful upon my return yesterday to find three letters from you. It was quite the best part of it all. And a most interesting trip it was. We went the first day directly from here to Mukden, with only stopovers at Tientsin and Peiping for unloading boodle of one kind and another. The trip up was beautiful, being over the north China plain and the hills with their uniformly square villages and walls around them, and then the lovely coastline on the north which made me think of the Riviera. North of Peiping we followed the Great Wall along the mountains and down to the sea, which is the way to see it. Then came Manchuria. Its first impression, later confirmed, is that it is a great and wondrously beautiful land, an empire worth fighting for. It made me think of the great plains areas of the States, a land where a man could live and be happy.

Mukden itself was a grim, gray spectacle, and a wasteland. I have seen clean destruction aplenty, but never anything quite as degraded as that place. It was never a beautiful city, being the Jap idea of modernism, but now it is just horrid. On top of that it rained the entire time I was there and most of it was under two feet of water and mud. The famous Yamato Hotel was, however, rather nostalgic, making me think of the National. So much so that one night I woke up convinced I was in 219 and very full of you. The usual warning to guests on the desk had one wonderful paragraph: "Guests are invited to make merry and to play musical instruments only until 10 pm and particularly 12 pm on week-ends. It is forbidden to gamble, smoke opium or indulge in other disreputable pastimes. . . ."

I am glad that the first draft of the play is done [*Another Part of the Forest*], trust that all goes well, and that you have a fine time in Truro. The farm sounds like fun in spite of all its troubles. Maybe some day you will let me do part of the work? Why is it that when you come near the end of an analysis you back away? Is it fear of what you may find out, or is it that people like the neurosis?

When she finished the play, Lillian devoted more time to politics. On 12 September 1946, Wallace gave the speech on foreign policy for which Truman fired him a week later, despite Truman's having read and approved it. Wallace emphasized the need for improved relations with the Soviet Union.[14] John noted the content of Wallace's speech, agreed with it, and condemned Truman for reneging on what seemed to have been prior full approval. John's view of foreign policy was entirely compatible with Lillian's, as was his admiration for Wallace; and his affection for Lillian remained full strength. This on 21 September:

> I just received an urgent wire that Wallace has just finished resigning. Well . . . Some things about this business puzzle me, and a lot more I would like to talk with you about. I guess it just about adds up to having the last redeeming feature of the Truman administration fade out. What comes now? My poppa done brung me up not to put things in writing. Then I got careless and started writing you what I wanted to; then you put the fear of the Lord back in place. Usually I find it difficult to contain myself, but I reckon it must be that way. With you I like to blurt out what is on my mind. About China there is little to blurt out any more except that all is now unmitigated gloom. It seems to me Chou's last blast closes the door on anything that might have been possible. Maybe it never really was anyway. I suspect that from now on out all here is downhill in the wrong direction.
>
> Your Sept. 7 came in last night to end the long dry spell, and welcome it was, darling. I am glad of what you say about Zilboorg and of the way the play goes. And of course I am deeply disturbed about some other things you say. It is not true to say I have no plans for returning, even though it has been delayed—just as everything else has been in the Dept. Personnel is now four months behind in transfers. It frightens me to realize I have been away eleven months now. Time has frightened me this year as it never has before. As for you and me, time apart is of course not good. I do not believe that if we have together what it takes that time in itself will destroy so long as it does not run too long and there is reason for it. Of course it does not do good.

On 24 September he wrote her that he had let loose another blast at the Department for procrastinating about his transfer, and indicated that he would be happy to buy into *Forest*. He doubted that his few thousand dollars would be of great benefit, but wanted to invest in it if appropriate. He again commiserated with Marshall, who was deeply hurt by Communist blasts at his integrity; this John thought to be terrible.

A week later, Wallace again topped John's writing agenda, and again John spoke of him favorably:

> One gathers that the Wallace affair has been a real explosion, though it is hard here to know how to evaluate the reports we get on it. I suspect many of them of being loaded, and I find it difficult to believe that the American people are as solidly against him as the editorials would lead you to think. If they are I give up. I may be foolish, but the full text of his July letter to the President struck me as about the most sensible thing I have seen on the subject. And there is damned little that can fit that category. But it can hardly be screwier than what goes on here. The correspondents have been busily engaged the last few days in putting cheery little stories about the coming peace. Where they get the stuff God only knows. Maybe it is the last optimism of a tubercular, for we are just about at the bottom of the barrel. If the stories that go out from here are representative of what you read at home you must be getting a ghoulish picture of politics in these parts. Makes me think of a crack in a recent New Yorker: Are you a hard drinker? No, it is the easiest thing I do. [1 October 1946]

His despair at what was happening in China was reinforced by a report from Nat Peffer, a Sinologue who was later to contribute the most incendiary portions of the *China White Paper*:

> Peffer is back from a two months' junket in the south. He is normally a cagey guy who sees this side and that and weighs them both judicially. This time he has come back full of anger and bitterness such as I have seen in few men, saying that whatever we have seen of terror and brutality in such places as Kunming is nothing compared to Canton; that Americans are universally hated; that this is now a Govt. which has only one possible peer in the world—Spain; and that if we think we can build China as a base for another war we will in the end find the enemy not only in front but also behind. Something terrific has happened to him and he tells a terrific story—like something out

of Jeremiah. I think today is a good day to have him tell it to Marshall. [4 October 1946]

Despite the fact that she herself was directing *Another Part of the Forest*, Lillian continued politicking during the fall of 1946. The FBI chronology of her misdeeds during this period has three paragraphs blacked out, again for "national security" reasons, so we do not know everything she did that agitated the director of the FBI. But we are allowed to know that in October she supported the formation of a Citizens Committee for Decent Department Store Wages, which would seem to be innocuous enough, unless one accepts the Bureau's antilabor bias. And on 26 October, the National Council of American-Soviet Friendship sponsored the "World Freedom Rally—USA-USSR—Allies for Peace," for which Lillian's name appeared on the reception list. On 14 November she put her prestige behind a movement to desegregate the theaters in Washington, D.C.; thirty-three playwrights, lyricists, and composers released a statement threatening to withhold their works from D.C. theaters unless doors were opened to Negro patrons. Lillian joined Robert Sherwood, Maxwell Anderson, Irving Berlin, Ira Gershwin, and a bevy of similarly talented artists in this endeavor.[15]

None of her activities in the fall of 1946 were as significant for the future as two events with which she was not connected. The first of these neither she nor John was aware of. Louis Francis Budenz, double defector from Catholicism to Communism and back to Catholicism in the fall of 1945, came to the attention of HUAC and began the career of public witnessing that made him the most destructive force of the inquisition. On 18 October Budenz made a radio speech in Detroit. In Walter Goodman's account, Budenz "said that American Communists took their orders from a secret agent of the Kremlin. This disclosure was made in the language of The Shadow [a radio character of the day]: 'This man never shows his face. Communist leaders never see him, but they follow his orders or suggestions implicitly.'"[16] J. Parnell Thomas, chairman of HUAC, casting about for something to spice up lagging (read *unnewsworthy*) HUAC hearings, immediately announced that Budenz would appear before the Committee. It was, says Goodman, a "life buoy" for Thomas; "It was his [Budenz's] inclination to melodrama that brought him to the Committee's attention in the fall of 1946."[17] Not for six years did Lillian realize what Budenz did to her when he got fully engaged in his career as an informer.

The second fateful event was the midterm election of 1946. Sniping at Rooseveltian programs, at the Communists, and at big labor were Republican staples in that election. Republican National Chairman B. Carroll Reece set the election theme in June: "The choice which confronts Americans this year is between Communism and Republicanism." The Democrats, he said, were "committed to the Soviet Union."[18] When the votes were counted, Republicans controlled Congress for the first time since the Hoover presidency. In California, Richard M. Nixon won a seat in the House of Representatives by redbaiting Jerry Voorhis, who had resigned from HUAC in disgust. Joe McCarthy rode into the Senate on a wave of anti-Communism, and HUAC came into its own.

Forest opened in Baltimore in early November, moved to Detroit, and then played at the Fulton in New York on 20 November. It was a solid success.

October 1946 brought a respite of sorts for John in Nanking. Nothing dire seemed to happen. He had a succession of letters from Lillian, and expressed pleasure that Lillian had had a wonderful steak fry with the Zilboorgs, where he wished he could have joined her. He exulted in two cables from her in one week. He read, and enjoyed, Arthur Kober's story in *The New Yorker*, as well as John Hersey's *Hiroshima*. He sent her a check for his investment in *Forest*. And on 29 October 1946, the Embassy was favored with a visit from Henry Luce:

My Dearest Darling: This noon just before going to lunch with a lot of very elegant and for the most part foolish people, I was standing out in front of the Ambassador's house quite happily splashing in a puddle of water with the young and very attractive son of the counsellor [W. Walton Butterworth] when along came Mr. Henry Luce on his way into the house, looking very unshaven, unwashed, unpressed and quite unlike his handsome pictures. So there we stood exchanging banalities, his I hope more incoherent than mine. He was carrying a copy of *Life* and finally asked me, since it had the series on Stuart, if I would mind seeing that he got it since he did not know when he would see him again. (I later found out that he was on his way to have lunch with Stuart. Don't ask me . . . I don't know the answer either). Anyway, after he left I was leafing through the magazine when suddenly, darling, you rose up out of it and everything inside me moved all at once. It was as though you had reached up and touched my face and were in my arms and very close. And ever since then I can see nothing else before my eyes. And should you walk in the door this minute it would not surprise me. That picture is almost as lovely as you, and for it I feel quite kindly toward Luce, even if his trip out here bodes no good that I can see. He brought me a little piece of you, and that is worth more than the unpleasant things of the day.

There was other good news. Lillian cabled that the opening of *Forest* in Baltimore had gone well. From the way she worded it, John thought this a good omen. It was followed by a cable from Detroit, where the play had gone the next week; Lillian sent two letters about these productions, along with press clippings, and best wishes for the tenth.

While on the road with *Forest*, Lillian was cut off from active politics. When she returned to New York, affairs of the ICCASP again caught her attention. Harold Ickes resigned as executive chairman on 12 November. There is still argument over the reason for the resignation, but Ickes's distaste for establishing a separate political party to run Wallace for president was undoubtedly a factor. Curtis MacDougall believes ICC's inability to pay Ickes the stipulated salary was important; whatever the case, both John and Lillian regretted the resignation.[19]

Then on 10 December, John received the bitterest letter yet; Lillian said Harriman told her that John did not want to come back, and that she had known this for a long time. Harriman obviously had great credibility with her; John was sorely challenged to counter this new charge of indifference. He wrote the same day:

I suppose one can deceive oneself, but I don't think I am doing it when I say that I do want to come back. Also I know that words can be pretty flimsy and that in the end only the fact can persuade. When I left the States I really did think I would be back before this time. My mistake was in thinking that the Department would of course live up to what it said it would do, and in not foreseeing the results which would come from the confusions in Washington and China. It may sound feeble, but I think it is true that this game here has to be played out. The General came out here for sixty days and he has been here a year and he literally does not know when he will leave. Never having failed before, he cannot yet bring himself to admit he has failed this time. My being still here is partially related to that, partially to the appalling immobility in the Department, and partially to something having gone wrong somewhere along the line that I don't know about yet. There are, or can be, implications in this long separation, and they are not good for us and they rather appall me, but I do not agree that it is because I have not wanted to come back.

He did not hear from her again until 25 December. Lillian did not repeat her accusations about his intentions; she was again suffering with her teeth, needing more pulled, and she agonized over a review of *Forest* by Brooks Atkinson in the *Times*.

John also had his woeful litany:

> Chou's recent speech in Yenan can only be interpreted as closing the door on negotiation, except on terms which only the insane can imagine anyone would accept. Actually, I think they have somewhere along the line decided they don't want a settlement. And in that I think they are making a terrible blunder. They will have to pay for it, and so will a lot of other people. It is an ugly sight to watch a country increasingly being forced into one extreme or another, as is happening in so many places. It makes any form of decent liberalism seem hopeless. For us in China the problem is as simple and the solution is difficult; but I reckon we bought it.
>
> Peffer leaves shortly for the States and should be back by the end of January. I'll ask him to call on you and give you the lowdown on what transpires. I don't agree with everything he says, but I think you will find him interesting. Like most of us here he is dreadfully pessimistic about what the future holds, fedup with a corrupt Govt. here, and completely disillusioned with the honesty or integrity of the communists or of their intentions anymore to do anything but provoke chaos, for their own partisan ends and in disregard of the cost to anyone else. There, I fear me, I must go along with him. Their actions now are unjustified from any standpoint, and can only be called irresponsible. They had absolutely nothing to lose by conciliation. And a great deal to lose by what they do do. It is all an unhappy and tragic business. So is the rest of the world for that matter. [25 December 1946]

This was the first of many anti-Communist diatribes. Lillian did not respond to it. It was more than a month before he heard from her again, and there was apparently no mention of politics in her letter.

But there were politics in New York. The ICCASP and the National Citizens Political Action Committee, after two months of negotiations, held a convention from 28 to 29 December at which they merged to form the Progressive Citizens of America. Lillian took part in the merger, and was to be on the letterhead of the new organization.[20] Nineteen forty-seven was waiting in the wings.

Cold War, Cold Romance

John began 1947 with a silk-purchasing expedition. However strained relations with Lillian had become, he did not neglect the little gestures of affection. Silk was scarce in postwar China, and good silk almost unobtainable. John used the clout of the American Embassy, China's only hope for salvation, to get some Nanking tribute silk, handwoven and in magnificent colors, allegedly taking three men a week to make a yard. He had difficulties deciding which color would best go with her hair; apparently he judged well.

Lillian responded with presents from New York's best shops, including a "monumental" pipe, which he valued for years; other gifts were ties, sweaters, and a scarf. He was beginning to feel like a "ragpicker's poor relation"; because he had come out to China with a limited wardrobe, and more recent arrivals came with trunks and fancy clothes, these were particularly welcome.

In January, General Marshall was appointed secretary of state, to John's great approval. It would mean, he thought, new firmness and direction in foreign policy; Marshall, he told Lillian, "understands the Russians without illusions." As for the Chinese Communists, they were by now beyond the pale; they had "no intention of compromising" and made a "welter of attacks on the U.S. and the General which were preposterous" (17 January 1947).

Whatever direction in foreign policy Marshall would provide, Lillian was not about to go along with it. She sent John the usual greeting for 10 February, but she spent much of her time working with the dissident Progressive Citizens of America (PCA). On 28 February PCA formed a theater division, with José Ferrer and Lillian as co-chairs. The theater division activities were basically bread and butter concerns, such as working conditions, taxation of theater tickets, and racial discrimination, but they included attention to the Federal Fine Arts Bill and the activities of UNESCO.[1]

Lillian was also active in the PCA women's division. Its February schedule featured a month-long political workshop in New York, with two hundred participants. It sent lobbyists to Washington and held a "Fashion is Politics" show with Faye Emerson Roosevelt as guest speaker and six Broadway actresses modeling clothes. Lillian also spoke at the tenth anniversary dinner of the Friends of the Abraham Lincoln Brigade on 12 February.

Lillian told John about these activities and hinted that with the current state of the world, the United States was the place to get in on the action. He agreed with this, but noted that because of the burgeoning witch-hunt in Washington, which was reported with relish in the KMT press, many of his colleagues were disinclined to go home. Things were safer in China—or so it seemed. But he was still committed to coming back, still riding the Department about a transfer.

Lillian had a visitor from China in February, writer Richard Lauterbach. Like Harriman, he voiced the opinion that John wanted to stay there. Lillian was much perturbed. The many acquaintances who had seen John and reported to her that he did not want to return were having an impact. She wrote him on 4 February, doubting, challenging, demanding "answers in full." He did not receive this letter until March 10.

The twelfth of March was a fateful day. President Truman called for aid to Greece and Turkey to help them resist Communist aggression, thus forcing a serious Democratic party split and causing a serious quarrel between John and Lillian. But John did not yet know about Truman's speech when, also on 12 March, he wrote his lengthy "answers in full" letter. The first part of what he wrote was an intellectual justification of precisely the theme Truman had sounded. In theory, it was a justification Lillian would have to agree with, since John put so much emphasis on democratic forms and the necessity for retaining the right to get rid of any government that "pushed people around." In specifics, however, since she saw intolerance in the United States as pushing people around, and since she believed the necessity for peaceful relations with the Soviets to be the only common ground on which to build any kind of tolerable society, his arguments did not carry conviction. This brought on the first serious intellectual breach in their relationship.

At least a third of John's letter on the twelfth dealt with his personal situation:

As for the personal part; you are quite right that I wanted to come to China. It was a great opportunity professionally, and has proven to be one of the best jobs any officer in the business has at present. The choice then was China or Argentina and the choice was obvious. Prospects for staying in the States were very small due to a lack of officers caused by the casualties and war and no recruiting during it. The bad part of that, it has developed, will not be over until summer when more moving normally will be in effect again. I could possibly have stayed, but only by a kind of representation that did not seem justified by the uncertainties in your mind or such hopes as you held out. However painful it may have been—and it was—you were rightly honest about it.

Also I wanted to stay here until Marshall was through. I am the only officer who saw it [the Marshall mission] and had a part in it from start to finish. It was a gallant cause, perhaps doomed to failure from the start, but worth the try. Now, I no longer wish to stay. I think I know the drift, some of it conscious, some not. I don't like it. It is dangerous. I have not the influence—probably no one has—to turn it. And I want out. I suspect that any interference now can only do harm; this thing must burn itself out to its destined end. So I would go where the dice have yet to be loaded. To blame what happens on bad luck or circumstances is foolishness. I don't think I have ever done that. I have been running away for some time, but from only one thing. And that is the decision as to what to do about the boys. I cannot go back; and I shy from that which cuts me off finally. To have avoided decision is and has been wrong for me, for them, for everyone else involved. It has also not made decision in the future easier or less muddy. Perhaps I have been hoping for some deus ex machina solution which would absolve me of guilt for my original mistake. That, of course, only happens in books. What it has done to you does matter a great deal to me, and I am deeply sorry for it and guilty about it because, you see, I was in love with you when I came here; I am in love with you now. What I said then about you and me I still mean. Does this make any sense to you? I hope you will tell me. And if not I will try again.

Lillian did not immediately respond to this soul-searching. Letters between the two had now slowed to every two or three weeks.

But the pace of action in the United States had not slowed. On 22 March 1947, Truman, in response to continued Republican attacks on the Democrats as soft on Communism, issued Executive Order (EO) 9835, establishing a loyalty-security program for government employees. Neither John nor Lillian knew what this would mean for them; Lillian, however, as a member of Progressive Citizens of America, supported that group's opposition to the measure. Jo Davidson and Frank Kingdon were the PCA spokespeople on this issue, in addition to Wallace. They objected particularly to those aspects of EO 9835 which allowed an executive department to withhold from an employee under investigation the precise charges against him, and to also withhold the names of hostile witnesses. The PCA held that there was no crisis sufficient to rescind the ancient provisions of Anglo-Saxon law giving an accused the right to know the charges against him, to face his accusers in an open hearing, and to cross-examine them. PCA called this a "domestic Truman Doctrine," and opposed it vigorously.[2] In the climate of the times, their opposition was ineffectual.

John did not comment on the loyalty-security program in his now infrequent letters to Lillian. He believed, then, that it was innocuous. Here he began to part company with PCA.

EO 9835 was still an untested threat; what Lillian, and the PCA, most feared was aid to Greece and Turkey—the Truman Doctrine. Accordingly, PCA scheduled a "Crisis Meeting" for Madison Square Garden on 31 March 1947. Wallace was persuaded to address it, and nineteen thousand people paid to crowd the Garden for his speech. This was phenomenal; few political rallies charging admission fill the house, but the PCA rally was sold out three days in advance.

Wallace was blunt. The lead of the *Times* report read: "President Truman's program of 'unconditional aid' to anti-Soviet governments will 'unite the world against America and divide America against herself,' Henry A. Wallace declared last night."[3] The *Times* also reported that several thousand people were unable to get into the Garden. Those inside "cheered, applauded, hooted and whistled" as Wallace and other speakers attacked the President. One of the biggest applause lines was "Once we grant unconditional loans to the undemocratic governments of Greece and Turkey . . . every fascist dictator will know that he has credit in our bank." PCA was riding high.

In April, Lillian joined other Jewish intellectuals in paying tribute to Marc Chagall in a dinner at the Delmonico Hotel. This found its way into her FBI file, possibly because Chagall was regarded by the FBI as subversive, more probably because other speakers at the dinner were the cultural attachés of Czechoslovakia, Poland, and the Soviet Union.[4] There is no record of what Lillian said at this dinner.

There is a month's gap in John's letters to Lillian, and by the time he wrote on 20 April, new political developments stirred his ire. He generally supported aid to Greece, thinking the opposition to it—and this could only mean PCA—hysterical and "building it up into a lot more than it really is." His sharpest criticism, however, was reserved for Wallace's new venture: a speaking tour of Europe where Wallace roundly condemned American policy at stops in England, France, Sweden, and Denmark.

This tour of Wallace's drew the wrath of almost the entire political establishment, including dozens of members of Congress, and Lillian's friend Harriman. Ed Flynn also weighed in against Wallace, calling him one of the "lunatic fringe that every party has to contend with."[5] John agreed; his letter of 20 April to Lillian said, "I furthermore think it is most unseemly of Wallace to make the kind of speech he does abroad. If he disagrees, let him do it at home."

In response to the widespread criticism of Wallace, seventy of his American supporters sent a letter to French leaders who were wavering in their intended sponsorship of Wallace's appearances in Paris. The letter claimed that Wallace's proposed visit to France would set a "pattern of . . . one world and the free interchange of opinions between the leaders of the people of all nations of good will." Lillian signed this letter, along with Van Wyck Brooks, Norman Corwin, Arthur Miller, Elliott Roosevelt, and Rexford Tugwell.[6] Whether she had received John's opinion of Wallace's foreign statements by the time she signed the letter we do not know.

When John heard from Lillian again, she was vacationing in Florida and Havana; her report was upbeat and nonpolitical. He responded in kind. But her next letter, of 22 April, which he received in eight days, carried bad news. Her father was deteriorating, and *Another Part of the Forest* had closed earlier than anticipated. This perhaps contributed to a long gap in her professional writing; she was not to produce another play for five years. But the copy of *Forest* she sent John was inscribed "To John, Because, because, and maybe next time, this comes with much love, and is lonesome for him. Lillian, March 1947." She also sent him a year's subscription to *The New Yorker*.

Her letter of 22 April was definitely political. She discussed the current feelings of PCA leaders that the breach between them and the Truman Democrats was now too wide to close, and perhaps a third party was necessary. John did not object to this opinion; he only commented: "If someone with imagination could break out of the fetish, I would think a third party would go. Everyone has always said it wouldn't, so it never occurs to anyone that it might. At least it would serve to break a kind of deadlock" (13 May 1947).

The tone of his letters was now definitely cool, compared with the passionate tone of those written a year earlier. He did, still, insist that he wanted to be with her, and there were allusions to their earlier happy times. But these were few and muted. John was, in fact, beginning to keep company with Hilda Hordern, Ambassador Stuart's secretary.

Lillian's next letter, which reached Nanking on 20 May, defended Wallace's speeches in England. She was fired up with the prospects of a Wallace race for the presidency. John now responded more acerbically:

I did not mean that Wallace has not the right to speak out. If he feels something is wrong he has an obligation to do so. But considering his past official position there is something about his doing so abroad that leaves a bad taste in my mouth. Furthermore, I think it was bad politics from his standpoint and such reports as I have seen rather suggest that he was not well received abroad for that reason. This may be scanty information. For example, certainly none of our news reports give any suggestion that he is drawing the audiences you say he is. On the contrary, they all speak of the growing opposition to him. Sometimes you wonder what to believe. [20 May 1947]

Several more letters from Lillian discussed politics without raising John's hackles. He was still suspicious of her reports that Wallace was getting a tremendous reception on a speaking tour. John commented on Dean Acheson's leaving the Department of State (temporarily, as it turned out— Acheson came back later as secretary) and expressed approval of Robert Lovett, one of Lillian's good friends, as Acheson's replacement. Two months later Wallace was to attack Lovett in another Madison Square Garden rally.

Lillian did get under John's skin with one barb. His letter of 1 June said: "This reminds me of something you said a while back, something so startling it escaped me at the time. Anent the PCA you asked me if I didn't believe in peace. Really, now! You surprise me, and sound like the *Nation*. I hope you won't mind if I heckle a bit, sweetie pie, but it does sound a bit like the old saw that there should be a solution in India, and the way to cure unemployment is to have everybody working."

They were both traveling in July: John on a long swing around China, Lillian to a UNESCO conference in Paris.

Lillian was still, in 1947, committed to the idea that cultural exchange was a useful mechanism for increasing international understanding. Consequently when UNESCO planned an international theater institute, and invited twenty-six delegates from various countries to Paris for a founding conference beginning 28 July, she accepted her invitation to participate with alacrity. J. B. Priestley of Great Britain was chairman, and the conferees discussed ways of improving the flow of acting companies and play translations across international boundaries.

Lillian thought the conference a great success. Interviewed by the *Times* upon her return, she called the meeting "extremely fruitful," and praised the participants for their vision and dedication.[7] Four years later, when she was again seeking a passport from Ruth Shipley, she referred to the Paris conference, stating that "Mr. J. B. Priestley would testify to the fact that I acted with sense and discretion, and in the best interests of my country."[8]

The FBI did not agree. New York SAC Edward Scheidt included in her file a *Journal American* story noting that while the Soviet Union had not joined UNESCO, it was participating "wholeheartedly" in the international theater institute. Therefore, the theater institute had to be under its control. And behold: "A notorious Communist fellow-traveler is included among the American representatives to the conference. She is LILLIAN HELLMAN, playwright, whose affiliations with red fascist groups and movements would fill a proscenium arch, according to files of the House Committee on Un-American Activities."

To be fair with Scheidt, he also included in the Hellman file a statement Lillian made while in Paris: "Politically I am a liberal. I choose to think that that means that I believe more in the rights of the working man than I believe in any other rights."[9] Perhaps one should not give Scheidt credit for this after all—claiming to be a liberal would not endear Hellman to his boss.

When Lillian wrote John about the conference, she was not optimistic. The State Department had leaked its unhappiness with her as a delegate, and this got back to her. John thought this curious and of no great import.

John's travels in China were with the military attaché, and his observations were incorporated into one of the documents that became a part of the report of the Wedemeyer mission. Secretary of State Marshall, smarting under Republican charges that the United States was letting Nationalist China go down the drain, sent Lieutenant General Albert C. Wedemeyer on a fact-finding mission to evaluate the state of affairs, with a view to sending further aid to China. Wedemeyer's report was of the "curse on both your houses" genre, with harsh words for both the Nationalists and Communists. John did much of the staff work for the Wedemeyer mission, some of which is in *Foreign Relations of the United States*, volume 7 for 1947. John's specialty was Sino-Soviet relations; his report of 1 July contains his first clear statement of belief that the Cold War had now reached Asia: "The Chinese Communists are a strong and effective extension of Soviet foreign policy and as such, a threat to the existence of any democratically inclined National Government of China, and therefore, a threat to the interests of the United States. Since the largest non-Russian Communist army in the world can be counted on to serve Russian purposes, the Kremlin can afford the luxury of taking, for the time being at least, a negative official attitude toward China."[10]

Marshall did not release the Wedemeyer report, since it contained a recommendation for UN trusteeship in Manchuria which Chiang would resent; for years afterward the suppression of this report was held by reactionaries in Congress to be proof positive that the Democrats were hiding their complicity in the fall of Chiang.

At the same time he reported these sentiments officially, John was writing Lillian his private thoughts about the behavior of the Russians. They were not complimentary. Molotov had been "shameless" at the Paris meeting of foreign ministers, and it was now clear that "the Russians for their own ends are prepared to precipitate chaos all over Europe. I think it is damned disgraceful. It will be more than interesting to hear what you pick up in Europe on this score" (29 July 1947).

His growing estrangement from Lillian did not keep him from seeking gifts for her. At Sian, he bought a belated birthday present that he thought to be much better "than the junk in Nanking: a Tang Dynasty tomb figurine of a court lady with a high head-dress. I think she is very sweet" (1 July 1947). She reciprocated with four packages from Saks and one from Dunhill, which made him feel luxurious.

Her letters to him from Paris touched no political wounds. When he got her first letter from New York upon her return, however, he fired back a long lecture. The political view to which he now subscribed, diametrically opposite to hers, signaled an estrangement of major import. What they had of personal and physical compatibility was no doubt still there. The companionship they enjoyed could still be revivified. But they were now on opposite sides of that great philosophical rift that tore the fabric of American society with the onset of the Cold War. His argument of 11 September was as clear a statement of the case for resisting Soviet aims as can be found:

> In my letters I suppose I have been trying to convey an idea, and
> have been avoiding saying it in so many words because I know such
> things are most difficult to explain in writing and are so easily misun-
> derstood. But since you have noticed it, I will try and beg your
> indulgence if the explanation seems inadequate. I do, in fact, think
> you are wrong about events and about a lot of people. A great many

conceptions that seemed valid prior to 1939 are no longer so, and perhaps never were except as useful expedients. A world which today is weary unto death and irritable is now looking down the throat of the most gigantic struggle it has ever known. As a result everyone is scared to death and a lot of people are doing a lot of foolish things, with no one having a monopoly on nonsense. Whatever the antecedents, reasons or alibis, justified or otherwise, the fact is that we are today faced with a situation which is relatively simple and whose solution is extremely complex. It is furthermore a situation which is not of the choosing of the United States, even if we have at times unwittingly compounded it. Whether the Russians are honestly motivated by fear of external aggression (and I believe that fear to be without justifiable basis), or whether their actions are the logical outcome of their rigid and narrow ideological blinders (probably one reacts on and develops the other), it is plain by now that the United States is faced with an expanding Slavic power which is completely without scruples of any kind. Unless something is done to contain that expansion it will engulf the world. I, for one, am not attracted by the kind of world they have demonstrated, particularly during the last two years. I think a few examples will illustrate the point.

The evidence is pretty incontrovertible that the regimes in the Soviet satellite states in Europe are ruthless dictatorships which would be turned out over night if the majority had any freedom of choice . . .* I don't see how it is possible to see evil design in the Marshall plan; and yet Molotov at Paris shamelessly and cynically junked the whole thing despite any fancy explanations from Alvarez del Vayo for what can only be interpreted as the objective of prolonging and deepening the economic misery and collapse of Europe in order to install communist regimes in power all over and based on the firm, and so far unprovable, belief there will be an economic collapse in the US. I cannot see that the communist record anywhere in Europe shows Europe would gain anything by it, if for no other reason than the absolute suppression and denial of all political liberties and civil rights which to my mind are the most important things in life . . . In China, the communists have never had the slightest intention of making peace or reaching a compromise. Even Anna Louise Strong admits that. They aim for the whole thing at any cost. They have done many good things for the peasants, but no one voices an opposition

*All ellipses in this letter are Melby's.

view more than once. That is beyond doubt. It is academic whether there is any direct line to Moscow, the fact is everything they put out and every view they express might just as well have been written in Pravda. In Manchuria the Russians did a job from which the area will not recover for decades. Then in violation of all agreements they saw to it that the communists took over. Russian slaughter of the Mongols, who never did them any harm, is one of the most monstrous, if lesser known, crimes of our time . . . In Korea they are sitting tight in their own zone until we leave ours and then the army they have trained will unquestionably move in and take over as things now stand . . . In Japan they have obstructed wherever possible without ever making a single constructive suggestion. How can you interpret all this?

If it is for the greater glory of the Russians, the answer is obvious. If it is for ideology, then I want no part of an ideology which, despite the fine talk about the people, is so indifferent to individual welfare, sets up a small group which presumes to decide what the majority wants, and to that end eliminates any vestige of opposition in any field, and at the same time produces the shoddy kind of intellectual life the Russians now have. I wish you could see the press translations from the Moscow literary papers. There are times when I find it hard to believe they are not trying to be funny as, for example, a lot of yammering about the social content of Prokofiev's latest quartet, the purge of the writers' union (I know some of those people), the rumpus over Picasso. On top of that there is the political propaganda, a large part of which is just downright lying.

All this is by no means to say that we have any monopoly on the angels. We have made plenty of mistakes and we will doubtless make more. We are supporting a lot of bad boys here and there, but that is no reason for turning their countries over to something worse from which there would be no appeal. And withdrawal of our support in a lot of areas would mean just that. Where we have failed is in not ensuring better regimes or in improving our own techniques. It is also unfortunate that a lot of people at home are taking advantage of the times to do ugly things. In time reaction will bring its own revolt, though it is hard to say how long it will take. It is also unfortunate that so few liberals realize they in the end take the heaviest rap from the communists who are seldom gentle with social democrats.

Sooo . . . be it nationalism or ideology or the former using the latter, the implications seem inescapable, and actions confirm implications. Unless you can go down the line with the ideology as correct and inevitable, you must oppose it. And I cannot agree with it as correct or inevitable. If life has any meaning, or personality any validity, then it can hardly be that narrow and restricted or hemmed in from possibilities of individual growth. The expansion of one people at the expense of all others is death. You may remember that in the thirties a lot of people said that if only you give Germany enough it would be satisfied. The German people also thought the world would be better for their domination. Their mistake was in forgetting to ask the world what it thought.

Darling, this has been a long spiel. So fire back at it. I have probably left a lot of things unsaid, but I hope this is not too bad. Now I shall put in some lettuce seeds, play with the pooch, have a drink and dinner, and go to bed wishing you were here. Much, much love, my dear.

As a specimen of marketplace argument, John's justification of the Cold War is highly persuasive. It may lack the sophisticated theorizing of George Kennan's "Sources of Soviet Conduct," and there is in it no hint of the providential mission that "history plainly intended" us to bear.[11] It is a stripped-down, empirical, participant-observer recital of events as John saw them. What cosmic irony that it was written for Lillian Hellman by a lover who two years earlier had shared her accommodationist views.

It was two months before John got a response to this. Lillian had, meanwhile, been busy. She was participating in the road show of *Another Part of the Forest*, which opened in Philadelphia on 22 September. As we know from her memoirs, nursing a play to performance was a traumatic and demanding task for her. Perhaps it was the play, perhaps it was involvement in politics, perhaps it was simply the awkwardness of responding to such a magnum opus; whatever the cause, Lillian did not answer John's letter until the end of October. Would that *her* argument had survived. But we do know that she took offense at his Cold War credo from his answer of 7 November:

I have your letter in reply to my long job. Neither one was easy to write and I don't think I agree with some of the things you said, at least not without some fuller explanation as to what you really mean. It is difficult, if not impossible, to explain and elaborate a lot of such things in letters. Written words mean varying things to different people and by the time that is realized the moment of explanation has passed. They must be talked. Of course I realize what all this implies of a personal nature, and that is the hardest part. On the other hand, I see nothing to be gained, and much to be lost, by pretending that one is what one is not. It is a luxury ill to be afforded. If something really does block a relationship, that difficulty is not solved by overlooking it. You can either have it in spite of the obstacle, or you can't. Half of the answer to that question belongs to you. This being the anniversary of the revolution, one must now betake oneself to the International Club with all the other official stuffed shirts to assist in commemorating it over the foul liquor which is traditional in Nanking. I'll have a drink of my own before going and one for you, the happy days we had before, and the hope we shall have happy ones again. Much love, John.

John said nothing to her about the cable Ambassador Stuart had received from the Department of State praising John's reports on the Chinese Communist Party, the third such commendation he had received in a year's time.

On 25 October 1947, the PCA held another rally, this one timed to coincide with the House Un-American Activities Committee hearings featuring the Hollywood Ten—actually nineteen at that stage. The PCA held two sessions, one at the Hotel Commodore, where seven speakers tore into HUAC and Representative J. Parnell Thomas for violating the constitution and bringing Congress into disgrace.[12] At an evening rally in St. Nicholas Arena on the twenty-sixth, with 7,500 people inside the hall and another 1,500 turned away for lack of space, Senator Claude Pepper declared that HUAC was undermining Americanism, and if successful in intimidating Hollywood, would take on the press, radio, and finally the pulpit. Lillian said many of the same things. Two paragraphs of FBI comment on the meeting are blacked out: national security.[13]

Wallace, meanwhile, made charges that must have caused Lillian a bit of uneasiness, especially his repeated attacks on Harriman and Lovett. Wallace did not claim that these were evil men; they did, however, represent investment bankers and big business. "The role of investment bankers," he said, "should be limited and controlled by the Government and the Government should not be controlled by investment bankers."[14]

There was again a month's gap in letters. When John wrote on 10 December, he responded to her nostalgia and plaintive questioning:

Not only do I remember Thanksgiving and a party and dancing, I also remember a black skirt, a gold blouse, a honey colored pin, and even darker eyes. More than that I remember that today is the tenth of December. The appalling part is that it was three years ago, and that is too long from any viewpoint. I really had not thought it would be this way. I don't suppose I knew what it would be, but not this and not here. And you are right that it is time we saw each other and talked, which would take some time for catching up on the intervening period.

And what do I feel? In many ways I am confused. The attrition of time and space, the impact of other people have blurred much, have made many things seem unreal, as though dreamed. . . . This I do know; there is in me a deep, deep affection and warmth for you. But perhaps this is not good enough? And if anyone loses the right to ask it is I.

What was probably Lillian's most trenchant statement of her basic Americanism appeared in the December 1947 issue of *The Screenwriter*. This was an attack not only on HUAC, but also on the cowardly Hollywood stars who groveled before HUAC and sought only to preserve their jobs and salaries. It was entitled, appropriately, "The Judas Goats." She identified some of her targets by name: Adolphe Menjou, Robert Taylor, Gary Cooper, Leo McCarey, all of whom had made fools of themselves before the inquisitors. They participated knowingly in the congressional circus. Her prose was passionate, her contempt scarifying. All of it deserves to be read; here I quote only the paragraph that expresses most clearly what she perceived to be true American values.

But why this particular industry, these particular people? Has it anything to do with Communism? Of course not. There has never been a single line or word of Communism in any American picture at any time. There have never or seldom been ideas of any kind. Naturally, men scared to make pictures about the American Negro, men who have only in the last year allowed the word Jew to be spoken in a picture, men who took more than ten years to make an anti-Fascist picture, those are frightened men and you pick frightened men to frighten first. Judas goats; they'll lead the others, maybe, to the slaughter for you. The others will be the radio, the press, the publishers, the trade unions, the colleges, the scientists, the churches—all of us. All of us who believe in this lovely land and its freedoms and rights, and who wish to keep it good and make it better.[15]

This gem never appeared in Lillian's FBI file. Perhaps the Bureau's net did not cover *The Screenwriter*. Perhaps J. Edgar Hoover could not deal with such intense invective. Wright, in his biography, says that the article may have been counterproductive, since it insults the Hollywood producers, who might have been able to intercede "between the Hollywood imperiled and the witch-hunters."[16] True, but it misses the point. Hellman despised them all.

In New York, the Wallace campaign surged ahead. A 15 December PCA Executive Committee meeting, with Lillian in attendance, voted eighteen to one (the lone holdout was Frank Kingdon of New Jersey) to urge Wallace to run for president on a third-party ticket.[17] Two days later, a small subcommittee of the PCA Executive Committee, including Lillian, called on Wallace at his headquarters in the McAlpin Hotel to inform him of their action. He was amenable. On 29 December in Chicago, he announced that he would lead the ticket of a new Progressive party.

Defeat with Wallace, Defeat with Chiang

During 1946, John wrote Lillian 255 pages of closely typed letters; hers to him were more numerous but on smaller paper. In 1947, John wrote fifty-two pages; Lillian probably twice that. During 1948, he wrote just seven pages; Lillian's letters decreased correspondingly. They were now going separate ways, and politics loomed larger in the few letters they did write.

Lillian wrote years later, in *Scoundrel Time*, that while she saw a third political party as necessary, she had "not wanted all energies turned toward a presidential campaign. I had thought we would concentrate on wards, districts, even neighborhoods, building slow and small for a long future, and I disagreed that so much energy and money, all of it, in fact, was being gambled on a man about whom I had many doubts."[1] But in 1947, she had been part of the delegation urging Wallace to run, and in the euphoria and enthusiasm of January 1948, she was swept along with the other members of PCA.

The Progressives did not expect Wallace to win. They expected him to get a substantial vote (projections ran up to 10 million) and to force the Democrats to moderate their headlong drive toward confrontation with the Soviet Union. Lillian was not put off by John's disdain of Wallace; she wrote John of the widespread enthusiasm for Wallace, and of the spirit of the second annual convention of the PCA, from 16 to 18 January 1948, in Chicago. Lillian was elected one of the vice-chairmen of the Party.[2]

John was not impressed. When he wrote her on 3 February, after thanking her for his Christmas present, explaining in more detail the T'ang dynasty tomb figurine he had sent her, and complaining about the turmoil in China, he let his feelings out about the new candidate:

> I am sorry to say I think Wallace is making a damned fool out of himself. It is too bad because he has offered much and still has much to offer, but this way it is being destroyed. His statement a few days

ago accepting communist support at best was naive. How can he think, as he says he does, that this means they support him and not their own program? Isn't the record clear enough by now that they will simply use him for their own ends and that those ends are bad? The public record alone should be enough to persuade that those ends are simply an extension of Soviet power, and that they will never hesitate to use any means available to secure that extension. Wittingly or otherwise, Wallace is being used for that purpose. However good his intentions and integrity, I don't quite see what it has to do with Jeffersonian democracy.

Contra Wallace, contra Hellman. But he still signed off "I miss you much, much always."

Lillian's major contribution to the Wallace campaign may well have been in February, at a luncheon of thirty-five wealthy women hosted by Elinor Gimbel at the Ritz-Carlton. Lillian was featured speaker. Curtis MacDougall in *Gideon's Army* describes the event: "Her address, in pamphlet form, was one of the most widely distributed pieces throughout the summer. In it, Miss Hellman pointed out that French and Spanish women had supported fascist programs and candidates, and that American women had not shown sufficient awareness of the threats to democracy in their nation. She spoke for peace, criticized the bipartisan 'get tough' policy, pleaded for racial tolerance, and vigorously denied that the party was controlled by Communists."[3]

In addition to this address, Lillian signed a letter from the National Institute of Arts and Letters to the Speaker of the House of Representatives, dated 12 February, protesting HUAC's hearings on subversion in Hollywood. This letter was thrown up to her in 1952 when she was called before HUAC.

John wrote her again, on 1 March. He was livid about Wallace and Czechoslovakia. John had befriended Jan Masaryk at the San Francisco conference, and recalls a conversation with him outside the opera house, just before Masaryk returned to Prague. Somewhat ominously, Masaryk said, "Well, John, its been wonderful to know you. I guess we'll never meet again." On 25 February 1948, the news reached China that the Communists had seized power in Czechoslovakia. John was much affected by this.

Wallace spoke on the Czech situation at a Minneapolis rally on 27 February. The Czech coup, he asserted, was in response to American "get tough" policies; we could expect the Soviets to get tough with neighboring states so long as the United States was warmongering. This comment set

John off, and he wrote Lillian: "I don't know who is advising Wallace, but he is certainly giving him some bum poop. This latest outburst of his could hardly be more inaccurate. He simply does not know whereof he speaks when his facts are as completely off base as I know they are in this case. It gives one to wonder about the rest" (1 March 1948). By the time John wrote this, his friend Masaryk was dead—suicide, said the Russians; defenestration, according to most Westerners.

But the most significant report in John's letter was a brief reference to his Shanghai excursion of late February to speak to the National Catholic Educational Conference of China. His text was picked up by the National Catholic Welfare Conference in the United States, which issued a press release some weeks later: "Shanghai, March 18. The strongest public condemnation of communism so far uttered by an American diplomat in China came from John F. Melby, secretary to the U.S. Embassy in Nanking, in his address at the National Catholic Educational Conference here. He pointed to a 'great similarity' between nazism and communism, calling the latter 'in a sense the greater of the two challenges.' He described communism as an 'iron helmet over the minds of men.'"[4]

Four years later this news release was entered in John's defense against charges that he was soft on Communism. He did not tell Lillian what he had said to the Catholics at Shanghai. His letter of 1 March was the last one he wrote until August. And on 1 April, as if to validate his Shanghai speech, the Russians blockaded Berlin.

John had by now come to terms with the peculiar work habits of Ambassador Stuart, and as the officer with the longest unbroken tour in China, John drew ever more important assignments. His hope at the time, however, was to attend the National War College in the fall of 1948, after taking the statutory three months of home leave to which he was entitled. But he was short of the minimum age the military set for War College students, and the State Department could not secure a waiver. Stuart took advantage of this impasse to cable Secretary Marshall on 30 March 1948: "With Melby not going to War College, hope you can find some way let me retain him here. With the prospects Soviet mediation China situation his vast background and ability are desperately needed to bulwark political section. Melby, himself, wants to stay and question statutory leave could be raised later."[5] Marshall agreed; John was kept on.

Lillian was unaccustomed to chastity. She and Dash had not been lovers since 1945, and she had been carrying a torch for John anyway. Now, in the spring of 1948, with the long silence from John and their bitter disagreements over Wallace and the Cold War, she launched into a new affair. Wright offers a colorful account of her new paramour, an ex-Communist longshoreman by the name of Randall Smith.

Smith's report on Lillian is as much about her character and personality as about her sensuality. He was fascinated by her. "The thing that drew me to Lillian was her honesty and integrity. There were no petty lies, no petty bullshit. No, Harry Bridges was like that. You sense integrity in someone, not so much by what they do or say, but the *shadow* of what they do or say. You overhear them on the phone, then you hear them relate the conversation later, that's what I mean by 'the shadow.'"[6]

Not only was Lillian's "shadow" admirable, Smith also found her a paragon of independence. He had been a Communist and knew the disciplinary demands of the Party. When Smith talked to Wright in the 1980s, it was inconceivable to him that Lillian could have been a Communist. She wouldn't have tolerated the discipline.

It was even difficult for her to tolerate the cacophony of voices in the Wallace campaign, though she gave it her best for a while. On 2 May, she represented the theater section of the National Council of the Arts, Sciences, and Professions (NCASP) at a Baltimore meeting. On 8 May the New York State Women for Wallace held their founding conference. There were about fifteen hundred people present, and the candidate gave the address. He proposed, far before its time, a constitutional "equal rights" amendment to eliminate discrimination against women; he also wanted to extend social security to 20 million families not then covered.[7]

Five days later in Detroit, Canada Lee and Lillian warmed up the audience for Wallace. There was opposition to Wallace's appearance in Detroit, and his party was guarded by more than a hundred police; but the rally came off without incident. Wallace concentrated his fire on Republican Senator Arthur Vandenberg, who was popular with Truman Democrats because of his support of bipartisan—and anti-Soviet—foreign policies.[8] The Wallace party went on to Hollywood, where 32 thousand people crowded Gilmore stadium to hear him.

On 8 June, Women for Wallace hosted a dinner for two thousand at the Hotel Commodore in New York. According to MacDougall, "There were two roomsful of children with babysitters, and the place overflowed with food and entertainment." Elinor Gimbel wrote Wallace's speech on this occasion; Lillian worked on the food and entertainment.[9]

According to an FBI informant, Lillian spoke her own piece nine days later:

[deleted] that on June 17, 1948, the National Council of the Arts, Sciences and Professions (NCASP) sponsored a meeting at Carnegie Hall, New York City. At that time LILLIAN HELLMAN, writer, stated that the "TRUMAN Loyalty Order is legalizing spying on the American people." She also stated that "this cold war is in many ways worse than a hot war. They are using this cold war hysteria to destroy, in the name of Americanism, our way of life in a more ruthless manner than the fascists of Germany ever dared." Miss HELLMAN reportedly closed with the questions: "What business have we to be in Greece? Why are we sending them guns and soldiers and helping the fascist government there to murder Greek patriots? Why are we arming the Turkish Government, a government which was aiding Germany during the war? Why do we refuse Israel? Are we, the people, so stupid that we will let a few politicians do with us what they please?"[10]

The FBI informant may have exaggerated Lillian's purple prose a bit here; it is hard to believe that she thought the Truman administration more ruthless than the Nazis. Unfortunately, the *New York Times* did not cover this seditious assembly.

The rest of June and most of July, Wallace and his crew prepared for the Progressive party convention to be held in Philadelphia on 23 July. This gathering was like no other political convention since that of the Jacksonian Democrats in the 1820s. Senator Glen Taylor of Idaho, who was to be Wallace's running mate, was the only senator present; there were two members of the House of Representatives. The rest were grass roots supporters. Most of these 3,240 delegates, three times as many as had attended the Republican convention, twice as many as were at the Democratic one, were there because they were true believers.

The dominant analogy used by reporters to describe the Progressive party convention of 1948 was "revival." It was like a Billy Sunday rally, lacking only a sawdust trail. There was hard bargaining behind closed doors by the platform committee, but there were real discussions on the floor before a platform was adopted. Unfortunately for the Wallaceites, a platform amendment proposed by three Vermonters and designed to emphasize that the party did not endorse Soviet foreign policy, failed of adoption because party leaders thought their independence of Communism was adequately spelled out in other planks. Reporters seized on the failure of the Vermont amendment to paint the party as a stooge of the Russians. Anne O'Hare McCormick, prominent syndicated columnist, described the convention rally in Shibe Park: "It was a striking spectacle, but there was something in the atmosphere, in the play of lights, in the dark mass of shouting people, that was too reminiscent for the comfort of observers who had witnessed similar scenes of acclaim for a potential 'savior' in Rome in the Twenties and in Berlin in the early Thirties. . . . In a way the genuine emotion behind it makes the fanfare more disturbing."[11]

We do not know what Lillian thought of the convention. We do know what John thought. On 10 August, when he wrote Lillian his third letter of the year, he had a lot of ground to cover. He had traveled widely in China and Southeast Asia, often with Ambassador Stuart; he had watched the Nationalist government sink further into incompetence. He had received his trunk from Moscow days, which Lillian had stored and then shipped on to him. And he had followed the course of Stateside politics:

> The political scene at home seems to have been good fun the last few months. I thought Truman turned in a good account of himself and showed very considerable savvy. The boys who just automatically write him off are making a mistake in my humble opinion. But of course the best show must have been Br'er Wallace. What he and many of his lack in good sense and realism they make up in noise. Wallace himself makes less and less sense to me, though there are plenty of the followers who know exactly what they are after. I am afraid there is altogether too much of the whole rabble-rousing business which is strangely and uncomfortably reminiscent of the early days of the Nazi party.

Could there have been a more pointed insult to a zealous antifascist?

Lillian was aware of Communist participation in the Progressive party. As she tells it in *Scoundrel Time*, Wallace took her aside one day in early autumn and asked her if it were true that many of the important people in the Party were Communists. She laughed; he must have known this.[12] And the chances are that he did, that his question to her was not quite as simple and naive as she remembered. The role of Communists in his movement was an issue, both within the movement and without, from day one. Wallace could not have slept through it.

Scoundrel Time went on to report a meeting she had with three Communist leaders, in which she urged them to withdraw their men from Progressive party councils: "You have a political party of your own. Why do you want to interfere with another political party. It's plain willful meddling and should stop because it is going to fail." The response of her auditors was evasive; they could not get the Communists to withdraw from Progressive councils because they had no control over other members.[13] Lillian did not indicate whether she believed them; she did say that nothing changed. But Wallace's blindness about Communist participation in the Progressive party began to irritate her.

She had not developed any new ideas for writing. John had been berating her about Wallace. Wallace, she thought, had been obtuse about the Communists. With her enthusiasm for the Wallace campaign waning, she took Wallace's wife Ilo, who detested the Communist hangers-on in the campaign, for a month's visit to Martha's Vineyard. This brought a needed rest, but no real satisfaction. She decided to go abroad.

The circumstances of this trip are best described in her letter to Ruth Shipley of the Passport Office, dated 23 September 1948:

Dear Mrs. Shipley:

On September twenty-second I received from M. Kosanovic, the Ambassador from Yugoslavia, a letter extending to me on behalf of the Committee of Culture and Science of Yugoslavia an invitation to attend, as their guest, two premieres of my play THE LITTLE FOXES, to be performed at the National Theatre in Belgrade on October fifth and tenth.

Before I make any decision about the trip, I wanted to find out from you whether my passport, #77535, issued on June 13, 1947, so that I could go to Paris as a delegate to UNESCO, would now be valid for travel in Yugoslavia.

If I went it would be necessary to leave October first or second and thus I must apologize for asking you for as quick a reply as possible. It is my feeling—although I am reluctant to spare two weeks from my own work—that perhaps any small aid I could contribute to good cultural relations between our two countries might be worth the trip.

My thanks to you now, and for your kindness in the past.[14]

Remarkably, this request was granted the next day. Perhaps by then the State Department already wanted to capitalize on Tito's break with Stalin, which had occurred in June.

With such speedy approval of her trip, Lillian decided to swing by Prague on her way to Belgrade.[15] There she talked with the vice-premier, Zdnek Fierlinger, about John's friend Masaryk. This conversation was not eminently satisfactory; Masaryk, according to Fierlinger, had not welcomed the Communist government installed in February, but had decided to cooperate with it because there was no alternative.

With Tito, Lillian was a big hit. He wanted to talk about the Wallace leghorns she was raising; she wanted to talk about his break with Moscow. They eventually talked about both. As would be expected, Lillian's sympathies were with the Yugoslavs; the Soviet Union was just another bully trying to enforce Communist orthodoxy on an unwilling neighbor. It was, to her, a typical case of authority pushing people around. Her attitude was at variance with that of candidate Wallace, who at the Progressive party convention described Yugoslavia as "a feudal country" where the peasants supported Tito in his dispute with Russia because they wanted to keep ancestral lands.

The performance of *The Little Foxes* did not delight her; she thought European directors "always direct American plays with actors jumping up and down, moving from chair to chair, running up staircases, as if we were a people who spent our lives like sandpipers." It was a reaction similar to John's when he saw her plays performed in Moscow.

In her free time she tried to talk to ordinary Yugoslavs, especially those who were not fully committed Communists. She was impressed with their standards of morality, and when she reported her trip in the *New York Star* in early November, she emphasized that "the Western World had better stop sneering and try to understand" these people, for they hardly fit the stereotype of debauched Communists.

Wright makes much of the claim that Lillian pulled her punches in her articles on the Yugoslav trip, not grilling Tito on the reasons for his break with Stalin, thus showing a "reluctance to make any public utterance that might damage the Russians."[16] She had been told by Mr. Prica of the Yugoslav foreign office that it was not necessary for her to be easygoing in her talks with Tito. As she put it in an article for the *New York Star*, Prica said:

> "You didn't have to be so tactful, you could have asked him anything you wanted." This was the first time in my life anybody had ever said such a thing to me, and I was delighted. I said, "Would you mind writing that on this envelope? that I was tactful? There are many people at home who will say I am a liar unless they see it written down. When you say tactful you mean that I could have asked him about the Cominform fight?"
>
> "Certainly you could have asked him. I think he would have told you."
>
> I said, "But I don't think you should ask a man if he has been unfaithful to his wife," and I was pleased to see him laugh. Prica and I

sat for a long time at lunch and he told me that the Yugoslav Communists were deeply puzzled by the Cominform attack, felt it to be completely unjustified, its accusations unfair and untrue. He said they felt deeply allied to the Soviet Union, would go on feeling allied to it, go on being convinced that a mysterious misjudgment had been made. . . .

These discussions of the Cominform fight make me a little uncomfortable: There is an aimlessness in talking about what you don't know. . . . I have a feeling it is simply a disagreement between two Socialist states and the rest of us have been naive in deciding that all Communists think alike, all the time, all their lives, as if they were robots. . . .

The Cominform statement seemed to me—and I have now read it several times—to be of a very general nature, written in words you use when you send a letter to somebody who is waiting for it and will understand it.

But if a stranger picks up the letter he will not understand, and is not meant to. I am that stranger to the Cominform letter; I don't understand the words. And I suspect most other foreigners are in the same position.[17]

It is hard to make a pro-Soviet position out of this. Lillian's articles about her Yugoslav trip are in fact typical of her style. As in her memoirs, she writes overwhelmingly about people, and on this trip it was of the sentimentality of the Germans returning home on the plane she took across the Atlantic, of the inebriated Irishman who approached her in the Shannon Airport bar, of the Dutch in Amsterdam and how they reacted to German invasion, of the Czechs and their recent takeover by the Communists, and of course about individual Yugoslavs in banks and stores and on the street. Lillian was, as in her plays, first and foremost interested in people.

After Belgrade, she stopped in Paris. Norman Mailer had told her about a brilliant new play, *Montserrat* by Emmanuel Robles, then in performance at the Theatre Montparnasse. She saw the play, was entranced by it, talked to the author, and bought the American rights. She arrived back in New York on 28 October, and for the rest of 1948, she worked furiously preparing a version of *Montserrat* for American audiences; she was to direct it. Wallace's campaign was forgotten. The big Women for Wallace luncheon on 26 October at the Commodore took place without her.

On election day, Wallace went down in disgrace. Truman, as John had thought, pulled it out, 24 million to Dewey's 22 million. For Wallace, slightly more than a million votes were counted.

In China, John watched the final disintegration of the Nationalist regime. The Communist steamroller was beginning to move; by the end of October 1948, all communications between the Nationalist-occupied parts of China and Manchuria, which was coming rapidly under Communist control, were cut. On 31 October, John and Dave Barrett, formerly with the American Observer's mission in Yenan and now assistant military attaché at the American Embassy, went to the airport to see if they could get a plane to fly them north for a firsthand inspection of the war zone. They had a long wait. John says, in *Mandate*, "The reason soon became apparent, as Chinese Air Force planes began to shuttle in from the north. Dave impassively watched several of them disgorge their contents, and then somewhat pompously announced: John, I have seen all I need to see. When the generals begin to evacuate their gold bars and concubines, the end is at hand."[18] The Nationalist retreat became a rout.

John was finally ready to leave China. He had been there three long years. On 12 December, for the fourth and final time that year, he wrote Lillian. He was coming home, by way of Manila, probably arriving in Washington early in 1949, "and so before long I really will be seeing you." He was feeling "almost shy" about the States, since so much would have changed:

> Also there has been an election whose results please me immensely and seem to have been a shock to a good many people. I can hardly say I thought Truman would win, but I have thought all along it would be a very close race. There was always something wrong about Dewey, and something about Truman which spoke with the voice of Main Street and that is what most people want in their saner moments. It would have been unforgivable if a larger Wallace vote had changed the outcome as it came all too close to doing anyway. You won't like this, but I was pleased that Wallace made as poor a showing as he did. A better showing would have been disturbing because of what Wallace, deliberately or otherwise, had come to stand for.

Some of these words John would later take back. Wallace had stood, among other things, for modifying the Truman loyalty-security program to give government employees under suspicion the right to confront accusers.

Lillian did not rejoice in Wallace's poor showing, but it was no great tragedy to her. She had a different tragedy on her hands: Hammett. She neither saw nor phoned him for months on end in 1948. But she got reports—from his housekeeper, from the few friends who called on him, and from Randall Smith whom she sent to see him. Diane Johnson in her book says Hammett became so drunk during this time as to be un-endurable.[19]

When Lillian wrote the introduction to *The Big Knockover* in 1966, she acknowledged that things were so bad she "didn't want to see the drinking anymore." But by 1980, when Johnson was well into her biography of Hammett, Lillian was no longer able to admit the depth of her sometime estrangement from Hammett. Johnson had Lillian's approval for the biogra-phy; it was in a way "authorized." But Lillian found fault with Johnson's writing, quibbled about little things, tried to keep her from interviewing people who might give a negative picture of the Hellman-Hammett rela-tionship, and demanded that she interview people whom Johnson did not believe could contribute to her story. Johnson wanted to write Hammett's story primarily from his letters. She says, in an article in *Vanity Fair*: "But it became clear that the plot of the biography Lillian Hellman envisioned was a story in which the hero had been waiting for her all the years until he met her, and he would be a hero who merited the patience, wisdom, and expense lavished on him by the heroine, and who, despite his cruelties, loved her underneath all along. She wished, as anyone might, to read an improved version, or a heroic version, of her life."[20]

The version Johnson wrote was unimproved—it presented fully the breach between the famous mystery writer and the famous playwright. But Lillian's "heroic" side was included, and her heroism was nowhere clearer than in December 1948 when Hammett had delirium tremens. Hammett's housekeeper phoned Lillian: Hammett was going to die if Lillian didn't come get him. At first, Lillian refused to go. But conscience, or pity, or the memory of happier days changed her mind. She went to Hammett's cottage, dressed him, got him in a taxi and took him to her house. She called a doctor: Hammett, the doctor said, had the DT's. She could calm him down with paraldehyde until he was fit to go to the hospital. This she did, and Hammett spent Christmas and New Year's in the hospital. The doctor told him he could never drink again, and he didn't.

On 15 December 1948, the day Alger Hiss was indicted for perjury, John left Nanking; he arrived in San Francisco on 30 December.

Loyalty in the Wings

On the surface, 1949 began placidly. Dash came back from the hospital and spent his time recuperating at the Pleasantville farm. Lillian worked weekdays in Manhattan, furiously adapting *Montserrat* for American audiences.

John arrived in Washington on 4 January, checked into the Department, and began getting acquainted with his new assignment: the Philippine desk. He wrote Lillian on 16 January, thanking her for a Christmas cable that had followed him from China, indicating that the changes in American society were neither so great nor so challenging as he had feared, and telling her that he was to go to El Paso on leave for a month and would contact her when he returned.

From El Paso he wrote her again, mostly about how his two boys had grown, commenting on her various trips, and promising again to contact her from Washington. But this promise proved difficult; his wife came back to Washington with him, leaving the boys in Texas. This he had not counted on.

Lillian phoned him on 12 March, and the conversation was cordial: no politics. He told her that his wife had taken a separate residence and was filing suit against him. The filing, however, took longer than expected, and his wife remained in Washington.

The Truman loyalty-security program, meanwhile, was grinding steadily ahead. Routine reports on all foreign service personnel were now accumulating in State Department security files. On 18 January, cables went out over the name of Robert Lovett, Lillian's old friend, as acting secretary of state, to the embassies in Moscow and Caracas: "URGENTLY REQUEST REPORT ON JOHN FREMONT MELBY, SUBJ LTR NOV 5, 1948, FROM CHIEF, DIVISION OF SECURITY." On 9 March, a similar cable, this time over Acheson's name, went to the Embassy in China. The answers were all highly favorable; John was loyal, hardworking, discreet, and went by the rules.[1] He was unaware of these inquiries, though the State Department was undergoing that microscopic scrutiny which later led to a spate of resignations and firings.

Indeed, some of John's colleagues were already under public attack. John Carter Vincent, a China specialist who was at that time head of the China desk in the Department, was attacked by Alfred Kohlberg in his pro-Chiang *Plain Talk* magazine. Senator Styles Bridges of New Hampshire asked the Department for its file on Vincent. Vincent, a southern conservative, had made a wartime trip with Vice-President Wallace, who was acting as a personal emissary of President Roosevelt, to Soviet Siberia and China. Kohlberg and his friends believed that Vincent had influenced Wallace to oppose Chiang.[2]

John Stewart Service, still under scrutiny for his part in the *Amerasia* affair, underwent another loyalty hearing; there was no publicity about this, but it was known within the Department. And on 31 May, the first trial of Alger Hiss began. Hiss was a pillar of the foreign policy establishment; he had been present at Yalta, served as secretary general of the United Nations founding conference in San Francisco, and then went to the Carnegie Endowment for International Peace as president. Whittaker Chambers fingered Hiss first as a Party member, then as a spy. Richard Nixon, as a member of the House Un-American Activities Committee, was instrumental in bringing Hiss to public attention. At the time, neither Melby nor most of his colleagues saw the Hiss case as crucial.

Lillian, although disillusioned with electoral politics, kept up her support of left wing causes. The National Council of the Arts, Sciences, and Professions, lineal descendant of the ICCASP, held a rally on 9 January at the Commodore to urge the abolition of HUAC; according to the FBI, Lillian contributed $250 to the cause.[3] On 11–12 February, she was one of the sponsors of an antibias rally in Washington. These minor activities attracted no great attention, but HUAC and Hoover noted them. None of these things had put her directly in the cross hairs of the inquisitors. On 25 March, all this changed.

NCASP, with much advance fanfare, invited foreign guests to a three-day peace conference.[4] Its opening event was a gala banquet at the Waldorf-Astoria; the whole operation has gone down in the history books as the Waldorf Peace Conference. Professor Harlow Shapley was chairman of the dinner, and when Joe McCarthy regaled the Senate about the Waldorf conference a year later, McCarthy focused his ire on Shapley. Lillian was at the head table, along with her friend from Moscow, Dmitri Shostakovich. Shostakovich and other Russian intellectuals had been kind to her when she visited them; she was now kind to Shostakovich. It was a photograph of

Lillian and Shostakovich at the Waldorf Peace Conference dinner that captured editors' fancies across the country and spread Lillian's name before a mass audience hitherto largely unfamiliar with her.

A different group of intellectuals, led by Sidney Hook, organized a counter-conference, enlisting almost as many Cold War supporters as there were peaceniks inside the Waldorf. In the bitter terms that were by now common currency among the contending factions, Hook depicted Shapley, Hellman, Frederick Schuman, Leonard Bernstein, Norman Mailer, Arthur Miller, Albert Einstein, Thomas Mann, and their collaborators at the Waldorf as hypocrites and tools of the Soviet Union. Hook called his organization Americans for Intellectual Freedom. The visiting Russians and others from Eastern Europe were not free; therefore, they were unworthy of talking about peace.

Two thousand pickets protested outside the Waldorf, led by the Catholic War Veterans. They jeered, insulted, and flashed placards reading "Keep the Communists out of America," "Go Back to Russia Where You Belong," and "You Can't Have Culture Without Freedom." The Waldorf area was barely kept free of violence by the police.

For five days, news of the conference dominated the New York papers. Norman Cousins, generally hostile toward the conference, was nonetheless allowed to speak his mind at the opening banquet. He was not bashful. As *Newsweek* told it in the issue of 4 April 1949:

> A few minutes after Cousins had seated himself in the ballroom, Shapley asked him what his subject would be. Cousins gave him a copy of the speech. Shapley looked at the first page, then the second. His jaw dropped. He rushed over to Lillian Hellman, the playwright. Then he dashed back to Cousins and got another copy. He and Miss Hellman read the speech together, conversing earnestly.
>
> They discussed it for about fifteen minutes. Shapley returned to Cousins. "Norman," he said, "it's been an awful lot of work to start this conference . . . but if this is the speech you want to make . . ."
>
> When Cousins started talking, a stunned silence fell on the crowd of 2,000. The reason for the pickets outside the Waldorf was not that Americans oppose peace, he assured the foreign delegates. The pickets were protesting the auspices under which the conference was being held—"a small political group," the Communist Party, which "owes its primary allegiance not to America but to an outside government." Jeers, boos, and hisses broke out all over the ballroom.

"I ask you to believe that this group is without standing and without honor in its own country," Cousins declared. . . .

At the speakers' table, Shostakovich jabbered excitedly in Russian to his colleagues. He was mystified by the booing. Reason: Soviet audiences don't dare boo Soviet speakers; in all his life he had never heard it done before. . . .

After Cousins had finished, Miss Hellman rose: "I would recommend, Mr. Cousins," she said tartly, "that when you are invited out to dinner, you wait until you get home before you talk about your hosts."[5]

The two days of panel discussions and resolution writing that followed the banquet were hardly less incendiary. New banners appeared among the pickets: "Kill the Red Killers," "Shostakovich Jump out of the Window." Dwight Macdonald, Mary McCarthy, and Robert Lowell attended conference sessions seeking opportunities to expose the Russians' lack of intellectual freedom.

Hook and his friends made the knee-jerk assumption of the inquisition: those who worked with Communists, even in a peace conference, were no better than the Communists. This assumption is hardly borne out by the records of the conference. As would be expected, the remarks of Soviet and other foreign Communists held strictly to the Party line. Some of the American participants, however, were not afraid to take positions critical of the Soviet Union. Professor Schuman thought both the United States and Russia blind to the fact that no one would win World War III. Several panelists attacked Russia's Trofim Lysenko, Kremlin-favored geneticist who proclaimed the irrelevance of heredity.

But the outstanding voice of moderation and common sense at the conference was that of Lillian Hellman. If she was, by virtue of appearing with Communists, still a fellow traveler (see definitions of this term in Appendix 1), she was clearly not a blind adherent of the Party line. As she told the conference:

> Nowadays on the Right it is fashionable to pretend that only Russia is at fault. I am sorry to say that there are too many on the Left who pretend that only the United States is at fault.
>
> It no longer matters whose fault it is. It matters that this game be stopped. Only four years ago millions upon millions of people died, yet today men talk of death and war as they talk of going to dinner. He who has seen a war and plans another must be either a villain or a

madman. This group of intellectuals can do no worse than statesmen. We want to declare that there still are men and women in the world who do not think it dangerous or radical to declare themselves for the continuation of life. . . . We place ourselves among those who wish to live, think, and breathe, to eat and play and raise their children, among the millions who want to be a little use and have a little pleasure and bear a little sorrow and die a little death, close to someone who has loved them in decency and in peace.[6]

Lillian's prose at the Waldorf has not achieved wide circulation. This is unfortunate; it is hard to find a more eloquent justification for the pursuit of détente with a totalitarian Russia.

The resolutions adopted by the conference were bland; their essence was that war is bad. Lillian was right in saying that the resolutions were valuable only in that they defined an area of agreement on peace among many persons of widely diverse views on other subjects.

Years later, after the publication of *Scoundrel Time*, Murray Kempton looked back on the conference and its outcome with equanimity. "The Waldorf Conference," he wrote, "was beset with more obloquy than it deserved. . . . What had been arranged might less enthusiastically be described as a discussion between Americans who spoke critically of their government and Russians who could hardly have offered theirs any such treatment and safely gone home. It is doubtful that the Waldorf Conference provided any historical lesson more significant than that Lillian Hellman got in trouble because she attended it and Dmitri Shostakovich risked worse trouble if he hadn't."[7]

A month after the conference, HUAC published a condemnation of the affair listing the "red-front" affiliations of the sponsors. Lillian was listed in the thirty-one to forty affiliations category. Hammett gloated to her that he made a more prestigious group, the forty-one to fifty category. One of Hammett's credits was the Crown Heights Committee for a Democratic Spain. He could not remember where Crown Heights was.

Six weeks after the conference, an unknown informant went to the FBI with a charge far more potent than mere participation in a peace conference. Lillian was linked with Gerhart Eisler.

On 6 May 1949, Gerhart Eisler went down to Manhattan Pier 88, bought a twenty-five-cent visitor's ticket to board the Polish liner *Batory*, and walked up the gangplank. Unlike most visitors, he did not leave the ship when it sailed. Once it was safely past Ambrose Light, he reported to the ship's purser and bought a ticket to Gdynia, Poland.

When the *Batory* routinely radioed its passenger count back to the Gdynia line office in New York, a stowaway was mentioned. This report by law had to be forwarded to U.S. immigration officials. They asked the steamship company who the stowaway was. "Gerhart Eisler, German, disembarking Gdynia" was the answer—and the resulting international furor added significantly to America's Cold War trauma, and to Lillian Hellman's FBI file.[8]

Gerhart Eisler was not just a casual stowaway; he was a Comintern agent, believed by many to be the chief agent in the United States, and he was free on bail from 1947 convictions for passport fraud (perjury) and contempt of Congress. Eisler's struggles to overturn these convictions had made him a headline figure. On 14 April 1949, he took his case to the United Nations, probably more for the purpose of propaganda than in the belief that U.S. courts would yield to UN pressure. UN Secretary General Trygvie Lie refused to see Eisler. On 18 April, the U.S. Court of Appeals in Washington upheld his conviction for lying on a passport application. He was facing a year in jail; boarding the *Batory* was an easy escape.

The Department of Justice, stung by the flight of such a high-level fugitive, immediately requested the British to intercept Eisler when the *Batory* put in at Southampton and extradite him back to the United States. The British were at first amenable, and the *Batory* was greeted by a contingent of Scotland Yard agents intent on seizing Eisler. There were also a hundred reporters and cameramen intent on recording their efforts.

Polish diplomats and the *Batory's* captain protested, but after a brief struggle, Eisler was carried down the gangplank and lodged in Southampton jail. He issued an angry statement: "I am the first prisoner of the North Atlantic Pact, this unholy alliance of reaction." *Time* described the Eisler case as "hotter than a sheriff's pistol."[9]

Subsequent British actions did not cool it off any. When Eisler came before the chief metropolitan magistrate, Sir Lawrence Dunne, in Bow Street Court, Dunne held that Eisler had not committed perjury as defined by British law and set him free. He left shortly thereafter for East Germany, where he was lionized by the Communist regime. Eisler's parting shot at his chief American tormentor, Attorney General Tom Clark, was that the attorney general was "America's biggest fool." Clark seemed to accept the description. On 1 June, he said, "I am the dumbest man in the country for letting Eisler escape."[10]

Lillian Hellman did not remember ever meeting Gerhart Eisler, though she knew his brother Hans, a musicologist. However one of the FBI's nameless informers told the Bureau that she had given a dinner for Gerhart the night before his escape, and that Lillian was a close friend of Gerhart's wife, Hilde.[11] This gem lay buried in the files totally unknown to Lillian. It was influential in all subsequent evaluations of her loyalty.

At the same time Eisler was jumping bond, John Melby was detached from the Philippine desk for a temporary writing assignment: he was to be the chief compiler of the *China White Paper* of 1949.[12] This 1,054-page document was intended by Secretary Dean Acheson and his boss, President Truman, to answer the swelling Republican castigation of the Democrats for the "loss" of China, and for being soft on Communism generally. In Acheson's view, Chiang, despite generous American aid, had simply lost the support of his people. The Communists had not so much won as the Nationalists had collapsed. The *White Paper* was designed to present overwhelming evidence to the effect that Chiang, not the Truman administration, had "lost" China. Who more appropriate than Melby to compile and edit such a document?

It was a massive undertaking stretching from April to August, with eighteen-hour days and many weekends. John was assisted by W. Walton Butterworth and Philip Sprouse. When the document was near completion, Ambassador-at-Large Philip Jessup was assigned to do final editing; John's old friends Nat Peffer of Columbia and Till Durdin of the *New York Times* were secretly brought into the State Department to give advice on how it could be most persuasive.

When Acheson wrote his memoirs in 1970, he reflected on his motives in commissioning the document.

> Justice Felix Frankfurter used to say that I was a frustrated school-teacher, persisting against overwhelming evidence in the belief that the human mind could be moved by facts and reason. . . . Early in the year [1949], while talking with the President about congressional and press criticism of our policy in China, I suggested that much of it flowed from ignorance of the facts. General Marshall had been reluctant to present the full facts for fear of hurting further the Generalissimo's declining fortunes. It was now clear that the Nationalist regime on the mainland was on the verge of collapse and that American disengagement from support of it as such must follow. Let us, I urged, prepare a thorough account of our relations with China, centering on the past five years, and publish it when the collapse came.[13]

Acheson could not have been more wrong. The massive documentation of the *White Paper* was totally irrelevant to the political problem of the fall of Chiang Kai-shek. The *White Paper* was read by few, convinced even fewer, and enraged Chiang's American supporters. But John was fortunate; his authorship of the *White Paper* was never publicized, while Jessup, who only did last-minute polishing, got all the public blame.

There was public blame aplenty. The core of the Senate China bloc, Styles Bridges, Pat McCarran, William Knowland, and Kenneth Wherry, issued a four-page blast at the *White Paper*. The Hearst, Scripps-Howard, and McCormick newspapers tore into it with a vengeance. Congressman Walter Judd claimed it was a fraud, and a *New York Times* editorial supported him. Alfred Kohlberg's American China Policy Association took up the cudgels and issued "A Partial List of Omissions and Errors in the State Department White Paper on China."

In the 1948 election, Truman managed to neutralize the Communist issue by deprecating Wallace and positioning himself in the center of American politics. His loyalty-security program and the firm anti-Soviet position he took in Europe insulated him from Republican attacks. In mid-1949, with the furor over the *White Paper*, Truman and the Democrats began to lose control of the Communist issue; the last half of 1949 was a disaster for them. Every month brought some new hostile development.

In July, the first Hiss trial ended with a hung jury. The right wing believed that Hiss was guilty; the courts must be Communist influenced.

In August, the self-serving *White Paper* came out, but publicity given it only made the administration look worse.

In September, Truman announced that the Soviet Union had exploded an atomic bomb. We were now no longer sole possessors of the ultimate weapon.

In October, Mao Tse-tung proclaimed the People's Republic of China; Chiang had been effectively driven off the mainland. This was particularly traumatic for Americans. The Chinese had now rejected Christianity and frustrated the whole American effort to preserve the Open Door and lift China up to modern civilization. Michael Novak, in *Choosing Our King*, captured dominant American emotion after the fall of Chiang precisely: "Ain't no hate like Christian hate."[14]

In November, the second Hiss trial opened. Now the devil would get his due.

In December, rubbing salt into the wound, Mao went to Moscow to negotiate a treaty of friendship and mutual assistance.

How, reasoned the Republicans, could the administration be so blind as to oppose the Soviet Union only in Europe? Hadn't Lenin said that the road to Paris leads through Peking? Wasn't it abundantly clear that the Democrats were putting on a show of anti-Communism in Europe in order to cover up their surrender to Communism in Asia? And wasn't this surrender only to be accounted for by treason? It became clear that the Republican road back to the White House, cruelly blocked in 1948 by Truman's fluke victory, lay through hammering at the Democrat's loss of China.

Largely because of the fuss over the Waldorf conference, Lillian achieved status during 1949 from the ever-vigilant American Legion. The Americanism division of the Legion issued a blacklist of 128 persons "whose past activities make them unsuitable or inappropriate for Legion sponsorship." These "Untouchables" were all members of the "Communist Conspiracy."[15]

Lillian did not grieve over Legion disapprobation; she did grieve over the silence from John. She told friends that she could not understand why he had not made an effort to see her; from her standpoint, political disagreements could not cancel out entirely the affection they had known in earlier years. Dash was now behaving appropriately, firmly on the wagon, enjoying the satisfactions of the Pleasantville farm. For part of the summer, Lillian rented a place at Gay Head on Martha's Vineyard, and Dash went with her. Lillian liked the Vineyard so much that she eventually made the Vineyard her main residence, but she still missed John.

Both at the farm and at Gay Head, Lillian worked hard on *Montserrat*. Again she decided to direct. The play opened in early October with trial runs in Princeton, Philadelphia, and Detroit; when it came to New York on 29 October 1949, the response was lukewarm. It ran only until 29 December.[16] But Lillian was already at work on *The Autumn Garden*, which was to be one of her best plays; the *Montserrat* failure she brushed off as just one of those things.

John returned to the Philippine desk after publication of the *White Paper*. The Communist (Huk) rebellion in the Philippines was heating up, and he soon became a major voice in determining the American response. In November he flew to Manila on a military mission.

John was uneasy about his relations with Lillian, more worried than she about their political differences. He had neglected her since his brief note of March, when he told her he would see her soon. The *White Paper* extravaganza, which kept him at the Department for eighteen-hour days, and troubles with his wife had combined to prevent an attempt to see her. Returning from the Philippines, he wrote Lillian a three-page letter from Tokyo, telling her of his intervening troubles and activities. His major news was that the same day the *White Paper* was released, the Hearst press in Washington carried a story entitled "Prominent Local Diplomat Sued by Wealthy West Texas Society Matron"; his wife was asking for separate maintenance and custody of the two boys (letter, 12 December 1949).

There was nothing of politics in his letter. He told her that the picture of her with Shostakovich at the Waldorf conference was "exceedingly handsome and stirred many things"; he did not comment on the conference. He concluded by saying that 1949 had been "an unhappy year that had to come sooner or later. Any ideas?" and signed it "Affectionately, John," He had written her only four times that year, and seen her not at all.

Hot War, Hot Witch-Hunt

There were at least four full-scale shocks to American equanimity in 1950. In January, Alger Hiss was convicted of perjury, which meant treason. In February, Joe McCarthy took charge of the burgeoning inquisition. In June, war between a Soviet surrogate (North Korea) and the United States broke out, convincing even hardened peace lovers that the Russians had finally decided to go for world conquest. In November, Chinese Communist "volunteers" smashed the U.S. Eighth Army in northern Korea, terrifying normally sensible people and destroying what little hope was left for an accommodation with the Russians. By year's end, the language of all news media was apocalyptic.

Under the surface, the Truman administration was establishing and arming the national security state, but publicly, Truman appeared to be concerned only with developing strength in Europe, the heartland of Western civilization. Asia-first Republicans, egged on by General Douglas MacArthur, held that we should concentrate on smashing Communists in Korea, where *they* had chosen to fight—and, if necessary, destroy Communist China in the process. This battle between Europe-first Democrats and Asia-first Republicans continued until Richard Nixon went to Peking in 1972. Lillian wrote in *Scoundrel Time* that Nixon was the "unwanted but inevitable leader" of Cold War anti-Communists; certainly in the 1950s this was true.[1]

The Truman blueprint for winning the Cold War was a document called NSC-68.[2] It was secret, as befitted the new national security mania; had it been public, perhaps McCarthy's broadsides might not have been so lethal. But even had NSC-68 been public, Truman, Acheson, Lovett, and Marshall were no match for McCarthy's demagoguery. McCarthy, emphasizing a nonexistent menace from internal subversion, won the battle for media coverage. So powerful was this poison that, when Melby's time before the inquisitors came, no conceivable record as cold warrior could have saved him. Nonetheless Lillian was right, years later, in *Scoundrel Time*, when she fantasized about what she "really wanted to say to Mr. Wood [Chairman of HUAC]: 'There is no Communist menace in this country and you know it.'"[3]

The appeal of McCarthy's successful demagoguery was understandable. On the face of it, Truman had called in 1947 for resistance to Communist aggression everywhere. Why had we not resisted in China? Why were we not going all out in Korea? General Omar Bradley's later answer that Korea was "the wrong war, at the wrong place, at the wrong time" was no answer at all to an Asia-firster.

And there were certain missteps by the administration. When, on 12 January 1950, Secretary Acheson delivered a major speech defining the U.S. defense perimeter in Asia, and placed South Korea and Formosa outside that perimeter, he unwittingly handed the Republicans a time bomb.[4] After the Korean War broke out in June, Republicans could claim that Acheson had invited the attack by notifying the world that we would not defend Korea. This had to be seen as subversion. That General MacArthur had concurred in setting this defense perimeter was unnoticed at the time, and irrelevant afterward. Acheson made the speech.

On 21 January 1950, a jury of his peers found Alger Hiss guilty of perjury.[5] The significance of this case to American politics is difficult to exaggerate. Hiss, in the view of American liberals, joined Sacco and Vanzetti as a martyr to anti-Communist fanaticism. Acheson fueled the flames; he told reporters, after the conviction, that he would "not turn my back on Alger Hiss." Acheson was not, in this remark, claiming Hiss to be innocent; he was simply invoking Christian charity toward a friend. But Republicans got much mileage from the statement.

State Department employees sensed immediately that the Hiss conviction would mean trouble, not just for those Foreign Service officers who had known and worked with Hiss, but for all of them. Melby said that they all knew this would open the flood gates to charges of disloyalty and subversion. Every student of the period verifies this judgment: if Hiss could be guilty, no one was above suspicion.

Lillian in subsequent years became a friend of Alger Hiss. She mentions his case in *Scoundrel Time*, and it is an unfortunate passage: she implies that Whittaker Chambers could not have hidden anything in a pumpkin, since it would deteriorate; she overstates the illegibility of the microfilms he hid in the pumpkin; and she claims that none of them were classified.[6] Much may be said about FBI illegalities and chicanery in the Hiss investigation, and Chambers was a multiple perjurer, but her defense of Hiss does not wash. Despite Allen Weinstein's massive *Perjury* (a study of the Hiss case), the full truth may never be known. Lillian's anger at the witch hunt led her to make unwise statements.

From Hiss's conviction it was but thirteen days to the confession of atomic spy Klaus Fuchs. This brought in its train, on 17 July, the arrest of Julius Rosenberg, and later his wife Ethel.[7] Here again was a massive blow to American confidence, and a powerful stimulus to the inquisition. The Rosenbergs were not, like Alger Hiss, of the eastern elite establishment; but the crime with which they were charged was more serious. And they, like Lillian, were Jewish.

In 1950, few stopped to realize that all of the cases of espionage to date had actually occurred before the end of World War II, and that the FBI had so infiltrated the then puny Communist apparatus that it was leaking like a sieve. Since the fuss was current, the danger seemed current.

McCarthy sensed this instinctively. On 9 February, when he opened his crusade before the Republican Women's Club in Wheeling, he achieved what no Republican orator had yet been able to do: he so personalized the issue of subversion that his charges became front-page news. This master salesman of fraud did not address the issues of China policy, or of the defense of Western Europe, or even of maintaining internal security. There is in McCarthy's diatribes no coherent support of right-wing contentions such as "The Soviets aim to conquer the world," or "The State Department sold Chiang down the river." He went directly for the groin: he sold fear and conspiracy pure and undiluted. And every new headline made his wildest charge seem plausible.

On 14 February, Mao and Stalin announced the Sino-Soviet Treaty of Friendship, Alliance and Mutual Aid. On 20 February, McCarthy made his first major anti–State Department speech to the Senate. It was incoherent, interminable, farcical. But it attacked the Department so viciously that Democrats felt they had to respond. Their answer was a Foreign Relations Subcommittee chaired by Senator Millard Tydings, conservative Democrat from Maryland, which was charged with investigating the loyalty of State Department employees.

The Tydings committee met from 8 March to 28 June. During the course of the hearings, McCarthy named names. Among them were Harlow Shapley and Frederick Schuman, Lillian's associates in the ICCASP, the Wallace campaign, and the Waldorf conference. She knew these two to be loyal American citizens; the fact that they could be publicly pilloried was cause for disquiet. John, too, was put on alert; Schuman had been one of the directors of his dissertation at the University of Chicago, and he had used letters of recommendation from Schuman when applying to the State Department.

But the McCarthy target with the most significance for Lillian was a China scholar she had never met: Owen Lattimore. McCarthy pulled out all the stops against Lattimore: he told the Senate that Lattimore was the top Russian agent in the United States, the "boss of the ring of which Alger Hiss was a part." These charges were ludicrous, and after Lattimore appeared before the Tydings committee with a stinging counterattack, McCarthy seemed to be discredited.[8]

McCarthy was rescued shortly after Lattimore's appearance by the testimony of Louis Francis Budenz. Budenz, former underground member of the Soviet espionage apparatus and later editor of the *Daily Worker*, was one of the most voluble of the ex-Communist witnesses. He had never met Lattimore, never read Lattimore's writings, and never produced any evidence linking Lattimore to the Communist Party. Budenz indicted Lattimore by hearsay: other members of the Communist apparatus had told him to "consider Lattimore as one of them." This hardly supported McCarthy's claim that Lattimore was the top Soviet spy—but it did put Lattimore among the subversives. Budenz was backed by Monsignor Fulton Sheen, Francis Cardinal Spellman, and, at that time, by the Department of Justice. His testimony resurrected McCarthy.

Budenz had not met Lillian Hellman, either; it is unlikely that he had read any of her plays. Certainly he had no evidence linking her to the Communist party. Yet he told the FBI in 1950, again as hearsay, that she had been a Party member in 1937, and had organized Communist front groups then and subsequently in furtherance of orders issued by the Party. Lillian was one of four hundred "concealed Communists" he claimed to know.[9] Budenz later (1954) published the same charge, watered down a bit, in his book *The Techniques of Communism*. This Budenz accusation, and the "dinner party for Gerhart Eisler" story, were the major bases for the belief of Melby's Loyalty Security Board that Lillian was a Communist. (For an analysis of Budenz' credibility, see Appendix 1.)

In 1950, Lillian did not know of the Budenz charge against her, nor how it and his charges against Lattimore would affect her life.

In addition to sharing the calumnies of Louis Budenz, Lattimore's case was significant for Lillian in another way. When she got her 1952 summons to appear before HUAC, she turned to lawyer Abe Fortas for advice. He gave her that freely, suggesting the strategy she eventually followed. But Fortas could not serve as her attorney before HUAC; he was handling Lattimore's case, and he told her that "neither he nor his firm could take my case because they were representing Owen Lattimore and Lattimore could hurt me or I could hurt Lattimore."[10] Fortas thereupon put her in touch with Joe Rauh. The outcome may have been the same, or even better, as Rauh was superb in guiding her through a demanding ordeal. But she was forced to change lawyers because Budenz, seconding McCarthy, had brought Lattimore into the arena.

The Tydings committee eventually condemned McCarthy on a straight party-line vote, but before its report was ready, the most significant event of midcentury intervened.

On 24 June 1950, Kim Il-sung launched his North Korean army across the 38th parallel, with Soviet connivance, upon the poorly prepared South Koreans. Within a week President Truman had ordered, and the country firmly supported, American defense of the South. Herculean achievements followed swiftly and gloriously. The Pusan perimeter held, MacArthur masterminded a daring counterattack at Inchon, and American troops pushed swiftly into North Korea.

There was, for a brief period, a chance that the opprobrium fastened upon Harry Truman for his indifference to Chiang would be lifted, a chance that Truman would be forgiven for past mistakes and be recognized for what he was: a vigorous opponent of Communism. The Korean War sent many who were skeptical about the Soviet threat into the Cold War camp; even Henry Wallace changed his mind after Korea. But at the height of euphoria, in November, things began to come unglued. Despite clear Chinese warnings that no American troops would be tolerated north of the 38th parallel, the U.S. and the UN, heady with victory, gave the word to reunify Korea by force. MacArthur, told to keep American troops away from the Yalu, disregarded instructions.[11] All hell broke loose.

It is difficult to remember more than three decades later the intensity of the trauma Americans felt when the Chinese charged MacArthur's finest soldiers and sent them reeling back to the south. The demoralization that followed is unpleasant to contemplate even from a distance of thirty-five years. *Time* spoke of the "abyss of disaster . . . the worst defeat the U.S. had ever suffered."[12] *Newsweek* felt that "it might become the worst military disaster in American history."[13] Every issue of the *New York Times* that December breathed crisis and disaster. For twenty-two days, *Times* Korean War headlines averaged five columns in width. Truman threatened the use of nuclear weapons. Atrocity stories appeared: on 3 December, a *Times* headline read "Survivors Say Foe Burned G.I.s Alive." An editorial of 4 December claimed that the situation was "reminiscent of the days when Hitler's armies started on their own march of conquest. . . ." On 24 December, the Reverend Edmund Walsh, vice-president of Georgetown University, said we were morally justified in using the A-bomb for a preemptive attack on Russia. Governor Thomas E. Dewey of New York instructed his civil defense leaders to prepare for "a possible million evacuees" from urban areas in the event of nuclear war.

And so it went. To the writer's mind, the most revealing, albeit pathetic, symbol of the panic was the *Times* story of 19 December headed "Skiers in Northwest United as Defense 'Guerrillas' in Case of Invasion."[14] Oregon and Washington skiers were preparing to defend the mountain passes against a Communist army.

While the Korean War unfolded against the backdrop of McCarthy's charges, another peddler of devil insurance was operating in the Senate. Patrick Anthony McCarran, nominally a Democrat, was as steady, systematic, and prestigious as McCarthy was flaky, disorganized, and disreputable. McCarran had adopted the cause of Generalissimo Franco in Spain during the thirties, and was so openly pro-Franco that he was dubbed the "Senator from Madrid." He also turned against the Roosevelt administration by 1940, and hated Harry Truman with a passion. His attack—along with Bridges, Knowland, and Wherry—on the *China White Paper* in 1949 was only one of his many collaborations with like-minded Republicans.[15]

Now, in September 1950, McCarran's Internal Security Act passed both houses of Congress. It was a repressive measure, equating dissent with treason, denying passports to American citizens who belonged to Communist-tainted organizations, and requiring such groups to register with the government; it also enabled the president to establish concentration camps for "subversives" in time of national emergency. Korea created the climate in which such a bill could pass. When Truman vetoed the Internal Security Act, Congress immediately overrode his veto.[16]

And in the 1950 elections, the witch-hunters seemed to have a great deal of influence. McCarthy campaigned strenuously against Millard Tydings in Maryland and against Scott Lucas in Illinois (Lucas was the Democratic majority leader who had appointed the Tydings committee). Both men lost. Sophisticated analyses have since shown that McCarthy's influence on those elections was minor, but at the time, he seemed to be a giant killer.

Thus the concatenation of events in 1950 created a national demand for scapegoats: Acheson, Hiss, Lattimore, the Rosenbergs, even Shapley and Schuman were among the candidates.

John Melby was not. He was beginning to take a major role in the Truman administration's quiet but sustained military buildup to counter the Soviet challenge.

This buildup began with a joint State-Defense review of the Cold War, starting in February and lasting through March. Acheson persuaded Truman to authorize the study; Paul Nitze was its guiding spirit. What Nitze and colleagues produced was a blueprint for quadrupling the nation's defense budget, from 13.5 to 50 billion dollars. Their document, NSC-68, was approved by the secretaries of State and Defense on 7 April 1950, and by the National Security Council (hence the title NSC-document 68) on 14 April.[17] One of the forces behind the approval of NSC-68 was Lillian's old friend Robert Lovett.

NSC-68 was a blueprint for precisely the kind of anti-Soviet policy that Henry Wallace had opposed. It assumed that Stalin had a plan for world conquest similar to Hitler's, and it argued that Soviet domestic tyranny was proof of the existence of this plan (the Korean War had not yet begun). It went far beyond George Kennan's call for containment of Soviet expansionism; it was Manichaean, alarmist, mindlessly anti-Communist. NSC-68, being a Democratic plan, assumed that the pressure point for Soviet expansion was Western Europe, but it did not neglect Asia. In Acheson's "defense perimeter" speech of January, the Philippines were included in those territories we would defend.

Melby, as head of the Philippine desk, was on the first team for the containment of Communism in Southeast Asia. Volume 6 of the *Foreign Relations of the United States* for 1950 carries seventy-one pages setting forth his views, memos, reports, and activities. On 2 February, he wrote a memo for Acheson's signature, delivered to President Truman, about how Philippine President Quirino could be made more effectively anti-Communist. On 23 March, he wrote recommendations for Acheson on the composition of a proposed economic survey mission to Manila. On 20 April, he wrote another memo for Acheson to give Truman, suggesting ways to handle the Communist Huk rebellion. There were dozens of other memos and plans. Throughout this period, John was working closely with United States Ambassador Myron Cowen in Manila.

Of course Acheson and Secretary of Defense Louis Johnson were concerned about more than just the Philippines; all of Southeast Asia was considered ripe for Communist plucking. In May, Acheson recommended, and Truman approved, a program of economic and military support for French reconquest of Indochina. There was little the U.S. could do about Communist insurgency in Malaya, since this was a British problem and the British were handling it vigorously; but Thailand, Burma, and Indonesia were also worrisome to the administration.

Consequently, in early June, Acheson and Johnson agreed that a high-level survey mission, under the auspices of the Mutual Defense Assistance Program, should go to Southeast Asia to determine how the U.S. could best aid that area in resisting Communism. Heading this mission was the ablest, most experienced, and most dependable cold warrior Secretary of State Acheson could find: John Fremont Melby. Melby had the temporary rank of ambassador; his military counterpart was Graves B. Erskine, commanding general of the First Marine Division. The Melby-Erskine mission (MEM) was appointed and most of its plans made before 24 June; war in Korea vastly heightened the importance of MEM but did not affect its genesis or itinerary. The assignment of heading this mission was, as State Department gossip quickly relayed to all and sundry, a plum.

MEM left Washington on 7 July for Saigon, Singapore, Bangkok, Manila, and Djakarta (a visit to Burma was cancelled). The mission returned via Europe, reaching Washington on 31 October. It was a four-month tour de force.[18]

John responded to this sobering assignment with long work days and intense effort. He assumed that the only way he could get maximum performance from the six State Department subordinates accompanying him was to outwork them, which, according to General Erskine, he did. Erskine's affidavit to John's Loyalty-Security Board three years later was an encomium; the Marine general became John's staunch supporter.

Three sections of the MEM report were particularly significant for John's future: the section on the Philippines, the one on Indochina (Vietnam especially), and an analysis of U.S. intelligence capabilities in the area.[19]

On the Philippines, John was by then a recognized expert. With Cowen's help, he set forth a program for shoring up the Philippine economy, strengthening the capable young administrators President Quirino was pressured into appointing, and equipping the Philippine military forces for their continuing battle with the Huks. These, and later recommendations he made when he reassumed his post as head of the Philippine desk, were mostly implemented and generally successful. John got no small part of the credit for the vast improvement in Philippine conditions during the 1950s.

The recommendations on Indochina were another story. American relations with that unhappy land were handled through the French Foreign Office, since Indochina was a French colony. Acheson's aid to the French for their war against the Vietminh was due primarily to the necessity of maintaining France as a loyal member of NATO, rather than to any analysis of the realities of Saigon and Hanoi. John and his mission soon came to believe that this was an error.

John's cables from Saigon anticipated by more than a decade most of the pessimistic reports from dissenters during the Kennedy-Johnson administrations. He was lucky in his Vietnam fact gathering. The French high commissioner, Léon Pignon, and the commanding general of French Forces, Marcel Carpentier, were dedicated imperialists, convinced that the MEM was out to subvert their world, and sure that if MEM exposed French weaknesses, Washington would revert to its historic anticolonial stance. But Melby and Carpentier discovered that they had been in Brazil together and could talk easily and confidentially in Portuguese. This circumstance gained Melby priceless intelligence.

As a cable of 25 July from John to William Lacy, head of the Southeast Asia desk, put it:

> Carpentier upon discovering we both speak Portuguese opened up to me on IC [Indochina] situation as follows:
>
> VM [Vietminh] problem cannot be solved by military means alone. French by proper application of force can break back of Viet Minh military strength, but basic problem it represents will crop up again in same or other form. Hatred of French is so deep-seated and traditional that French incapable of selling that political, economic and propaganda follow-up required to make military successes stick. Only Vietnam can do this and Bao Dai, though intelligent and aware of problem seemingly lacks requisite determination and training. Some new and vitalizing element should be injected into situation within predictable future. VM only group in IC possessing driving faith in its own cause. All Viets secretly pleased with VM success in bogging down French since distaste for white man greater than any other fear.[20]

So much John suspected from the "official" sources available to his mission; Carpentier's confidential disclosures confirmed his suspicions.

In the final report of the MEM, John extrapolated some of his findings in Vietnam to the entire area: "The overwhelming motif of Southeast Asian thought and emotion is nationalism." To him, the Vietnam situation was China all over again, a Communist movement that had captured the banner of nationalism, opposing a weak and corrupt leader kept in power by white men. The French could not win; they could frustrate Ho Chi Minh only by guaranteeing Indochina complete independence and by nurturing an effective indigenous leader to take over from them. Neither French nor Americans could win in Indochina: "White troops will always be associated with colonialism."[21] This was not a welcome conclusion to a government mightily concerned with placating France.

General Erskine concurred with Melby. Unlike the Krulak-Mendenhall

Mission to Vietnam, which reported two diametrically opposite conclusions to President Kennedy a decade later, the military and civilian leaders
of MEM were in agreement.

Dean Acheson listened to Melby's report on the mission at a meeting of
undersecretaries on 8 November. As *Foreign Relations* records, "Mr. Melby
was complimented by the Secretary for his excellent presentation."[22] Com-
pliments, in this case, did not mean acceptance. U.S. support for the
French Army in Vietnam continued and increased. NATO was more important than Southeast Asia.

The third outcome of MEM resulted from what was initially a tangential
assignment. Assistant Secretary Dean Rusk had asked John to make a
confidential assessment of the accuracy of American intelligence from this
area. Rusk had reason to be concerned. Information reaching Washington,
particularly from Saigon, was often contradicted by events within days of
its arrival. This was not surprising, since the American government had no
Vietnamese language officers, Southeast Asia was an assignment good people never chose to apply for, and until World War II, nobody thought the
area would ever be important.

John found that indeed U.S. personnel in Southeast Asia were ill-in-
formed about events in the countries to which they were posted. This was
true of all agencies. In his final report, he said that the level of intelligence
production there was so bad as to approach malfeasance.[23] This negative
evaluation rapidly reached the Pentagon and the CIA. Coming from a
diplomat, such judgments were highly incendiary, particularly to Lieutenant General Walter B. "Beedle" Smith, newly installed and prickly head of
the CIA. Smith had been brought into the Agency by Truman precisely
because CIA had not been getting accurate or sufficient data. Smith was
now afraid that this hostile report would reach CIA enemies on Capitol
Hill, or perhaps would give J. Edgar Hoover ammunition in his continuing
war with the CIA. Reverberations of Smith's choler reached Acheson, who
called Melby in, explained the situation, and advised him to visit General
Smith for a smoothing of ruffled feathers.

Melby remembers his December 1950 session with Smith vividly. Allen
Dulles, assistant director of the CIA, later to become director, sat silent in a
corner while Smith excoriated Melby. Smith's concluding blast: "Young
man, either you are a genius, in which case you'll be promoted very fast, or
you're a fool, in which case you'll be fired." Melby was calm, but did not
retreat from the severity of his judgment. Within months, there was a
complete change in intelligence personnel in Southeast Asia.

Melby may have been damned at the CIA, but at the State Department his reputation soared. He had brought off a difficult task with aplomb, and with approval from the military. Furthermore, the Soviets had attacked him personally and his mission generally. To diplomats cringing under McCarthy's charges of being Commie lovers, any sign of Soviet displeasure was welcome. Melby's efficiency reports for the year were glowing.[24]

John and Lillian met again in 1950 for the first time since the painful parting five years earlier. Lillian went to New Orleans in January to visit her aunts, gathering material for her next play. En route she stopped off in Washington; she and John lunched together, and she stayed at his apartment in Georgetown. Despite their dissonant political positions, each still found the other good company. They talked of people they had known in Moscow and New York, of music and theater, and of their respective travels. John mentioned that he was seeing Hilda Hordern, who had been Ambassador Stuart's secretary in Nanking, with some regularity.

Politics was handled casually; Lillian expressed some of her disaffection for the Wallace campaign, and John did not push his contempt for Wallace. Lillian gave him a copy of *Montserrat* inscribed "For John. With much love. Lillian, Jan 1950." She invited him to spend a weekend at the Pleasantville farm should he have opportunity.

In mid-March he accepted her invitation and came to the farm. Dash was then in California, and John and Lillian were alone. It was a relaxing and pleasant weekend for John; his legal dispute with his wife had been trying, and puttering around Lillian's animals was therapeutic.

The weekend was not without incident. They discovered, to their surprise, that the old chemistry still worked, and they slept together. As Lillian later told John's hearing board, "The relationship at this point was neither one thing nor the other; it was neither over nor was it not over."[25]

Apparently both regretted the renewal of their former intimacy. Lillian expressed her feeling this way: "It was obvious that it had been wrong to resume the relationship, and that it was not going to work, and that we had both been right in thinking that it had come to an end previously, and we had made a mistake in thinking it was not at an end at this minute."

However they felt about the affair at Pleasantville, they determined to maintain their friendship. Toward the end of March, John visited his parents in Bloomington. He wrote Lillian from there firming up an arrangement to see her again in New York on his return. The Bloomington letter was mostly about his travel schedule, and it instructed her not to get up early enough to meet his 6:00 A.M. arrival at La Guardia. Then there is this line: "As for where we go, I leave that to your appraisal of the local Gotham situation & the counsels of discretion" (30 March 1950). He took a room at a hotel; they dined, walked around Manhattan, and went to a show. He stayed only thirty-six hours in New York.

Lillian now began working hard on *Autumn Garden*. He remembers seeing her again for lunch in April when she came to Washington to use the Library of Congress; according to her later testimony to John's State Department Loyalty-Security Board, she did not remember this. By June, she had completed a first draft of the play. Dash then returned from California and moved in at Pleasantville; by all accounts, it was a good summer for both of them. She and Dash had not been lovers since the war, but he took a keen interest in her work and made a major contribution to *Autumn Garden*. She wrote in *Pentimento*:

> I was at a good age; I lived on a farm that was, finally, running fine and I knew that I had found the right place to live for the rest of my life. Hammett and I were both making a lot of money, and not caring about where it went was fun. We had been together almost twenty years, some of them bad, a few of them shabby, but now we had both stopped drinking and the early excited years together had settled into a passionate affection so unexpected to both of us that we were as shy and careful with each other as courting children. . . . I guess it was the best time for me, certainly the best time of our life together. Now, I think that somewhere we both knew—the signs were already there, Joe McCarthy was over the land—that we had to make it good because it had to end.[26]

Some hangovers from Lillian's Progressive party activity remained that summer. She was still on the party's executive committee, which in July was struggling with a statement on the Korean War. Wallace was deserting his former anti–Cold War stance, and at an executive committee meeting on 6 July, he supported resistance to North Korea. Lillian backed Wallace, but there was no decision that day. Two days later the committee met again, finding itself still stalemated. Lillian then moved to establish an ad hoc committee to work out a resolution satisfactory to Wallace. This was done, but Wallace reneged on the agreement. Three weeks later he resigned from the Progressive party.[27] There was not much left of it, and it gradually disintegrated. Lillian's participation also declined. She concentrated on *Autumn Garden*.

John and Lillian exchanged letters several times during the summer of 1950. His letters from Saigon (31 July) and Singapore (25 August) were his usual fascinating travelogues. Vietnam was too disrupted by the French-

Vietminh war to be enjoyable, but he raved about Laos and Cambodia: "I think these two places may well be the most enchanting lands in the world." From Singapore he wrote: "We have changed our schedule so often very little mail has caught up with us. One letter from you in Saigon. The Russians in any event have been watching with interest and making some very rude remarks indeed on the Moscow radio. It seems I am a very nasty person, even dangerous. Highly flattering. And what is this I hear about Wallace leaving the Progressive Party. I have heard nothing more than the fact and that apparently it was over Korea. Interesting."

John did not contact Lillian when he arrived back in Washington at the end of October. His divorce was now final; he and Hilda Hordern were seriously thinking of marriage. Lillian phoned him in December; the conversation was cordial, and he responded with a Christmas letter. They were now, so it seemed, just old friends.

Riding for a Fall

Nineteen fifty-one was a bad year for federal employees. Louis Budenz and Elizabeth Bentley, the most voluble of the ex-Communist informers, continued naming names of those they claimed had served the Soviet Union. Philip Jessup, John Paton Davies, Jack Service, and O. Edmund Clubb were under fire from the Asia-first Republicans (and Pat McCarran).

There was another big spy case under adjudication. William Remington, a Department of Commerce economist, like Hiss an establishment WASP, was on trial for espionage as a result of Bentley's accusation. Remington was billed by some as another Hiss. Bentley's accusation against him did not hold up by itself; in February 1950, Remington won a nine thousand–dollar libel settlement against Bentley. Only brutal pressure on Remington's ex-wife, causing her to change her original testimony, gave the government case any credibility at all. But the pressure was brought, Ann Moos Remington capitulated, and on 7 February 1951, a jury found Remington guilty.[1]

On 9 February, with much fanfare, McCarran's Internal Security Subcommittee operatives seized the files of the Institute of Pacific Relations.[2] These files had been thoroughly searched already by the FBI, who had found nothing significant in them; but the senators were excited. McCarran predicted there would be a sensation when the contents of the files were revealed.

On 29 March, the explosive Rosenberg case resulted in a conviction. Both Julius and Ethel were sentenced to death, with execution set for 21 May. Appeals delayed the executions, and the turmoil of the Rosenberg case fueled the witch-hunt for another two years, until they were finally refused clemency by President Eisenhower and executed on 19 June 1953. As with Hiss, belief in the innocence of the Rosenbergs became a litmus test for liberals.

In April 1951, the Asia-first/Europe-first quarrel brought another terrible shock to Americans. Douglas MacArthur, firmly believing that the war in Korea had to be taken to the enemy, even the Soviet enemy if necessary, had been sending influential American media and politicians statements expressing his disagreements with Truman's policy of limiting the war. MacArthur wrote a letter to Representative Joseph Martin, House Republican leader on 19 March, criticizing management of the war, and Martin released this letter to the press on 5 April. This was seen by Truman, backed by the Joint Chiefs of Staff, as insubordination. On 10 April, MacArthur was fired.[3]

There has to be a separate scene in any account of the inquisition for the firing of MacArthur and the furor that followed. The histrionic hero of Corregidor and Inchon climaxed his career in a blaze of glory. He came home to mass adulation. It began in San Francisco, progressed across the country, and culminated in his address to a joint session of Congress. Those who were present in the chamber of the U.S. House of Representatives on 19 April 1951 claim that the effect of his "farewell speech" outshone by far previous performances in that setting by Franklin Roosevelt, Winston Churchill, and even Madame Chiang.[4] The impact of "Old Soldiers Never Die" on the public was only slightly less electrifying. Even now, listening to a tape of the performance, one can understand how MacArthur's eloquent prose reverberated in a frustrated country.

To millions who found Joe McCarthy's crudities unpalatable, MacArthur's dignified eloquence rang true. If Democratic treason had previously seemed too unlikely an explanation of Communism's gains, MacArthur's masterful rhetoric made it credible. The Korean War could have been won, he claimed, had the right decisions been made in Washington. "Why, my soldiers asked of me, surrender military advantages to an enemy in the field? I could not answer."

But of course he could, and did, answer. So eloquent was the answer that the screws of national security were tightened another notch. There was talk of impeaching Truman. From 3 May to 27 June, in secret joint session, the Armed Services and Foreign Relations committees of the Senate took testimony on the military situation in the Far East. All the principals appeared, all the charges of treason and of selling out to and being soft on Communism were thoroughly aired. In their final report, the senators leaned toward the view of events presented by MacArthur.[5] Truman's popularity dropped to a new low.

As if there had not been provocation enough for a long-suffering public, the MacArthur hearings were hardly over when Pat McCarran and his Senate Internal Security Subcommittee began their year-long hearings into how the Institute of Pacific Relations had come under Communist influence and engineered the downfall of Chiang Kai-shek, the North Korean invasion, and the defeat of the Eighth Army. The same cast of villains was pilloried: Acheson, Davies, Jessup, Lattimore, Schuman, Service, Vincent, and Wallace. There was even mention in the McCarran committee's final report of Lillian's good friends John Hersey and Archibald MacLeish. The major witness was again Louis Budenz, with Elizabeth Bentley a close second. Some of Lillian's "Commie fronts" were also featured: American League Against War and Fascism, American Peace Mobilization, Little, Brown and Company (Lillian's left-wing publishers), Russian War Relief, Voks, and so on. The McCarran hearings went on for a year, with frequent headlines.[6]

However frantic the pace of burgeoning suspicion, the first eight months of 1951 were very good for John Melby. His advice was sought, and heeded, on how to deal with Communist advances in the Philippines and Southeast Asia. His memos were reference points even for those who disagreed with him.

On 15 January, he wrote a five-page memo suggesting how to implement the administration's plans for containing Communism in the Philippines; most of it became policy, after an internal fight with foreign aid officials who thought Melby's position leaned too heavily on military aid.[7]

John was also much sought after as a State Department spokesman. During the early months of 1951, he filled six to eight requests from citizens' groups across the country for a State Department speaker to explain American policy in China. Remarkably, he was not required to submit the texts of his speeches to the Department for clearance, as was usual. He was presumably an effective representative of an otherwise discredited department; after one speech in St. Louis, he overheard two ladies discussing his performance. They were surprised: "He sounds like a normal American."

On 31 July, John's annual efficiency report was written by his immediate superior—a conservative Virginian, William S. B. Lacy—and endorsed by Livingstone Merchant. Lacy thought John should be promoted to Class II and expressed his reasons glowingly:

> I have no hesitancy in asserting that Mr. Melby is one of the ablest officers I know. During the past year he has served as Officer in Charge of Philippine Affairs and as such he has made the major contribution

to the development of our new policy toward the Philippines which as of this date has proven remarkably successful. This has required initiative, imagination, resolution, and a great deal of courage.

Mr. Melby was jointly in charge of the Melby-Erskine Mission which visited the Philippines, Indochina, Thailand, Malaya, and Indochina in the summer of 1950. . . . That this mission was a success is due in large part, according to General Erskine, to Melby's powers of analysis, synthesis, and his skill as a practical diplomat.

I can record that Mr. Melby discharged these difficult tasks with remarkable success; the economy of the Philippines, moreover, is already showing indisputable signs of recovery. . . . Mr. Melby played a major role in the difficult and dramatic negotiations which resulted in the United States–Philippine Treaty for Mutual Defense and which resulted in the recession on the part of the Philippine Government from their highly emotional opposition to the Japanese Peace Treaty. . . .

I recommend that Mr. Melby be promoted.[8]

To which encomium Livingstone Merchant added, "Mr. Melby is just about the ablest officer I know in his class." John was promoted, in August, to Foreign Service officer Class II.

John and Lillian had only casual contacts in the early months of 1951. Both had other interests; Lillian her chaste superintendency of the now sober Hammett, John his comfortable relationship with Hilda Hordern, Ambassador Stuart's former secretary and also, for several weeks, secretary to the Melby-Erskine mission.

John does not believe he was in love with Hilda, certainly not in the intense way he had been with Lillian. But Hilda was attractive, a great complement to his Foreign Service ambitions, and he was the marrying kind. On 26 January 1951, John and Hilda were married in Washington. A dozen or so of their close State Department associates attended the wedding. Hilda knew about John's affair with Lillian and knew that he was still fond of her.

When Lillian was in Washington one day in February, she and John lunched together. It was their first meeting since the summer of 1950, when he had left on the long Southeast Asia mission. There was much to talk about: he reported on his travels and on mutual acquaintances he had seen; she talked about the changes in Hammett and about her new play, *Autumn Garden*. If she was upset that John had married again, she did not show it. They discussed the political climate of the country and found common ground; both despised HUAC, the persecution of the China hands, and the increasing tempo of scapegoating.

Autumn Garden opened in Philadelphia in late February and moved to the Coronet in New York on 7 March. Lillian was proud of the play, and it was a critical success, even though it only ran for 101 performances. But one group had no use for it: the Communists. The *Daily Worker* of 15 March panned it as a "Retreat from the World of Reality." *Garden*, according to the reviewer, showed "the great scenes of futility with which the middle class, as a whole, tends to react to the world crisis of capitalism."[9] There was no "world crisis of capitalism" for Lillian Hellman; there were only two hostile, aggressive superpowers, each fearful that the other would attack.

Lillian, as usual, sent John an inscribed copy of *Garden*: "For John as always and as before. Lillian, May 1951."

With *Autumn Garden* on the boards, Lillian spent more time at the farm. Hammett went to California in April, largely on business, but the major outcome of his trip was meeting and falling in love with his granddaughter Ann. Surprisingly, he was allowed to bring Ann, still a baby, back to New York with him. Lillian adored the baby as much as he. When Hammett's daughter came to reclaim Ann and take her back to California, both Dash and Lillian were distraught. The joys of Pleasantville in summer, however, were great consolation.

July brought trouble to Pleasantville, and brought John and Lillian back together. Hammett was one of four trustees of the Civil Rights Congress, an organization concerned primarily with providing bail for left-wing activists who might get in trouble with the law. Eleven Communist leaders were convicted under the Smith Act in 1949 for conspiring to overthrow the U.S. government; they were bonded by the Civil Rights Congress, and were free pending appeals until a Supreme Court decision in June 1951, at which time they were ordered to appear. Four of the Communist leaders failed to appear to serve their sentences.

Immediately government officials began to suspect the trustees of the Civil Rights Congress of hiding the fugitives. A contingent of FBI men, apparently without a warrant, showed up at Hellman's farm where Hammett was living to look for the missing Communists. The FBI discussed this visit when preparing a blind memorandum sent by the FBI to McCarran's Senate Internal Security Subcommittee, which requested a report on Hellman. A. H. Belmont of FBI headquarters notes that certain material in her file was not forwarded to McCarran "because of the questionable reliability of the informants." One of the items not sent to McCarran reads:

On July 4, 1951, [name denied] had received information from a very reliable source to the effect that the eight [*sic*] Communist Party fugitives were in hiding at the farm of Lillian Hellman, Hard Scrabble Road, Pleasantville, New York. When interviewed by Bureau agents on July 5, 1951, Hellman denied knowing any of the fugitives and a search was made of her property with negative results. This information is not being included in the blind memorandum as the original source of information is not known and the results of investigation proved negative.[10]

Searches were also made of the homes of other trustees, with no results. So the trustees were called into court to answer questions about the fund, the fugitives, and the contributors who had put up the money. Frederick Vanderbilt Field was the first to appear; he was uncooperative at a hearing on 6 July and was indicted for contempt of court. His millions did him no good.[11]

Hammett was the next to be called. Lillian argued with him that he should simply tell the court that he did not know where the fugitives were, and did not know anything about the contributors to the fund. He objected on principle to telling the court anything; consequently he too was held in contempt, arrested, and sentenced to six months in a federal prison.

Lillian describes Hammett's ordeal in her memoirs, as does Diane Johnson in *Dashiell Hammett: A Life*.[12] Hammett realized, as Lillian probably did too, that there was little that she could do for him, and that making a fuss over his imprisonment would hasten the day when she too would be called before the inquisitors. So Hammett sent Lillian a note by his lawyer: "Do not come into this courtroom. If you do, I will say I do not know you. Get out of 82nd Street and Pleasantville. Take one of the trips to Europe that you love so much. You do not have to prove to me that you love me, at this late date."[13] She knew he was right; she booked passage to Europe. This brought up an old, thorny question: could she get a passport? In the climate of the times, it was doubtful. Ruth Shipley was still in charge. But that old curmudgeon had yielded before; Lillian went to see her. It was not an acrimonious visit, and on 13 July 1951, Lillian wrote Shipley one of her inimitable persuasive letters:

Dear Mrs. Shipley:

I filed an application for a passport and discussed the matter with you yesterday. As I told you, I have been hired by Hoche Productions of Paris to adapt for motion pictures Ibsen's play "A Doll's House." I am most anxious to write this motion picture not only because it is a most distinguished play and could be a fine picture, but because I need to work and I need to earn the money. Most certainly I do not intend, and shall not, take part in any political activity of any kind: I wish to go to Europe only to work on the movie and to supervise and possibly direct the London production of my last play, "The Autumn Garden."

I am not a Communist. I am not a member of the Communist Party. In the past I have been a member of many left wing organizations but, while I may have made many foolish decisions in my life, I have never done anything which could be called by any honest person, ugly or disloyal or unpatriotic. For the last few years—I am not sure of the exact time, it might be a little more than two years or a little less—I have had no participation in any group of any nature or kind unless I include the distinguished organization of the Institute of American Arts and Letters of which I am an elected member, or my trade organization, the Author's League of America, of which I am a governing member. (It is more than possible that my name is still, however, carried on the rolls of some organizations: at this minute I could not truthfully say which organizations, nor do I think my rather careless records at home would help me to be more accurate.)

I have carried a passport for many years and I believe that I have carried it well both as a citizen and as a writer. In September of 1944 I was invited to The Soviet Union as the cultural representative from the United States. (Mr. Eric Johnston, I believe, had previously been invited in the same capacity as representative for American business.) I was reluctant to make what was a dangerous flying journey across Siberia and into a country at war, but I believed, and so did many people in Washington, that it was my duty to make whatever contribution I could to the war effort. And I did make a contribution. Mr. Harriman, whose guest I was in the American Embassy, told me on the day of my departure that he was reporting to Washington that my visit had been the most useful in the making of good relations of any foreigner who had been to Moscow. I know that Mr. Harriman will remember the report and will be glad to tell you that he so remembers. (I tried this afternoon to reach Mr. Harriman but he had left his office and did not return.) But Mr. John Melby who was also living in the Embassy at the time, will, I am sure, be glad to verify what I have written here, and perhaps will give you any other details of the trip that you might wish to know.

My next trip to Europe was in 1947 when I went to Paris as

American delegate to UNESCO's about-to-be formed Theatre Institute. I am convinced that the English delegate, and chairman, Mr. J. B. Priestley would testify to the fact that I acted with sense and discretion, and in the best interests of my country. As a matter of fact, Mr. Priestley told me that I had been chosen as American delegate because my plays are well known in Europe and I had, therefore, been the chief reason for the arrival of important European theatre names.

And now forgive me for these boasts which I do not like to make about myself. I write them here as proof of my loyalty to our country—I am indeed sad that such proof should ever have been needed—and my absolute conviction that I have never been, nor could ever be, any part of any action that I considered disloyal to my country. The truth is that I am a rather old-fashioned patriot, although for a true patriot those words need not be written because they are implicit in the person and are too good to be flaunted about.

My thanks for your kindness and courtesy to me. I was due to leave New York tomorrow and any delays are dangerous to my contract. Therefore I hope that you will find it possible to issue my passport in time for me to leave within the next four or five days.

> I am most grateful to you.
> Lillian Hellman[14]

Immediately after her visit with Shipley, Lillian attempted again to get in touch with Harriman; he was out of the country. Her next recourse was to John. She called him at the Department and arranged to meet him that day. She told John that Shipley would probably contact him to verify what she had said about her Moscow visit, and they discussed her options should Shipley refuse. Lillian then returned to New York.

John was questioned about this incident by his hearing board two years later:

Q: Did you hear from Mrs. Shipley after that?

A: No. Mr. Nicholas called me.

Q: Who is Mr. Nicholas?

A: He is one of the men in the Passport Division. I don't know specifically what his job is, but he works on special cases I believe. He called me and asked me what I knew about the trip [Lillian's trip to Moscow, 1944]. He said he could not find much in the files.

Q: What did you tell him?

A: I told him, as far as I knew of what she had done there, how long she was there.

Q: Was there any other conversation about Miss Hellman, Mr. Melby?

A: The only other thing I remember was he asked me if I had any reason to believe she was a Communist, and I said "Not as far as any evidence I have." And he said "Well, I don't have any information either, beyond a long list of organizations over past years," and that was all there was to that.[15]

We have no record of what went on at the Passport Office after Nicholas's call to John. Three weeks later, on 2 August 1951, Shipley cabled Lillian: "Passport valid British Isles, France for four months being sent Rockefeller Center Passport Agency. Call there this morning."[16] Lillian was late getting away, but she made it. Had she applied six weeks later, the outcome might have been different. The HUAC testimony of Martin Berkeley came on 19 September.

The House Un-American Activities Committee had found Hollywood fertile territory for getting headlines since Martin Dies was chairman in 1940. Lillian had not been in HUAC's main line of fire, since she was primarily a playwright living in New York most of the time. After the widespread publicity she received during the Waldorf conference, it was inevitable that she would be caught up in any future Hollywood dragnet.

HUAC's purpose was not to discover who had been producing pro-Communist movies. It was instead to hold degradation ceremonies, as Victor Navasky calls them. The FBI already knew who had been working with and in the party. So did the committee. What the degradation ceremonies, or purification rites, were intended to accomplish was primarily to make the committee members look good, appearing to be guardians of public morality and American virtue. Hence the more names that a witness named, the more purification and publicity.

Martin Berkeley, like Budenz and Bentley, was a generator of long lists of names. There are various counts of how many persons he claimed had been Communists in Hollywood; Navasky's figure of 161 is probably accurate.[17] Berkeley originally denied to HUAC that he had been a Communist, but quickly reversed himself and promised to cooperate. There was, he said, an organizational meeting of Communists at his house in June 1937; Lillian Hellman was there.

Lillian did not remember ever meeting Martin Berkeley; Dash told her she might have been at a luncheon party with him at some time. But she definitely was not at his organizational meeting; Ring Lardner, Jr., who was there, says Lillian wasn't.[18] Berkeley, in fact, was wildly inaccurate. In his testimony, quantity was the enemy of quality; Navasky says that Berkeley made at least a dozen misidentifications. William Wheeler, HUAC staff investigator, tried to persuade Berkeley not to mention so many people; "I told him not to do it, but his ass-hole lawyer, Edward Bennett Williams, insisted."[19] Few of Berkeley's colleagues had a good word for his character or credibility. Isobel Lennart noted: "Martin Berkeley I always thought was a pig when he was a Communist and a pig when he stopped being a Communist."[20]

Like the run of McCarthyite charges, truth never caught up with the original smear. Berkeley's identification of Lillian as a Communist was duly entered in her FBI file, serial 56. It was the Berkeley testimony that brought her to the attention of HUAC.

Lillian was in Europe when Berkeley testified, and was unavailable for immediate rebuttal. She was also unavailable for an equally serious event that occurred on 27 September, eight days after the Berkeley testimony: John got an interrogatory from the State Department Security Office.

An interrogatory is a list of questions, sent by Security to officers about whose loyalty or security there is suspicion. The recipient is requested to respond to whatever the Security Office asks; if his answer is acceptable, that is the end of the matter. There is no "case." If the answer is not acceptable, the Security Office issues a set of charges and arranges a hearing, after which decisions are made as to the officer's suitability for further government employment.

John was astounded at getting an interrogatory. His performance had just been rated superlative, his promotion had come through, and he was an integral part of the American campaign to frustrate Communist ambitions in Southeast Asia. Yet so many Foreign Service officers who had been in China were going under that he should not have been surprised. Anyone who had served the treasonous Democrats was fair game, and to have served in China made it worse. True, most of the China hands who were hauled before loyalty-security boards during this period had been in China during World War II and run afoul of Patrick Hurley; all of them also had additional liabilities, such as writing glowingly of the Chinese Communists, or publicly deprecating Chiang Kai-shek, or sharing documents with unauthorized persons. John had done none of these things.

Nor did his interrogatory emphasize China. The first three questions dealt with Lillian Hellman. What was his relationship with her? What did he know of her political beliefs? Was he aware of her Communist sympathies and activities? These, it seemed to him, were easy to answer. He and Lillian were good friends, formerly lovers, who had drifted apart. Her political and economic beliefs were confused, naive perhaps; Harriman called her a fellow wanderer. Melby knew she had joined a number of pro-Soviet organizations, but so had thousands of respectable people when the Russians were our allies. There could be no problem here.

The next four questions seemed even easier. Why did you use Frederick Schuman as a reference on your application to the Foreign Service? What did you know about Schuman's beliefs? Were you aware, in 1936, of his advocacy of Communist candidates? Were you aware since 1936 of his Communist affiliations? These too were simple. He had given Schuman as a reference because Schuman was one of three professors who had supervised his Ph.D. dissertation at Chicago. Of course he knew that Schuman was left-wing and that he was a joiner of Communist-sponsored organizations, but John did not believe him to be a Party member or to be disloyal to the United States.

Next question: In China, you were an admirer of the Democratic League, which was a Communist front. What were your opinions and knowledge of the League? Aha, here it was, buried, in a camouflage of trivia—the Chiang Kai-shek supporters were after him. John Leighton Stuart—fifty years a Christian missionary and then Melby's superior as ambassador—Stuart, the soul of respectability and uprightness, had inadvertently caused him to come to the attention of the inquisitors by assigning him to liaison with the Democratic League. The Democratic League was *not* Communist, he had *not* of his own volition sought it out, and Stuart would testify to his complete innocence. (Stuart later did precisely that.) That would settle the matter.

The remaining questions were of the "Are you now or have you ever been" variety. He could answer them with gusto. No, he was not now, had never been, a party member, or a sympathizer, or a joiner of fronts. His one gesture of sympathy with our Soviet allies had been a statement of support, approved by Averell Harriman, for Russian War Relief.

John was not greatly worried about such an insipid interrogatory. He consulted friends in the Department, especially Myron Cowen, then reassigned to Washington. Cowen sent him to a lawyer, John Burke, in New York. Burke had no experience in loyalty-security matters, but advised John that he should respond confidently to the interrogatory. As far as his

relations with Hellman were concerned, he need not go into detail. It was
not necessary for him to give a complete history of their affair, just some
illustrations of the times they had seen each other.

So he prepared his answer by himself, on his own time, without breaking
stride in his continuing intense involvement in Philippine affairs. Seven full
pages of his answer—twice as much as he devoted to any other question—
were spent on an analysis of the Democratic League. Eight days after the
questions came, his answers were in the hands of the Department Security
Office.

But it was curious that he was under question at the same time as Lillian
was named in public testimony as a Communist, and while Dash was in
jail. So he wrote Lillian, telling her there had been questions about their
relationship. She wrote back saying that she was sorry, was there anything
she should do? He said he would let her know. Then he was off on a trip to
Southeast Asia, visiting the Philippines and serving as adviser to the American delegation to the South Pacific Commission, meeting at Nouméa, New
Caledonia. He returned to Washington in early November. There was no
response from the Security Office. Surely he was home free.

On 20 November 1951, forty-six days after he had submitted his answers, the bombshell came in the form of a supplemental interrogatory. It
was a bit nasty in tone. "With reference to question No. 1 of the Board's
original interrogatory, it is alleged that you visited Lillian Hellman during
the spring of 1950 at her home in Pleasantville, New York. If so, please
relate the circumstances, the reason for, and the nature of the visit." That
was all. Nothing on China, Schuman, or his relations with the Communist
party.

This new development shattered John's complacency. He had told nobody in the spring of 1950 that he was going to Pleasantville. No one
had been at the farm that weekend; Dash was in Los Angeles, Lillian's
farmer was away. John had phoned a friend in the Marine Hospital on Long
Island and had identified himself to the operator; perhaps Lillian's phone
was tapped. Orwellian images crowded into his mind: Big Brother *was*
watching!

John had to assume that the information came from the FBI. But who
was the FBI watching, him or Lillian? Surely not him. He had broken no
laws, joined no suspicious organizations, signed no pro-Soviet petitions,
made no public attacks on American policy, and since 1946, had been a
pillar of anti-Communist rectitude. He had been commended for his penetrating analyses of the Communist threat in Asia, had been head of the
prestigious Melby-Erskine mission to Southeast Asia, and had been con-

gratulated by the secretary for his report. There was only one possible conclusion: Lillian was under surveillance. She had done something he did not know about to arouse FBI suspicion. Perhaps it was during the Wallace campaign. Perhaps it was in connection with the Waldorf conference. Perhaps she had served the Communists before he met her in some way she had never told him about. Perhaps the order of questions in his original interrogatory had been significant, and he was under the gun because of Lillian rather than because of his activities in China.

This new interrogatory not only caused him to wonder if Lillian might have been an active Party member, it enhanced the apparent credibility of government intelligence. John had every reason to belittle much intelligence collection abroad; indeed, his castigation of American fact gatherers in Southeast Asia while on the MEM had been severe. But now, in FBI jurisdiction, somebody knew more about him than he thought possible. And if they knew he had been at Pleasantville, they must know a lot about Lillian.

John could not know, in 1951, what future developments would prove about the shoddiness of many FBI files. J. Edgar Hoover was still on a pedestal, perceived by most Americans as incorruptible and omniscient. Alan Barth's skeptical "How Good Is An FBI Report?" was not to appear in *Harper's Magazine* until 1954. The first of the FBI's professional witnesses to be indicted for perjury, Harvey Matusow, was not exposed until 1954.[21] Richard Rovere's "The Kept Witnesses" did not appear in *Harper's* until 1955. From then on the credibility of the FBI suffered steady erosion, culminating in David Garrow's 1981 exposure of FBI lying in his book *The FBI and Martin Luther King, Jr.*, and in Penn Kimball's chilling *The File* in 1983. All John knew, in 1951, was that the FBI was right about his being in Pleasantville.

John would later learn, when the allegations about Lillian came tumbling out during his hearings, that the FBI was a vast vacuum cleaner, sucking up the bad as often as the good—its agents listening, as Penn Kimball put it, to "busybodies, crackpots, ideologues, well-meaning patriots, the genuinely alarmed, the envious and the scorned. Agents in the field wrote it all down. . . ."[22] John did not know that yet; he did know that his professional standing was under attack because of his affair with Lillian. He had to talk to her about the new developments. He phoned, and she agreed to come to Washington.

They were puzzled about several things. Was his case connected with Martin Berkeley's attack on Lillian? With Dash's recent notoriety? Was their mutual acquaintance with Fred Schuman a factor? Was the supplemental interrogatory a genuine indication that his relations with Lillian were the important matter, or was this just another smokescreen for the ubiquitous China recriminations?

They could not know. John and Lillian discussed how to respond to the new interrogatory. What was he to say about the "nature of the visit" to Pleasantville? John did not think that even security officers had a right to pry into intimate details of law-abiding citizens' private lives. He did not want to embarass Lillian by telling government snoops that their romance still had an ember glowing.

The inquiry at one of his loyalty-security hearings reveals what they decided:

> Q: Did Miss Hellman, when you talked with her in November 1951, ask you not to mention what had happened at Pleasantville?
> A: Rather, I would say, we agreed between us it was a regrettable thing of great embarassment to us both and we wanted to forget it and we hoped that nobody else would ever have to know about it.[23]

So he said in the answer to his amended interrogatory that the Pleasantville visit had been purely social, and filed this answer with the Security Office on 29 November. Again there was a long silence.

John went back to his Southeast Asian affairs; Lillian was now absorbed with nursing Dash back to health when he got out of jail on 9 December.

On 13 December 1951, John Stewart Service was fired from the Department of State, after sixteen years as a diplomat, on the basis of lies about him disseminated by the Chinese Nationalist Foreign Office in Taipei.[24] He was given no opportunity to confront his accusers. This event was a terrible omen.

The Cauldron Boils

Nineteen fifty-two was to be the year of deliverance for the Republicans. Thomas Dewey might have blown their 1948 chance to capture the White House by being low key and polite; this time there would be no such mistake. The campaign would be fought out along the lines of the "K_1C_2" slogan—Korea, Communism, and Corruption.

Aggressive anti-Communist leaders of the Republican party were in the ascendancy. McCarthy, having survived the early disasters of the Tydings hearings, was now riding a crest of popularity due partly to the Korean War and partly to the escalating concern about spies and subversives. McCarthy's enemies in the Senate were getting nowhere in their efforts to censure him. William S. White explained what all this meant in a *New York Times* column of 27 January:

> The upshot of all this has been to leave Senator McCarthy in a place of indisputably increased power and prestige in the Senate. More than a year ago he was mortally challenged by one of its most entrenched Democratic veterans, Senator Millard E. Tydings of Maryland, who denounced Mr. McCarthy's State Department charges as a fraud and a hoax, and in 1950 Mr. Tydings fell at the polls.
>
> Ambassador at Large Philip C. Jessup had been an early McCarthy target, and at the last session of Congress the Senate omitted to act on Mr. Jessup's nomination to our United Nations delegation after a Foreign Relations Subcommittee had voted against him 3 to 2.
>
> These matters have not gone unnoticed in the Senate, and particularly in an election year.[1]

Even though John Stewart Service had been fired in December, McCarthy was not appeased. On 5 January 1952, he released minutes of a Loyalty Review Board meeting from a year earlier in which Garrett Hoag of Boston, a board member, had complained that the loyalty-security program of the Department of State was "completely ineffective" because the Department had a "remarkable record of never having fired anybody" on loyalty grounds.[2] Hoag's statement was not accurate, since there had been quiet firings of people whose cases never reached the board, and since most separations from the service were achieved by making it clear to the employee that he had better resign before he was fired. But accuracy was not of interest to McCarthy: Hoag was talking his language, and McCarthy made a big splash with it.

And of course McCarthy's activities spurred increased publicity seeking by his competitors, McCarran's Senate Internal Security Subcommittee (SISS) and HUAC. McCarran achieved regular headlines with witnesses at his Institute of Pacific Relations hearings; HUAC outdid itself with more than a hundred days of public hearings at which more than three hundred persons testified during 1951 and 1952.

On 25 January 1952, McCarran announced that John Carter Vincent, one of Budenz's targets, was being called back from Tangier to appear before the SISS.[3] They wanted Vincent to explain his part in the fall of Chiang Kai-shek. On 31 January, President Truman added fuel to the flames at a news conference by charging that McCarthy was "a pathological character assassin who needed no information to make accusations against others."[4] McCarthy retorted: "The time and words [of the president] are almost the same as when the House Committee on Un-American Activities was exposing Alger Hiss. They are almost the same as when I was exposing John Service."[5]

Two weeks later the John Paton Davies case was in the news again; Lyle H. Munson, former CIA agent, testified before the SISS that Davies had tried to get three people identified by Budenz as Communists on the CIA payroll to give "consultation and guidance" in developing Asian policy.[6] That same week, in what appeared to the witch-hunters as an incredible display of arrogance, Secretary Acheson ordered Vincent returned to duty as minister in Tangier with the "full confidence and best wishes" of the State Department.[7] It is hard to imagine a more direct challenge to the McCarthy-McCarran-HUAC forces.

John and Lillian watched these events with apprehension. In mid-February 1952, Lillian was in Washington for the opening of *Autumn Garden*. She phoned John, offered tickets to the play to him and his wife, and arranged to meet him to talk over her involvement in his security investigation. They apparently met twice. Neither remembered specifically what was discussed, but their sense of impending trouble was strong.

Days later, when Lillian was back in New York, their fears were realized. She has described in *Scoundrel Time* the 21 February appearance at her apartment of the Federal marshal with a HUAC subpoena. This led to her conference with Abe Fortas, who could not take her case but who suggested a strategy for dealing with HUAC and who put her in contact with Joe Rauh; Rauh then got her appearance postponed until May and began work on her defense.[8]

She saw John again when she was in Washington consulting Rauh. They canvassed the full range of subjects HUAC might ask her about. Foremost in Lillian's mind was a danger that the committee might probe extensively into her activities in Moscow in 1944 and 1945, which would bring in both John and Averell Harriman.

In *Scoundrel Time*, she says:

> Both Rauh and I believed that my wartime trip to Russia, about which I have written in another book, would be the center of the Committee's questions. . . . In Moscow, I had stayed for months in the embassy as the guest of Averell Harriman, who was our ambassador. Both Rauh and I believed that the Committee would ask me about that visit in their open antagonism to the Roosevelt period. The Fifth Amendment has catches: if I were asked if I knew Harriman or President Roosevelt, I would have to say yes because I could not claim that knowing them could harm me; but if I were asked if I knew Chaplin or Hammett, for example, I would have to refuse to answer because they could, in the eyes of the Committee, incriminate me.[9]

She does not mention her concern about Melby in the final draft of *Scoundrel Time*, though she included it in the first draft. As she wrote John in September 1975, when she was preparing the final draft, "You were in the first draft, that was why I wrote to you for info., but somehow our history both touched me and pained me and in the second draft I took it out because I couldn't figure out how to do it" (letter dated "Saturday" from Vineyard Haven).

Since Lillian's romance with John had never got into public print, she and Rauh thought perhaps HUAC might not know about it. She was determined not to tell them about it; publicity at this stage could seriously affect his loyalty-security hearings. As for Harriman, he was preparing to seek the Democratic presidential nomination; any mention of him before HUAC would be the kiss of death. Comments on *Scoundrel Time* usually assume Lillian was most anxious to avoid naming any people she had known in Hollywood or in the many left-wing organizations she had supported. This was not the case. *Lillian wanted primarily to protect Harriman and Melby.*

Lillian was quite prepared to tell HUAC about the many left-wing organizations she had belonged to, her participation in the Marxist study group in 1938 and 1939, her part in the Wallace campaign, and her sponsorship of the Waldorf Peace Conference. She was not prepared to talk about her friends and associates. But she did not want to hide behind the Fifth Amendment, which would create a suspicion of guilt. The problem she and Rauh faced was how to get the committee to allow her to talk about her own past without naming other people. Because of a recent Supreme Court ruling on the use of the Fifth Amendment, this was a complicated matter. They did not settle on a strategy in March.

Meanwhile the drumbeat of charges and accusations against John's and Lillian's friends continued. On 25 February 1952, McCarran wrote a strongly worded letter to Attorney General McGrath demanding the prosecution of Davies.[10] The next day, Lattimore began his lengthy testimony in the witness chair of the McCarran Committee, beginning with a long statement of his background and beliefs, which included the assertion that Budenz was a perjurer and that the SISS was conducting a kangaroo court. For the twelve days of Lattimore's testimony, he was page one copy.

Despite the security investigation, John continued his key involvement in Southeast Asian policy. William Lacy filled out John's efficiency report on 8 March; it was as enthusiastic as the year before. Melby was "devoted to the American Foreign Service, prepared to perform difficult and disagreeable tasks and able to improvise solutions to problems on his own initiative . . . has an encyclopedic knowledge of Far Eastern Affairs. . . . No adverse factors. . . . I should be delighted to have Mr. Melby serve with me at any post. In my opinion, Mr. Melby is ready for greater responsibilities, and should be promoted." This year the report was endorsed by Ambassador U. Alexis Johnson.[11]

The day after Lacy so vigorously praised Melby, the *Times* carried a story that gave great comfort to Foreign Service personnel. Acheson reversed a negative finding of the Department Loyalty-Security Board:

> Official acknowledgement this week that Secretary of State Dean Acheson had reversed an unfavorable ruling by his loyalty and security board brought the harsh light of Congressional inquiry once again on the already bruised and battered State Department loyalty-security program.

O. Edmund Clubb, a Foreign Service officer since 1928 and a China expert in recent years, was found by the State Department's loyalty-security panel to be a security risk. Secretary Acheson, on the word of a "most experienced and trusted" official who had restudied the whole record, overturned the panel's decision and cleared Mr. Clubb of the security stigma. . . .

Now Congress, or at least influential members of it, wants to know "how come."[12]

Here was a precedent that, in a worst-case scenario, would be comforting to John. He was still waiting on a response from the Department to his amended interrogatory filed in December 1951, and assumed that no answer was good news; but given the pressures on loyalty and security boards, it was nice to know that the secretary was willing to support meritorious officers in spite of adverse findings.

In late March, Joe Rauh conferred with Frank Tavenner, HUAC's chief counsel. Rauh conveyed Lillian's determination not to involve other people in her testimony though willing to speak freely about her own past. Tavenner was not sympathetic; Budd Schulberg had tried to do the same thing but had been persuaded to change his position. Tavenner suggested that perhaps Lillian would find it easier to talk about her acquaintances in executive session than she would in a public hearing. Rauh apparently did not comment on this. What became clear to Rauh was that the committee wanted to show how the Communist party sought to control the thinking of its members, particularly in the entertainment and literary fields. Lillian, according to Tavenner, was known to be a Party member.

When Lillian wrote *Scoundrel Time*, she did not remember Rauh telling her about this meeting with Tavenner. In 1975, Rauh sent her a copy of a memo he wrote about it dated 26 March 1952.[13] It is inconceivable that her memory is correct. He must have discussed it with her shortly after it happened. What he told her must have been largely responsible for her growing anguish as the date of her appearance neared.

John and Lillian needed to talk again. John was heavily occupied with Southeast Asian affairs, and could not come to New York. Lillian, for some reason, did not want to come to Washington again. When John mentioned that he was scheduled to give two lectures to the Philadelphia World Affairs Council on 4 and 5 April, she responded that she had been wanting to see some friends in Philadelphia, and that perhaps they could meet there. It was agreed.

John arrived in Philadelphia on the morning of Friday, 4 April 1952. He checked into his hotel, spoke to the World Affairs Council meeting, and then went to meet Lillian at her hotel in late afternoon. They dined together, walked around the town a bit, and had a nightcap in her hotel; then he returned to his. Neither noticed the FBI agent following them.

On Saturday John spent the day at the council meeting; Lillian visited friends in the suburbs. They met again around four o'clock. Again they dined and then went up to her room for a drink. The free-floating conversation of earlier years gave way to the exigencies of her subpoena and his interrogatory: If his loyalty-security people knew about the weekend at Pleasantville, did HUAC also know? What did HUAC know about her other than the many organizations she had supported and the infamous Berkeley testimony? Why was she being called now? Could his affair with her really be the one salient item in John's case when Service, Vincent, Davies, and Clubb were under fire for events in China? And could she refuse to take the Fifth, refuse to talk about people she had known, and still escape indictment for contempt of Congress? The hours passed, the physical attraction that originally drew them together returned full force, and John stayed all night. The next morning, Lillian returned to New York, John to Washington. Neither of them knew that the FBI had Lillian under surveillance.

Elia Kazan preceded Lillian before HUAC, on 10 April. He had already appeared once, in January, behind closed doors. Kazan admitted then that he had been a Party member for two years in the 1930s, but refused to talk about other members. The committee was now interrogating him again; he had had a dramatic change of mind: "I have come to the conclusion that I did wrong to withhold these names before, because secrecy serves the Communists and is exactly what they want. The American people want the facts and all the facts about all aspects of Communism in order to deal with it wisely and effectively. It is my obligation as a citizen to tell everything that I know."[14]

The Committee released Kazan's testimony the next day. Not content with this avenue of confession, Kazan purchased space in the *New York Times* of 12 April 1952 to bare his soul. What he had to say seemed pointed directly at Lillian. After giving the details of his brief Party membership during 1934 to 1936, of his disgust at Communist tactics and at their suppression of personal opinion, and of his rejection of everything the Party stood for, he dealt with the long lapse between leaving the Party and telling what he knew:

> The question will be asked why I did not tell this story sooner. I was held back, primarily, by concern for the reputations and employment

of people who may, like myself, have left the party many years ago. I was also held back by a piece of specious reasoning which has silenced many liberals. It goes like this: "You may hate the Communists, but you must not attack them or expose them, because if you do you are attacking the right to hold unpopular opinions and you are joining the people who attack civil liberties."

I have thought soberly about this. It is, simply, a lie.[15]

Lillian was one of the readers of Kazan's *mea culpa*. It did not change her mind a bit; she called it "pious shit." She believed that in the climate of the times, naming names could do nothing but "bring bad trouble" to anyone connected with the witness. She was determined not to join the bandwagon of namers.

Exactly two weeks after Kazan's public confession, Special Agent Francis W. Norwood of the FBI took testimony from an unnamed informant, at a place whose location is still withheld by the FBI, which testimony added to the charges against Melby. The informant had been one of John's diplomatic colleagues; he did "not desire to testify before a loyalty hearing board." He did, however, desire to bring down John Melby. This informant claimed that John had "rewritten all of Dr. John Leighton Stuart's dispaches to make them fit the policy of aid to the Chinese Communists"; had as a mistress in the American embassy in Nanking a woman who was firmly pro-Communist; and had attended a special dinner at Communist headquarters in Chungking in February 1946.[16] It took one month for these new allegations to filter through to the security people in the State Department; this was a record for bureaucratic interchange. One of these charges eventually showed up in John's hearings.

HUAC brought Edward G. Robinson back for a reappearance on 30 April; like Kazan, he had changed his mind and repented of his earlier recalcitrance. Robinson now begged for forgiveness and absolution.[17] His was a classic degradation ceremony.

Lillian loathed it also.

On 30 April, John's long wait came to an end. His answers to the interrogatories were not acceptable. From the State Department Loyalty-Security Board he received a letter of charges. There was only one: "that during the period 1945 to date, you have maintained an association with one, Lillian Hellman, reliably reported to be a member of the Communist Party." The regulations for dealing with the charge were simple: he could answer in writing under oath, submitting affidavits or other documents within thirty days. He could have an administrative hearing on the charges before the Loyalty-Security Board if he asked for it within fifteen days. He could appear before such a hearing personally, be represented by counsel, and call witnesses.

What he could not do was far more important. He could not see the material in the Department file, could not see FBI reports, and could not know who had given evidence against him. In his case, however, the supreme barrier was none of these limitations; it was the prohibition against any inspection of the "evidence" alleging that the person with whom he was guilty of associating, Lillian, was a Communist.[18] This was the rock upon which his efforts in seven long hearings foundered.

It was time, now, for serious legal advice. John talked to friends in the Department, especially Myron Cowen. The substance of the advice he got was: Hire the most conservative attorney you can find, and do just as he tells you. John was put in touch with Arthur Scharfeld, a very successful practitioner before the Federal Communications Commission. They began the long process of reconstructing a chronology of John's meetings with Lillian. Since the board had noted that John left out the Pleasantville visit in his answer to the first interrogatory, it seemed desirable for him to list every time they had been together. This again required Lillian's cooperation.

John and Lillian talked by phone several times; on 16 May, five days before she was to appear before HUAC, she came to Washington. *Scoundrel Time* records that she went to Washington early only to get out of New York, but this is not the whole truth; she wanted to see John.[19] Between the shopping and aimless wandering she mentions in *Scoundrel Time*, she helped John prepare his case for the Loyalty-Security Board, and he helped her refresh her recollections of Moscow. They met on 19 and 20 May; this was probably the time when they exchanged the letters they had written each other, Lillian insisting that if HUAC asked her to produce any letters she had from John, she wanted to be able to say that she had none.

On 19 May, Clifford Odets appeared before HUAC. Odets had taken Lillian to dinner earlier in the month to talk to her about what he was going to say to the committee. At dinner he was all bravado; Lillian says in *Scoundrel Time* that Odets "pounded on the table so hard that his wineglass spilled, and he yelled 'Well, I can tell you what I am going to do before those bastards on the Committee. I am going to show them the face of a radical man and tell them to go fuck themselves!'"[20] But on 19 May, the bravado disappeared, and Odets groveled.

The day of Odets's testimony, John got an amended letter of charges: there were two new ones. One was about China—the claim that he had kept company with the woman friendly to the Chinese Communists. The other new charge was that he had been a regular reader of the *Daily Worker* in El Paso during 1937; but, the letter went on, the informant who made the *Daily Worker* charge had no question about Melby's loyalty. All this was puzzling; the new charges were so ridiculous that it almost seemed as if the Board had to throw in something else just in case the Hellman association was satisfactorily explained. John was furious. He had, sporadically, read the *Daily Worker*. What conscientious Foreign Service officer hadn't? But he was not a subscriber, and if one fact about his professional life was clear, it was that he was not a subscriber to Communist doctrine either.

While John was wrestling with these new charges, Lillian and Joe Rauh were deciding on a strategy for her HUAC appearance. Rauh's first plan was for Lillian to "refuse to answer, on grounds of self-incrimination, any and all questions with respect to Communist views, activities, and associates . . . and later issue a statement to the Press."[21] The statement to the press would explain that she was quite willing to talk about herself, but due to the complexities of Fifth Amendment precedents, she would then be compelled to talk about others or risk contempt. Two drafts of such a statement survive in the Rauh papers at the Library of Congress, one written by Lillian (undated but mailed 17 April 1952) and another written by Rauh (dated 14 April).

By 30 April, when Rauh wrote Lillian a long letter, he thought that in addition to releasing a statement to the press after the hearing, she should write the committee before the hearing, offering to tell them anything about herself if they would agree not to ask her about other people. Rauh sent her a draft of such a letter. He told her he did not expect the committee to agree to let her testify on such a limited basis, but if they did, it would be advantageous to her.

The main thrust of Rauh's long letter of 30 April was to convince Lillian that previous drafts of the statement she would release to the press were inadequate. In Lillian's draft of 17 April, she acknowledged that she had "joined" the Communist party in 1938 by attending a Marxist study group, where she "saw and heard nothing more than people discussing the history of Marxism and the events of the day." She left this group in 1940 because her "maverick nature was no more suited to the political left than it had been to the conservative background from which I came."[22]

Rauh thought she was too cavalier about her Communist associations:

> The more I read your draft statement, the more it seems to me that it is so little critical of the Communist movement in America that it will be generally considered an acceptance of it. Please don't take

offense, but your statement is likely to be compared by unfriendly sources to a lady retiring from the Republican Party because she is tired of politics, although she still thinks Bob Taft is a dear, sweet thing. Such a retirement from the Republican Party might be possible in Newport or Southampton, but I do not see how it is possible for you to have that sort of retirement from Communist politics. The statement almost seems to equate membership in the Communist Party with membership in a ladies' literary society or "good works" club. This may have been your experience, but few will accept it.

Let me ask you a couple of specific questions about your statement that will help make this point clear: Isn't it a little naive to say that the Communists at their meetings just talked about the latest books they had read or at least naive to suppose this would be believed? When you say that you drifted away from the Communist Party because you seemed to be in the wrong place, doesn't it have a certain air of getting into Schubert's when you wanted to be at the Majestic? When you refer to the Communists as people who were going your way, don't you just confirm what the House Committee is setting out to prove about you?

Now I know from our talks that these implications are not true. You made it quite clear in our talks that you genuinely disagree with the activities of the Communist Party in this country and recognize that you were wrong in ever joining the Party. I believe your refusal to say so is based on your feeling that somebody might think you were saying so because you were afraid of public opinion rather than because that was your true view. It seems to me that you should no more refrain from saying things for that reason than you should actually say them because you were in fact afraid of public opinion. To my mind, your own statement does you an injustice.

I must say that, on looking back at the draft statement we sent you, I find that it is not as strong as I now believe we should have made it. It was, however, a minimum based on things you had actually said to me. I think you should seriously consider whether a forthright declaration that you had been wrong in joining the Communist Party, including reasons, is not the only road to follow here.[23]

No subsequent drafts of the proposed press release survive; so we do not know to what extent Lillian yielded to Rauh's arguments. They continued to work on this statement, which was in the end not issued, as well as on a letter to Chairman John Wood, right up to the time of the hearing. Rauh drafted the letter to Wood, and much of the final version was Rauh's original text. But Rauh says that the one pristine Hellman addition was the famous phrase "I cannot and will not cut my conscience to fit this year's fashions."[24] The final version of the letter appears in *Scoundrel Time*; she asked that she not be required to tell about other people and thus not forced to take the Fifth Amendment.[25] Chairman Wood's prompt answer: No.

John Melby was privy to all these deliberations, and Lillian thought that Harriman should also know that she was to appear before HUAC since she was worried that her connection with him might be brought out. Rauh was therefore asked to talk to Harriman. This he did on 11 May. As he wrote Lillian the next day, "Mr. Harriman was grateful for the thoughtfulness in giving him this information, but did not feel that there could be any real embarrassment, as his action at the Embassy in Moscow had been both official and appropriate."[26]

The twenty-first of May, the day of Lillian's appearance before HUAC, is enshrined both in the lore of the committee and in commentaries on the inquisition. Lillian's own description is indispensable, but it is only part of the story. Her fears of involving John and Averell Harriman in unwelcome publicity are not hinted at in *Scoundrel Time*, nor are the hours she spent with John worrying about how their situations might be connected. These were not fanciful fears. While HUAC was fixated on the exposure of pink movie stars and writers and knew little about foreign affairs, Tavenner did have access to FBI files that identified Melby as one of Lillian's visitors. (J. Edgar Hoover always publicly proclaimed that FBI files were never given to anyone outside the executive branch, and a paper record of refusal of all such requests was created. The reality is that Hoover leaked files to Congress, sympathetic journalists, and anti-Communist crusaders like the American Legion.)[27]

One wonders why Tavenner (or one of the committee members) did not ask Lillian about John Melby. To connect her with a clandestine visit from an important State Department officer would have been, in the climate of 1952, dynamite. There was indeed much in her file that would have made news. Yet she was dismissed after a mere thirty-seven minutes; one has to assume that Joe Rauh's clever handling of the "I will not cut my conscience" letter unnerved the committee, so that they were anxious to be rid of her.

Lillian's enemies still take delight in pointing out that she was not really the first person to attempt to avoid naming names without invoking the Fifth, and they also emphasize that her eventual use of the Fifth was not legally justified, since what she could have told the committee could not have incriminated her.[28] This latter is a picayune claim; in a choice between jail and invoking the Fifth to protect other people, surely the questionable usage is warranted. As to her pioneering the "moral" response, she may not have. She just did it with class. Murray Kempton in his *New York Review* analysis of *Scoundrel Time* had it right: "The most important thing is never to forget that here is someone who knew how to act when there was nothing harder on earth than knowing how to act."[29]

She did not take the Fifth consistently, however. She answered questions as to whether she was a Communist in 1952, 1951, and 1950: she said "No." Before that, she took the Fifth.[30] Court interpretations of Fifth Amendment usage were obscure; Lillian's understanding was that there was a three-year grace period, beyond which she could not answer questions without losing the Fifth Amendment privilege, but up to which she could respond. She did not understand why this was so, and she acknowledges in *Scoundrel Time* that Fifth Amendment regulations were confusing. The question of her apparently inconsistent usage came up in John's State Department hearings, and was thoroughly aired.[31]

Lillian's use of the Fifth has established itself in our tribal memory. When, in December 1986, super patriot Lieutenant Colonel Oliver North (and others) took the Fifth about his part in the arms-to-Iran deal, columnists found the comparison with Hellman's usage thirty-four years earlier to be the best way to establish a link with history. Charles Krauthammer, writing in the *Washington Post*, noted:

> Liberals, once so enamored of the Fifth Amendment, now have discovered its inconveniences—just when Oliver North needs it. It turns out, you see, that the privilege against self-incrimination was created in the 16th century to protect free speech and religious liberty and, later, in the debates on the ratification of the Constitution, was identified with protection from torture and inquisition, and we're far past that in our history, so who needs it now that Lillian Hellman doesn't, and if Ollie North is such a hero why won't he fry for his country? Something like that.[32]

After the hearing, Rauh sent Lillian off with his assistant, Daniel Pollitt. Lillian records in *Scoundrel Time* that she and Pollitt went to a restaurant for a drink; Pollitt says this was at the Statler. Rauh came along shortly; the mood was upbeat. Rauh insisted they had outfoxed the committee at its own game, and that this would be the end of the matter. There had been no discussion of Lillian's connection with Harriman, and of course none of John. And she was not—yet—cited for contempt. When Lillian got back to the Shoreham, she called John, and he came by for a few minutes to hear how it had gone.

Then Lillian went back to New York, and to straitened circumstances because of the blacklist. It was, as she wrote, a tough spring.

And despite Joe Rauh's upbeat assessment, while she had indeed out-foxed the committee, her "victory" angered inquisitors of all stripes and intensified the desire of Hoover and others to "get" her. This was, later, the reaction of State Department officers who served on John's hearing boards. They felt she had tricked HUAC, reneged on her promise to tell all about herself, and demonstrated again her true Communist commitment. Until much later, when Lillian became a heroine to those who opposed the inquisition, her triumph over HUAC simply increased her visibility as a target. Perhaps the HUAC hearing triggered the interest of the CIA in her activities.

Since John's answers to his interrogatories were not satisfactory to the Loyalty-Security Board, a hearing was set for 26 June. He began to work seriously with Scharfeld, preparing to answer in person not only the charges about Lillian but the additional, ridiculous ones. At the Depart-ment, he was moved from the Philippine–Southeast Asia section to serve as assistant to Myron Cowen, who was now responsible for Mutual Security Administration activities in the Pacific area. Apparently the impending hearing did not lower the quality of his work; Cowen continued to support him strongly.

In mid-June, John's father's best friend died; there was to be a memorial service near New York. John's presence was much desired, and he went up for the service. While he was there, he stopped by Lillian's for lunch. She knew of no further developments in her case, and he told her of what he was doing to prepare for his. He did not know whether she would be called to give testimony to his board; Scharfeld, so far, did not think so. She was quite willing to appear if asked.

On Thursday, 26 June 1952, the State Department Loyalty-Security Board met at 10:00 A.M. in room 1210 of the New State Building, to deliberate In the Matter of John Fremont Melby. Howard Donovan was chairman; Lehman P. Nickell and James W. Swihart were the other mem-bers. The board was assisted by John W. Sipes, its legal adviser. Scharfeld and his assistant, Theodore Baron, accompanied Melby.

John was not overjoyed with the choice of Donovan as chairman. He had known Donovan, did not think well of him, and had once vetoed a sugges-tion that Donovan be appointed consul general in Singapore, a post Donovan desired. But the luck of the draw, the assignment of interesting jobs, had been with John so consistently that he could not now complain. Anyway, he was confident. Whatever could be said about Lillian, John's professional record was without blemish. An impressive array of Department stalwarts had provided affidavits attesting to his loyalty and discretion; five of them were to appear as witnesses at the hearing. And there were other exhibits, such as the National Catholic Welfare Conference press release on his anti-Communist speech, and a photostat of a *Daily Worker* article attacking him. With his rock-ribbed reputation for anti-Communism, he and Scharfeld were sure that no puny guilt by association with a playwright, who was also a friend of eminent officials, could do him in.

The Budenz Agenda

There were two agendas before Howard Donovan's board that June day. One was Arthur Scharfeld's agenda: to prove his client, John Melby, eminently fit for the Foreign Service of the United States because of his competence, loyalty, and trustworthiness. The other agenda was Louis Budenz's, as it reached this hearing through FBI and State Department channels: to vilify and disgrace all of the four hundred "concealed Communists" he knew about by hearsay, *and with them their friends and associates.* Budenz was not present at the hearing and probably never heard about it. But without Budenz, Donovan would have been without a substantial agenda.

Donovan began with the relevant departmental regulations.[1] John's answers to the interrogatories, and to the charge of association with Lillian, were entered in the record. Then Scharfeld began his presentation.

The case made in Melby's behalf can only be described as formidable. The same superlatives which, appearing in his efficiency reports, had rocketed him to the top of the Foreign Service now reappeared in personal testimony and affidavits, accompanied this time with equally firm statements about his loyalty. Scharfeld skillfully mustered this evidence.

Lewis Clark, career minister in the Foreign Service, who had been Melby's immediate superior in the Nanking Embassy:

Scharfeld: What is your opinion of Mr. Melby with respect to his loyalty to the United States Government?

Clark: Well, I have never noticed—I mean, the question would never have arisen in my mind that there was any doubt as to his loyalty to the United States. I mean, I have absolutely nothing or no reason whatsoever to suspect him of any disloyalty. . . .

Scharfeld: What would you say with respect to the matter of security, his tact and discretion in matters which were handled within the scope of your supervision?

Clark: I am not aware of any failure to be discreet. I mean, I would never have questioned his security anyway; it would never cross my mind to question it.

Scharfeld: You mean you had complete trust and confidence in him?

Clark: I had complete trust in him.[2]

William S. B. Lacy, director of the Office of Philippine and Southeast Asian Affairs, John's superior during the period when he worked on the Huk rebellion:

Scharfeld: What is your opinion, specifically now with respect to Mr. Melby's loyalty to the United States Government, his consideration of the interests of the Government, and the matter of security?

Lacy: Well, as I set forth in an affidavit I wrote, I have no doubt whatever about his loyalty to the Government of the United States. I regard him as an unusually competent officer. I would think his integrity unassailable and I have never heard of any instance in which anyone suggested that he lacked discretion in dealing with highly secret matters. Is that a responsive answer?

Scharfeld: Yes, sir, thank you, sir. . . . He has been associated with you in the Department in the past. Would you want him to serve with you again?

Lacy: I should be delighted.[3]

Joseph B. Phillips, deputy assistant secretary for public affairs, who had been public relations officer for Eisenhower in North Africa, served on Ike's staff in Europe, later worked under Harriman in the Moscow Embassy, and whose wife Treacy had been so sure that Lillian loved John:

Scharfeld: Did you have trust and confidence in Mr. Melby at the time of your association in Moscow?

Phillips: I certainly did.

Scharfeld: Do you have now?

Phillips: I certainly do.

Scharfeld: Would you want to be associated with him again?

Phillips: I think it would be a pleasure and a benefit. I have always thought of Mr. Melby as a very capable officer.

Scharfeld: What is your opinion with respect to his integrity, loyalty, and security?

Phillips: To answer the last one first, when I came to Moscow I naturally was eager to learn what was going on, and I remember very distinctly that Mr. Melby made it quite clear to me that I had to find out from the Ambassador, not from him. That sticks in my memory. As to his loyalty and integrity, I have never had any reason whatsoever to question either of them.[4]

Not all the affidavits and testimony were available at this first hearing, but there were four others similar in import to the ones above. Ambassador Cowen was extremely supportive, stating that John would be his first choice as an assistant for any post he might have; Cowen had requested that John be assigned to him in his present work, as mutual security administrator, and later requested that John be sent with him to the U.S. Embassy in Belgium. John was clearly the finest officer Cowen had ever worked with.[5] Ambassador Stuart's assessment was almost as complimentary; he claimed that his Embassy in China could not have functioned well if Melby had not been totally loyal and discreet.[6] Averell Harriman was not as effusive, perhaps because he was then an active candidate for the presidency of the United States.[7] Certainly his belief in John's integrity was in no way weaker than that of the other ambassadors whom John had served. (Twenty-eight years later, it was Harriman's insistence alone that compelled the bureaucracy to restore John's security clearance.) Richard H. Davis, at that time officer in charge of Soviet affairs, was also adamant that John was the quintessence of professionalism: he found John "absolutely trustworthy, experienced and astute" as a Foreign Service officer.[8]

In addition to these witnesses, Scharfeld presented as evidence a series of documents demonstrating John's anti-Communism and effectiveness as a spokesman for American interests. There was a copy of the report on the probability that the Chinese Communists would work closely with the Soviet Union that John wrote for General Wedemeyer on Wedemeyer's 1947 mission to China.[9] The National Catholic Welfare Conference press release touting John's anti-Communist position in his Shanghai speech of 18 March 1948 was entered in the record.[10] There was a long analysis John wrote for the State Department's policy planning staff assessing the ideological position of the Chinese Communists, in which John debunked the claim made by some journalists (though never by State Department officers) that Mao and his people were not real Communists but "mere agrarian reformers."[11] Attacks on John by the *Daily Worker* completed the documentation.[12]

At the end of Scharfeld's agenda, the evidence of John's loyalty and security was overwhelming. There was no questionable incident in his career, no hint of sympathy with Communists, no charge of indiscretion with classified material, no accusations of espionage, no leaking of sensitive material to left-wing journalists—nothing to tarnish the record.

The questions addressed by the board to witnesses were routine and mechanical. The board members were obviously not interested in Scharfeld's agenda. He was wasting his time and theirs. They wanted to get to the only matter that concerned them: his association with Lillian. Thus after Scharfeld's witnesses had been politely heard, after the documents had been introduced, the real hearings began: quizzing John about why he had associated—nay, why he had been *in love* with—this damnable Communist.

Melby was sworn in, and John W. Sipes, counsel to the board, started the questioning.

> Sipes: Mr. Melby, in connection with Exhibit No. 8, the affidavit of Mr. Harriman, did you acquaint Mr. Harriman, in connection with your request for this affidavit, with the nature of the charges in this proceeding?
> Melby: He was aware in general, yes.
> Sipes: Was he aware that you were charged specifically with a relationship with Lillian Hellman?
> Melby: Yes.
> Sipes: Do you know why he did not observe or comment on that in his affidavit? I don't see that he did. I just read this. Did he make any collateral comment to you in that connection?
> Melby: No. He was aware of what was going on in connection with me. He said that he would put anything in the affidavit that I wanted that we thought would be helpful. So we suggested that he leave out any personal references in view of his particular situation at this time.
> Sipes: In other words, you did not ask him to comment on his judgment or his impressions as to Miss Hellman's political orientation during the time he also knew her in Moscow?
> Melby: That's correct. . . . I showed him those portions which concerned Miss Hellman and he told me at that time that he thought it was a proper answer. . . . And his only comment on Miss Hellman, when he said of course he would do anything I wanted, was "Of course, I never knew her to be or believed her to be a Communist at all—a fellow traveller in the days gone by, yes, but I never had reason to believe it was more than that."[13]

Sipes then led John through a review of his youth, education, and early service, including questions about whether his parents were Americans, what church he belonged to, and whether he was active in political clubs in college. Then Sipes returned to Hellman. Had John "disclosed to her any facts, information, or data contrary to security regulations or contrary to the best interests of the United States?" No. When had his relationship with Miss Hellman ceased to be romantic? Probably during 1947. Had the relationship since then been anything but platonic? No.[14]

There followed a long series of questions in which Sipes tried to find out why there had been *any* relationship with Lillian once the romantic affair was over. The hidden premise of these questions was not clear to John or attorney Scharfeld yet, but one can see it in the transcript: *Since anyone could tell that Hellman is a Communist, or at least a fellow traveler, how could a judicious government servant associate with her in any way?* These questions went on for most of the afternoon:

Sipes: Mr. Melby, did you ever ask Miss Hellman if she had ever been a member of the Communist Party?

Melby: Yes, and she said that—this was in 1945, in 1952 she repeated it again, that in the period of 1938 and 1939 she had been interested in a small Marxist study group of intellectuals in New York, that she presumed that during that brief period that constituted membership, but that was her only connection with the Party, that she dropped out of this group sometime in 1939. . . .

Sipes: Did you believe her answers to your questions on those occasions?

Melby: In 1945 I knew so little about her organizational affiliations that I didn't have any opinion on it then. I didn't know what she belonged to. And a lot of the groups that I suppose she might have mentioned were groups I wouldn't know how to identify. . . . There is the National Council of the Arts, Sciences and Professions which I believe is a separate organization, in which Miss Hellman was originally active too. I don't know whether it has become a Communist front organization, though I have heard that it has. And I understand Miss Hellman has been inactive or completely out of that thing, I believe, for two or three years anyway.

Sipes: That is perhaps what I had in mind. I think that organization had some function at the Waldorf Astoria in 1949 which attracted a great deal of attention.

Melby: That's right. What the tie-in was between that and the Indepen-

dent Citizens Committee I don't know. One may have been kind of a
successor to the other. But a great many people involved in the one
that had the function at the Waldorf, particularly after that show,
dropped out.[15]

There were questions about whom John had met at Lillian's place. He
named as many as he could remember: Mr. and Mrs. Arthur Kober, Louis
Kronenberger, Dr. Gregory Zilboorg, William Wyler. Had he met Paul
Robeson? "I met him just in passing, that's right, but not at any function, as
I recall."[16]

Donovan: Did Miss Hellman ever mention to you her friendship with
  Gerhart Eisler?
Melby: No.
Donovan: Did you ever meet him at Miss Hellman's home?
Melby: Never. I never met him.
Donovan: I raise that question because, according to information be-
  fore the Board, she gave a dinner party for him just before his sud-
  den departure in 1949, and according to our information, she is a
  very close friend of his. [This was not correct. The FBI informant
  claimed she was a close friend of Mrs. Eisler.]
Melby: I have never heard her mention him.
Donovan: She never mentioned him?
Melby: No.
Sipes: Did you ever meet Mrs. Gerhart Eisler?
Melby: No.[17]

The board wasn't buying this. Donovan and Swihart undertook a little
hostile examination.

Donovan: Mr. Melby, in your reply to the interrogatories from the
  Board you state that you never had any reason to believe—I'm not
  quoting exactly but I'm trying to give you the purport as I understand it—that you never knew or understood or believed that Miss
  Hellman was a Communist. Now, in view of the associations she had
  and her membership in, I won't attempt to count the number of
  Communist front organizations—I'm trying to rationalize that statement, how you could say that you didn't realize that she was a Communist. The fact that she didn't have a card in her handbag wouldn't
  mean much.
Melby: I said that she was not a Communist in 1945. As I say, I knew
  very little about the organizational connections. She told me then

that she was not and had not had anything to do with the Party since 1939, the statement which she repeated to me in 1952. And I had never heard anyone refer to her as a Communist, although she certainly followed a left wing line but not as a member of the Communist Party.

Swihart: Right on this point, Mr. Melby, I notice that in your reply to the first interrogatory of the Board and also in your amended reply of May you do have quite a lengthy analysis of Miss Hellman's political beliefs, which are the same in both. In fact, I think you say, amongst other things, that it didn't take you very long to perceive that she had a definite interest in and sympathy with Communism in the Soviet Union and you also say that you felt she was probably a left winger and a fellow traveler. And then you have told us orally that she had told you in 1945 that she assumed she had been a member of the Communist Party in 1938 or '39 as a result of participating in this Marxist study group. Now, as an individual with considerable political sophistication, as your dispatches show here, what kind of proof does one really need? It seems to me you have made out a pretty good case yourself right on the basis of your own statements that she may very well have been a Communist. . . .

Melby: Well, I think that on the basis of her views that she might have been, yes; but what she told me then, at that time that I knew her, was that she was not. She was never interested in Soviet politics as politics; that she was a socialist economically, yes, or thought she was. I'm not sure what one was. Certainly she thought she was one. She was very sympathetic to the Russian people and what was going on in the war. I think that that emotional reaction led her to condone things for the Russians that she would not condone for her own country. And I think that her horror at war led her to attribute better motives to the future of Russian foreign policy in terms of peace and war than I would have, and I think better motives then than she would now. . . .

Donovan: Well, how would you diagnose her answers to the House Committee on Un-American Activities a few days ago? She declined to answer whether she has ever been a member of the Communist Party. That isn't technically the way the question was put, but it seems pretty obvious, at least to me, that her answers to those questions were tantamount to admission that she had been a member of the Party.[18]

John then explained Rauh's belief that there was a limitation on her ability to answer questions without losing her Fifth Amendment privilege. Rauh told her that she could answer about Party membership for 1952 and 1951, but not farther back than that.

> Sipes: On that point, Mr. Melby, you in explanation or rationalization of Miss Hellman's answers before the House Un-American Activities Committee—her refusal to answer the third question . . . whether she was a member of the Communist Party in 1950, which she refused to answer—you explained to the Board the theory of her case as mentioned by her lawyers, and so forth, as the statute of limitations. I would like to put into the record at this point that the Board has information from reliable sources that Miss Hellman was a secret member of the Communist Party in 1950, which might be another explanation of why she didn't answer that question.*[19]
> Melby: It might, if that be true, yes, certainly.

The grilling on Lillian's memberships, acquaintances, and the secret contents of her file was beginning to unnerve John. He was asked about her relationship with Joe Curran, who according to the board was supposed to be a friend of hers. John knew nothing about Curran. Donovan pressed on. "We are trying to find out what sort of people you knew through Miss Hellman because the information the Board has about a great many of Miss Hellman's friends is not very flattering to Miss Hellman."[20] John could only repeat the names of people whom he met through her. The Board came back several times to Paul Robeson. John insisted he had only met Robeson once.

By late afternoon, the board had still not laid all its cards on the table. The full Budenz agenda came out finally from the board's counsel:

> Sipes: I was wondering if it would surprise you that the Board has reliable information that she not only went into a large number of these organizations which we have enumerated here in the records but actually participated in the organization and creation of a number of them on direct and specific orders of the Communist Party. Does that surprise you in any way in your judgment of Miss Hellman?
> Melby: Yes, it certainly would.
> Sipes: Assuming that would be true?

---

*This was not true. The board had no such information. Budenz *gave* his testimony about Hellman in 1950, but he had not been in the Party since 1945, and did not claim that Hellman was still a member.

Melby: Yes, it certainly would; that she had done it on the orders of the Communist Party, that really would surprise me.[21]

This charge would, of course, have surprised anyone who knew Lillian. That she had been a fellow traveler was clear; that she was under Party discipline was quite another matter. Sipes's introduction of this blockbuster held it to be "reliable information." John had no idea at that time who had provided this claim. Budenz was never mentioned in his hearings. John had to assume this came from her FBI file; if this new claim was as well grounded as the report about his visit to Pleasantville, and Lillian really had acted on Party orders, he was in trouble.

The Budenz charge was not emphasized in this first hearing; only later did its significance become clear. Sipes presented it ex cathedra and moved on to other things.

The Philadelphia meeting of April 1952 interested the board very much. They wanted to know if John had told anyone in the Department that he was to meet Lillian there; he said he had told his immediate superior, Myron Cowen. Then came this question:

Donovan: Why was it necessary for her to consult you in connection with her subpoena before the House Committee on Un-American Activities?

Melby: What she said to me was that she wanted to know if there was anything in particular that I wanted her to do or say or not say if I or Mr. Harriman, or Mr. Harriman through me, were brought into the investigation.

Donovan: Did she ask you specifically how she should reply to a question if they asked Miss Hellman if she knew you?

Melby: Yes.

Donovan: Since the question wasn't raised and perhaps it was academic, how would she answer it?

Melby: I told her she should tell the truth.

Donovan: Did she consult Mr. Harriman about matters like that too?

Melby: She said she was going to. Whether she did, I don't know. I think she probably did.[22]

There was desultory questioning about his reading the *Daily Worker*, about whether he had any allegiance to the Communist party, about the attitude of the American Embassy in Moscow toward the Russians in 1944, and about his relationship with the allegedly pro-Communist woman in China. Always and inevitably the questioning came back to Lillian.

John was greatly disturbed by the seeming solidity of the board's evidence that Lillian was a Communist. He could not know how phony were the anonymous reports—of people who would not give public testimony —about her dinner for Eisler, her forming front groups at the Party's request, and her active membership even as late as 1950. The board's attitude was clear: they accepted these as gospel.

Perhaps it was already too late to convince this board that he had not been careless in talking to Lillian, that he had picked up no red virus from her, that he had, as he said, disagreed with her on important issues in foreign affairs. The board was clearly hostile. Scharfeld's request that the record be kept open until Dean Rusk had a chance to come down from New York to testify on John's behalf was agreed to, but if Rusk's testimony was to mean no more than that of the other dignitaries who had spoken for John, the whole exercise was useless. It would probably be useless even to call Lillian; she would not be allowed to inspect and rebut the evidence against her either.

Toward the end of the hearing, Sipes brought up the future attitude John intended to take toward Lillian. His question invited John to participate in a typical degradation ceremony, which, if handled correctly, could lead to John's clearance, just as naming names by the witnesses before HUAC led to their avoiding the blacklist.

> Sipes: I had better go on to the answer to a question by your counsel as to your future intentions with reference to your association with Miss Hellman. I believe you answered to the effect that you didn't see any reason or cause for continuing them. I wonder if that is as categorical as you wish to make that answer for the purpose of these proceedings. What is your intention with reference to your future association?
>
> Melby: I have no intention. That was an unfortunate choice of words. I have no intention of seeing her and I see no reason or cause for it.[23]

This, on the face of it, was a victory for the inquisitors. The heretic had confessed his error and promised not to repeat it. But the language of the promise was still not, as Sipes put it, "categorical." John had not said "I will never see her again under any circumstances."

Had he been categorical, had he shown some degree of contrition for ever having associated with such a Communist, *perhaps* he might have been let off with only a wrist slapping. But the McCarthys and McCarrans were still putting the pressure on the State Department to come up with some honest-to-God firings, the loyalty-security people were still under the gun, and the political climate pointed to more, not less, pressure for conformity and personal purity. Perhaps no promise John could have made would have changed the board's attitude.

The board adjourned, at 4:05 P.M., until 30 June 1952, at which time it would take testimony from Dean Rusk.

"Are You Defending Miss Hellman?"

Tuesday, 30 June 1952, Howard Donovan and colleagues resumed hearings In the Matter of John Fremont Melby.[1] It was a late afternoon meeting, scheduled to accommodate Dean Rusk, who had left the State Department four months earlier, and was to be inaugurated the day after the hearing as president of the Rockefeller Foundation. Rusk was known, around the Department, as a man who kept his opinions to himself, who was capable of seeing all sides of an issue—a prestigious, astute, canny man. Had he left State as a sinking ship, in these waning days of the Truman administration? Some thought so. Certainly none of the opprobrium for the loss of China attached itself to Rusk. Later, as secretary of state, he was to be Lyndon Johnson's stalwart defender of the Vietnam War.

Rusk worked with John Melby while Rusk was assistant secretary of state for far eastern affairs, from April 1950 to December 1951. It was he who selected John to head the Melby-Erskine mission. Did he now have any doubts as to the wisdom of that choice? Not at all. For half an hour, he responded to Scharfeld's questions about John's politics, his loyalty, his discretion, about whether Rusk always agreed with John and whether John's ideas had been useful. The answers were always the same, with no doubt or equivocation: This is a good man, and I trust him completely. His contribution to the American program for resisting Communist influence in the Philippines and Southeast Asia had been major.

> Scharfeld: What is your personal opinion with respect to Mr. Melby's ability as a Foreign Service Officer?
> Rusk: I consider Mr. Melby a man of very considerable ability, abilities that go beyond his age and class in the Foreign Service. The fact that he was selected to head the Melby-Erskine Mission is an example of that ability. I feel that as he matures in the Foreign Service he will

undoubtedly be given responsibilities of the very highest sort before
he winds up his career. . . .

Scharfeld: Would you say then that you had complete confidence in
him, in so far as using discretion and tact for such information of
top classification?

Rusk: Why, I demonstrated complete confidence by the fact that he
regularly received such papers and documents, and I do not recall
any instance of mishandling of documents or any lack of security
which would cause me to want to review that confidence. As a matter of fact, I recall no instance where the matter ever came up for
discussion.

Scharfeld: Would you want to be associated again with Mr. Melby in
any official capacity?

Rusk: If I were back in the Department of State—which I hope the
kind fates will not bring about for the immediate future—I should
be delighted to have Mr. Melby associated with me again.

That was the end of Scharfeld's questioning. One might have expected
the board to probe Rusk seriously about Melby's relations with other
people; one might have expected some testing of the Budenz agenda and
the Eisler gossip, some effort to find out why this conservative statesman
had such laudatory things to say about a man who deliberately associated
with a Communist writer. One would have thought that the board would
take Dean Rusk seriously. They did not. *No member of the Board had a
question or comment for Rusk.* Sipes lamely asked for the dates of the Melby-
Erskine mission, hardly solid probing. He got his answer, and the witness
was excused.

Scharfeld had two other items on his agenda that day. Affidavits had
arrived from Livingstone T. Merchant, who had served with John in China
and was now serving as deputy for political affairs to the United States
special representative in Europe. The other was from W. Walton Butterworth, then ambassador to Sweden, formerly minister-counselor in the
Nanking Embassy. These affidavits were more of the same: they testified
that John was loyal, secure, brilliant. The board did not care.

John was again brought in for questioning. There was only one area of
questioning: Hellman, ever Hellman.

Had he seen her since the day of her HUAC appearance? No. Had she
phoned him since her HUAC appearance? No. Had he phoned her since
her HUAC appearance? No. Had either written the other? No.

But he had seen her plenty before the HUAC appearance, and the board was obsessed with this.

> Donovan: I have asked this question before, Mr. Melby, and I know it is repetitious, but I'm going to ask it again. It's important that it be clear in the minds of the Board. What was the purport or purpose of her meeting with you in Philadelphia? Will you state that?
>
> Melby: It was concerned solely with her subpoena to appear before the House Committee and her desire to know what she should do or what she should say in the event that I should be brought up in that hearing.
>
> Donovan: And your reply to that inquiry was what?
>
> Melby: That she should tell the truth.
>
> Sipes: As I understood your testimony the other day, Mr. Melby, Ambassador Cowen knew, or you told Ambassador Cowen before you went up to Philadelphia that you were going to see Miss Hellman. Is that correct?
>
> Melby: That's correct.
>
> Sipes: Did he make any suggestion to you at that time as to whether you should enlighten anybody else in the Department in the Security Division, or anybody else like that, with reference to the contact with Miss Hellman?
>
> Melby: No. The only thing he said was that if anything was necessary he would take care of it. . . .
>
> Sipes: Well, in the event of future recall of Miss Hellman before the House Un-American Activities Committee or perhaps her being called before the Senate Judiciary Subcommittee on Internal Security, do you feel that it might be necessary for you to further reconstruct dates and one thing and another to the extent that you would have to have an additional meeting with her?
>
> Melby: No, I see no need for anything further on anything that I know of, no. She was interested in the one thing, what she should say about me, and she knows what I think.
>
> Donovan: Well, then, the Board interprets that statement to mean, Mr. Melby, that you have no intention of seeing Miss Hellman again.
>
> Melby: That's correct.

Score two. But the board was still not satisfied. There were all those shady characters who had been good friends of Lillian.

Donovan: There are several other questions I'd like to ask about Miss Hellman and her associates. As I remarked the other day, she had a rather wide circle of friends, and I'd like to know if you ever at any time met any of these people at her home or at any other place socially when you were with her. Dorothy Parker?

Melby: Once, just once.

Donovan: What was the nature of that, just a social contact?

Melby: Just a cocktail.

Donovan: Clifford Odets?

Melby: Never, I never met him.

Donovan: Ruth McKinney?

Melby: I have never met her either.

Donovan: Donald Ogden Stewart?

Melby: I have never met him.

Donovan: Ralph Ingersoll?

Melby: I have never met him.

Donovan: Richard Wright?

Melby: I have never met him either.

And so on through a host of names: Michael Quill, Mrs. Burton Emmett, Steve Nelson, employees of the Soviet Consul in New York. John had never met them.

But he had met Dorothy Parker. One can imagine the raised eyebrows from the conscientious inquisitor. One has to assume that the point of all this interrogation was to determine the extent to which this Foreign Service officer would have been sullied, contaminated, and corrupted had he met these devilish people. Yet this hearing board was not atypical of the times; heresy was abroad in the land, and wasn't it the duty of all true Americans to bring to book not only the heretics, but their friends, and their friends' friends?

Lehman P. Nickell, who had little to say so far, now took over questioning. He wanted to make sure that they had an account of every single time John had seen Lillian since his return from China. And was that lunch, or dinner? And are you sure? And could it really be that you did not see her in 1949 *at all*? Whose initiative was it when you had lunch in January 1950? Did she call you, or did you call her? Could it have been lunch and dinner too?

James Swihart also had a line of questioning. Had John omitted some of their meetings from his first accounting "on the grounds that you were a gentleman and you felt you had to make sure it would be an appropriate thing for you to do?" This Swihart worried for five minutes, and it was taken up then by Sipes. John answered that he had not consciously done so: "There was no intention to withhold it, sir." The Pleasantville visit he had forgotten; anything else he had left out because, in his first answer, he was not trying to list every single meeting; and he gave only the ones he thought might be significant to the board. It was a bad answer. This board, this inquiry, was not to be content with gaps or omissions in the record. A heretic could be purged only with full and complete confession.

The dinner party for Gerhart Eisler came up again. Was John there? No, he couldn't have been; he did not see Lillian in 1949.

> Donovan: Miss Hellman never mentioned Eisler to you in any way, shape or form?
> Melby: Never.
> Donovan: Would you consider that as out of character on Miss Hellman's part to have a dinner party for Gerhart Eisler who was out on bail?
> Melby: Who was out on bail?
> Donovan: Yes.
> Melby: I don't know enough about him to say.
> Donovan: I said, considered out of character for Miss Hellman, not out of character for Eisler.
> Melby: No, I understand that. She would give a dinner party, I think, for anyone whom she had known who had been a friend.
> Donovan: Even though he might be pending deportation?
> Melby: On the kind of charge that I understand Eisler was pending deportation for—and I don't know very much about his case—unless he had been a close personal friend I don't think she would. If he had been a close personal friend, she might, yes.
> Donovan: Well, the point is she did, so the assumption is that he was a close personal friend. The reason we are asking all these questions, Mr. Melby, is since you were associated with Miss Hellman, it's only natural to suppose that some of her associates were your associates. In other words, it's something that has to be cleared up definitely, and that is the reason we are trying to find out about this. As I said before, this was a rather wide circle of friends of Miss Hellman's.
> Melby: Yes.
> Donovan: I have just one last question, Mr. Melby. Do you today consider yourself in any way obligated to Miss Hellman to such an ex-

tent that she might conceivably bring any pressure to bear on you
with reference to any material you shouldn't disclose to her?
Melby: I do not.

It was then 4:45 P.M. Scharfeld was told to present his summary. In a
court of law, it would have been a tour de force. After highlighting the
impeccable support John had from those who had worked closely with
him, Scharfeld came to grips with the Budenz agenda, without knowing
who had fingered Lillian as a Communist, and without being able to
confront these claims directly:

> Although it now appears from statements that the Board members,
> as well as Mr. Sipes, have made here that the Board has information of
> Miss Hellman's alleged Communist affiliations as far back as 1944,
> such information was never communicated to officials at the [Mos-
> cow] Embassy. In fact, the steps taken by our government to faciliate
> Miss Hellman's movement and activities would seem to indicate the
> exact opposite. This is true as late as 1951, when Miss Hellman
> obtained a passport to travel to Europe despite the well recognized
> policy of the Department not to issue a Passport to anyone suspected
> of Communist affiliations or membership in the Communist Party.
>
> It must be assumed, therefore, that responsible persons in the
> Department didn't give credence to the reports and statements which
> the Board now indicates were in the files of the Department. Under the
> circumstances, a reasonable person could reliably assume that Miss
> Hellman was not a member of the Communist Party, as she had
> informed Mr. Melby in 1945 and again in 1952. In any event, what-
> ever association there has been or had been since 1945 has been of the
> most casual character and, as you have heard Mr. Melby state under
> oath, has been discontinued and will be discontinued.
>
> The Board's inquiries further seem to be pointed at the fact that Mr.
> Melby's initial and supplemental reply to the interrogatories was not as
> completely in detail as his recent amended reply of May 19. . . . When
> Mr. Melby, in his initial reply, didn't discuss the intimate details of his
> relationship with Miss Hellman it was no more than his failure to
> understand that this was what the Board wanted. There is obviously a
> natural reluctance on the part of anyone to go into the fine details of
> personal relations, and particularly is that true when the relationship
> is between a man and a woman having a romantic affair. Moreover, as
> a layman, Mr. Melby didn't comprehend that the inquiry was intended

to encompass the minute details of that relationship. In trying to present his own case, I believe he was simply proving the old adage that one who represents himself, has a very foolish person for a client. . . .

Mr. Melby made perhaps his greatest mistake in not seeking legal assistance immediately upon the receipt of the Board's first interrogatory and certainly after getting the second. When he did seek such advice it took him many days and weeks to refresh his recollection by repeated questioning and examination on all phases of his life since 1944, and I think also prior to that time. By the time he prepared and submitted his amended interrogatory he had all facts assembled that it was humanly possible to piece together and these that have been given to you are as complete as they could possibly be made. . . .

What the members of the Board will now decide will determine the future life and career of a fine officer and whether our country can continue to derive the benefits of his efforts in a field where we are always in need of loyal, competent officers and public servants.

The hearing was concluded, the chairman announced that the record would be kept open several days for additional affidavits, and the witness was excused.

Scharfeld had labored in vain. The record was not complete yet; even had it been, the board's mind would not have changed.

Never see Lillian again? Impossible.

Joe Rauh's diary records that John and Lillian met in his office three days later, on 2 July.[2] Rauh wanted to see Lillian about possible future problems, and he thought he should also know the extent of Lillian's involvement in Melby's case. What he heard was disturbing. John's case was *nothing but* Lillian. Rauh no longer remembers what agitated him the most, but it was likely the assemblage of secret evidence against Lillian, the evidence that had so unsettled John. Rauh asked John whether he could see the transcript of John's first hearing; John consulted Scharfeld about this, and Scharfeld said no. Rauh never saw the transcript, but he got a description from John of what the State Department loyalty-security people thought about Lillian's "Communist" record. There seemed little that Lillian could do at the time.

John and Scharfeld were beginning to disagree on how to handle his case; the problem was whether to call Lillian as a witness in any future hearing. John was stunned by the picture of Lillian's clandestine Communism that the board accepted. This was not the Lillian he knew. As he explained his feelings in a later hearing: "My first instinctive reaction to the thing was, I'm in no position to prove or disprove these things but certainly anybody accused is entitled to an opportunity of denying them and explaining why they are wrong or refusing to explain, in which case there is a presumption that they may be true, which, even without thinking, evolved in my mind—at least give her a day in court on it."[3]

And in their conference with Rauh on 2 July, Lillian expressed strongly the desire to appear before John's board to answer their charges. She knew those charges to be false. She did not want them uncontradicted on the record—any record. There was still the chance that she might be called before McCarran's Internal Security Subcommittee, where she could not count on the skill of Joe Rauh, or the blundering of Congressman Wood, to get off scot-free. The Senate outfits were tougher, and she was convinced that anything in State Department files would be available to the senators too.

If John was distressed at the derogatory material about Lillian, Lillian herself was outraged. She knew she had not hosted a dinner for Gerhart Eisler; she had her secretary go over her engagements carefully for the period before 9 May 1949, and there was no record of such a dinner. She still did not remember ever meeting Eisler. As for being a close friend of his, as Donovan claimed, this was risible. Nor was the Budenz charge that she had organized front groups at Party behest any more plausible. (Neither did she know that Budenz was the informant peddling this canard.) None of her activities had ever been undertaken because of the Party. As to active Party membership in 1950, this was made up out of whole cloth. If she could confront these lies head on, surely she could at least convince the board that they were questionable.

Scharfeld, however, opposed having Lillian appear for John. He had discussed this possibility with Sipes. As Joe Volpe later put it, "Sipes scared hell out of Scharfeld" about putting Lillian on. The Donovan board's mind was made up; she was a Communist. Anything she said would only further damage John's position. This controversy continued as long as Scharfeld was John's lawyer.

There was another conference in Rauh's office between John and Lillian on 12 July. We cannot be sure what was discussed, but it was probably still the implications for Lillian of derogatory material in Donovan's possession. In *Scoundrel Time*, Lillian writes as if the HUAC hearings of 21 May 1952 ended her involvement in such things until the summer of 1953 when she was in Europe; this is not correct. Her several trips to Washington to meet

Rauh, and sometimes John also, indicated that her lawyer, at least, was worried about what might come next.

One event of summer 1952 eased Lillian's concerns somewhat; on 26 July, during the Democratic National Convention, Harriman withdrew from candidacy for the presidency. He later ran for, and was elected to, the governorship of New York; his political ambitions did not end in 1952. But worries about involving him in the inquisition became less immediate.

While it was clear that Donovan and the board had made up their minds that Lillian was a Communist of the most dangerous kind, perhaps they had not yet decided what to think of John. They called him in for a third hearing on 15 August.

The board, according to Donovan, had discovered certain discrepancies in John's statements. On 19 May, he had sent to the board an amended reply to his interrogatories, giving as the last date on which he had seen Lillian 5 April, in Philadelphia. When the board quizzed him about this on 26 June, he did not tell them about his subsequent meeting with her on 21 May, the date of her HUAC hearing. The board set out to investigate this discrepancy during the hearing of 15 August:

> Donovan: You saw her on May 21, but you didn't tell the Board about it. Now, that is a point that must be clarified because after all it is bound to create some doubt in minds of the Board.
> Melby: Yes, sir, I realize that and after I had seen the transcript I realized really how bad it looked when it was in cold print.[4]

John explained that he had not thought the brief meeting after her hearing to be of any consequence. She had merely told him that nothing had happened before HUAC that involved him or Harriman; of this John said, "To me, it was just simply passing by to make sure that there wasn't more trouble with things I didn't know about and might not know about otherwise." Sipes was not about to buy this.

> Sipes: When you saw her in April in Philadelphia, that was in connection with her prospective appearance before the House Un-American Activities Committee in which there was at least some worry or some concern that your name might be brought up one way or another, and that was really the reason for the meeting?
> Melby: This is correct.
> Sipes: That, of course, I can see is a matter of considerable consequence and something you would very definitely remember. The next meeting, as you have testified, was in Washington at which she

reported to you the outcome of this very serious matter in which
you might personally become involved. It seems to me that by the
same token, that would be of considerable consequence and a matter that would likely stick in one's mind. Here she is reporting to
you, so to speak, on the outcome of this matter in which you might
well have been involved.

Melby: Yes, I can understand that, but the completely negative result of
her own meeting with the House Committee, not only as far as I was
concerned, or Mr. Harriman, or anything else, I gather—but I just
dismissed the thing from my mind figuring I had been on the wrong
track all along there, and things that were of interest or of concern
to me were yet to come, and so I just blanked the thing out.[5]

The board did not believe him. Like a dog worrying a bone, the board
came back again and again to the chronology of their meetings:

Donovan: You see, Mr. Melby, the Board's concern arises from the fact
that your association with Miss Hellman is the crux of the whole
problem; therefore, the Board has been greatly concerned about
your lapse in memory and anything pertaining to Miss Hellman, and
it is difficult to understand why a meeting on May 21st could be
overlooked. That is what we are trying to clarify and the reason for
these questions because, as I say, it is obvious that apart from Miss
Hellman there isn't much to talk to you about.

Melby: May I say one other thing, Mr. Chairman, in connection with
this lapse of memory. At the time that I saw her in May, I was still
under the impression of my picture of her as I had known her, as
mutual friends had known her, namely, as a left wing liberal, or even
as a plain left wing without being a liberal, a circumstance which
would make her one kind of person. Had I known then what has
developed in these hearings, namely, the assertions of her secret
membership, assertions of her activities which are completely new
to me, I would not have then in May seen her even in my own defense . . . so I say seeing her in May and believing at that time that
she was one thing would make it much more easy for me just simply
to dismiss the meeting as of no consequence.[6]

Then it was back to her appearance before HUAC. Why did she need to
discuss that with John? What could he possibly tell her, other than what he
claimed he had—namely, that if his name, or Harriman's name came up,
she should tell the truth? This did not necessitate a meeting; he could have

told her that over the telephone in a matter of minutes. Or it could have been done by letter. And why was she so worried about appearing before HUAC?

> Melby: I don't know why she was.
>
> Donovan: Didn't she tell you?
>
> Melby: No, she said then—what she said was that she didn't know why she was being subpoenaed or what the material would be or what the reason was for calling her.
>
> Donovan: Do you think she was telling the truth when she said that, Mr. Melby?
>
> Melby: I thought so at that time; in the light of what has come out in the hearings I guess not. She must know herself what information is here.
>
> Donovan: With the information at my disposal, I can well understand why she was so concerned about being subpoenaed by the House Committee on Un-American Activities.[7]

Here is the master flaw on which the whole loyalty-security program broke down, the assumption contrary to the whole spirit of English common law: because of the overriding needs of state security, informants must be protected; and the rights of the accused—even of guilt by association—to confront the purveyor of charges face to face, to cross-examine that person, challenge his credibility, examine his accuracy record—these common law rights no longer count. Donovan, and the board, were invincibly seized of a "Truth"—that Lillian Hellman was a Communist and had done the Party's bidding to the detriment of the United States. John had willingly associated with Lillian. He would not now abase himself sufficiently, purge himself, swear categorically that he would never ever see her again. Thus he was guilty too.

The board did make some progress in breaking down John's faith in Lillian. He was beginning to accept their "Truth," even to the extent of deploring her refusal to tell HUAC everything they wanted for *their* degradation ceremony.

John's account of the advice he gave her about what to say before HUAC reflects these misgivings:

> Sipes: You are familiar, I take it, Mr. Melby, with the offense known as suborning perjury. Did it enter your mind that Miss Hellman might get herself involved in such a matter as that?
>
> Melby: What is suborning perjury?

Sipes: Inducing someone else to perjure himself. I am wondering if you
were familiar with such an offense as that. Were you on guard
against anything of that sort?

Melby: Certainly, and if she had asked me what she should do I would
have told her to tell the truth on everyone, but she didn't ask me
about anybody but myself. If she had asked me if she should name
the people with whom she had been associated in 1939, I would
have said "yes." As it turned out, she did not do so and was obviously reluctant at that time.[8]

The next line of questioning concerned John's efforts to keep his superior, Ambassador Cowen, informed about his dealings with Lillian and the
board. Donovan now wanted him to repeat exactly what he had told Cowen
about the trip to Philadelphia and about his meeting Lillian after her HUAC
appearance. This took up half an hour. The questions were endless: How
had they arranged the meeting? Had he phoned her beforehand? What
precisely (again) had he told Cowen? When had he told Cowen? Did he put
it to Cowen in such a fashion as to obtain Cowen's clearance to go, or was he
just casually mentioning it? What did Cowen respond? How did Cowen
react when told afterward about the meetings? When did Cowen leave
Washington for his new post in Brussels? Did John report to Cowen on the
21 May meeting before his departure? Did Cowen know about this board's
charges against John before giving him clearance to see Lillian in Philadelphia? How could Cowen have known about the charges since John hadn't
received them until after he had left for Philadelphia? (John's answer: "Well,
the word 'charges' is a loose use of the word. He knew of the interrogatory
and my answers to it and where the matter stood.")

Then came the axe. The Board had corresponded with Cowen, who did
not remember clearing the Philadelphia trip with John. Moreover, Cowen
had left the country on 21 May and could not have been consulted in
advance about the meeting at the Shoreham on that date. The probing
continued:

Sipes: The Board is left with considerable difficulty to understand your
testimony that you cleared, or that you informed at least, Ambassador Cowen about your contact at the Shoreham on May 21st . . .
when Ambassador Cowen had already left Washington, D.C. and
had left the United States on May 21st.

Melby: I don't remember the details of telling him except that I know I
told him because my relationship with Mr. Cowen was such that I
would never do anything without his knowing of it. It may be on

this one particular item that I wrote to him of it afterwards. As I say, that whole incident was passed off as something of no consequence. . . .

Donovan: Are you sure, Mr. Melby, you brought it to his attention in such a way that it was not just a casual mention of something you were going to do? I mean, you said you deliberately told him.

Melby: Absolutely. . . .

Sipes: You told us he said in so many words, "Sure, go ahead."

Melby: Yes, that is correct.

Sipes: Do you think he'd likely forget something like that? You said he knew about Lillian Hellman by reputation, at least, he knew who she was, etc. He knew you were at least the subject of interrogation by this Board, and here you are actually consulting with him as to whether you should see her in Philadelphia because of this sub-poena, etc. Do you think that is the kind of thing Ambassador Cowen would likely forget?

Melby: He could, yes.[9]

There was more; it was wearisome. Scharfeld sensed immediately that the matters of notifying Cowen, and his response, were of great moment to the board. He asked if the statement the board had from Cowen could be put in the record so that he and John would know precisely how the matter had been put to Cowen. This request Donovan declined. Scharfeld could get his own statement from Cowen; the Board's evidence was not to be released.

There followed a series of questions by Sipes about how often, where, and under what conditions John saw Lillian during the summer of 1945. Nothing new came out. He then moved to 1949, 1950, 1951—did the board have *all* the contacts? Was it lunch or dinner? Who initiated the meeting? Who made the phone calls? Was there one, or two, phone calls in 1949? How many visits to Pleasantville in 1950? Why had he seen her in New York so soon after visiting the farm? How had he arranged to visit her—by letter or telephone?[10]

But it was not yet over. Sipes went back to John's statement that he initially thought the significant matter in his hearing would be China and hence had downplayed the Hellman connection.

Sipes: You say there were a number of questions about China, and you didn't think [Hellman] was the primary matter. The first question in the interrogatory was devoted to Miss Hellman, was it not?

Melby: Yes.

Sipes: And of course, the second interrogatory was devoted to Miss Hellman.

Melby: Yes.

Sipes: . . . [in your interrogatory] you mention a telephone call from New York concerning a passport matter, and that in July of 1951 you saw her for a few minutes concerning this passport matter. Now, you had mentioned in your first interrogatory at page A-10 only the telephone call about the passport after she had obtained it. You didn't tell us about the telephone call in advance of the passport matter, but I am wondering, Mr. Melby, what was the necessity for her to see you in July of 1951. I would assume that you told her what, in her telephone call from New York, was her recourse about passport matters. Why was it necessary for you to see her personally in July 1951?

Melby: There was no particular necessity for it. She just said that she had come to town on that, and asked could I stop by her hotel for a minute.[11]

Looking back from the vantage point of the 1980s, when the pursuit of heretics is no longer of such cosmic importance as it was in 1952, it is hard to understand the picayune detail this board insisted on. It is even harder to understand why they felt that John should have known, by 1949, that this prominent playwright—close friend of such prominent families as the Lovetts, Harrimans, and Herters—was anathema to any right-thinking government servant. Donovan again:

Donovan: Mr. Melby, another point that has caused the Board some concern in this connection is this: After it was made clear to you that we were very much interested in Miss Hellman, we find it very difficult to understand why you did not take the trouble to inform yourself about her. There is plenty of material available, and it seems to me, and I think to the other members of the Board, that you should have had ample warning, certainly by 1949, as to what Miss Hellman was, or is.

Melby: Not by 1949, not the nature of the information you have here. I was abroad during that time. I was abroad until 1949. I had no way of hearing anything about her at all, not anything about her activities. Once I was back here, 1949 to 1950, I had no personal interest or personal reason for going into the matter, because I had only the most casual kind of association. I had never heard anyone refer to her, the people who knew her, in terms other than the picture that I

had had of her. In fact, I remember one conversation on the problem of the liberal in American society who, from the best of motives,
has been made a tool of Communist activities and Communist propaganda, unwittingly so, and I remember Mr. Bohlen in this connection citing Miss Hellman as a good illustration of that, and the need
for those of us who know something about this Communist business
to do something to make them see the nature of the Communist
conspiracy.[12]

Donovan seized that opening to once again put into the record the secret
testimony of Louis Budenz: that Lillian received "orders from high Communist officials" to initiate Communist-front organizations. After that, he
threw in the claim that in June 1938 she had attended the Tenth National
Congress of the Communist party in New York. Then Donovan's conclusion: "These two facts alone explain our concern. There are a great many
people who think Miss Hellman has never left the Communist Party, and
the Board is confronted with a very difficult problem. The record speaks for
itself—your continued association with her."[13]

The record also shows that under this pounding, John's answers were
confused, contradictory, and incomplete. Swihart, who had scored few
points in the inquisition up to now, took a stab at unnerving the victim: "At
page A-43, you state that in February or early March, 1952, Miss Hellman
wrote you that she had been subpoenaed to appear before the House Un-
American Activities Committee, and that you replied, et cetera. Now, at
page B-74, you indicate there that she telephoned you that she wanted to
see you about this matter. Now, which was it, telephone, letter, or both?
Take as much time as you like, Mr. Melby."[14]

Indeed, take as much time as you like. And if you sort out your recollections on this one, the inquisitors will come up with another dozen events
on which you may not have perfect recall, or on which you may have
changed your story as the enormity of your one-time lover's seedy past is
displayed to you. And if you do not crawl before us in submission, we will
cast you into disgrace.

But what if the victim makes no mistakes? What if he turns on his former
amorous associate, condemns her with even greater fervor than the inquisitors, swears on a stack of Bibles never to see or talk to her again? Will he
then be restored to the ranks of the pure, as were those who groveled
before HUAC?

At the end of this day of grilling, John's composure was shattered.
Donovan ended the proceedings with the bottom-line question:

Donovan: In your statement, in the statements of the amended interrogatory, the Board has felt some concern that you were defending or explaining away Miss Hellman, which, of course, it is your privilege to do, but frankly, with the information we have, we find it very difficult to accept your interpretation of Miss Hellman's political views, her activities, and so forth. These just don't fit in with the picture. Would you care to comment on that again?

John gave in to the pressure:

Melby: Yes. I was not in any sense attempting or trying to defend her. I was only defending myself and the association, in the sense of trying to explain my understanding at that time of what her views and activities were. I never had any evidence or suggestion during that period of disloyalty to the United States.

Granted that I disagreed with some of her political views. They were never expressed to me, nor did they come to me from other people in terms that would lead me to believe that she would put the interests of someone else ahead of the United States. That opinion of mine seemed, in my mind, to be confirmed in that it was the opinion of other people of known reliability, known reputation, who shared the same view that I had. Had I had any, the slightest, suggestion, to say nothing of knowledge, of this kind of activity and views that have come out here, the association would have been discontinued permanently, automatically, and right then and there.[15]

So the board had won. John was converted to the government's view of Lillian as subversive, as someone with whom a foreign service officer *could not* associate—and keep his job. Scharfeld obtained permission to enter further information from Ambassador Cowen, and the hearing adjourned.

Security Risk

Adlai Stevenson was selected by the Democrats as their standard-bearer for the 1952 presidential election. In the climate of the time, it was not a good choice. Stevenson had given testimony in the Hiss trial, asserting that Hiss's reputation was good. While Stevenson was governor of Illinois, the legislature passed the Broyles Bill, requiring loyalty oaths of public employees and making it a felony to belong to subversive organizations. Stevenson vetoed the bill, asserting that "the whole notion of loyalty inquisitions is a national characteristic of the police state, not of democracy." This immediately put the McCarthyites on notice; the slogan "K_1C_2" (Korea, Communism, and Corruption) filled the Republican need for anti-Stevenson rhetoric superbly.

Dwight Eisenhower emerged triumphant from the Republican convention. This was a brilliant choice, for political purposes; Ike was not as conservative as the Asia-first Republicans wished, and he was much too Eurocentric. But where else could they get a leader with the ethos and charisma Ike radiated? The convention offered a foretaste of things to come; McCarthy addressed the gathering on the second night. His followers created pandemonium, snake-dancing with placards in red reading "Hiss," "Lattimore," and "Acheson." McCarthy's speech was less incendiary than usual, but his followers didn't mind; they did, after all, want to win, and a certain decorum was called for.

With Ike at the top of the ticket, the second spot had to go to a red-baiter. It was Nixon. Lillian usually expostulated "Nixon" in the same breath with "McCarthy," and at the time, there was some justification for this. In *Scoundrel Time*, she asserts, of the writers and editors of *Partisan Review* and *Commentary*, that "their Cold War anti-Communism was perverted, possibly against their wishes, into the Vietnam War and then into the reign of Nixon, their unwanted but inevitable leader."[1] It is hard to see this as a perversion. The Nixon of the 1950s *was* a McCarthyite.

But Eisenhower was in control. The salient question was how he would behave. Ike was known to despise McCarthy, but such was that worthy's power that Ike hesitated to cross him. The paradigmatic event of the campaign gave little comfort to moderates and government employees.

It happened in Wisconsin. Ike wanted to avoid speaking in Wisconsin, where he knew he would be obliged to appear side by side with McCarthy (as he had been forced to do with the equally loathesome William Jenner in Indiana) and would be forced to endorse McCarthy; or, his advisers believed, endanger a Republican victory in that state.[2] The campaign managers, however, scheduled Ike for a major speech in Milwaukee. At the suggestion of Arthur Hays Sulzberger, publisher of the *New York Times*, Ike included in the speech he prepared for Milwaukee a strong endorsement of General Marshall. McCarthy had said that Marshall was a traitor.

There was furious argument about the Marshall endorsement as Ike's campaign train rolled toward Milwaukee. Wisconsin Governor Walter Kohler wanted the Marshall paragraph deleted, as did several Eisenhower aides; Ike fumed, sweated, and agreed. The mimeographed text, with the Marshall paragraph included, had already been released to the press; thus when Ike gave the speech without the Marshall reference, McCarthy (falsely) claimed credit for its deletion. This skirmish was front-page news; McCarthy's clout appeared unassailable. Eisenhower looked to be the appeaser.

McCarthy campaigned widely in 1952, always including his scurrilous attacks on Democrats as soft on Communism. The high point of his rhetoric was a television address from Chicago on 27 October. It included the usual quota of falsehoods, such as that the *Daily Worker* backed Stevenson. What went down in history, however, was McCarthy's malevolent reference to "Alger—I mean Adlai," which, in case some dimwit missed it the first time, he said twice.[3] It was an ugly campaign, with ominous portent for John and others who had served under the Democrats.

Despite the firm injunction from his board that he have nothing whatsoever to do with Lillian, John saw her again on 22 September 1952. Rauh called her down once more. All we know about this meeting is from a later hearing before John's board:

> Sipes: What was the nature of the meeting in Rauh's office on September 22? I don't believe you dilated on that one as yet.
> Melby: It was purely and simply, in so far as the time I was there, to find out if there had been any developments, any decisions, if there

would be any further activity in it where she was particularly
concerned. . . .

Volpe: How long were you there, Mr. Melby, at Mr. Rauh's office?

Melby: Oh, a half or three-quarters of an hour, if I remember.

Sipes: Is that the extent of your seeing her or having any contact on
September 22?

Melby: Yes.[4]

John, still wondering if it would be desirable to have Lillian testify so the
board could see that she was not a wild-eyed radical, argued fruitlessly with
Scharfeld. Scharfeld's position was that the ground rules had been established firmly; the board was obliged to accept FBI files and would not
admit testimony tending to discredit them. But one avenue Scharfeld did
want to explore: getting Cowen to give evidence that John had kept him
informed. In late October, Cowen had occasion to come to Washington.
Accordingly the board met again on 31 October, Cowen being the only
order of business.

His opinion of John had lost none of its glow:

Cowen: . . . Mr. Melby had my complete confidence, and I regarded
him as an exceptionally competent Departmental officer, and that
was the reason for my asking that he be assigned to me when I came
back to the Department last year. And I had also asked or discussed
with the Department the possibility of his coming to Brussels with
me. . . . From the security standpoint, I have never had any reason
to doubt Mr. Melby's complete integrity, and on the contrary, I have
had many reasons to have complete confidence in him.[5]

Then the questioning turned to whether John had consulted and informed Cowen about seeing Lillian on the two occasions in dispute. The
board's information on this had come from a security officer of the Paris
Embassy, who went to Brussels to talk to Cowen and to Jameson Parker,
Cowen's assistant. As Scharfeld and John suspected, this officer had not got
things quite clear. In regard to the Philadelphia meeting, the questioning
went:

Scharfeld: Do you have trust and confidence in Mr. Melby at the
present time?

Cowen: Yes, I do. I am disturbed about these matters you are talking
about now, the trip to Philadelphia. I am disturbed because I don't
recall it. And when I was here in the Department two or three days
ago, Mr. Melby came to see me. He was very insistent that he had

told me of his April trip and of his purpose in seeing Miss Hellman. I still don't remember his having done so.

Scharfeld: Well, would you say the fact that you do not recollect it under the conditions that you were working at the time would indicate that he had not told you?

Cowen: No, I wouldn't say that at all. I am only sorry that I don't remember it. . . .

Swihart: Mr. Ambassador, you said at one point that Mr. Melby, at the outset, did not feel this Hellman thing was perhaps of much importance.

Cowen: I didn't say the Hellman thing, I said the whole matter.

Swihart: I'm sorry. I was going to say, he did talk a great deal to you about it?

Cowen: Oh yes.

Swihart: I was just wondering about the consistency.

Cowen: He regarded her as, sort of a misguided liberal, I would say. I asked him pointedly if he thought she was a Communist. He said, "Definitely not. It's impossible." . . . I will be very glad to read to the Board, if you like, what Mr. Melby had to say in his letter [to Cowen in Brussels].

Donovan: That has not been available to the Board, and it might be pertinent, if you care to read it, Mr. Ambassador.

Cowen: I will read what is pertinent. This is a letter from Mr. Melby to me, dated August 18:

"Somewhere along the line, something seems to have gotten off track. Just how serious it is, I do not know, but I fear the worst. The session last Friday was about as rough as anything I have been through, consisting, as it did, of what seemed to me to be picking on small inconsistencies. It may be that this was done as a test of credibility. If so, I doubt if I came out very well. Every small point was sooner or later blown up into something of a major issue. What really seemed to interest them most was the part concerning you.

In my testimony of last June 26th, I referred to a trip to Philadelphia, following a speaking engagement in Bloomington. I was in Philadelphia April 4 and 5, the primary purpose of the trip being two speeches I was making before the World Affairs Council. Incident to this trip, I twice saw Lillian at her request, and in connection with her forthcoming subpoenaed appearance before the House Committee. In answer to a question, I told the Board you had previously been aware of this trip, and had raised no objection—In fact, I seem to recall that you wanted to go along with me. I am, incidentally, enclosing that part of the transcript which refers to this incident.

Last Friday, the Board reverted to this incident, and particularly your awareness of it. They indicated considerable scepticism on my version, despite my insistence that I very clearly remembered the conversation, which I do. As a final shot in this incident, the Board indicated that it had wholly reliable information that you never knew anything about it. All efforts on our part to find out just why they were so sure, and how they allegedly knew this, were unavailing. Certainly there was an implication they had gotten it from you, but they never admitted it, nor if so, in what form or context. It is all very puzzling. Since we do not really know what they are driving at, we are holding the hearing open until we can get something from you. As soon as we get the transcript of the Friday hearing, we will send you pertinent parts of it, along with a series of questions.

The ominous note was the Board's attitude that we could do this if we wished, but they already knew as much as they thought they needed to know. I suppose this can be read either as indicating disinterest, or that they have already made up their minds. By this time, I am so confused that I doubt if I could correctly give you the time of day."

That is the end of the letter.[6]

It was a mistake to read it. The board's feathers were considerably ruffled. At the time of the previous hearing, the board had depended on the report of the Paris security officer, which turned out to be wrong in three respects. And here John was revealed accusing the board of nitpicking, of having a closed mind, of deciding on insufficient evidence. Cowen no doubt meant the best for John; but despite his positive comments about John's integrity, the overall impact of his appearance was to alienate the board.

Cowen seemed to sense that what he read from John's letter had not set well, and he tried to recover by again emphasizing that he frequently tuned out people who were talking to him while he was busy, and that Jameson Parker did relay many messages to him from John, and vice versa. *He trusted John implicitly*, he said. The board did not.

Scharfeld reported to John what had transpired at the hearing. It was a gloomy report. One ray of light appeared. Two days before the Cowen hearing, Brad Connors, one of Acheson's assistants, came to see John. The secretary of state, said Connors, heard that the board was going to render an adverse report. Acheson, however, who remembered John's contribution to Southeast Asian affairs with gratitude, disagreed with the board. John was to appeal and, as Acheson had done with Ed Clubb, he would reverse the board. There was only one problem with this; if the Republicans swept the elections, Acheson's reversal could not be made to stick.

As predicted by Acheson, on 3 November 1952, John received a notice of suspension from duty, on the grounds that he was a security risk. While this was anticipated, it still hurt to see it in cold print. With his record, his devotion to the cause, his brilliance in planning and carrying out Cold War strategy—now to be unfit for service. It was a crushing blow.

Eisenhower was elected president the next day. Statistically, McCarthy-ites could take little comfort. Joe ran in Wisconsin and came in last among the six Republican statewide candidates. Several of McCarthy's strongest supporters in the Senate were defeated. But the Republicans won a Senate majority; McCarthy could look forward to a significant chairmanship.

What mattered to John and Lillian was their perception of a coming escalation of the inquisition. John's immediate move was to get a new lawyer. Scharfeld must have misread the board; Cowen's appearance had not saved him. Perhaps now he needed someone with experience in loy-alty-security practice. The someone he went to was Joseph Volpe, Jr., who had spent many years as deputy general counsel and then general counsel to the Atomic Energy Commission (AEC).[7] Volpe had handled the AEC's 1947 investigation of the loyalty-security of J. Robert Oppenheimer; at the time John approached him, Volpe was representing Oppenheimer in secu-rity matters.

Volpe had learned the hard way that FBI files were untrustworthy. When he was with the AEC, it did not accept the testimony of confidential informants without careful investigation. Many of the informants whose charges wound up in FBI files were neighbors who bore a grudge, or who exaggerated their charges to enhance their importance to the FBI. In many cases, Volpe and his AEC colleagues had forced the FBI to produce an informant, and, under cross-examination, the charge was found to be baseless. Volpe had seen witnesses under oath in AEC proceedings explic-itly repudiate statements that the FBI reported them as making. Had Volpe been able to compel the State Department to produce the informants who so blackened Lillian's name, the outcome of the Melby case might have been different; but the system did not permit this.

Volpe not only knew the fallibilities of loyalty-security witnesses, he had another advantage: Sipes had also worked for AEC, and they knew each other. Volpe was insistent that Lillian be brought in to testify before John's board. It was clear to Volpe, after reading the transcripts of John's hearings, that there were only two ways John could possibly get the negative decision reversed: John could repudiate Lillian totally—grovel as did so many of the Hollywood witnesses before HUAC and explain away his association with Lillian as nothing more than sheer physical attraction; or he and John could attempt to convince the board that the FBI reports were false and that Lillian was not the dangerous person anonymous informants had made her out to be. The first course was clearly out; John would not countenance it. Somehow, they had to change the board's picture of Lillian Hellman. They also had to deal with John's failure to inform the board with alacrity every single time he saw Lillian; this clearly agitated Donovan and Sipes greatly.

For much of November, Volpe studied the transcripts, talked to John, and prepared his case. On 1 December 1952, he saw Walter Scott, assistant to the deputy under secretary of state, to request that the case be reopened. Scott told him that the findings in the case were under review and that action by the deputy under secretary would be announced shortly. So it was, the next day. The deputy under secretary upheld the board's decision. The Secretary had the last word, but at that stage, John was to be fired.

December was an ominous month. McCarthy was bragging around the country about how the skunks were now really going to be cleaned out of government. Against the advice of President Truman, Attorney General James P. McGranery brought Lattimore before a federal grand jury in Washington and, on 16 December, obtained a seven-count indictment for perjury. Big headlines. Another Hiss case. Roy Cohn's runaway grand jury in New York issued a presentment claiming that the United Nations was honeycombed with disloyal U.S. employees and that Department of Justice officials were covering up for them. The House Committee on Tax-Exempt Foundations had Dean Rusk on the carpet to explain why so many pinkos got foundation grants. Rabbi Benjamin Schultz presided at a luncheon in McCarthy's honor, hosted by the Joint Committee Against Communism. McCarthy spoke, claiming that the reds were already trying to infiltrate the Eisenhower administration. The Civil Service Loyalty Review Board found that there was reasonable doubt as to the loyalty of John Carter Vincent, and that much-investigated diplomat was again called home. Lauchlin Currie, prominent aide in Roosevelt's wartime White House, was brought back from Colombia, where he had emigrated, to appear before the Lattimore grand jury. Budenz appeared before the House Committee on Tax-Exempt Foundations, naming philosopher Corliss Lamont, of Columbia University, and editor Carey McWilliams as Communists. The new McCarran-Walter Immigration Act went into effect on 24 December, and the first ship to dock in New York after that, the French liner *Liberté*, was forced to keep 271 sailors on board, without shore leave over Christmas, because they refused to answer questions about their politics as required by the law. Dozens of similar Cold War headlines dominated the news.

Lillian described many of the events of the summer and fall of 1952 in *Scoundrel Time*. She told of her triumphal narration of *Regina*—Marc Blitzstein's opera based on *The Little Foxes*—of leaving the farm, of the ridiculous dinner with Henry and Ilo Wallace, of her "affair" with a rejected suitor of her youth. She did not tell of her continued involvement with John's struggle and the additional conferences in Washington. Nor was it completely clear that she herself was through with the inquisition. Since she was blacklisted, there was nothing for her to do in Hollywood. Her state of mind precluded generating a theme for a new play, which seemed to be the only outlet for her.

Kermit Bloomgarden came to her rescue. Why not revive *The Children's Hour*? The idea took hold; as Richard Moody put it, she was "in need of some income and desperate to raise her voice against the outrages of HUAC and McCarthy."[8] *Children's Hour* had as its theme the evil done by girlish gossip; in 1952, audiences would easily recognize this evil as akin to that of McCarthyite gossip. The play opened at the Coronet on 18 December and ran for 189 performances.

The success of *Children's Hour* was some, but not much, consolation for the venom she knew to be lurking in her government files.

By the end of December, Volpe was in command of the tangled history of John's loyalty-security hearings. He wanted to talk to Lillian, to see what kind of impression she might make if she were to testify, and to ask directly what her connections with so many left-wing organizations had been. Rauh accordingly called her to come to Washington, and on 27 December, Rauh, Lillian, and Volpe met in Rauh's office. At some point in the discussion, John's presence was desired; Volpe called John and he came to Rauh's office, where he stayed for a short time.

As Volpe later described the 27 December conference,

> Miss Hellman's point at that time was that she would be willing to appear providing she was given an opportunity to testify to all matters that concerned her or involved her activities or political affiliations. I was in no position at the time to assure Miss Hellman of anything with respect to her testimony. And for that reason this gave rise in her mind to some questions about whether she would be willing to appear or

would be willing to provide an affidavit. There was also the matter of Pleasantville and Philadelphia which, for obvious reasons, Miss Hellman found extremely distasteful to discuss. Mr. Rauh made clear at that time it would probably not be necessary to discuss Pleasantville and Philadelphia except to the extent we would want her testimony as to whether or not there were any other occasions when the same thing happened, these two episodes would be taken care of by Mr. Melby's testimony and she would not be subjected to any embarrassment or humiliation if she could appear.[9]

The 27 December conference was not conclusive. Lillian and Rauh met again the next morning. Lillian was still uneasy about what she would be allowed to say if she were to appear, and she wanted to talk to John about it. Rauh called Volpe again to ask if John could come over to Rauh's office, and Volpe agreed. The three of them met for an hour or so; Lillian seemed amenable to giving testimony.

Then John made a big mistake. Lillian was ready to fly back to New York. It seemed rude to put her in a cab to go catch her plane. John drove her to the airport. When this event came out in a later hearing, some member of the board underlined with a heavy black marker the statement in the transcript "I drove her out the airport" and put an exclamation mark in the margin opposite.[10]

When Volpe requested formally on 8 December that an appeals board be appointed in the Melby case, there were still fifty-two days of Acheson's tenure left. The lame-duck Truman administration, however, had many things to deal with other than the fate of a little-known, albeit brilliant, Class II Foreign Service officer. And clearing from the record fraudulent accusations against a female playwright was hardly on the agenda either. It was 23 January 1953, three days after Eisenhower took office, before an appeals board was constituted and functioning.

First Appeal

In hindsight, one might think that John Melby should have expected no quarter from an Eisenhower administration. Ike had shown during the campaign that his personal scorn for McCarthy would yield to political expediency. And what political expedient was more important, in early 1953, than fulfilling a campaign pledge to get the pro-Communists (which included those who *associated* with Communists) out of government?

One might also say that appeasing McCarthy was a political expedient of the first rank. Philip M. Stern's foreword to the transcript of the Oppenheimer hearings captures accurately how powerful this senator was:

> It is difficult, in retrospect, even for those who lived through it, fully to recapture the fear this powerful demagogue, Joseph McCarthy, aroused, and not merely among the unsophisticated. Men of strength, good sense, and self-respect suddenly found themselves accepting McCarthy's frame of reference and his "guilt by association" line of argument. As an example of the lengths to which this went, Democratic senators, searching for a lawyer to serve as counsel for their investigation of the so-called "Army-McCarthy" controversy, turned down a distinguished Pittsburgh attorney on the ground that his *firm* (although not he personally) represented Alcoa, which in turn had sponsored a television program critical of Senator McCarthy. [Italics in original.][1]

But Eisenhower was a unique president. After a lifetime in the military, Ike came to the White House with a firm commitment to a hierarchical chain of command in administration. He believed that one delegates authority and does not interfere with subordinates' decisions unless there is strong reason. If a subordinate insisted on forcing his superior to make a choice, fine; Ike wanted the potential choices, and the subordinate's evaluation of them, laid out clearly in a one- or two-page memo. Ike's cabinet was to have real power.

The subordinate who ultimately controlled John's fate was Secretary John Foster Dulles. If ever there were a secretary of state who should approve of and reward John's stellar contribution to opposing the Communists in Southeast Asia, it was Dulles. Like Nixon, Dulles could not be outflanked on the right. He had none of the liabilities of his predecessor. Many expected that he would use his righteous anti-Communism to slap down the Wisconsin demagogue. Leonard Mosely notes in his book *Dulles*:

> There was no doubt that McCarthy had responded to the mood of the country with his wild charges of treachery and deceit. A large portion of the population thought he was right. A minority thought he was a cheat and a liar and a traducer of reputations, but were afraid to say so.
>
> One would have thought, however, that the exception would have been John Foster Dulles. As a pillar of the Church and an upstanding believer in Christian charity, a man of impeccable morals with a life-long reputation as an unsullied Republican and supporter of the American Way of Life, he seemed the ideal crusader capable of riding out and puncturing the gibbering monster and demonstrating that he was nothing but a bag of wind.[2]

Thus it seemed plausible on 26 January 1953, when Volpe took the Melby case to the Department of State Appeals Board, that guilt by association might yet be ruled out, and justice prevail.

The board constituted to hear the Melby appeal consisted of Ambassador Lowell C. Pinkerton (chairman), Thomas C. Mann, and Richard F. Cook. These were thoroughly conventional diplomats. Pinkerton and Cook seemed willing to listen to reasons why the record so far was incomplete and why the case should be returned to the Donovan board for additional hearings. Mann was quite different. As he revealed himself in this hearing, he was not only ultraconservative, but was also running scared before the McCarthyite assault on the Department of State. Mann could not understand why an officer of the Department of State would spend any time at all in the company of "a person whose loyalty to the United States was suspect." Sexual attraction he could understand; anything other than that had to indicate either disloyalty or carelessness on Melby's part. Mann gave John a very hard time indeed during this hearing.

There were basically two issues Volpe wanted to raise with the Appeals Board. The most important issue was really a fundamental challenge to the whole basis of the loyalty-security procedure: Was the Board obligated to be sure of its evaluation of Lillian Hellman as a dangerous Communist? On the face of it, this issue had been settled by the terms of the appeal hearing. As Pinkerton wrote in a letter to the lower board on 23 January 1953, "Counsel for Mr. Melby indicated that he wished to introduce evidence concerning the loyalties and political affiliations of Miss Hellman. Mr. Volpe's request that this issue be heard by the Loyalty Security Board is denied." Volpe knew that this request was the guts of the matter. He knew that, if only by indirection, the board had to be forced to modify its picture of Lillian as a dangerous subversive.

Here the crucial role of the counsel to the boards, John Sipes, becomes clear. He was the expert guiding the board members in the rules of the game. His guidance, in this case, was inimical to Melby.

Sipes came into the State Department in August 1950, when the Hiss conviction, McCarthy's onslaught, and the outbreak of war in Korea made the need for a tough security counsel pressing. State, Sipes's new client, needed to produce credible evidence of cracking down on loyalty and security risks. The more people fired, the better Sipes and his superiors would look. The man Sipes worked for, however, General Conrad Snow, chairman of the State Department Loyalty-Security Board, had a low key approach to problems of employee clearance. Snow's forte was inducing questionable employees to resign, as he put it, "due to administrative pressure."[3] This kept disloyal and risky employees out of the Department; there was no other Hiss case, nor any proven subversive. But Snow's technique produced no statistics to advertise how State was cleaning out the Commies.

Even worse, these quiet removals of suspect employees did not show up as "cases" referred to the Civil Service Commission Loyalty Review Board. Other government departments, in contrast, flooded the Loyalty Review Board with cases. Thus when the ferocious Communist hunter Hiram Bingham, former Republican senator from Connecticut, took over as chairman of the Loyalty Review Board four months after Sipes began work for the State Department, Bingham found what seemed to him clear confirmation of McCarthy's charges: there wasn't any loyalty-security program in the Department. It hadn't fired anybody. The place was full of Alger Hisses.

It took Bingham only two months after he assumed office to come charging over to see what was going on in the State Department program. On 21 March 1951, Bingham met with General Snow, John Sipes sitting in, and delivered his charge: he "expressed dissatisfaction with the record of the Loyalty Security Board of the Department of State because according to the record the Loyalty Security Board had taken adverse action in no cases whatever from 1947 to 1951."[4]

Snow, taken aback, struggled to explain how his program had been effective despite the absence of countable "adverse actions." Perhaps he succeeded in convincing Bingham that all was safe at State, perhaps he didn't. The memo Snow wrote about their confrontation is upbeat and reassuring.[5] But Counsel Sipes got a clear message: the high brass now wanted quantifiable *results*. The appearance of toughness was more important than the reality. Six months later, when John Melby got his interrogatory and began his series of hearings, Sipes sounded like the typical "fire them all" security officer.

Sipes's guidance of John's hearing boards most significantly affected John's fate in the area of whether rebuttal of secret testimony was to be allowed. When Pinkerton denied Volpe's request to introduce evidence concerning Lillian's loyalties and political affiliations, the hand of John Sipes was at work. He must have misled Pinkerton; some hearing boards did allow persons charged with guilt by association to offer evidence that their associates were loyal citizens, and Sipes knew it.

On 20 and 21 October 1952, three and a half months before Melby's Appeals Board met, Joseph M. Franckenstein, an employee of the Office of Public Affairs of the High Commission in Germany (a State Department operation), was examined by a Loyalty-Security Board meeting in Bad Godesburg.[6] The heart of the case against Franckenstein, as against Melby, was guilt by association with an alleged Communist. In Franckenstein's case, this was his wife, Kay Boyle Franckenstein. Kay Boyle, like Lillian a well-known writer, had supported the Waldorf conference, signed an appeal of the Joint Anti-Fascist Refugee Committee, and was charged with Communist party membership by an unknown informant. (She later learned who this was: Louis Budenz.)

Sipes had to know that the Franckenstein Board, which was also set up by his office, had permitted Franckenstein's attorney, Benjamin Ferencz, to call several witnesses for Kay Boyle. These witnesses, and Boyle herself, were thoroughly cross-examined by the Board in Germany. The result was a unanimous verdict supporting Franckenstein's loyalty and security, *despite Ferencz's ignorance of the names of the informants against Boyle and Franckenstein, and his inability to examine them.*

The favorable result of the Franckenstein hearing did not stick. Franckenstein was fired under the guise of a reduction in force. He fought the firing but lost on appeal because of a nasty "Opinion of Security Counsel" written by Sipes and S. H. Lay.[7] Franckenstein then appeared before

Thomas Hennings's Senate Subcommittee on Constitutional Rights with a great deal of favorable publicity and obtained the support of Judge William Clark for a suit against the State Department; in 1957 Dulles reversed the negative security finding and reinstated him in government service.[8]

We do not of course know that the Melby board would have come to a different conclusion had it been similarly open-minded about hearing evidence on Lillian Hellman. Sipes was in direct control of the Melby board, and he preempted such a result, just as he later managed to engineer a reversal of the favorable finding on Franckenstein. But Volpe would have made a good case; the witnesses he wanted to present supporting Hellman's loyalty were top drawer.

At least Volpe's determination to confront the issue of Lillian's loyalty changed John Melby's outlook significantly. Under Scharfeld's guidance, John was required to accept the fact of the board's negative picture of Lillian without protest. Volpe was now encouraging protest. They both knew that the rules set by Pinkerton would not change; they both expected that the original board, if it heard an appeal, would not countenance a frontal assault on the FBI gossip. But with Volpe as his attorney, John could at least challenge and belittle this rigid and authoritarian procedure. And John was no longer impressed with the credibility of FBI evidence. Volpe convinced him that Lillian might never have been a card-carrying Communist, that the great vacuum cleaner in this case had sucked up a great deal of trash.

Volpe's technique in dealing with the official picture of Lillian was subtle and exquisitely timed. He did not raise the matter immediately; it came in first at page thirty-nine of the hearing before the Pinkerton board. Volpe was discussing the incompleteness of the record as it came from the lower board; Sipes wanted to clarify what he meant:

Sipes: When you say "some things that are not in this record," you mean Miss Hellman's testimony or merely instances and explanations of issues actually dealt with below?

Volpe: I mean, Mr. Sipes, Miss Hellman's testimony, for one thing. It seems to me that, in an important sense, is at the heart of this problem. What kind of a person is this? Is she the dangerous character that she has been portrayed to be in the hearings in this case? . . . Now, as I said before, I don't know what the truth is. I would be happy to repeat what I have learned in discussing the case with her, but I think the only appropriate way for getting at that problem is to hear her testimony and for the people in the Department who are going to have responsibility for passing judgment on her testimony to see it, question her, cross examine her on the things she is going to say. . . .

. . . I think what happened here is this: Mr. Scharfeld discussed the question of bringing Miss Hellman in as a witness. Mr. Sipes, as he has just stated, perhaps scared the living daylights out of Mr. Scharfeld, and it was for that reason that he decided that the only way to handle this case was to assume the things that were being said about Miss Hellman were true. Now, gentlemen, when I told Mr. Sipes that I had in mind calling Miss Hellman, he expressed some amazement. Fortunately or unfortunately, I have never been able to decide which, I have had some experience with these matters inside the government. I have read many of these reports. I have seen these references to reliable informants. I have some idea of the rather tricky nature of so-called derogatory information. . . . I don't think I need to sit here this morning and dwell at any length on the dangers involved in accepting as gospel, the statements or the charges of even so-called reliable informants. Now perhaps I don't have the sense Mr. Scharfeld has; perhaps it's this reason that I would barge in where angels fear to tread, but I have seen this sort of thing before. I don't know whether Miss Hellman has been a se-cret agent of the Communist Party, but I do know she is prepared to testify and by God, I know of no other way to get at the truth of an allegation or charge except to hear the testimony of the people who are involved. I wish it were possible, and I assume that Miss Hellman would wish it were possible, to call before this Board the people who made these charges.

Mann: Counsel, I would like to hear from you on the relevance of Miss Hellman's testimony to the issues in this hearing. Do you—is it your intention or expectation that you would prove she is a loyal American citizen, or are you proceeding on the theory that politics was not discussed in her associations, or some other theory? I'd like to know. I'd like you to explain the relevance to this hearing here. . . .

Volpe: . . . I would simply hope through her testimony to do two things. One of them quite modest: namely, to demonstrate to the Department that there was never any reason for Mr. Melby to sus-pect that Miss Hellman has been a dangerous person, a devious per-son, the conniving person that these allegations make her out to be. I would hope to do that not only through Miss Hellman's testimony, but through the testimony of other witnesses.

Mann: Excuse me, which other witnesses?

Volpe: Who have known Miss Hellman as Mr. Melby has known her.

Mann: Which other witnesses?

Volpe: Averell Harriman, Louis Kronenberger, Mrs. Christian Herter, people who have known her. People who are quite honorable, quite respectable, and have known Miss Hellman for years, have been entertained in her home, have spent weekends at her farm; but who, I'm sure, would never have continued this association had they any idea that she was a secret agent, or a secret member of the Communist Party.

Mann: Well, the second issue?

Volpe: The second is this. I hold no brief and I would make no particular effort, but there is at least a chance, it seems to me, that if Miss Hellman appears and testifies, through her testimony it might be possible to create at least a doubt that she has been the dangerous person that people say she has been. I'm not prepared to believe that what Mr. Sipes has said is that, no matter what Miss Hellman testifies to, nobody in this Department is prepared to believe her. I don't think he even intended to say that, I don't think he would ever have that in mind, and I think that all Mr. Sipes has intended to say is that it's going to be a tough hurdle for someone to jump—for Miss Hellman to jump—or anyone else to jump, if there is to be a denial, a refutation of the information that is available to the Department.

Sipes: Let me just clarify one thing. Counsel mentioned that I expressed, or showed, some amazement at the suggestion that he made in proposing to call Miss Hellman. I might say that such amazement stemmed not from the idea of Miss Hellman as a witness to testify as to what the association exactly was between herself and Mr. Melby, as to the contacts, or as to what they discussed, as to what the purposes were, and things of that kind; but rather from the thought of Miss Hellman as a witness in her own defense, and the thought that we, or that the Board below, might be put in the position of having to try out the accuracy or inaccuracy of information in its possession concerning Miss Hellman which, to me, seemed to be somewhat inappropriate inasmuch as this Board, or the Board below, neither one, are investigative bodies; and I think Counsel will understand that if we were in that position with respect to every person mentioned in proceedings of this kind, we would be in an endless process.

Volpe: Mr. Sipes, all I can say in answer to that is this: As long as we are going to have loyalty and security programs, . . . I don't think we can go to too much trouble in any case where the future of a man is concerned, and should it turn out that this case will depend upon a judgment of whether or not . . . Miss Hellman has been a dangerous person, if that decision should affect Mr. Melby's future, then I don't think there are any lengths that this Department could go to that are too great to establish the truth.

Sipes: Let me say I agree with you one hundred percent.

Volpe: Even to the point of calling witnesses. I hate to go into this but I think I need to make myself clear on it. For roughly eight years I was in the Atomic Energy Program, and this was a devilish problem for us; but, at the same time, there were some of us who felt that where a man's life and his reputation were at stake, and that is really what is at stake in these things, there wasn't too much that could be done to determine the truth. We asked the FBI in cases to produce the witnesses, and I would like to say right here and now, and you can verify my statement by checking with the FBI, in one case we can say thank God we got those witnesses before the Board because what they said to the FBI agents was not what they were prepared to say when they were under oath and subject to cross examination. And these were reported to be reliable informants.[9]

It was a valiant effort. Volpe exposed the inherent weaknesses of unidentified and unexamined informants. He even secured from the reluctant Sipes an acknowledgement that truth should be established in loyalty-security proceedings. But it was to no avail. Somebody's head had to roll. The FBI was a hallowed institution. The board was not going to be bothered, neither this one nor the original Donovan board. Lillian might testify, but they did not want to hear that she was a loyal citizen.

Volpe had, nonetheless, opened the door a crack. The inquisitors could not admit that they were closed to new evidence. Sipes protested that if the board were not satisfied with the evidence in its possession, it could ask the FBI for more. But there was no promise and no expectation. Underlinings and marginalia in the transcripts of this and other hearings show that the boards were contemptuous of claims that Lillian might be something other than what FBI files showed. The boards were, and would remain, invincibly ignorant.

While Volpe was preparing the appeal, he conferred several times with Sipes. Possibly because they were old friends from AEC days, Sipes told Volpe something he had not told Scharfeld: FBI surveillance revealed that John had spent the night in Lillian's room at the Barclay Hotel in Philadelphia on 5 April 1952. The Board had not yet confronted John with this.

John had maintained that his relationship with Lillian after 1945 had been purely platonic; the Barclay incident cast doubt on this claim. Because of this, and because of John's failure to identify and report every time he had seen Lillian, there was much doubt as to his candor with the board. Dealing with this doubt was almost as important to John's case as was Lillian's alleged Communism.

John and Lillian both regretted the reappearance of their former passion at Pleasantville and Philadelphia, and hoped that it need not be known to anyone. Volpe counseled against this strategy; he believed that complete candor was necessary. The two amorous incidents had been regrettable lapses; John had lied about them to protect Lillian and his wife-to-be from embarrassment, and the board could be made to understand this. What had happened did not make John a security risk. He had told Lillian no secrets, and there was no challenge from anyone to his professional discretion. John agreed that he should now tell the Appeals Board the whole story.

Volpe introduced this matter after a brief review of the times John had seen Lillian since his return from China:

> Volpe: . . . Now it was John Melby's testimony about this particular period that I think got him in hot water, and the next questions are how and why. The answer is this: Melby was trying to protect his wife. He was also motivated by the quite natural reluctance that any individual experiences when he is confronted with the problem of discussing a matter which is so very personal. He thought that what he had done had no real or important bearing on the inquiry that was being made by the Department into the question of his loyalty to the United States and eligibility for continued employment in the Foreign Service. It was quite a personal experience and it was all the more troublesome because it was an experience that was not as it had been during the period in 1945 when he thought he was in love with Miss Hellman and when there had even been discussion of marriage.
>
> When the hearing started in this case, Mrs. Melby was in ill health. She still is. Melby has been most anxious to spare her any further distress or any additional cause for emotional upset. He had looked upon this particular chapter as something he regretted very much and as something that he would in some way have to make up to his wife in their future relations. He did not realize or appreciate its relevance to this case until it was too late. . . . I believe we can

show that he was not motivated by any dishonorable or sinister purpose when he responded to the questions as he did. It would be our hope that a full explanation and amplification of the record would persuade the Department that Melby's behavior was at least understandable in the light of all the circumstances. Miss Hellman is most anxious to set the record straight. She respects and admires Melby and is distressed with the thought that she might be responsible for destroying his future in the only work he has known and the work he loves dearly. She told me that she regretted this recent chapter just as much as Melby did because it was clear that the close relationship which had once existed between her and Melby back in 1945 was gone. If Miss Hellman appears as a witness, she has assured me that she will answer any and all questions that the Department might want to ask her about her views or her actions. . . .

Mann: Counsel, I would like to ask another couple of questions, if I may. You mentioned that Mr. Melby, or at least you inferred, that Mr. Melby was somewhat reluctant to discuss his relations with Miss Hellman because he was trying to protect his wife. Now as I understand you to say he married his present wife in January 1951. Did you intend to infer that there were amorous relations between Mr. Melby and Miss Hellman after 1945?

Volpe: I did.

Mann: And that Mr. Melby's testimony in that respect was not correct at the original hearing?

Volpe: That is correct.

Sipes: On that same point, Mr. Mann, I believe there is testimony in the record that your wife knew about your trip to Philadelphia in April of 1952. Isn't that correct, Mr. Melby?

Melby: Yes.

Volpe: That is a correct statement. I have talked with Mrs. Melby about it. She has always known, she has known from the beginning, and she knew at the time these meetings took place that her husband was seeing Miss Hellman. . . . the crux of this problem is whether this silly, stupid indiscretion which really is at the bottom of the questions and no doubt arose as a result of his conduct in responding to questions, whether or not that is to be the reason for destroying this man's future. It has nothing to do with the loyalty, it has nothing to do with political activities, it has nothing to do with security. This is another reason why I hope the Board will hear Miss

Hellman's testimony. I don't know whether you would be in a position to judge where the truth lies with respect to these charges that
were made against her. But I would hope that you could find it possible to believe her testimony that never was there anything between
her and Melby that would give rise to any question of loyalty or security. I questioned Miss Hellman at length about that and he never
talked shop with her, she never asked him and I think before we are
through a good and sufficient argument could be made that she
should be believed on that score, and Melby should be believed on
that score, because you have the testimony of his colleagues who
have testified as to his discretion, honesty, integrity.[10]

Then Mann, with bulldog tenacity, picked up the question of why, after
1945, there should have been any association whatsoever between John
and Lillian.

Mann: What I'm interested to know is this: Would you testify on a
rehearing, that the principal reason you continued to have relations
with Miss Hellman after 1945 was because of this amorous attraction between you, or would you testify that that was only incidental?
Melby: That was purely incidental. Such relations as we have had, beginning with 1950, have been, well, what little there was, have been
just that of people who have been good friends and who casually see
each other, and there's been really very little of that since mid— or
the fall of 1951. The principal reason for the association has been
connected with this proceeding and that of, as I say, erstwhile
friends who still feel friendly to each other, having no reason not to
feel friendly to each other; whose paths haven't crossed, and whose
work is different.
Mann: Well, would you say after 1945 your relationship was predomi-
nately intellectual rather than the other, or—
Melby: Yes, I suppose intellectual and friendly, of people who have artistic and literary tastes in common and like those things. Just enjoy
each other's company socially when it comes about, but—
Pinkerton: In April, 1950, when you stayed at her house in New York,
that weekend was devoted to just talk, was it?
Melby: Yes, the theater, and I hadn't had—I'd been out of the country a
long time and I hadn't had much opportunity for theatre or things
like that, and that's all there was. . . .
Sipes: You have testified now, or have indicated that you would testify,

that there was casual or intermittent sexual relations after the 1945
period—after October 1945. Now, my question is—up until what
point did that go on?

Melby: Never after Philadelphia.

Mann: I have one other question: Was she attracted to you until what
time, in your opinion? I want to say this. I hesitate to ask these questions; it's just as embarrassing to me as it is to you, but our duty is to
find out why this relationship between you and Miss Hellman—
that's what we are trying to do—why she was attracted to you? Let
me put the question this way—after 1945?

Melby: I don't know.

Volpe: Mr. Mann, perhaps I can help on that. I have talked with Miss
Hellman about this aspect of the case and you can well imagine it
was most difficult. The story is simply this: That this would be Miss
Hellman's story if she were subjected to examination on this phase
of the case. They were in love, or at least thought they were in love
in 1945, when Melby left for China in October 1945. This was the
state of affairs between them. They were two people in love. While
he was in China letters started dropping off. . . . When he got back
to this country she had no intention of pursuing Melby; she was
content that he had met someone he was in love with; planned to
marry; she was aware of the rather unfortunate circumstances of his
first marriage and she wished nothing for Melby but happiness and
well-being for the future. At the same time, she admired him and respected him, and was fond of him as a person. When he went to
Pleasantville for a weekend, Miss Hellman's testimony would be that
there was no intention of having amorous relationships—it was just
two old, good friends getting together to enjoy some of the things
they had enjoyed before—talking about books, talk about plays, talk
about artistic things, as Mr. Melby has said. It happened—she said
she regretted it and Melby regretted it.

When he stopped off in New York in April, nothing happened.
They were going to be good friends, she hoped some day she could
meet his wife, and be a friend of hers. John wasn't married yet, but
he told her he'd planned to be married. Nothing happened between
them from Pleasantville down to April 1952, when they met in
Philadelphia.

The meeting in Philadelphia was not for the purpose of having a
rendezvous. She was genuinely and sincerely concerned with what
might happen at the hearing before the House Un-American Activi-

ties Committee. She knew, for example, that John had been in China and people who had been in China were under attack and it occurred to her that she might be asked questions about him. This was what was in her mind. She was also concerned with Averell Harriman, but she didn't want to go to Averell Harriman, but knowing that John was a friend of his and would see him occasionally, she wanted to talk with him about that. They met Friday afternoon, or late in the afternoon; they had dinner together, he took her back to her hotel; they had a nightcap and he went home. Late the next day, as John has said, they met for dinner, had some drinks, he took her back to the hotel as he had done the night before. It was his intention to go back to his hotel, it was never her intention that he stay. They had a few drinks and then, as those things will happen, it happened. And that's all there is to it. . . .

Mann: . . . What I'm trying to get clear in my mind is a clear, logical explanation of why a personal relationship should have continued after 1945 when the amorous aspects of that relationship were only incidental.

Volpe: Well, in 1945 when Melby knew her well and saw her often, he certainly had no suspicion that she was anything more than a fuzzy liberal and as he has already indicated, they were both interested in many other things and I assume he was attracted to her and she was attracted to him as individuals, as a person; he did not see her for almost five years. He is back in this country approximately one year, about a year, and did not see her. There were telephone conversations, Miss Hellman told me, when I talked with her, that she was kind of puzzled. After all, they had been good friends; she thought that even though Melby had now found, was now interested in another woman and planned to marry her, there was no reason for them not to continue to be friends.

Mann: What reason was there why they should be friends? That's what I'm getting at—the positive aspect rather than the negative aspect probably.

Volpe: Well, I assume the same reason why most of us have friends and that is some respect, admiration, fondness for the other person as a person. They were, I think one might safely say, intellectually they were compatible and no doubt found many things to talk about that were of interest to both of them. . . . I realize Mr. Mann why you're asking the question and I'm trying my best to answer it.

Mann: I'm really looking for light.

Volpe: I'm fumbling, but I think it's a little bit easier to explain why
people become enemies than it is to explain why people are friends.
Mann: Well now, let me put the question in this way. Mr. Melby answered in response to one of the interrogatories, "I have been aware
of Miss Hellman's Communist sympathies, and I have disagreed
strongly with her point of view." Now, if there was no affinity there
on political subjects and the sexual relationship was merely incidental, then I would like to know precisely what the attraction was.
They disagreed on politics, they were not interested in each other
personally, except in an incidental way. What was the interest?[11]

Mann did not give up. Six more times in this hearing he came back to his
wonderment that there could have been any basis for John's seeing Lillian if
no sex was involved. They didn't agree on political subjects; so what
precisely were the "strong platonic interests" that held them together?
Again, did they discuss politics after Moscow? Didn't it bother John that he
was on friendly terms with a person whose loyalty to the United States was
suspect? If Lillian had Communist sympathies, wouldn't the Communists
call her in to question her about what she learned from John? Why did she
break with the Progressive party? It was clear that at the conclusion of this
hostile grilling Mann would not vote for a rehearing.

From 10:35 A.M. to 1:45 P.M. the Pinkerton board sat on the "Appeal to
the Secretary of State In the Matter of John Fremont Melby." The chairman
told Counsel Volpe that the Appeals Board would take his request for a
rehearing before the lower board under advisement and he would be
notified of their decision.

There was no celebration for John and his attorney.

Hellman as Witness

However much Thomas C. Mann may have objected to giving John another chance, the Appeals Board voted two to one to do exactly that. Late in the afternoon of 23 January 1953, the day that John's appeal was heard, Pinkerton phoned Joe Volpe and told him that an order had already gone to Donovan to hold another hearing. A copy of the order was in the mail to Volpe.

It was a limited victory. Pinkerton's text read:

Gentlemen:

On January 23, 1953 the Loyalty Security Appeals Board heard Mr. John Fremont Melby and his attorney, Mr. Joseph Volpe, Jr., present a request that the proceedings be reopened to take certain additional testimony and for the amplification of the record. . . .

After careful consideration of this request, under Section 396.13 of the Regulations and Procedures of the Department of State, the Loyalty Security Appeals Board determined that the matter should be remanded to the Loyalty Security Board for the limited purpose of providing Mr. Melby with appropriate opportunity to correct, amend or amplify the existing record of his testimony concerning the nature and extent of his relationship with Miss Hellman. The testimony of any witnesses should be limited to this issue.

In addition, counsel for Mr. Melby indicated that he wished to introduce evidence concerning the loyalties and political affiliations of Miss Hellman. Mr. Volpe's request that this issue be heard by the Loyalty Security Board is denied.

In remanding this case for the limited purpose stated, the Loyalty

Security Appeals Board does not imply any judgment on the merits of the case.

Lowell C. Pinkerton
Chairman
Loyalty Security Appeals Board[1]

January 23, 1953

This left a big unsettled question. Would Lillian be willing to testify under these conditions? Would, in fact, her testimony now conceivably do any good? The Donovan Board was firm in its belief that she had been a full-fledged Communist—nay, might even still be one.

Volpe felt that Lillian's performance before HUAC had been impressive enough that even if she could not undertake a frontal assault on the malicious FBI reports, she could create some doubt in the minds of the board members as to whether she really was a dangerous person. And there was the further benefit: they *might* accept her word, partially, as to whether John had been indiscreet in talking with her, and whether the affair between them was now over. Volpe noted that in one of the early transcripts one of the members had wondered if Lillian still had some hold on John that would cause him to betray confidential information. Surely talking with her for an hour would dispel that misgiving.

There was much discussion between Lillian, Rauh, and Volpe. Tentatively she decided to appear. She needed to spend some more time in Washington anyway. She had an offer from Alexander Korda to do a movie script, and this would require that she go to Europe. Passport clearance again. After the HUAC hearings, none of the hostile witnesses had been able to get passports. When she consulted Rauh, he told her she should go see Ruth Shipley in person. Lillian scheduled a meeting with Shipley for the morning of 4 February, leaving herself plenty of time to work with John's lawyer.

John's hearing with the Donovan board was now set for 5 February. Donovan was called out of town because of the illness of his father shortly before the scheduled time, but, after canvassing alternative dates, Volpe and the other board members decided that if the hearing were not held as scheduled, it could not be held for months. Donovan could read the transcript; if he had questions, he could get in touch with Volpe.

There remained the difficult matter of whether the board would hear Lillian. Volpe got in touch with Sipes again. Sipes felt that Lillian could appear, not as a witness to refute the FBI charges against her, but only to talk about her relationship with John.

Lillian was not happy about this, but since John and Volpe wanted her, and Rauh approved, she decided to go ahead. As with her previous appearance before HUAC, she wanted her opinions of the whole process on the record, no matter what happened in the hearing. She and Rauh drafted a letter to Donovan.

February 2, 1953

Dear Mr. Chairman:

Mr. Volpe has asked me to testify at the hearing concerning John Melby. Most certainly I am willing to do so. Ever since I knew I had been spoken of in connection with Mr. Melby's hearings, I have wanted to testify and have been puzzled that I was not called upon to do so. But these matters are not within my field and I have little knowledge of them.

As a writer and a dramatist I have taken part in political activities, particularly those directed to the maintenance of peace. But most certainly I have never engaged in anything that was disloyal or subversive, nor have I ever witnessed such conduct on the part of anybody else at any time. Therefore it is impossible for me to believe that association with me could possibly cast any doubts on the career of Mr. Melby, and I most strongly resent any suggestion that such could be the case.

I am prepared to come before you, as might any other good citizen, to tell you anything you might wish to know about myself or about my friendship with John Melby. I hope you will feel free to ask me any question about my political activities, and I will answer in full truth. I wish to help in coming to a decision about a government servant. But in coming before you I want to make one point completely clear: my testimony about my friendship with John Melby is in no sense and to no degree an admission on my part that I have been guilty of any wrongdoing; nor do I feel that his association with me could possibly be deemed a relevant consideration of his trustworthiness as a United States government employee.

I should like your assurance that this letter, or any similar statement that I might make concerning the subject matter of this letter, will be put into the record when I testify on Thursday.

Sincerely yours,
Lillian Hellman[2]

And so it was put into the record, Lillian at her feisty best, to lie buried until 1985.

On 4 February 1953, Lillian went to see Mrs. Shipley. *Scoundrel Time* has a vivid description of this confrontation. Lillian sat silently listening to Shipley read the list of suspect organizations she allegedly belonged to:

> Mrs. Shipley had not finished the list when she looked up and said, "Tell me, Miss Hellman, do you think most of the friendly witnesses have been telling the House Un-American Committee the truth?"
>
> It was a most surprising question. I said no, I was sure they had not, many of them had been coached to confess what they had never done and had never seen.
>
> Mrs. Shipley said, "Edward G. Robinson, for example?"
>
> I said I thought so, but I wasn't sure. But there were others, Martin Berkeley, for example, who said that I had been at a Communist meeting in his house. I was never at his house and didn't believe I ever met him.
>
> I said, "The kiddies have been playing games on all of you, Mrs. Shipley, and you deserve the tricks they played because you pushed them into it."
>
> Mrs. Shipley did not seem angry. She was thoughtful as she riffled through the rest of my file, seemingly looking for something she knew was there. Then she said, "I've suspected many of them were lying. They will be punished for it."
>
> I said, "I don't think that's the way the world is going. It's people like me who need jobs. That's why I came here, not wanting to come."
>
> She said, "I can see that," and was close to a smile.[3]

Shipley questioned her as to whether she engaged in political activities in Europe. Lillian replied "No." Shipley then asked her to write a letter to this effect and promised that a passport would be sent to her that week.

After her meeting with Mrs. Shipley, Lillian joined John and Volpe in Volpe's office. Volpe told her he had forwarded her letter to the State Department Loyalty-Security Board, and they discussed what might happen in John's hearing the next day. During the course of the discussion, Lillian reminded John of a visit he had paid her, in New York in July 1952, that both of them had forgotten about; her secretary had remembered it, and told her about it just before she left New York. Volpe probed this newly recalled event; should they bring it to the attention of the board next day? He decided they should. Upset as the board members would be at yet another contact with Lillian that John had forgotten, it would be worse for John if the board knew about it from the FBI. (This was a mistake; the board had not known about it, and suspected even more that John was not coming clean.)

After the conference in Volpe's office, Volpe asked John to walk Lillian back to her hotel. He did, with all dispatch.

The fifth of February was the day for the sixth hearing in John's long series. Since Lillian was anxious to get her letter to Shipley, Volpe arranged for John to appear at the State Department hearing in the morning and for Lillian to come in at two in the afternoon.

Lillian spent the morning again writing an *apologia pro vita sua* for the head of the Passport Office, using Joe Rauh's facilities. It was, if anything, more pungent than the one she had written in 1951:

Dear Mrs. Shipley:

I have been asked by Sir Alexander Korda of London Films to come to London in order to consult with him about writing a movie script. There will be a consultation period of four weeks, after which we will sign an agreement guaranteeing fourteen to eighteen weeks of work on the script itself. (Sir Alexander has talked of a year's contract, but at this period I am not sure that I wish to remain in Europe that long). Under the proposed contract I am to be paid in dollars, pounds, francs, and liras.

I wish to repeat here our conversation of yesterday, and to do so under oath: I am not a member of the Communist Party and I have no affiliation with the Communist Party of any kind whatsoever. Any association that I did have in the past ended in the year 1940 and never from that day to this has it ever been resumed in any sense. In any case—although most certainly I do not wish to stand on technicalities—my association was of the most casual nature and never included anything more than the discussion of current events or books on philosophy and history.

I have, of course, since 1940 been a member of many left-wing organizations, but I have never done anything that could be considered disloyal or subversive. Nor have I ever witnessed such acts or heard such talk from anybody else. (If ever I had, I would have considered it my duty to have reported it to the proper authorities). I have known many people through these organizations, and otherwise, with left-wing views, but at no time in my life have I ever had political friendships. My relations with my friends, now and in the past, have been and will continue to be personal or professional.

I have always thought of myself as completely independent and, as any complete record would show, I have as often been in disagreement with Communists as I have with right-wing political people. I have often been attacked by Communists: I wrote the anti-Nazi play, "Watch on The Rhine," during the year 1940 and it was produced in March of 1941, during the period of the Nazi-Soviet Pact; a number of my other plays have been attacked by the Communist press and I myself have frequently been frowned upon. However, I do not wish to use such attacks, either from the political right or the political left, in the rather shabby way I think they have been used by many people.

Like most other people, I have made mistakes but I feel guilty of nothing and I am secure in the belief that I have never done more than exercise my rights as an American citizen. It was on that basis, and no other, that I joined the Progressive Party. I resigned from the Progressive Party as I have resigned from other organizations, when I felt myself in fundamental disagreement. As a matter of fact, since 1949 or early 1950, I have had no political activities of any kind and have entirely concerned myself with writing.

In July of 1951, in applying for a passport, I assured you then, as I assure you now, that my trip abroad is entirely made for the purpose of earning a living as a writer. During that trip of 1951, I was asked three or four times, in England as well as in France, to speak before professional groups. I refused all such offers, even though two of the invitations came from very conservative people. It seemed to me that I have given you my word on the nature of my trip and I kept that word even past the point where you might have believed it necessary. I do not ever wish to relinquish my rights as an American citizen to speak freely in agreement or disagreement, but as part of those rights, I have had respect for promises made in honor, and I will continue to respect them.

I would like to repeat here that I think of myself as a rather old fashioned patriot, and any good that I have done, or any mistakes that I have made, have been entirely due to my deep feeling for the place where I was born. I am only sorry that these words have to be written. I have believed them to be implicit in my work and have, in turn, believed that my work has an honorable place in the present American cultural scene.

I am, more than I can say here, grateful to you for the courtesy and kindness you have always shown me.

Sincerely yours,
Lillian Hellman[4]

The letter was notarized.

While Lillian was writing her letter to Shipley, John and Joe Volpe appeared in room 1210-H of the State Department Building. In Donovan's absence, James W. Swihart acted as chairman; Lehman P. Nickell was also present. The agenda was similar to that heard by the Appeals Board two weeks earlier. Volpe explained why he wanted John to appear again, and why he intended to call Lillian and John's wife Hilda in the afternoon.

Volpe also introduced affidavits from Jameson Parker and General Erskine. Swihart was a bit leery of receiving them and asked if the affidavits related to John's relationship with Lillian. Volpe assured the Board that Jameson Parker's affidavit concerned John's efforts to keep Ambassador Cowen informed of his meetings with Lillian. The Erskine affidavit, however, was a straightforward character reference; it did not concern Lillian. Volpe hoped, however, that the board would make an exception and receive it, which the board agreed to do. It is hard to believe that the board actually read Erskine's affidavit; that doughty marine general apparently believed that John was the finest Foreign Service officer he had ever met. But at least the board received it.

Swihart and Nickell listened skeptically to the new and more candid account of John's relations with Lillian. Sipes, having heard it all before the Appeals Board, had an agenda of his own. He could not believe that the United States government, in 1944, had extended the full hospitality of its Moscow Embassy to a visiting red-tinged playwright. Nor did he believe that Lillian's trip could have been beneficial to the United States. He queried John about these things; in the margin of the transcript reporting this discussion, there are bold question marks, probably made by Donovan later. Opposite John's claim that Lillian's report from the Russian war front had been "most useful," someone wrote: "WHY DID HELLMAN GET TO THE FRONT?" It was not exactly the way Volpe had expected this rehearing to go.

Marginalia reveal the consistent hostile attitudes of the board members. They did not believe that John had failed to contact Lillian immediately upon his return from China in 1949. They could not understand why he had gone to visit her in Pleasantville. They refused to credit John's statement that when Nicholas of the Passport Office called him about Lillian in 1951, Nicholas said that the Office had no information that she was a Communist. They did not believe that any of the meetings John had with Lillian were left out of his original statement inadvertently or because of faulty memory. They rejected the claim that Lillian had not known why HUAC wanted to question her. They did not believe that she was desirous of protecting other people when she testified before HUAC. They rejected John's statement that he saw her in Philadelphia for a reason other than to renew their affair. They did not believe that Averell Harriman told Adrian Fisher, State Department legal adviser, that Lillian was a "left-wing liberal" but not a Communist. They refused to credit Lillian's offer to HUAC to tell everything about herself. In the meticulous accounting of all the times since 1949 when John had seen Lillian, they underlined or made marginal comments about every one where he claimed that the meeting was to prepare for her appearance before HUAC or his appearance before the board. And one can sense, from the questioning, an almost prurient interest in the love life of this famous playwright. The transcript of the morning hearing, with John and Joe Volpe present, runs to seventy-three pages. There are thirty-two hostile or skeptical markings on these pages.

So they didn't believe John Melby about anything. Was it conceivable that they would believe Lillian Hellman?

John was not in the room when Lillian was sworn in at two o'clock; Volpe wanted her to testify without John present.

Volpe led off the questioning. Why had she gone to Moscow? Where did she live, how had she met John, when did she get to know him well? To these last questions, Lillian replied: "I don't think I have to say it is a difficult story to tell. All relations between human beings are difficult to talk about if one tells the truth. I didn't know Mr. Melby very well until I went to live in the Embassy. I did know him very well after I went to live in the Embassy. I think that we both fell in love in this period. I knew he was married and I knew it was an unhappy marriage. We found we had many common interests."[5]

She then briefly described her visit to the Russian front, the short stay in England, and John's passage through New York en route to the San Francisco conference.

> Hellman: He went out to the San Francisco Conference and came back, I think, some time in July of 1945, at which point I had a very bad accident and had taken a house in Easthampton, Long Island, with my secretary. John came down and visited a number of weekends or

a number of times during the week. I would have absolutely no memory of how many times—perhaps three, perhaps four, perhaps five. That was the summer of '45.

I think he went to China in October of '45, and the relationship was left on the basis that we both think over the whole thing, and if and when he got a divorce from his wife, we would probably get married—neither one of us, I think, committed to anything; neither one of us willing to be committed to anything. [Lillian was inaccurate here. John had been eager to make a commitment; Lillian was the one who held back.]

We wrote to each other a great deal during 1945 and during, I would think, 1946. In here I am quite rough about the dates. I wouldn't remember them exactly. I would think about 1947 I had a sense that the letters had changed in tone, for what reason I didn't know. I probably thought I knew. I was certainly unwilling to ask, and by 1948 it seemed to me quite clear that the whole relationship had changed and would not continue on the same basis any longer. I did have a letter from Mr. Melby some time in December or January of '49, saying that he was returning to this country and we would speak. I no longer remember who called whom on the telephone, but we talked on the telephone in January '49, and made no attempt to meet, since I suppose without saying it we both understood that the relationship had come to an end, and I imagine both of us are people who found no need to talk of the reasons for the end.

I did not see him through '49. I did have a letter from him in January of 1950, saying that he felt there was much that should be explained to me, and if I was free or coming to Washington, couldn't we have lunch or dinner. It was at this point, when I was doing research for a play called "Autumn Garden," and I was on my way to New Orleans, where I was born and had a family, I was on my way through Washington and did see Mr. Melby. I have no accurate memory of the conversation. I do remember his saying that he had attempted to patch up things with his wife and found it impossible, and he was in the middle of getting a divorce. It is my best memory that after I had done the research work in New Orleans, I came back to Washington and once again had lunch or dinner or a drink with him, although I wouldn't remember the time of day or how.

Some time in March of—perhaps because there was no long conversation about this relationship and perhaps neither of us are the kind of people who find it necessary to put decisions in words, the next meeting, as I remember it, was in March of '50, at which time I owned a farm about an hour from New York, and Mr. Melby came and stayed for a weekend. I understand that Mr. Melby told you about this weekend. I am sure I have no objections to telling you anything you want to know about this weekend but I understand that Mr. Melby has already told you the details of the weekend.

The relationship obviously at this point was neither one thing nor the other: it was neither over nor was it not over.

In April of 1950, Mr. Melby, about a month after the Pleasant-ville—about six weeks after the visit—Mr. Melby came through New York, I think coming from Illinois, and stayed at my apartment. It was obvious from both these visits that it had been wrong to resume the relationship, and that it was not going to work, and that we had both been right in thinking it had come to an end previously, and we had made a mistake in thinking it was not at an end at this minute.

I may say here, because the date coincides with a completely per-sonal decision of my own—which was that I was not a political per-son and should cease having any political activities of any kind, at which point I had ceased, around '49 or '50—that Mr. Melby in my relationship was never under any circumstances, never had anything to do with any political interest of any kind. I don't think we ever, as far as I can remember, discussed anything that was not in the news-papers of that day. I was never even very clear—because my own kind of curiosity does not take that kind of direction, I was not even very clear about what Mr. Melby's job was in Moscow, when I lived next door to him. I don't know what he did. I have never been sure what his job was. I didn't ask questions. It is not unusual for me not to ask questions. It does not occur to me to ask such questions.

I have gone through the last ten or twelve years knowing that I disagreed with a great many people, and I had a great many conser-vative friends I had gone to college with, grew up with, and was very devoted to, and there was no sense having any discussions which would turn out unpleasantly or sharply, and so I ceased to have them, and so Mr. Melby was in a long line of those with whom I have no political connection whatsoever.

After the visit of April 1950, not only did I have no political ac-tivities to discuss, but I wouldn't have discussed them in any case.

I think some time in the summer of June or July, Mr. Melby went on a mission to Southeast Asia, and he rang me up to tell me he was going, and as I remember, he wrote me one or two letters during the trip—very short letters describing where he was and when he was coming back—and I answered with several letters, both of us perhaps much too reluctant to say perhaps these letters should cease and we should cease seeing each other, but both of us at this point knowing it. And they did cease, the letters ceased, and I never heard from Mr. Melby nor did I ever get in touch with him until a half year later, when I came down to Washington and felt that enough time had gone by. I came down to Washington to do research work on a collection of Chekov, which I had been doing, and thought that perhaps it would be all right at this point to call John and find out how he was. I did call him and we did have lunch, I think at a hotel—I don't remember which hotel—and it was at this lunch that I learned that he had got married. And we had a perfectly pleasant lunch, in which I don't clearly remember what was said, but I clearly remember I felt I hoped it was a happy marriage and it would work well.

I didn't see him or write him, nor did he see or write me, until July '51, at which point I wanted a passport to do a French movie, and I came down to Washington to see Mrs. Shipley, saying that I was not a Communist, explaining in the letter, which is in Mrs. Shipley's records, a large part of my history, and came to the place at which I told Mrs. Shipley that I had been in—she asked me why I had been in Moscow, and I told her why I had been in Moscow, and I told her Mr. Harriman said it had been a valuable visit. And she asked me if I would call Mr. Harriman and ask him to tell her that. And I did call his office, and he had about an hour before getting on the plane to go to Persia. I said there were two other people I thought would vouch for this visit: Eddie Page and John Melby. She said she thought Eddie Page was in Berlin. I called John, asked him if he remembered Harriman saying this. He said, "Yes." He said, as a matter of fact, he thought he had written the letter for Mr. Harriman. He came around to see me and I told him about the passport. As far as I remember, somebody from Mrs. Shipley's office went to see him and he did vouch for the truth of the statement.

I went to Europe in July and returned, I think, in October. I think, although I am now very uncertain, that I had a letter from Mr. Melby in Europe, saying that he had been asked to fill out what I have been told is called an interrogatory, and that I had appeared in

the interrogatory; so that when I came back I called him, and I think
he was out of America. I think he was in Caledonia or New South
Wales; and I take it from the date that my secretary has given me
that when he got back he must just have called me and I saw him
some time around November of 1951, when he told me he had forgotten to mention in the interrogatory a weekend that he had
spent—*the* weekend that he had spent in Pleasantville in March. I
must say I found nothing very remarkable about this, because I
never can remember where I have been for weekends either; and he
asked me the details of the trip, of what time he had arrived in New
York, and whether we had gone straight to Pleasantville, and I did
the best I could to remember, which probably was not very accurate.

We talked chiefly about that and I did not see him again until a
year ago now, when I had a play called "Autumn Garden" in Washington, and I came to rehearse the play, to be with the play, and Mr.
Melby came to the hotel several times to see me, chiefly, I think, to
talk about his own interrogatory or the play. They were brief visits. I
was very busy in the theater most of the day and all of the evenings.

Some time in March I was subpoenaed by the House Un-American Committee, a record of which I have with me in case you would
like to see it.

At this point I was in Washington. I do not have any memory of—
and I do not know whether John has or not—of seeing Mr. Melby. I
have no memory of it. I came down to see Joseph Rauh, who is my
lawyer. Perhaps I saw Mr. Melby; perhaps I didn't.

In the first part of April Mr. Melby said he was going to be in
Philadelphia. I had said, however, whether I saw him or not, I said I
wanted to talk about my hearing, since I had no knowledge of what
would come up in it, whether the Moscow trip would. My own
memory is usually very bad and I wanted to talk about it with him.
He said he was going to be in Philadelphia and it would be very difficult for him to come to New York, and would I come down to
Philadelphia? One of my minor reasons for going to Philadelphia
was that I had promised to visit some friends of mine who lived near
there, and it seemed to be a chance to see him and do both. Because, I think, as I said before, the relationship is a confused relationship, I understand, or certainly I hope Mr. Melby has told you
about the Philadelphia visit.

From then on Mr. Rauh and my secretary have given me a series
of dates on which I have seen Mr. Melby; never, as far as any of us

knows, alone; always mostly with Mr. Rauh; several times with Mr. Volpe; always about either my hearing or this particular hearing.

I think in general that is the history of the relationship. There are really over the period not too many dates. It is an interrupted history. It is a confused history. Most certainly it is not black and white, nor do I want to claim that it is.

If you have read or seen or heard of my House testimony, you know that I was completely willing to testify about myself, and made such an offer, but I was not willing to inform on or involve other innocent people, and thus I had to act in a way that I did not wish to act, but which was under the direction of Mr. Rauh. There was no other way to take except the Fifth Amendment, which is what I took when the offer was refused. However, I am most certainly willing to answer any questions you would have, as I was willing to answer any questions that they would have. I have no secrets. I would be glad to tell you anything else you wish to know about the relationship. I think, as I said before, to make it black and white would be the lie it never has been, nor do I think many other relations ever are. I don't think it is as much of a mystery as perhaps it looks. It has been a completely, as far as any kind of—it has been a completely personal relationship of two people who once past being in love happen also to be very devoted to each other and very respectful of one another, and who I think in any other time besides our own would not be open to question of the complete innocence of and the complete morality, if I may say so, of people who were once in love and who have come out with respect and devotion to one another.

I would be glad to tell you anything else I can.

Volpe: Miss Hellman, during the period of 1945, when you had returned to this country and when Melby was awaiting orders to go to China, you saw a good deal of Melby in New York. Is that right?

Hellman: Partly in New York, partly in East Hampton, Long Island, yes.

Volpe: During that period, how did you and John spend your time when you were together in New York or out on the Island?

Hellman: I had had a bad accident and was in the hospital for a while, so that by the time I went to East Hampton I was leading a very quiet life of a picnic with friends, or dinner with friends, of going to bed very early. I was also working on a play. . . .

Volpe: Were there any political activities at this time?

Hellman: For me?

Volpe: I am not speaking now of your activities alone, but when John

visited you in New York or out in East Hampton, were there any political activities or meetings of any kind that he engaged in or not?

Hellman: Oh no, no. . . .

Volpe: Miss Hellman, on my way back from lunch today, it all of a sudden occurred to me that when you and John Melby meet you kiss
each other. I noticed that when you met John Melby at Joe Rauh's office. Would you mind explaining that?

Hellman: I can't possibly explain such a thing, Mr. Volpe. I kiss a great
many people I am fond of. I don't think one has any reason for just
kissing somebody one is fond of.

Volpe: I hope you don't mind my asking the question.

Hellman: In my years of my life I kissed my father each time I saw
him. I can't possibly know the reason. I think it frequently happens
between people who haven't seen each other for a long time and
who are fond of each other.

Volpe: I have no further questions.

Hellman: I didn't mean to stop your inquiry into the kissing. It is just
that I didn't know.

Volpe: Frankly, Miss Hellman, it occurred to me just as I was coming
back from lunch, and I might just as well tell the rest of it. It also occurred to me that perhaps someone in the past has seen you do this
and has attached to that some significance which is not there. That
is the reason I asked you the question.

Hellman: That is very possible.

Sipes: I would like to suggest, Mr. Volpe, I think Miss Hellman was
born in New Orleans, is that correct?

Hellman: Correct.

Sipes: It is a Southern custom, is it not?

Hellman: It is a Southern custom. I don't think I do it with people I see
every day, but I think I do with people I haven't seen for a long time
and I am fond of.

Swihart: I have no questions, Mr. Counsel, unless other members of
the Board have.

Nickell: I haven't.

Sipes: I have just one or two questions. If Miss Hellman has no objections, I would like to ask them. Do you recall, Miss Hellman, seeing
Mr. Melby in June of 1952 in New York?

Hellman: June of 1952? Yes, yes, I do. I am sorry that I skipped it. I am
looking at it here [indicating her notes].

Sipes: Could you tell the Board just the extent of your seeing him at that time, if you would, please.

Hellman: Yes. I don't remember this visit very clearly. I think he came up with his mother and father to go to a memorial service of some kind, and I know he stopped, I know he came into the house, because I remember my secretary getting him a couple of numbers on the telephone, and I don't any longer know whether he had a drink or lunch, but the visit was for an hour or two. But the reason it sticks in my mind is that she dialed two or three numbers for him. I have no other memory of the visit. It was a casual visit of an hour or two.

Sipes: Do you recall whether you had lunch or not?

Hellman: No, I don't. I remember being in the kitchen and fixing something, but I don't know what I was fixing—whether sandwiches or drinks. I don't even remember what time of day it was.

Sipes: But the visit was at what? Your apartment?

Hellman: Yes. I had not remembered this visit, which is why it is kind of stuck—my secretary reminded me the other day she had gotten a couple of numbers for him, she thought a number at an airport where he was saying goodbye to somebody that was leaving. She had trouble getting LaGuardia airport.

Sipes: Do you have any recollection whether he mentioned anything with reference to the status of his proceedings with reference to the State Department Board? I think we were in process at the time.

Hellman: I don't. It is most probable that he did, I would say, but I don't have any memory of it. This is a very confused period for me, probably because I had just gotten over being occupied with the House Committee, was thinking of going into rehearsal with a play, and any procedure here was kind of dim and confused for me. I am sure if it was true, he probably did mention it. I would think it was this period, because I notice Mr. Rauh's office has a meeting on July 2 in Mr. Rauh's office, and it must have been very close in there. I really couldn't say honestly that I remember any particular discussion on that particular day.

Sipes: I am not clear whether you have covered this point in your statement, as to your recollection of seeing him in May, right after your appearance before the House Committee.

Hellman: Yes, I did see him. I am sorry, I thought I said that.

Sipes: You may have. I am not sure.

Hellman: Yes, I am sorry if I omitted it. I was staying at the Shoreham Hotel. He came in once or twice to discuss my particular case. I actually had no idea at this point whether they would accept this offer or not, and if they had accepted it, I wanted to know as much as I could remember about the Moscow visit, and he did come in once or twice.

Sipes: While you were at the Shoreham?

Hellman: That is right.

Sipes: And prior to your testimony before the House Committee?

Hellman: Yes. I was here, according to Mr. Rauh's office, on 19, 20 and 31 May, and I would say he came in either once or twice.

Sipes: Do you recall whether you saw him or he saw you after your testimony?

Hellman: I don't recall. I really don't recall. I don't recall what time of day I left Washington. I left Washington almost immediately after testifying, so that would be doubtful, but I don't really remember. I might have seen him for five minutes. It is possible. I don't remember. The testimony was in the morning and I think I took an early afternoon plane back, but I am not sure of that.

Sipes: The times that he did come in, however many times it was, before your testimony, there at the Shoreham, do you recall whether that was your initiative or Mr. Melby's initiative?

Hellman: No, I don't. I would think it mine, since it was my trouble, but I don't remember. I would never think of it that way, I suppose.

Sipes: With respect to your meeting Mr. Melby in Philadelphia, in April of 1952, I am not clear, not too clear from your statement as to whose initiative that belonged.

Hellman: Nor am I, Mr. Sipes, since I never thought of it as one person's initiative or another. I wouldn't know. I couldn't answer that question honestly.

Sipes: You wouldn't recall whether he phoned you and suggested this meeting or whether you phoned him, or whether it was correspondence, or just how that came about?

Hellman: No, no, I don't remember whether it was by letter or telephone or what it was, or whose idea it was. My guess would be that in the light of the circumstances, it was probably both. I had just been subpoenaed, had no knowledge there would be a postponement at that point, and I wanted to find out all of my own history that he remembered, and it probably was mutual, that he also probably wanted to see me about it.

Sipes: I just have one question, Miss Hellman. I wonder if you care to
state, would state to the Board how you regard your present relationship with Mr. Melby?

Hellman: Oh, yes, I am perfectly willing to. I regard my present relationship as of a very old and devoted friend. That would be the way
I would think of it. How Mr. Melby regards it is not my business.
Certainly that is all it has been to me for a very long time, and that is
the only way I think of it. If I didn't think of it that way, I wouldn't
be here. This has not been a pleasant idea for me, and it was only
because I am very devoted to Mr. Melby and think that any reflec-
tion on his security is unjust that I was willing to come. I certainly
wouldn't come for anybody I didn't feel very close to and devoted to.
Beyond that I have no other feelings about Mr. Melby.

Sipes: I have no further questions, Mr. Chairman.

Nickell: I have none. . . .

Volpe: I have nothing further.

Swihart: All right. Thank you very much, Miss Hellman.

[The witness was excused. Mr. Melby returned to the hearing room at
this point.]⁶

"It has been a completely personal relationship of two people who once
past being in love happen also to be very devoted to each other and very
respectful of one another . . . two people who were once in love and who
have come out with respect and devotion to one another." Most of this
testimony of Lillian's is underlined in the board's transcript, and because of
it, John's fate was signed, sealed, and delivered. *Respect and devotion, between this Communist and this would-be diplomat?* Lillian Hellman, by being
honest, by acknowledging respect and devotion between herself and John
Melby, had killed his chances to continue in the service of the United States
government.

This time there were no reporters to carry Lillian's impassioned prose to
the public—as there had been at her HUAC hearing—nor to note that the
board was resolutely determined to ask her no questions about her political
beliefs and activities. Her plea to the board to ask her anything they were
concerned about was ignored. The system, or perhaps one should say the
indoctrination of the board members, triumphed.

Perhaps even more damning than Lillian's portrayal of her relationship
with John as one of respect and devotion was John's waffling about whether
he would see her again. In the early hearings, when he was "devastated" by
the evidence before the board about Lillian's secret activities, he was firm,

though not categorical, in his intention not to see her. Now this changed. Volpe's effective belittling of the anonymous FBI informants had stiffened John's attitude. The board's obdurate refusal to inquire into the accuracy of untested charges by unknown witnesses he saw as vitiating their implied claim to infallibility. John was contrite about his misleading answers to early board inquiries, contrite about the lapses at Pleasantville and Phila-delphia, but not contrite about his friendship for Lillian. That he was not is clear from much of his testimony at the hearing of 5 February:

> Volpe: Mr. Melby, is there anything about your relationship with Miss Hellman since 1950, when you first saw her again after your return to this country from China, down to the present time, that you have not mentioned or discussed in your testimony today before the Board?
>
> Melby: No, I don't think of anything.
>
> Volpe: Is there anything you would like to say with respect to your be-havior or conduct at any earlier hearings?
>
> Melby: There isn't very much that I can say, except that it was pretty bad. I remember that when you agreed to take the case, one of the first things that you insisted on was that I read over the entire tran-script. I was horrified at what was in it, the contradictions and inac-curacies, and in reading it I just couldn't believe that I had said some of the things that I had. I didn't see how I could. I don't know how to explain it except that I had come in here with one picture of what Miss Hellman was, and as charge after charge began to appear, I was simply stunned. I doubt if I could have been more stunned if the charge had been made that my grandmother had been an orga-nizer for the IWW. It just didn't fit anything that I had known or ever heard, any picture that I had. My chief reaction was, "Well, we have to get the other side of the story," and yet my lawyer at that time didn't want to approach it that way. I didn't know what I was doing or what to do on it. That combined with the relationship with my wife and what it would do—all I can say is that I just got pan-icky and terror-stricken and lost my head on the thing. As I say, in looking back over the transcript, there are things there that I don't even remember saying, and that I don't see how I could have said, and obviously I did. All I can say is that I just hope that you can un-derstand how that can happen to somebody in the awful fix that I was in.
>
> Volpe: I have no further questions, Mr. Chairman.

Swihart: Do you have any?

Nickell: No.

Sipes: No.

Swihart: A little earlier, Mr. Counsel, you had indicated you might put Mrs. Melby on as a witness. It is not necessary, from the Board's standpoint, but do you still plan to do that?

Volpe: Yes, sir.

Swihart: I see. I thought perhaps you were through.

Volpe: I really have one other question I would like to ask Mr. Melby.

Mr. Melby, will you tell the Board what your relationship has been with Miss Hellman since April 1952, and what it will be from here on out?

Melby: . . . It is, in view of events and circumstances, inconceivable that there could be, that there is really any basis left now for any friendship between Miss Hellman and myself. It is almost impossible to see any basis for even the most casual kind of social contact which might happen by chance—cocktail party, dinner, something—except in so far as my wife for obvious reasons was fully aware of it, agreed to it, and participated in it. That is hardly likely to be the case, so that I think it can be stated that there will be no association.[7]

"Hardly likely to be the case . . . I think it can be stated that there will be no association"—to an inquisitor demanding categorical denials, this wishy-washy terminology was light years away from what was acceptable. The only acceptable pattern for a repentant sinner was total repudiation of former contaminated associates. John failed this test.

When Hilda Melby came on, she confirmed her willingness to accept John's apologies and to let bygones be bygones: "Well, of course I was shocked and hurt and infuriated, but I feel that knowing John as I do that he couldn't possibly have told me if it hadn't been terribly important for me to know, and I wouldn't be here now if I didn't believe that it was as he said, that it was simply a lapse, that it was not a resumption of any affair. It was something that happened, and I believe that, and I feel—I am quite convinced in my own mind that that is ended."[8] There were no questions by the board. Hilda Melby was dismissed.

It was now Volpe's turn to summarize:

Gentlemen, I have spent many hours trying to figure out a way of not only presenting this testimony so that it might do Melby justice, but I have also spent a lot of time trying to figure out what I might say to this Board to help you in the determination you will have to make, and though the temptation is great to make speeches about the cause of the issues involved, I don't think that is going to help anyone. I suspect that if John Melby had come forward last year and had said, "Look, fellows, I am in a pickle. I will be happy to tell you anything and everything I know about Miss Hellman and my association with her. I am in this predicament, however. There were these two transgressions. I have regretted them. They really meant nothing. They were the result of animal instinct and human frailties rather than anything else," my guess is John wouldn't be here today trying to persuade you gentlemen and others who will be concerned with this case that there is any reason to question whether his continued employment in the Foreign Service would constitute a security risk. He undertook to refrain from talking about an episode or two episodes that were extremely personal, not only to him but to Miss Hellman because—and I am convinced of this—I think no man would ever feel comfortable about talking of such things, and I think John had no way of anticipating that his decision not to discuss these two episodes would ever create the kind of weird and no doubt mysterious picture that finally evolved from his testimony before this Board. . . .

I was convinced, as I hope you will be, that there has never been anything in this relationship that would give rise to any question of security, either directly or indirectly. I am also convinced, as I hope you will be, that the romance or love affair that existed between Melby and Miss Hellman ended some time when John was in China, and that Pleasantville and Philadelphia were episodes that are very hard to explain. He has made it abundantly clear, I think, that he regretted the fact that it happened, and I think it is also clear that Miss Hellman regretted it. You must remember that John has known Miss Hellman as a thoughtful and long and sensitive friend. It was not an episode that anyone would be willing to talk about. She is a woman of stature and prestige, and I think Melby's reluctance—well, I think the saying is "kiss and tell"—in this case is understandable.[9]

A few words about John's love for his work and his unblemished record, about the board's having based its previous decision on an incomplete story, and the hearing was over.

When Lillian reported to Joe Rauh afterwards, the only comment Rauh remembers was "That Volpe is a queer duck. Why in the world would he ask me about kissing John Melby?"[10]

Fired

After John's hearing of 5 February 1953, Lillian returned to New York expecting momentarily to receive the passport Shipley had promised her. It did not come. On 19 February, she wrote again:

Dear Mrs. Shipley:

I am most anxiously awaiting my passport. I am unhappily in the position of being unable to make any plans, and possibly endangering my contract by not being able to give a "Yes" or "No" answer.

I dislike worrying you again, but I would be most grateful if it could be sent to me within the next few days.

My warm regards to you,

Lillian Hellman[1]

Shipley's office received this letter the next day.

Ruth Shipley's passport barony was one of the federal bureaucracies that brooked little interference from transient elected officials, or their equally transient appointees such as secretaries of state, attornies general, and the like.[2] Shipley was much like J. Edgar Hoover; he too had established himself as largely beyond the control of mere presidents. Shipley had held this job since 1927. She had good contacts on the Hill; passport requests of congressmen were speedily processed, and they were allowed to give the impression to constituents that their requests were speeded up because of the congressmen's intervention with Shipley. President Roosevelt called her a "wonderful ogre."

Through most of her years in this post, Shipley labored without much publicity. In 1952 this changed. She denied Linus Pauling, prominent chemist at Cal Tech and later the winner of two Nobel Prizes, a passport to go to a scientific conference in London. The conference was to discuss the chemical structure of biological molecules; research presented at the conference led to the discovery of DNA. Had Pauling been able to attend, his own research in this area might well have been stimulated and might have led to an unprecedented third Nobel Prize.[3] But Pauling had belonged to several organizations listed by the attorney general as Communist fronts, and Shipley decided that his travel abroad was not in the best interests of the United States. The intellectual community was much upset by this denial. Her Pauling refusal induced the faculty of Reed College, in Portland, Oregon, to contact Oregon Senator Wayne Morse. Morse investigated the situation, decided that the Passport Office was "tyrannical, arbitrary, and capricious," and made a floor speech on 6 June 1952 excoriating Shipley and her ultimate superior, Dean Acheson. Morse made extensive use of a *Washington Post* editorial sharply critical of the Passport Office for its frequent denials based upon secret evidence that citizens could not confront or rebut.[4]

Morse's attack provoked strong defense of Shipley by Senate powers who shared Shipley's fervent anti-Communism, among whom Pat McCarrran was most supportive. When *Colliers* carried an article about Shipley in July 1953, McCarran was quoted as giving her credit for many features of the McCarran-Walter Immigration Act. She returned the compliment: "I think the McCarran and Un-American committees have done a grand job."[5]

Shipley's anti-Communism was shared by her two brothers, one of whom, Frank Bielaski, had worked for the Office of Strategic Services and was instrumental in pushing the *Amerasia* prosecution. The other brother, Bruce Bielaski, was a former FBI agent; between them they added considerably to Shipley's voluminous files on American citizens who had applied, or might apply, for passports. She was alleged to have data on more than twelve million people, filling 1,250 filing cabinets.[6]

Not only Pauling, but Paul Robeson, Rockwell Kent, Edward G. Robinson, Corliss Lamont, Leonard Boudin, and a host of other left wingers were denied passports by Shipley. In the period from May 1951 to May 1952, she withheld passports from approximately three hundred citizens. All the hostile Hollywood witnesses before HUAC were on her blacklist.[7] In Lillian's case, there was special reason for Shipley to be hostile. Lillian had visited, and written favorably about, the Spanish Loyalist forces, and had been active in the Friends of the Abraham Lincoln Brigade. The Russians had used passports of dead members of the Brigade illegitimately for Soviet operatives entering the United States; this not only offended Shipley's basic anti-Communism, but also frontally challenged the integrity of her office.

Furthermore, Shipley had in her possession all the FBI gossip about

Lillian: the 5 July 1949 report on the Eisler dinner, the 27 July 1950 Budenz charges, and the summary report issued to Pat McCarran on 4 December 1952. As Lillian noted in *Scoundrel Time*, Shipley read to her from the long list of suspect organizations to which Lillian had at one time lent her name. It was, therefore, of consummate significance when Shipley again approved a passport for Lillian in 1953. There is no doubt whatsoever that Shipley disbelieved the FBI materials.

In fact, Shipley and the Passport Office probably checked into Lillian's record on their own, not trusting FBI informants. Lillian told John that Shipley had said, "One thing we have done is to check with the entire politburo of the American party, and there isn't a single member who knows anything about you." It is hard to believe that the Passport Office reached all the party leaders, but the ones they did reach would have said they knew nothing about Lillian. There was nothing for them to know.

In 1953, however, Shipley was working for the Eisenhower administration. The only possible explanation for her failure to deliver a passport to Lillian as she had promised is pressure from above.

Above, in this case, might have been Secretary Dulles. Despite the high hopes that Dulles, because of his religious background and overt piety, would stand against the inquisition, he turned out to be as craven as most politicians when confronted with McCarthyite power. Within days of taking over the State Department, he issued a letter to all Department employees calling for "positive loyalty" to the policies of the government, with the clear implication that they had not in the past given such loyalty. In the two public cases left to him by the outgoing Acheson, John Carter Vincent and John Paton Davies, he got rid of them both, despite vigorous pleas from most of the eastern foreign policy elite. And Dulles acquiesced in the appointment of Scott McLeod, former FBI agent, then administrative assistant to Senator Styles Bridges, as chief of State Department security. McLeod and McCarthy worked closely together. When Ike nominated his friend Charles 'Chip' Bohlen as ambassador to the Soviet Union, McLeod not only recommended against Bohlen, but also leaked his opinions to Senate friends. Dulles was aghast and seriously considered firing McLeod; but in the end Dulles bowed, keeping McLeod on, and, in 1953, McLeod was Ruth Shipley's boss.[8]

Given Dulles's peripatetic ways, McLeod probably exerted the most pressure on Shipley in the Hellman case. And despite Shipley's independent ways, despite her clout with the same group of right-wing senators to whom McLeod related, she found herself compelled to use an administrative dodge to put through the approval of Lillian's passport. She claimed that she issued it because of time pressures that prevented her from consulting the security file on Lillian. On 26 February 1953, in an obvious maneuver to cover herself in case McLeod, Dulles, or any other snooping superior gave her a hard time about it, she dictated a "memorandum for file": "The time given Miss Hellman for the consideration of this work was very limited and the file was out of our hands too long for me to consult SY [Security] before granting the extension if she was not to lose her contract."[9]

She approved the renewal of Lillian's passport until 1 August the same day; Lillian got it and wrote her a note of thanks on 28 February. Shortly thereafter, Lillian left for Rome to work on the script for Korda.

John, meanwhile, was waiting. On 24 February 1953, the Loyalty-Security Board "determined that its previous decision to the effect that John Fremont Melby constitutes a security risk to the Department of State and that his removal from employment in the interest of national security should be affirmed."[10] The decision was relayed to Volpe on 9 March; should John still want to appeal the decision, the Loyalty-Security Appeals Board would hear him on 13 March. After a flurry of conferences, John and Joe Volpe decided to appeal. Pinkerton had given them another chance before; perhaps it was worth trying again.

The 13 March session was the seventh hearing "In the Matter of John Fremont Melby." Pinkerton, Mann, and Cook assembled for a final look at the record, this time with Lillian Hellman's testimony before them.

Volpe was concerned that he did not know on precisely what grounds Donovan and his board had acted; therefore he felt obliged to cover them all. He began his long statement by acknowledging that John had responded inappropriately to the first interrogatory because he thought the crucial item was China rather than Lillian Hellman; that he appeared to defend Lillian, unaware that the board had made up its mind about her; that John had answered his first two interrogatories somewhat carelessly, without advice of counsel; and that John had received bad advice in preparing for his first four hearings. The board listened politely.

Or perhaps one should say that the board appeared to listen politely. The board was, in fact, deaf to everything except the FBI gossip about Lillian, and the respect and affection John and Lillian still had for each other. Occasionally a board member would ask a question revealing that he, too, shared the lower board's assumptions: no loyal American, especially a Foreign Service officer, would knowingly associate with a *Communist*. Ambassador Cowen may have had it right when he later told Melby, "If you'd just been sleeping with your secretary, they'd have thought nothing of it. But Lillian Hellman, my God, that's something else."

Volpe dealt with whether John had kept Ambassador Cowen informed of his contacts with Lillian; the evidence now, with Cowen's extensive testimony, was clearly sufficient to establish that John had tried to inform Cowen regularly and candidly. The Pinkerton board did not respond.

Volpe also covered the two instances, Pleasantville and Philadelphia, when John and Lillian had resumed their former relationship; he argued that these were lapses which had not been repeated since, and that they did not compromise John's long record of security consciousness in any case.

Then Volpe got into the tortured question of when John and Lillian had seen each other, and why some of those times had slipped John's memory. Here Sipes had some questions to ask:

Sipes: Did I understand you correctly that the June 1952 contact in New York was one of forgetfulness, that is, with respect to not telling the Board about it? Is that correct?

Volpe: It certainly is. . . .

Sipes: Do you recall whether or not in the course of your seeing Miss Hellman on that occasion you discussed in any way your case that was coming up before the Board?

Melby: No, I do not remember discussing it.

Sipes: The hearing then before this Board was the first hearing, on June 26, 1952, which according to the dates, was less than a month after you had seen Miss Hellman in New York in her apartment. The Board, as you no doubt recall, stressed at great length and sought repeatedly to get your statement on the last time you had seen Miss Hellman, which we finally established as May 21, I believe the day of her testimony before the House Committee. My question is, could you provide this panel with any more rationale of how you could conceivably have forgotten a contact at her apartment in New York less than a month before, when it had been made clear to you . . . that the Board was interested, actually literally, in the last contact, regardless of whether you regarded it as important or not?

Melby: I can't add anything except that it was just plain forgetfulness. My main interest in the trip had been this memorial service which had gone very hard with my father. He had taken it very hard, it upset him terribly, and I just plain forgot the other things I did.

Sipes: You don't recall whether you had lunch at Miss Hellman's apartment?

Melby: I think I stayed there for lunch, as I recall.

Sipes: Have you read Miss Hellman's testimony in connection with her
recollection of that visit?

Melby: No, I have not.

Sipes: You have discussed it together with Counsel and Miss Hellman
prior to Miss Hellman's appearance before this Board, I take it, from
what Counsel just said.

Melby: I don't remember that we went into any detail of that kind.

Sipes: That is all I have, Mr. Chairman, on that.[11]

This was the June visit that only Lillian's secretary had remembered, and
John had volunteered it to the board when he was reminded about it. Yet
Sipes did not credit John for reporting it.

For two and a half hours, Volpe strove valiantly. He summarized the
testimony to Melby's competence, loyalty, and security, and argued for the
merit of returning him to active duty. The question of Melby's truthfulness
about Pleasantville and Philadelphia he brought up again in closing:

Volpe: Now, you will notice that I omitted making any reference to the
fact that Melby had not told the whole story in the earlier hearing.
The reason I omit that in connection with this question of security is
that while truthfulness, veracity, are certainly pertinent, relevant in
determining whether or not an individual is a risk, I think there is
enough in this case to persuade the Department that Mr. Melby is a
person of unquestioned veracity, honesty, and truthfulness. This has
been the testimony of all of the witnesses who have appeared, and
his not having told the whole story should be treated not as raising
any serious question of defect of character, but rather a perhaps
foolish, stupid, but nevertheless to a considerable extent understandable reluctance to talk about something that was very personal
and, as he has said, something that tormented him for some time.
And, as I indicated earlier, if this case were reduced to this one single point, what should the Department do with Melby because he
did not tell the whole story the first time? Then my feeling is that it
would no longer be a security question, but rather a question for
some disciplinary action. But I have assumed that in arriving at the
conclusion that Melby's continued employment in the Department
would constitute a risk to security, the Board did not arrive at that
decision on the ground that having withheld the story he can no
longer be trusted, because if that were the point, then I think I
would urge that in considering the security question on that ground

you should take into account his long period of service, the faithful way in which he has served during this 15- or 16-year period, what his colleagues thought about him and what they had to say about his honesty and veracity. I think the Loyalty Board must have been concerned with other aspects of the case when it arrived at its conclusion.[12]

After ten minutes of trying to show that Lillian could not possibly have any "hold" over John that would cause him to betray a trust, Volpe was through. Pinkerton thanked him for his "eloquent presentation," and asked Mann and Cook if they had any questions. They had none. The members of the board had had none throughout.

But Sipes had some questions. The day before, he heard that John had come to his old office in the State Department building to collect mail, to dictate a memorandum requested by Adrian Fisher, and to confer with Philip Jessup (at Jessup's request) about disposition of documents used in compiling the *China White Paper*. Since John was under suspension at the time, Sipes thought that he should not even be in the building. Sipes grilled John about it for fifteen minutes.

Volpe was horrified. John had never been told not to come to his office; he had been explicitly informed that it was all right to pick up his mail. And if Fisher and Jessup requested his help, how could he not come to their offices? Sipes's concluding burst of hostility, capped by his insistence "that Mr. Melby on the adjournment of this hearing take the matter up with the personnel authorities and find out what his terms of reference are when he is under suspension" drew from Volpe his first and only sharp remark:

Volpe: Mr. Sipes, we won't have to do that. I would instruct Mr. Melby that he is not to set foot on 21st Street, if you like, until this matter is disposed of and I am sure he would be glad to stay away from the State Department or the proximity of the State Department if anybody had told him to do that. I have nothing further, Mr. Chairman.

Pinkerton: That completes the evidence and we will take the matter under advisement and let you know in due course the judgment of this Appeals Board.[13]

While Lillian was preparing to leave for Europe and John was in Washington waiting to hear the outcome of his appeal, Hammett was called before the inquisition again. This time it was the top tribunal: McCarthy's Senate Permanent Subcommittee on Investigations. At the hearing of 26 March 1953, Chairman McCarthy and Counsel Roy Cohn wanted to know about Hammett's books, why they were in U.S. Information Service Libraries, and whether this was a good idea. Hammett got off some sharp lines. Asked whether he thought Communism would be a good form of government for the United States, he observed (accurately) that Communism "is *no* form of government": Hammett had read Marx and knew that, according to the master theoretician, the government would wither away. And when McCarthy asked Hammett if he thought that providing books by Communist authors in the information program was a good way to fight Communism, he answered, "If I were fighting Communism, I don't think I would do it by giving people any books at all." McCarthy did not follow up on this answer. Hammett had taken the Fifth on questions dealing with his own relations to the Party; the Committee dismissed him in frustration.[14]

Hammett was not the only one called before the inquisition. Unbelievably, anti-Communist hysteria actually intensified in these early months of the Eisenhower administration. Every day, there were four or more stories in the *New York Times* about reds, Russian plans to conquer the United States, or domestic subversives. The administration and the witch-hunters in the Senate feuded for a month over Ike's nomination of Chip Bohlen as ambassador to the Soviet Union (Bohlen was finally approved). McCarthy inaugurated his attack on subversives in the Voice of America and our overseas libraries; Cohn and Schine set off on their whirlwind junket of Western Europe, to unanimous European derision. A Senate resolution attacking the Soviet Union for breaking its wartime agreements sputtered and died. General Van Fleet claimed that U.S. forces in Korea were short of ammunition. HUAC called dozens of witnesses, many of whom invoked the Fifth. The Senate Internal Security Subcommittee, now under William Jenner, was busy ferreting out subversives in education; it also heard Herbert Philbrick, FBI plant in the Communist party, accuse six Boston clergymen of being Communists. McCarthy and Harold Stassen feuded over how best to stop Western trade with the People's Republic of China. Friends of Julius and Ethel Rosenberg continued to fight for a reprieve. The Supreme Court barred Abraham Isserman, one of the lawyers who defended the eleven top Communist leaders in the Foley Square trial, from practicing before it. The Lattimore trial was postponed until October, and Johns Hopkins University abolished the Page School of International Relations, which Lattimore headed. Lewis K. Gough, national president of the American Legion, said that the United States should use the same tactics in opposing Communism as the Russians used in opposing capitalism. Attorney General Brownell issued regulations for registration of suspect groups as subversive and began his list of Communist fronts. Et cetera.

John was hardly surprised when, on 22 April 1953, he was formally terminated by the Department of State.

Loyalty-Security boards do not release reasons for their actions. In cases that have attracted much public attention—such as those of John Stewart Service, John Carter Vincent, and John Paton Davies—we know a great deal from congressional investigations, partisan journalists, and records kept by high government officials, most of which are ultimately released. We know why Service was fired from the record of Senate deliberations found in the papers of Styles Bridges. We know about Vincent's case because Dulles was forced to make a public statement, and the Alsop brothers published many columns about Vincent. We know about John Paton Davies from congressional investigations and Dulles's records.

John Melby's case never became public; none of these sources are available. There was some State Department leakage to his friends. Sipes told Joe Volpe that the major reason for John's dismissal was his lack of candor before the board; the members thought him untrustworthy. Ray Thurston, a Foreign Service officer who had worked with Howard Donovan in India, told John that Donovan said: "Damn it, if Melby had just said he had slept with her and that was all there was to it, that would be one thing. But he kept telling us how much they had in common intellectually, and that bothered us like hell."

Probably the best indication of how the board felt is an analysis of the underlinings and marginalia of the various hearings, particularly the sixth hearing, the record of which Donovan had to read carefully due to his absence on the day it was held. There are forty-one such markings on the transcript of the whole sixth hearing. Fourteen of these indicate that Donovan (or another member, if they are not his markings) believed that the association between John and Lillian had been closer than they admitted, or that it had gone on too long after they ceased being in love. Twelve markings indicate disbelief of claims by Lillian, John, Harriman, or others that she was not a Communist but a misguided liberal. Nine markings indicate skepticism of John's claim that he could not remember some detail the board asked him about. Three show that the reader thought John should have known Lillian was a Communist and avoided her. One indicates concern that he misrepresented their relationship at Pleasantville and Philadelphia; one is unclassifiable. The overwhelming evidence is therefore that the board acted primarily on the belief that Lillian *was* a Communist and that John had been, and still was, much too close to her. It was guilt by association, in pure form.

Sipes's claim that the board decided against John only because he initially lied about Pleasantville and Philadelphia is not quite believable. The whole range of prosecutions and firings during the witch-hunt points to exculpation of falsehoods when the guilty party shows abundant contrition. Consider, for instance, the egregious perjuries committed by Whittaker Chambers before he finally admitted that he and Hiss had been involved in espionage. Chambers emerged a hero, and escaped prosecution, entirely due to his zealous conversion to the anti-Communist cause and his willingness to turn on his former comrades. Louis Budenz lived down ten years of fraud and chicanery by becoming more holy than the Pope.

Elizabeth Bentley, the ex–spy queen, made up numerous charges, one of which, against William Remington, brought on a libel suit that was settled in Remington's favor. This did not debase her standing as a witness; she mouthed the proper righteous indignation toward her former Communist colleagues. As Ralph S. Brown, Jr., notes in his monumental *Loyalty and Security* "the community generally condones . . . an unknown number of penitent liars."[15] Had John Melby been penitent, been willing to turn on Lillian Hellman, to moan about how she had taken him in, to join the board's castigation of her as a dangerous subversive, there is little doubt that he would have been cleared.

The board's recommendation that Melby be fired was not the final word; that belonged to the secretary of state. On 22 April 1953, Dulles upheld the board.

Surprisingly, there is no record in the Eisenhower Library of Dulles's deliberations in the Melby case. Dulles kept meticulous records. He made notes of even the most trivial things, such as his phone call to Senator McCarthy informing the senator that Carlisle Humelsine, undersecretary for administration in the Truman Administration, had resigned; McCarthy despised Humelsine, and Dulles wanted the senator to know about his going. Dulles recorded in great detail his anger at Scott McLeod for leaking information about the Bohlen file to various senators. Dulles had even recorded a conversation with his brother, Allen Dulles, and Attorney General Brownell about whether the three of them should go to a ball game as planned on 19 June 1953; the Rosenbergs were to be executed that night, and they decided it would make "terrific propaganda" for the left wingers for them to be enjoying themselves at that time.[16] On Melby's firing, nothing.

There is much evidence that Dulles personally dealt with all the adverse security recommendations. We have it on the authority of his sister, Eleanor Lansing Dulles, that on these matters "he felt that since the ultimate responsibility lay with him, he should examine the hundreds of pages of testimony himself. So he spent dozens of hours on the voluminous dossiers, reading most of them at home, occasionally consulting with some of his advisers or seeking more information."[17]

Equally positive statements come from John W. Hanes, Jr., a special assistant to Dulles:

> In the first couple of years, I suppose these security cases were as time consuming an individual thing as the Secretary had to do, because he did these himself when they finally came to him. The material in them is voluminous. Some of these cases, literally, had eight or ten feet of material and files. There are summaries, of course, but you never trust to a summary, really. I wouldn't. I mean, if you trust to a summary, you're trusting to the judgment of the guy who summarized it. I liked to look at the raw data, and the Secretary, being a good lawyer, did. . . . I suppose the average one of these cases would require him to spend something between eighteen and thirty hours going through, which is a hell of a thing for the Secretary of State to have to do, and in a well ordered universe it wouldn't happen. He did it. He did it very faithfully. And he did it as a good lawyer. He made his own decisions on these things.[18]

Dulles could hardly have avoided the case of a Class II Foreign Service officer.

But perhaps Dulles was really not so sedulous in reading the files on security cases. Had he read them all, he could hardly have been so ignorant about procedures. At a press conference on 24 November 1953, reporters questioned Dulles about the attitude of the Eisenhower administration toward basic rights of employees accused of being security risks. Ike had just given a speech asserting that a man should have the right to confront his accuser. One reporter reminded Dulles that Department of State employees had not had this right under Truman. Had this changed now? Dulles replied, "I believe that he does have, under the present loyalty program. . . . he has the opportunity for a hearing, in which he knows of the charges against him and who makes them." Reporters were skeptical, and pressed Dulles on this. Weren't the FBI informants still protected? Dulles waffled. Perhaps there might be a few cases where FBI material was withheld.[19] This exchange was revealing; Dulles knew very little about how his own loyalty-security programs were run. Certainly if he had read the Melby file, he would have known that no opportunity whatsoever was provided for John to confront his accusers, nor for him to rebut the anonymous charges against the alleged Communist with whom he associated.

Despite the fact that the Eisenhower Library indices list no reference to John or Lillian, there is a reference to Lillian that was discovered by Blanche Wiesen Cook. One of Ike's friends, Ward Melville, sent Ike a copy of a diary kept by an anonymous journalist who accompanied Adlai Stevenson on a worldwide tour in the summer of 1953. They were in Rome during the latter part of June. The diarist recorded:

> We then met Stan Swinton of the AP, who said that the effect of McCarthyism on the Embassy here has been insidious and that a great many specialists would like to resign mainly because their morale is shot and are only waiting to do so because resignations at this time are usually interpreted as a polite term for firing. One of Stan's acquaint-ances had just been refused an MSA [Mutual Security Administration] post because he had kept company with Lillian Hellman in 1932. This sort of thing is not calculated to create a sense of security among the staff.[20]

Refuse a post to a presumably competent man because he had "kept company with Lillian Hellman" two decades earlier? This no doubt repre-sented the true attitude of the Eisenhower administration, but one that it would not care to put on paper.

Perhaps Dulles skimmed the Melby file rather than reading it carefully, and he noticed that Lillian had been an outspoken opponent of Franco, whose cause Dulles had espoused in the 1930s as the member of Sullivan and Cromwell handling Franco's legal affairs. The anti-Franco zeal of John's lover could have settled the matter for Dulles without the necessity of studying the whole file.

The Eisenhower regime was not noted for its devotion to the arts and literature. Perhaps Ike and his millionaire cabinet were unacquainted with Lillian Hellman. But at the cutting edge of Ike's security program, where the objective was to pacify the Republican right wing, the operatives knew that Hellman had scored one on Chairman Wood, and they held it against her. Ike talked a good game about maintaining security "without besmirching the reputation of any innocent man," and, in his limp-handed way, Ike supported people like Bohlen against the witch-hunters. But Bohlen was a special case; he had played golf with Ike. Melby did not play golf. Neither did John Carter Vincent nor John Paton Davies—at least not with Ike. And there were no command performances of Hellman plays for Eisenhower.

As for the secretary of state, there is little doubt that, if Dulles got advice from subordinates, it was in line with the decision of the Melby board. Scott McLeod would have wasted no sympathy on Melby. And, in 1953, the undersecretary was John's old challenger, Walter Bedell Smith.

"Beedle" Smith would not have forgotten John's castigation of CIA intelligence personnel in Southeast Asia after John returned from the Melby-Erskine mission. Thomas C. Reeves in his biography of Joe McCarthy notes that Beedle was a "secret ally of McCarthy's."[21] Stephen E. Ambrose, in *Ike's Spies*, also calls Smith a McCarthyite, "looking for Communists under his bed at night."[22] Beedle would have despised Lillian—and fired any diplomat who slept with her, talked to her, lunched with her, or read her plays.

John considered, and rejected, going to court. This would have meant endless notoriety for their affair, embarrassment for Lillian, probably damage to Harriman who was about to be elected governor of New York, and demerits for Rusk, Erskine, Cowen—all the friends who had stood up for him. Joe Rauh believed that John could have got the decision overturned with enough high-priced legal help; Joe Volpe believes that in the climate of the time, John's perjury about events in Philadelphia would have been used against him.[23] Volpe is probably right. In the pietistic, vengeful atmosphere of the first Republican administration in twenty years, whose mission was to clean subversives out of government, anything could serve as an excuse to add one more firing to the burgeoning statistics.

The statistics appeared early in the administration, and they were startling. In October 1953, the White House announced that 1,456 persons had left the government payroll since Ike took over. This vague statement was clarified by Bernard M. Shanley, special counsel to the President, who claimed that "1,456 subversives had been kicked out of government jobs since the President assumed office."[24] As the 1954 elections approached, this figure grew. On 3 March 1954, Ike claimed that 2,427 security risks had been separated from government service.

The numbers escalated until the Civil Service Commission released figures covering the period from May 1952 through October 1954: 8,008 security firings were claimed. Donald Kemper, in *Decade of Fear*, explains what was happening: "To the public, the Eisenhower Administration, with its increased volume of alleged security separations, seemed to be striking sound blows to end the 'twenty years of treason.' This deceptive caricature of the Eisenhower security program led easily to the 'numbers game,' a Republican political device aimed at convincing the public that the Eisenhower Administration was busy ridding the federal government of Communists and fellow-travelers left over from the Truman era."[25]

What the administration was really doing was a bit less impressive. In 1955, a subcommittee of the Senate Committee on Post Office and Civil Service held hearings on the administration of the Federal Employees Security Program. Philip Young, chairman of the Civil Service Commission, appeared before the subcommittee. He admitted under questioning that less than 40 percent of the claimed number had been terminated; the rest had resigned. Those who had been fired were thought to be unreliable or unsuitable for various reasons, and most of them had been terminated under civil service regulations passed long before Eisenhower's presidency. And 40 percent of the entire group had been hired, not by the miscreants Roosevelt and Truman, but under Eisenhower.[26]

The Post Office and Civil Service made their own extensive search of personnel records, and announced in December 1955 that, through June 1955, only 343 persons had been dismissed under Eisenhower's Executive Order 10450.[27] After this, nothing more was heard of the numbers game.

The 343 dismissed by Eisenhower's Executive Order were, of course, only a small contingent of those caught up in the security net. Ralph S. Brown's conservative assessment of the overall impact of loyalty-security dismissals in the nation as a whole is that in the decade of 1947 to 1956, 11,500 persons in the United States were dismissed from a job, or were excluded from a calling. About 3,900 of these were federal employees.[28] Among them was John Melby.

Firings were only part of the story. Many people suffered in other ways. One of John's friends was Seymour Levinson, State Department finance officer. Taking advantage of obscurities in the regulations, Levinson returned the contribution John had made to the Department pension fund. Levinson was reprimanded and demoted.

One avenue of redress that John did explore was the Catholic church—at that time untainted by fellow traveling. Several of John's colleagues who received interrogatories had used their Catholic faith to help fend off the witch-hunters. John had good Catholic friends. One of them, Father Fred McGuire, then with the National Catholic Welfare Conference (NCWC), had known John in China and believed him to be the soul of discretion and anti-Communist valor. John asked Father Fred to explore the possibilities of securing a quiet reversal through Church contacts.

McGuire found this a difficult mission. His own organization, NCWC, was bitterly split between pro- and anti-McCarthyites. Eventually Father McGuire went to see Scott McLeod, whose response was chilling: "Look, I'm going to tell you for your own guidance and for Melby's welfare, if you pursue this matter, we'll turn the case over to McCarthy. He doesn't know about it."[29] End of project.

One can imagine the headlines had McCarthy gotten wind of this case: "Communist Playwright Enlists Services of High-Ranking U.S. Diplomat, Senator Asserts," "McCarthy Claims U.S. Secrets Passed to Communist Agent Within Walls of U.S. Embassy," or "U.S. Ambassador Implicated in Spying for Soviet, Says McCarthy." It is amazing that news of the Melby firing did not get to the senator. He had steady access to FBI files, and his "loyal American underground" functioned in the Department of State.

When I asked John in 1983 why his case had never become public when so much else had leaked, he responded:

> I knew a lot of newspapermen in Washington, and I thought they were all pretty good friends of mine. The only one who ever approached me about my firing was a man, whose name I don't remember, who was AP correspondent in the Philippines. One day he said, "Look, I understand there's some trouble." I said "Yes." He said, "Is there anything you want me to write about it?" I said "No." He said "O.K., then we forget about it." I think that among newspapermen there was a kind of conspiracy to protect me.

Rome, London, and Beyond

If the Cold War drove John and Lillian apart in 1947 and 1948, their mutual involvement in the witch-hunt brought them together again. Hilda Melby could sense it. On the record, for the benefit of the Loyalty-Security Board, Hilda put on a front of sweetness and light, willing to forgive and forget. Privately it was quite different. She had worked for the Foreign Service all her life, and was entranced by the prestige and perquisites of an embassy. She told John, "I would have been a wonderful ambassador's wife, and you've killed that possibility." Her resentment did not impel her to seek a divorce, and the marriage continued fitfully for fifteen years; but the affection of their courtship was gone.

The affection between John and Lillian, however, revived powerfully. They saw each other several times before she went to Rome to work on Korda's film. The clashing political beliefs responsible for their estrangement in 1947 had moderated. Lillian had dropped out of the Progressive party with its exaggerated view of Soviet innocence; John, having experienced the pathology of Cold War fanaticism, backed away from his earlier hard-line anti-Soviet position. By the 1960s, both he and Lillian were vigorous opponents of the Vietnam War.

Much of what happened to Lillian the summer of 1953 is described in *Scoundrel Time*, but much is left out, including fascinating events hinted at in her passport file, and equally revealing items in her letters to John. Most important, Lillian left out any account of her romance with John or of his firing. Despite the silence of *Scoundrel Time*, it is clear from her letters in the 1950s that she was still in love with John and wanted to share her life with him.

For one thing, the chemistry that had brought Lillian and John together in Moscow, reasserting itself almost against their will at Pleasantville and Philadelphia, continued strong. As John told me in 1983, "When we met, even after months of absence, we picked up right where we had left off." At one point during their bout with the inquisition they planned to escape to London together. John planned to divorce Hilda as soon as her health improved so that he and Lillian could, finally, marry. For Lillian, this was a reprise of her earlier affair with Ingersoll, and the parallel worried her. But her 1945 doubts about the durability of her bond with John had vanished.

Both of them knew that there were still obstacles in their way in addition to John's wife. From Lillian's standpoint, she felt responsible for Hammett, who was literally penniless because of Internal Revenue claims for back taxes. She felt an obligation to look after him.

From John's standpoint, money was crucial. He was out of a job from 1953 to 1955, living on the slim proceeds of his State Department pension refund. He was still paying child support for his sons; he could hardly afford another divorce, let alone help to provide for Lillian. Nor could he allow himself to be kept by her. But money was probably not the greatest inhibition. The only career to which John aspired was diplomacy. To marry Lillian then, in the heat of the inquisition, given the arsenal of misinformation that the FBI, HUAC, McCarthy, McCarran, and the right-wing press could use against her—and thus him too—would forever bar him from getting his security clearance restored. It was perhaps a classic choice for him: career versus love.

And Lillian was still, despite her passport clearance from Shipley, in trouble. Lillian began to suspect that her mail was being intercepted by the FBI. Consequently while she was in Europe in 1953, she and John corresponded through Lillian's secretary, Lois Fritsch, in New York. Each would write to Lois, with no other name and no return address on the envelope; Lois would then forward the letters from her New York address. This strategem was only partially successful; by bribing a hotel messenger, Lillian discovered that her mail was intercepted in Rome by the CIA.[1]

Lillian's trouble appeared to begin in June. She had then been in Rome a month; realizing that she would not be able to finish her work for Korda by the time her passport expired on 1 August, she wrote Shipley for an extension:

Rome, Italy
June 14th, 1953

Dear Mrs. Shipley,

I am writing to ask for an extension of my passport which expires the first week of this August, 1953. Because I have signed a motion picture contract, and am now writing the scenario, and because I have arranged for the production of two of my plays in London and Paris, it will be necessary for me to be coming back and forth for the next year.

I will still be in Europe when my passport expires and, in the light of past circumstances, I have thought it best to write to you and ask how I should go about arranging the extension. I have no permanent address here, so may I ask that an answer be sent to 63 East 82nd Street, New York City, and my secretary will forward it to me wherever I am.

I am sure I do not have to say that I have most strictly observed, in every particular, my letter to you of last February.

I am grateful for your past kindness to me, and I wish you a most pleasant summer.

Most sincerely,
Lillian Hellman[2]

The letter was received in Shipley's office on 18 June. Seven days later, Shipley wrote Lillian a letter directed to the New York address; "In reply to your letter dated June 14, 1953, you are informed that the Department has instructed the American Embassies at Rome, London and Paris to renew your passport for a further period of one year at such time as you may make application therefor." When Shipley's letter reached Lois Fritsch in New York, Fritsch dutifully forwarded it, unopened, to Lillian in Italy.

We do not know whether Shipley consulted her superiors on this, nor whether they gave her trouble if she did. There was no hiatus in the execution of the decision as there had been in February. The passport file shows that Airgram No. 3083, dated 25 June 1953, went to the American embassy in Rome, with copies to London and Paris. The routine sender was "DULLES," with Shipley's initials underneath. A notation at the bottom of the file copy says "Sent." The clerk who filed the cable, J. F. Simpson, also initialed it. It is inconceivable that this message did not go out, with copies to London and Paris: "Upon application, you are authorized to renew passport No. 491701 which was issued on August 2, 1951, to Lillian Hellman for a period of one year. The passport should be restricted for travel to the British Isles, France and Italy and necessary countries en route."

On 28 June, three days after Shipley had written Lillian that she *would* get a full year's passport renewal, the *New York Times* carried a story saying that Roy Cohn, acting for McCarthy's Permanent Subcommittee on Investigation, had announced that twenty-three persons were to be called as possible witnesses to testify on the State Department's overseas libraries and information centers. Cohn said the committee was having "great diffi-culty" locating some of the witnesses: "It is obvious they are ducking [my subpoenas]." Among those to be called, in the order listed by the *Times*: Rockwell Kent, Lillian Hellman, Dorothy Parker, Paul Robeson, Richard O. Boyer, Corliss Lamont. Who was ducking his subpoenas? Cohn would not say.[3]

Not knowing of the McCarthy story, in early July Lillian wrote John of her adventures. She did not like Rome in summer; it was too hot, and she could not accustom herself to taking a siesta. Yet she could not bring herself to leave. She was in as much demand for dinner parties as she had been in New York, but she liked her fellow diners less. At one dinner she met the sister of a prominent British politician who asked Lillian to read her war diary. Lillian did read the diary and told John in graphic terms that it revealed why Britain was in decline: the diary had favorable references to the Germans and snide remarks about Jews. Lillian was way behind in her writing, and dissatisfied with what she had written.

And she missed John: "I hope something good has happened for you this week. It is an odd crime that in all the years you couldn't come to New York, and now you can, I'm not there." Lillian also commented on the future. Hilda Melby was still sick that summer, and—shades of Ingersoll—John was hesitant to tell his wife how things stood with Lillian. Lillian also commented on this in her letter: "You don't give me much news of home life. How is Missy? [Hilda] Have you ever discussed future plans with her, or is it wisest and kinder to leave things alone now? I am sorry about the sale of the house—I would have guessed wrong that Republicans would pay more money. And now, darling, it is early morning and I must go to work before it's too hot to do anything. Lois will see you, and consult you, possibly before you get this. Forgive this letter—its all disconnected. And much, much love, always."

Lois was to consult John about Lillian's desire to make a quick and quiet trip back to the United States in late August to get the road show of *The Children's Hour* properly underway. She was afraid that if she came back, either HUAC, now under Representative Harold Velde, or Joe McCarthy, would call her to testify, thus preventing her from finishing her contract with Korda. Lois was to find out what John thought about this. John does not remember what he thought, and if he wrote Lillian about it, the letter does not survive. Lillian asked Joe Rauh the same question, however, and his answer is available. Rauh told her it was possible, but not probable, that she would be subpoenaed, depending on how much publicity she received. There was something else:

Another factor is whether either of the Committees is familiar with John's case. It seems quite certain now that McLeod himself made the adverse decision in John's case and is thus well acquainted with all the facts. This would certainly seem to indicate that the McCarthy Committee knows all about John's case and your "relation" to it. On the other hand, if this is true, why haven't they called John and had a Roman Holiday with him? Unfortunately, one does not dare make even the most discreet of inquiries about such a subject for fear that an inquiry would raise questions and result in actions that might otherwise not be thought of.[4]

Shortly after Lillian wrote her letter to John, the *Rome Daily American* carried the story about McCarthy's subpoena; in *Scoundrel Time* she writes as if she first learned of it ten days before her passport expired. This must have been on 21 July. At this late date, she still did not know that Shipley had ordered her passport renewed. The imminence of her passport's expiration and the shock of another subpoena upset her greatly, as she says in *Scoundrel Time*:

I knew that with the news of McCarthy, and no passport, Korda would not, could not go on employing me.

I started out for the cable office, deciding that I would send McCarthy my Rome address, but a few cups of coffee later I knew there was something the matter with that kind of showing-off because most certainly he knew that I was in Rome and where to reach me. When I realized that it had taken me an hour to figure that out, I knew that I had better not rely on my own judgments. I telephoned the office of Ercole Graziadei, a fine lawyer whom I'd met several times, a man who had a splended reputation as an anti-Fascist under Mussolini. He said that although I could not be sure of the newspaper story, it was now certain the American consul in Rome would not issue an extension of my passport. He also said that he believed Rome was not a good place for me because the Italian government often took their orders from Mrs. Luce and they could pick me up or harass me on an even lesser charge than evading a subpoena, or for using a passport that had expired. I said I thought I'd go back to New York immediately. He laughed and said he thought that was foolish: I would be giving up a job I needed, walking into trouble. Why didn't I go up to London for a few days, where the government didn't take orders from Washington, and try for an extension of my passport there?[5]

She took Graziadei's advice. The CIA tried to disrupt her plans, but she stayed far enough ahead of them to make it to London. Her adventures there are also recorded in *Scoundrel Time*; the American consul told her he could not extend her passport, but that he would have to refer the matter to Washington. We do not know whether Shipley's approval cable had gotten lost in a stack of papers at the Embassy in London, whether Ambassador Winthrop Aldrich refused to follow instructions from the Passport Office, or whether lesser officials were stalling. There is no record in Lillian's passport file that London questioned Shipley's 25 June order. But about five days after she first applied, the consul in London renewed her passport for three months, and she returned to Italy.

In Rome once again, she phoned Dash to ask if anything had transpired on the McCarthy subpoena; Dash told her that "there had been nothing in the New York newspapers about a subpoena" for her. He was wrong; he did not go back far enough in the *Times*, to the story of 28 June. But luckily for her, McCarthy had not carried through with his earlier intentions. Her worries, and the trip to London, had been unnecessary. But she did discover that a CIA operative, whom she calls Dick, had been behind her harassment and was regularly getting information from the hotel personnel about her.

It was obvious by now that having Lois Fritsch forward letters to Lillian unopened had disadvantages. Lillian wrote John again in late July, just before she left Rome, complaining about the disruption her passport renewal had caused and observing that if Lois had opened Shipley's letter and cabled Lillian the good news, her life would have been much easier. Despite her troubles, parts of this letter were upbeat. Ruth Shipley had once again been good to her; this continued to astound Lillian. James O'Sullivan, a friend of John's then working in Rome, had invited Lillian to dinner the morning after Rome newspapers carried the story about McCarthy's subpoena. Lillian thought this a brave gesture, even though she couldn't accept the invitation at the time. And, reflecting on the witch hunt, she remarked that the atmosphere in Washington was so poisonous that John wouldn't be able to take it even if he still had his job.

But Lillian was sorely tried by the loss of time over the passport matter and afraid that she wouldn't get her script for Korda done on schedule. She was no longer sure she would get back to New York in September as planned. As she wrote John, "Under ordinary circumstances, I would have come home a month ago: I am tired of Europe, sick of travelling, and forever sick of not living with somebody I want to be with. I don't know what can be done about that—I know only what I have known for a long time: this is no way to go on, and hard, hard for me. . . . And as soon as I feel a little more cheerful, I will write again. I am a crotchety old lady today who only wishes you were here, or I were there, or we were some place, in some kind of life. All my love, darling."

Lillian called James O'Sullivan before she left Rome. He and his wife invited Lillian to go with them to see the Harlem Globetrotters, then appearing in Rome. She turned this invitation down, but accepted dinner at a favorite restaurant. O'Sullivan, now a professor at the University of Louisville, says Lillian did not discuss her passport troubles.[6]

Lillian says little in her memoirs about the rest of 1953. From a letter to John of 19 August, we know that she left Rome for Biarritz ten days earlier with Frank and Kay Gervasi; he was a reporter for *Collier's*. The car had trouble, Lillian got sick on the trip, and the apartment William Wyler had rented for her in Biarritz was awful. She forfeited a large deposit on it and moved to the Miramar Hotel. The Miramar was fine, but as she wrote John, "I know only that I am tired of hotels, tired of being with people about whom I do not give a damn: that, of course, is the only real loneliness."

There was a mail strike in France while Lillian was in Biarritz. The hotel claimed they sent a courier to Spain frequently with letters to be mailed, but she wasn't sure if John would ever get hers. But if he did, she sent "love, and hope, and more love."

Lillian did finish her script in Biarritz and took it to London toward the end of August. She wrote John again just before she was to have a final settlement with Korda. Being in England, as always, improved her morale. She was again staying at Claridge's and got a letter from John there. Apparently John had hinted at something important developing in Washington, but was not specific. She was frustrated at his vagueness: "I wish to God there had been good news for you. You have taken it all with such grace and good nature, so much better than I have taken less important things."

As to England, she resented English criticisms of the United States. "But this is, as always, a pleasant land, if they could only do something about the climate. I don't know what made these people so reasonable, so undisturbed, so determined on liberty, but they have it all. If they could only cook and stop the rain. . . . I can't tell you, particularly since I've been here, how much I have wanted you to be here, too. It was two years ago now that we thought of it, and then everything began to pop. And how many years before that did we think of being together? The older I grow the more I am haunted by the need of people doing things at the time they should be done—and the less I seem to do them. . . ." [punctuation as in original]

John and Lillian did meet several times during the summer of 1953 after she returned from England, both in New York City and at Martha's Vineyard. John remembers having lunch with Robert Shaplen in Greenwich Village one day before he took a plane to the Vineyard. But despite the hopes which Lillian expressed in her letter from London, hopes that they both maintained for many years, they were never together again for any significant period. Partly this was because Hammett's health deteriorated. Lillian resented having to take care of him, despite the glowing account of their later relationship that she gives in her memoirs. And John's job search absorbed him almost completely.

At first after his firing, John felt that his skills and experience would be welcome in business; he might even be able to make some money. He rapidly discovered that Foreign Service skills were not readily transferable to anything else, and that having been in the State Department was the kiss of death. It did not matter how or why he had left; some employers to whom he applied were indifferent to the reason he was no longer in the Department. McCarthy had made working in the Department such a stigma that jobs were very hard to come by.

One of his first efforts, the job in New York to which Lillian refers in one of her letters from Rome, was with Standard Oil; it would have taken him to Cuba. After initial encouragement, he found they didn't really need a new man in Havana after all. It was the same everywhere. He tried the international departments of the big eastern banks: "Sorry, no openings now." This lasted from April 1953 to the summer of 1955; he was without work almost two years.

John had known Douglas Oliver, an anthropologist who was then at Harvard, and who was influential in promoting academic programs dealing with Asia. Oliver knew of a one-year research fellowship at Yale, for which he recommended John. Yale was not at that time a noticeably liberal institution; Communists were not tolerated on the faculty. One might have expected that a man fired from the State Department as a security risk might not have passed muster with the Yale administration; but John got the job, and during the academic year of 1955 to 1956, he began to get acquainted with what would eventually become a new career.

By 1955, Lillian had inherited some money and was in better financial shape. But she was still wary of the claims of the Internal Revenue Service, fearful that it would discover some new reason for confiscating her money. John remembers that she sent him five hundred dollars which he kept in his bank account in New Haven, mailing her cash as she requested it for Hammett's expenses.

At least once, Lillian interceded with one of her academic friends on John's behalf. He still has a copy of a letter of recommendation that she wrote for him to Harold Taylor, President of Sarah Lawrence College, but nothing came of it.

While John was at Yale, he was offered a chance to take part in a new operation that was much to his liking.

Jameson Parker, Ambassador Cowen's former assistant, and Eleanor Wolf, wife of a prominent Philadelphia attorney, Robert Wolf, were interested in establishing an organization to promote the study of Asian affairs at a grass-roots level. They felt that college was too late for Americans to learn something about the mysterious Orient, and they wanted to encourage broader education among the citizenry, especially in the public schools. In 1956, with John's help, they established the National Council on Asian Affairs, with an office in Philadelphia. They got financial support from John D. Rockefeller III, and for three years John was the director of the Council.

This was a task that John thoroughly enjoyed. His new Council did not duplicate the work of the by then moribund Institute of Pacific Relations, which had focused on specialist monographs; he held many seminars for high school teachers from all over the country. (His researchers discovered world geography textbooks that had more pages on the Netherlands than on the whole of Asia.) The Council used Asians living in the United States as instructors for these seminars and managed to establish courses on Asia in many public schools. The operation was clearly a success, but money was always a problem, despite Rockefeller's contributions. Lillian tried to be helpful in John's fund-raising. She wrote him in 1956 suggesting potential donors. One of them was Arthur W. A. Cowan, the eccentric Philadelphia attorney to whom she devoted a chapter of *Pentimento*. John went to see Cowan, who was pleasant but condescending: Cowan put his feet up on his desk, almost in John's face. No money was forthcoming.

Neither Lillian's suggestions nor other efforts to raise money kept the National Council on Asian Affairs on a sound financial basis. And in the late fifties, Rockefeller came to the conclusion that McCarthyism had so damaged all the professionals in the Asian field that the best thing to do was to start afresh with a whole new group uncontaminated by previous experience in China. He therefore withdrew his support of the National Council on Asian Affairs and started the Asia Society in New York. John and his co-workers never found the funds to keep the Council going; it folded in the summer of 1959.

During 1958, John talked with Pierce Gerety, a New York lawyer who had formerly been general counsel of the Civil Service Commission and was then a member of the United Nations Security Board. Gerety knew civil service regulations, and advised John that it was possible for an individual who had difficulties with one federal agency to apply through the Civil Service Commission for security clearance with other agencies. Gerety filed such an application in John's behalf, and on 11 August 1958, the request was granted.[7] But there was a catch-22; an agency seeking to employ such an individual had to consult with the agency from which he had been separated. That meant, in John's case, the State Department. Gerety soon discovered that the Department was unyielding, still suffering under the McCarthyite attack, and that State's veto was always acceded to. This blocked several applications John made for federal jobs during the next six years.

John kept Lillian informed of his Philadelphia activities, mostly by phone, occasionally by letters which have not survived. In 1959, he told her about his frustrations in trying to get government jobs. After he phoned her in June 1959, she responded with condolences and regrets for missed opportunities:

Sunday night

How very long since I have written to you. It was good to talk to you: I had just finished cooking dinner and feeling as if I wished there were some place to go, and regretted the ties that would have made that impossible, and wondering how they came about, and thinking how careless, nothing but careless, most of us are, and how carelessness accounts for most people, everywhere. That doesn't seem sad, it just seems careless. . . .

She closed, as usual, sending much love and an invitation to visit.

Something new now developed at Philadelphia. The University of Pennsylvania had many foreign students and little guidance for them on all the pitfalls of big cities and American folkways. After a Korean student was murdered on campus with much unfavorable publicity resulting, the university decided to upgrade the existing minimal job of foreign student adviser; John was hired for this. It was hardly the equivalent of an ambassadorship, but it gave John something respectable to do while he pursued better jobs. He served in this post for five years. The foreign student adviser duties kept John out of his office much of the time. In August 1959, after several attempts to reach him by phone at the university, Lillian sent this note on her letterhead postcard: "Dear Prof. Melby, I have called you twice. Can a non-PhD ask how you are, and where? A non-PhD."

John had known during the Eisenhower years that his chances of returning to government service were slim, but he still wanted desperately to take
up again the diplomatic work at which he had been so successful. Consequently when John F. Kennedy was elected president in 1960, his expectations soared. Lillian, then in London, wrote him a note from Claridge's: she
hoped that the Kennedy administration would be good for him—and for
the country.

For John and other Foreign Service officers who had suffered under
Dulles and Eisenhower, a return to a Democratic White House had to mean
a change for the better, possibly even restitution for previous wrongs.
When Dean Rusk was appointed secretary of state, John's fortunes seemed
much improved; Rusk knew John's work firsthand.

In December 1960, John wrote Rusk, expressing the hope that now Rusk
could deliver what Acheson had been unable to: a reversal of the unfavorable security decision. Rusk answered on 29 December, guardedly, saying
in a postscript, "I can't take up your main question until I am aboard." No
matter; John knew it would not happen overnight. He also wrote Averell
Harriman, who was to be ambassador-at-large; Harriman replied that he
would welcome John back in government.[8] It looked like easy sledding.

But the months went by, and nothing happened. The New Frontier
turned out not to mean new personnel policies, at least where security
matters were concerned. And Kennedy was not a friend of those who had
been fired during the McCarthy days; he had himself been close to McCarthy, as had Kennedy's father. During a campaign speech in Massachusetts,
Kennedy had attacked Lattimore and John K. Fairbank for selling out
China. Just as Kennedy postponed withdrawal from Vietnam for fear of
stirring up opposition before the 1964 elections, so he postponed doing
anything about the security wrongs of the 1950s.

The attorney general, Robert Kennedy, played a major role in this area.
When I talked to Dean Rusk in 1984, he explained that his inability to do
anything about John's case—or about John Paton Davies, who was also in
limbo—was due to Bobby's decisions. Bobby Kennedy was not a liberal in
those days; he did not sympathize with victims of the witch-hunt. He told
Rusk that anyone who had been a witness for an officer fired previously
could not deal with that officer's request for clearance. Rusk had been a
witness for both John Melby and John Davies; hence he was barred from
pushing their cases. Rusk told me, "I was sad about that. They had a right to
expect more of me as Secretary of State."[9]

So John was forced to deal with subordinates and politicians. He contacted Roger Jones, under secretary for administration, and Jones's succes-

sor, William Orrick; when this seemed to get him nowhere, John visited Pennsylvania Senator Joseph S. Clark, Jr., whom he had met in Philadelphia. For four years, Clark fought with the State Department bureaucracy to get John's security clearance restored.

There was always some reason why it couldn't be done—*yet*. Roger Jones said the real problem was not within the Department; it was the House Committee on Un-American Activities. That committee maintained, Jones said, a list of persons it did not wish promoted, and of persons it did not wish re-employed. Melby's name was on the list. Jones further claimed that there was a plant in his office to check on Department actions, that he knew who this was, but could do nothing about it. As of July 1962, Jones claimed that the Department had succeeded in getting only one name removed from the list.[10]

Even the Peace Corps, President Kennedy's pet project, was constrained by hangovers from the inquisition. John was intrigued by the idea of a Peace Corps and sought an interview with Bill Moyers, assistant to Director Sargent Shriver. Moyers and John hit it off immediately. Moyers wanted John to go to Indonesia as director of the Peace Corps operation there and proposed this to Shriver. Shriver sent to the State Department for John's file.

When Shriver saw the file, as Moyers later told John, Shriver said, "This is a lot of garbage. Forget it. He's all right." The one thing Shriver and Moyers were determined to avoid was hiring people who had any previous connection to the CIA. The Peace Corps had to be free of the taint of dirty tricks. John met this criterion. He was hired on the spot, on a temporary basis, to train volunteers preparing to go to Ceylon. He loved it.

But by the end of the Ceylon training, no approval for a regular appointment came through. John did not learn, and Bill Moyers no longer remembers, precisely how the appointment was killed.[11] John suspects it was the HUAC's influence.

Senator Clark and his assistant Harry Schwartz spent a great deal of time on John's case, heckling the State Department bureaucracy endlessly. Nothing moved; the matter was always "under consideration." On 16 June 1964, John wrote Rusk again:

Dear Dean:

After discussing the matter with Joe Volpe who is my lawyer, I am writing an appeal to you personally because I have quite frankly reached the end of ideas as to what else I can do about the shadow which has affected everything I have done professionally for the last eleven years. Even in my efforts to secure a position in the educational or other private internationally-oriented organization world with which I have been associated for some years, this has repeatedly been the case. In my present circumstances, there is no reason to assume other than that it will continue to be so, unless there can be some resolution of my security problem.

The situation is made more difficult by the fact that my profession of the practice of international relations, in which I have literally spent my entire life, has reached the point where sooner or later any form— and I emphasize this—of its practice touches some activity of our Government. In our world it could hardly be otherwise, in view of our country's international role and the inevitable interweaving of governmental with educational and foundation activities. This has been the principal reason I have persisted in seeking a clearance. (Another important one, incidentally, has been the effect on my sons. One of them had his commission in the Army held up for six months because of me.)

As you know, the Department about a year ago agreed to reconsider my case if someone requested it in connection with any particular job for which someone wanted me. I thought at the time that this would be easy to arrange in any of several directions. And, indeed, a substantial number of people have expressed more than passing interest in being helpful and have actually had job openings for which I was qualified. Some were in the Government; some were not. But here a pattern emerged. Everything would go well; agreement would be reached. Then the whole thing would vanish in embarrassment and with evasion instead of explanation. Obviously at the final moment of decision, people have been swayed by the security background, and have preferred to avoid involvement in the troubles of others and to play it safe, despite their previous and vigorous protestations that the errors of the past as a minimum have a right to be reviewed in this somewhat saner period. Naturally I can understand their reluctance in view of what we have all been through, but I cannot like or admire it.

The most recent case is illustrative. This past spring I have been negotiating with George Washington University about two jobs. Both interested me and the University was interested in me for either of them. One would have required a security clearance; the other would not. Early in May I had every reason to believe we had reached agreement and was so told explicitly; and then little by little there wasn't anything there on either job. Nor was there any explanation as to what had happened, only evasion and vague apologies. It was the same sequence that had happened before.

I have about concluded that it is futile to attempt to clear up this matter by this method, and that the only approach left is to go directly to the heart of the problem. I am, therefore, asking you for reinstatement in the Foreign Service. . . .

I believe that the total of my background and work, including what I have been able to do in recent years, has given me a rather unique experience to offer in international affairs and that I have something useful to offer. I can no longer see how it will be of much value in the future, however, unless this taint can be removed.

Sincerely,
John F. Melby

The answer came, six weeks later, from William J. Crockett, deputy under secretary for administration of the Department of State: we are studying your file. Four months later, in November 1964, John wrote Crockett to ask what was happening. Crockett's assistant answered; the boss was out of the country. On 5 January 1965, John wrote Senator Clark again; Clark again pressured the bureaucracy. Nothing happened. John wrote Crockett again in July 1965; no response. This went on for another year.[12] Finally, in early 1966, the State Department ordered a full field investigation of John by the FBI. This was completed by summer; no negative data were uncovered. Still the Department stalled.

By summer 1966, however, John had found surcease from his troubles. He went to Toronto to see friends who had formerly been in the Canadian Foreign Service, met John Holmes—also an acquaintance from State Department days—found that Holmes was now director of the Canadian Institute for International Affairs and was recruiting people to establish international programs in Canadian universities. One of the new universities, Guelph, wanted a Chinese program. John interviewed at Guelph, found the prospects exciting, and on 1 July, assumed the chairmanship of the department of political studies.

Joe Clark continued to needle the State Department for another few months; by then John was happy at Guelph, and Clark let the matter drop. Hilda did not want to move to Canada; she had a good job with the National Science Foundation. In 1967 she and John were divorced.

John's new job in Canada pleased Lillian. She wrote from Vineyard Haven on 8 July 1966, congratulating him and expressing again the belief that he was better off not being in Washington.

Lillian had by 1966 determined to do the memoir that became *An Unfinished Woman*. As with all of her writing, this meant lengthy research and visits to whatever locale she was writing about. Consequently, that summer she returned to Moscow, a trip that she describes in some detail.[13] On 14 November, back in New York, she wrote John again "That long pole of memory got deeply stirred, and I thought a great deal about you."

The 1966 visit to Moscow did not satisfy Lillian's urge to revivify the memories of her wartime trip, and she went again in 1967. This time she had as interpreter Maya Koreneva, a specialist in American literature and a member of the Gorky Institute of World Literature. Lillian established with Koreneva the same personal relationship she had in 1944 with Orlova; Carl Rollyson wrote Koreneva when he was researching his biography of Hellman, and got in return a rich, insightful sixteen-page letter.[14]

One of the incidents Koreneva relates shows that Lillian *could* be critical of the Soviet Union. Lillian was asked by Radio Moscow to do an interview for local broadcast, and she agreed to this. The first part of the interview went well, with Lillian expressing her strong opposition to the Vietnam War—a position that the Russians liked. Then she criticized the Soviets for something trivial, and the interviewers protested. She told them that she would not allow the interview to be edited for broadcast, and the whole thing was canceled.

Lillian and Maya Koreneva did not agree about Khrushchev. Maya approved his rehabilitation of Stalin's victims, but she was appalled at his buffoonery, as when he pounded his shoe on the table at the United Nations. Khrushchev was also not as generous to artists as Stalin had been; his views were vulgar. Lillian, in this instance, supported Khrushchev: he *had* eased the repressive atmosphere, and as for acting the clown at the United Nations, that at least showed he was human.

In Canada, John found the paranoia about things Chinese that still dominated American politics and academia much less potent. The Canadian government, not regarding Chiang Kai-shek as the savior of the Orient or Madame Chiang as Joan of Arc, had quietly made peace with Mao Tse-tung; trade and exchanges of personnel between Canada and the People's Republic were flourishing. In John's new position, he found that his manuscript on the fall of the Nationalist government, which no publisher in the United States had been willing to take, was indeed saleable. The University of Toronto Press published *Mandate of Heaven* in 1968; John dedicated the book to Lillian. When he was in New York shortly after publication, he visited her again. In December 1968, Lillian wrote him a note: she had enjoyed the book and enjoyed his visit. He should plan to come again.

For five years, John headed the political studies department at Guelph; when his term as Head was over, he continued as professor. This gave him, finally, an opportunity to work in the field to which he was devoted, although not as a servant of the United States government. He married again in Canada and settled down with his Canadian wife, Roxana, in a 150-year-old stone house in the heart of Guelph, where he still lives.

His affection for Lillian continued, as did hers for him. Almost every letter or note she wrote him included an invitation to come visit. When *An Unfinished Woman* was due from the press in 1969, she wrote: "You appear in the Russian stuff, and I think you will like your appearance." When she sent him a copy, her inscription was "For John with much love & because he is in, importantly, this book. Lillian."

In late 1969, Orville Schell, writer on Asia and one of the founders of the Committee of Concerned Asian Scholars (CCAS), began to put together a program for the CCAS meeting to be held in San Francisco the next April. CCAS was a group of young opponents of the Vietnam War, who saw in our involvement in that unhappy land the lingering influence of McCarthyism and of the "loss" of China. Most of the established academicians in the Asian field belonged to the conservative Association for Asian Studies, whose attitude toward Schell and CCAS was one of wariness. The Association for Asian Studies was meeting in San Francisco in April 1970, and CCAS met there at the same time, as a kind of appendage.

Schell wanted to produce a panel for CCAS that would consider the relationships between our China debacle, the inquisition, and Vietnam. Accordingly, in early December 1969, he wrote Lillian, John, Jim Peck (also a founder of CCAS), and John King Fairbank of Harvard, asking them to speak to his general topic and then discuss it among themselves and with the audience. Schell was not aware of the romance between Lillian and John.[15]

When John got his invitation from Schell, he immediately wrote Lillian. How did she know Schell? Would she participate on the San Francisco panel? She was sailing in the Virgin Islands at the time, but she answered John in January: "The conference sounds kind of interesting, but I don't quite know what I would be doing there. However, we might have fun together. If you hear more, or even if you understand anything, would you write me? My love to you and a happy year."

John knew about the Association for Asian Studies and was aware of the challenging CCAS; he wrote her what he knew about the conference. They both decided to go.

The CCAS program in San Francisco in April 1970 was jammed. Schell introduced the speakers, who made brief remarks. Lillian was the star; Jim Peck says that she was forceful, intense, eloquent, and had the audience in the palm of her hand.[16] But many in the audience, outraged at the conservatism of the Asian studies establishment and at the revelations of CIA money behind various scholarly foundations, wanted to castigate Professor Fairbank. Hostile questions and comments degenerated into pandemonium. It was not the kind of discussion Schell had planned on; he adjourned the meeting. Owen Lattimore was in the audience, but took no part.

Afterward, John, Lillian, and Schell went to the KRON-TV studios, where the station paid them fifty dollars each to record their views on China and Vietnam. All three signed their checks over to CCAS.

That evening John and Lillian went to a prominent Chinese restaurant. Danny Kaye happened to be there, and, as he frequently did, shared his culinary skills with restaurant patrons: he cooked their dinner that night. It was one to remember; John and Lillian never saw each other again.

The FBI recorded Lillian's appearance in San Francisco. Serial 72 of her headquarters file notes: "Information coming to our attention reveals Hellman's support of New Left and antiwar groups. According to information received in April, 1970, she was one of the speakers at the Second Annual National Conference of the Committee of Concerned Asian Scholars, described as a New Left-type group made up of students and instructors which is against the war in Vietnam and supports the government of Communist China."[17]

Nineteen seventy was thé second year of the Nixon administration. Lillian was alarmed by what appeared to be increasing repression of dissent and public debate. She had been teaching, first at Harvard, then at MIT, and it seemed to her that student dissidents had a legitimate message that Nixon and Attorney General Mitchell were seeking to stifle. She had long been inactive in politics, but the times seemed to cry out for some kind of action.

The American Civil Liberties Union, long a bulwark of the Bill of Rights, appeared to be weakening. During the summer of 1970, Lillian called together a group of like-minded intellectuals to form what became the Committee for Public Justice (CPJ). It was a stellar group; the first executive council included Robert Coles, Norman Dorsen, Burke Marshall, Robert B. Silvers, Telford Taylor, Jerome Wiesner, and Harold Willens. They hired an executive director, published a newsletter (*Justice Department Watch*), and discussed ways of countering Nixonian repression. Lillian's name on fundraising appeals assured funds for a decade.

The new committee announced its formation at a New York press conference on 17 November 1970. Most of the publicity centered on Ramsey Clark, attorney general in the Johnson administration, who had just published a book critical of J. Edgar Hoover. But Lillian's role in forming the Committee for Public Justice was duly noted. As the *Washington Post* put it, "Playwright Lillian Hellman, the principal organizer of the group, also spoke at today's news conference. She said she felt impelled to do something last spring because 'some of us thought we heard the voice of Joe McCarthy coming from the grave.'"[18]

Appropriately, the FBI, whose scurrilous gossip had caused Lillian so much anguish two decades earlier, was the target of CPJ's first full-scale operation. On 29 and 30 October 1971, CPJ and Princeton's Woodrow Wilson School of International Affairs held a conference on the FBI at Princeton. The agenda was a series of scholarly papers and discussions about the Bureau, in which the country's foremost students of civil liberties participated.[19] Lillian did not speak, but she derived much quiet satisfaction from hearing Frank Donner analyze the crudities and falsehoods of FBI political informers.

J. Edgar Hoover was invited. In a blistering four thousand–word letter to Professor Duane Lockard of Princeton, Hoover said:

> Thank you for your letter of September 28, 1971, extending to me an invitation for a representative of the FBI to "strongly defend the Bureau and its role" during the forthcoming October conference which will, in your words, focus "primarily on the Federal Bureau of Investigation." We were aware of the plans for the conference, having read the announcements in the press, and some related remarks, critical of the FBI, attributed to persons who apparently will be among the "judges" hearing this case. . . .
>
> While I should like to believe that the correlation between your own words casting us in the role of a defendant, and the critical remarks made by some of the "judges" before the fact-finding inquiry had even begun is one of pure coincidence only, you will understand from that coincidence why I immediately recalled with some amusement the story of the frontier judge who said he would first give the defendant a fair trial and then hang him.[20]

The last item released in Lillian's FBI file is a report on the members of CPJ's executive council. To the Bureau's chagrin, of the eleven people involved, six had never been investigated by the Bureau, hence were presumably "clean"; four had been investigated, cleared, and had served as officers of the federal government; only one, Lillian herself, appeared in Bureau files as subversive and on its Security Index.[21]

CPJ was active as a watchdog of civil liberties until 1982, when Lillian's health forced her to give up such efforts.

John and Lillian continued to write and talk on the telephone. In January 1974, he wrote her praising *Pentimento*; she responded with thanks and another invitation to visit. In April, she was excited by a visit John was about to make to his old haunts in China. She had wanted to go herself but had not been able to get a visa for the People's Republic. John wrote that he had seen her on a television program, for which he congratulated her; she responded: "I am glad you liked the Moyers show. For the first time in my life I liked myself on television. Moyers is, indeed, very good."

Later that spring Lillian made her last trip to Europe. She found John's report on his China trip waiting when she returned. It was his usual colorful commentary, for which she expressed thanks. But there was a troubling note in her letter, dated 10 June 1974: she had been diagnosed as having an irregular heart. This was the beginning of the series of illnesses from which she never recovered.

In September 1975, Lillian was struggling with the manuscript of *Scoundrel Time*. She tells us at the beginning of the book how difficult it was to write. One of the things she does not tell us is about her struggles over whether to describe the very large part John played in her clash with the inquisition. John was, by then, tenured at a Canadian university. Presumably, public acknowledgement in the 1970s of an affair that had peaked in the 1940s would have done him little harm, and she herself was well beyond serious damage by any of her former persecutors. Nonetheless, she decided to leave out entirely that part of her story; in a letter to John from Vineyard Haven that September she explains why:

> I am now through a second draft of the short book. Tomorrow my editor arrives. I am almost sure I will need a third draft. You were in the first draft, that was why I wrote you for info., but somehow our history both touched me and pained me and in the second draft I took it out because I couldn't figure out how to do it. I have never been in any doubt that I took our affair very seriously, but I didn't and don't know why the fact that it had no end, was so disturbing to me. Maybe because I just plain never understood and maybe you didn't either. In any case, my inability is the sign of the feeling that is still there, of course.

This is at best a misleading explanation. As Diane Johnson discovered, at this stage Lillian was determined that her life be written to her specifications. Hammett's role was to be that of the hero who "had been waiting for her all the years until he met her," and who "merited the patience, wisdom, and expense lavished on him by the heroine."[22] In this formula, there was no room for another hero or heroes—hence the banishing of Ingersoll, Melby, and lesser lovers. Rollyson puts it well: "How to make room for John when Dash has already been cast as her leading man?"[23]

So *Scoundrel Time* came out stripped of her part in his firing. It was a startling best-seller. John wrote congratulating her, and enclosed several Canadian reviews. When Lillian answered, on 26 May 1976, she concluded plaintively:

> These occasional letters we exchange do not substitute for a meeting. Is there no way we can ever manage that again? It is perfectly possible that you wouldn't want it, and it wouldn't be right. But I would like it if you would, and New York is a larger town than where you are.

They were not to meet again. By now seventy-one years old, Lillian began to suffer serious health problems, of which the most annoying to her was eye trouble. John was having eye problems too, and much of their remaining correspondence until Lillian's death was devoted to discussions of cataracts and glaucoma. John had the first operation, in 1977; his was largely successful and restored his vision almost completely.

In 1977, when Jimmy Carter, a Democrat, came into the White House, some of John's friends suggested that it was time to bring up the long-buried security clearance and see if perhaps the climate had significantly changed. Averell Harriman was the most insistent; he began to push for John's reinstatement.

By then, John's security file in the State Department had been routinely destroyed. Harriman demanded that it be reconstructed from Civil Service Commission records, the FBI, and the transcripts of John's loyalty-security hearings that still existed. By May 1978, the whole thing had been reassembled. Again bureaucratic inertia and skittishness took over, and nothing happened. Harriman prodded some more. The matter seemed to be stuck in the office of Ben Read, under secretary for management. Richard Holbrooke, assistant secretary for East Asia (which term replaced "Far Eastern affairs") was one of those pushing for John's clearance.

On 26 February 1980, Holbrooke wrote to Read:

Governor Harriman maintains his deep interest in the security clearance of John Melby and continues to express his dismay that we have been unable to give him an answer during the 17 months that this case has been under review. I understand that the security phase of the investigation is complete and that there is now some sort of legal question.

For whatever reason, the continuing delay is proving highly embarrassing to us. Can't we resolve this case or at least give a more definitive response to Governor Harriman and Mr. Melby?[24]

For once, the gears were sufficiently lubricated. Ambassador Samuel Gammon, newly returned to Washington from Mauritius (later executive secretary of the American Historical Association), was assigned by Read to handle the Melby case. He discovered the trouble: nobody was sure that the secretary had power to clear an applicant who once had an adverse ruling. Gammon obtained the services of Marc Ginsburg, who had been in charge of patronage in the Carter White House; Ginsburg's legal memo did the trick.[25] State Department security was forced to do a last-minute check, which included contacting the Royal Canadian Mounted Police; there were no adverse findings. In early November 1980, Secretary of State Edmund Muskie cleared John and put him on the payroll as a consultant.[26] John spent three months working on the Sino-Vietnamese conflict. The change of administrations in January 1981 automatically caused all consultants to be dropped, but this was no matter. The battle had been won.

While John was fighting the bureaucracy, and winning, Lillian was losing her battle against cataracts and glaucoma. Her last two letters to John, in October and November 1978, were typed in capital letters: she could barely read. She wrote John on 23 October, complaining about the eye operations she was facing, about the continuing glaucoma treatments, and the "misery of quarter-seeing everything." But she was excited that John was about to be rehired by the State Department. She wanted to know what she should say if the FBI came around asking about him. And she wanted him to come visit.

Lillian unfortunately never regained satisfactory sight.

John phoned Lillian for the last time in spring 1984; she was very ill, and John Hersey suggested to John that he should call. It was a sad conversation; Lillian knew her end was near, and she despised death as much as she had despised McCarthy. But John's call was welcomed; they talked about Moscow, and East Hampton, and the time of scoundrels. Lillian again invited John to visit, and he planned to go in the summer. But on 30 June 1984 Lillian died of cardiac arrest in the hospital at Vineyard Haven. She remembered John with a small sum in her will.

Was Lillian Hellman a Communist?

In the spring of 1953, six senior officers of the U.S. Department of State and the lawyer charged with advising them as security counsel answered the above question in the affirmative. They recommended that a brilliant Foreign Service officer of impeccable anti-Communist credentials be fired because of his association with Lillian Hellman, his refusal to renounce that association, his inability (which they saw as unwillingness) to recall each and every time he had met her, and his initial unwillingness to admit to two occasions when he had slept with her. These members of John Melby's hearing boards were not alone in that belief; probably most of the federal government in 1953 thought that Lillian was a Communist.

But what is a Communist? There are as many varieties of Communists as there are of capitalists. An attempt to sort out the nuances of Communist commitment and affiliation yields something like this: At the lower end of affiliation would be what are called "dupes"—people who are used by Communists, and support Communist causes, without knowing that they are doing so. Lillian was not accused of being a dupe; she did support many causes that were also important to Communists, but she knew the Communist position.

The next level of involvement is that of the fellow traveler. The definitive analysis here is David Caute's *The Fellow-Travellers*, a 1973 tome of 433 pages which describes "the twentieth century intellectual—artist, writer, educator, scientist—and his affections for and disaffections with Communism." Caute presents a number of useful definitions of "fellow traveler." One of them is that of Leon Trotsky, Commissar for Foreign Affairs in the Bolshevik government in 1918; when he reflected on the relations that might prevail between his country and the United States, he said: "America and Russia may have different aims, but if we have common stations on the same route, I can see no reason why we cannot travel together in the same car, each having the right to alight when so desired."[1] Trotsky later became disillusioned at the propensity of fellow travelers to "alight" precipitously and prematurely, but the "right to alight" is a stable defining characteristic of a fellow traveler's commitment.

J. Robert Oppenheimer acknowledged in 1943 that he had once been a fellow traveler, which he defined as follows: "Someone who accepted part of the public programme of the Communist Party, but who was not a member."[2] And as Caute notes, the overwhelming majority of fellow travelers were not members of the Party. Their services to the Party were three in number: "political journalism, membership of communist front organizations, and, where appropriate, the loan of their prestige, their lustre, the respect in which they are widely held."[3] Lillian was certainly a fellow traveler in her early years, though Harriman preferred the term "fellow-wanderer" in her case; the vital question here is when she chose to "alight."

Party membership is the next step up in commitment. The Melby hearing boards, taking their cue from the FBI, believed Lillian to have been a member, certainly in the past and probably in 1953. They further believed that the Party itself was an agent of the Soviet Union, and that membership therefore involved disloyalty to the United States.

Lillian told John Melby that she had been a member in 1938 and 1939 by virtue of the Marxist study group she attended, but that she had "severed all connections" with the Party in 1940. She does not say whether or not she had a Party card or paid dues; we will probably never know. But the 1930s are irrelevant to our question here, which concerns the period from 1944 on.

The final degree of commitment is being a Soviet agent, one who directly serves the Soviet government—in short, a spy or espionage agent. J. Edgar Hoover believed Lillian to be this also, hence his order to search her effects for evidence of subversive activity when she returned from Moscow in 1945.

What we need to decide is this: Was she, during the period of Melby's association with her, a fellow traveler, Party member, or Soviet agent? Let us look at three categories of evidence: her activities and associates, her personality and character, and the credibility of the FBI (and HUAC) testimony against her.

Lillian had published eight plays, written eight film scripts, and adapted four plays of other writers for screen or stage by the time she gave up theater for memoir writing. Most of this output had been produced by the time of the inquisition. Many of her original plays had a social message; one of them, *Watch on the Rhine*, was seized on by the FBI as showing pro-

Communist thought. Her FBI file contains numerous references to *Watch*, the earliest being in a summary report dated 16 June 1941: "The Daily Worker for April 4, 1941, carried a lengthy review of the recent play written by Lillian Hellman styled, 'Watch on the Rhine.' The review was extremely favorable. It is interesting to note that the theme of 'Watch on the Rhine' was the story of an underground fighter working for the overthrow of Adolf Hitler."[4]

Unfortunately, the FBI simply displayed its ignorance and bias here. *Watch* was produced on 1 April 1941. This was during the time of the Hitler-Stalin nonaggression pact; Germany and the Soviet Union were friends. The Communist party position on American foreign policy was basically isolationist, vigorously against aiding Britain in her war against Germany. The Party sponsored pickets at the White House to try to keep the United States from joining the war against Hitler. The theme of *Watch* directly opposed the Communist position; *Watch* was a powerful statement in favor of joining Britain in the war against Germany.

Watch put Communist party editors in a bind. They wanted to stay on good terms with Lillian, who had endorsed many Party fronts and might still support some of their future causes. But they could not endorse the theme of *Watch*; the Party line was rigid on this. So they compromised by praising the technical virtuosity of *Watch* as theater, and the skill of the actors, while damning the theme of the play. The FBI agent who wrote the paragraph cited above either did not know the score, or deliberately mis-represented what the *Daily Worker* said.

The *Daily Worker* review of 4 April 1941 was written by Ralph Warner. The first third of the review is indeed laudatory: "bears the same stamp of the skilled craftsman as 'The Children's Hour' and 'The Little Foxes' . . . carefully created and believable characters . . . deftness of line and swift-ness of scene . . . exactly the right actor in the right role. . . ." But then comes the demurral: "The play is written as if no war were then taking place in Europe." Hellman is right to pick on Fritz Thyssen and other backers of Hitler, but "additional ideas would have rounded out the picture—and 'Watch on the Rhine' definitely needs such added clarification."

What clarification did the *Worker* think was needed? Explication of the Party line on the war and Russia:

For Miss Hellman has skirted the question of war without eliminating it as a possibility; she has avoided mention of the working class as the leaders in the struggle for the better world, and nowhere does she indicate that a land of socialism has already established the permanent new life of peace and freedom, morality and comradeship and is the greatest guarantee that the ultimate struggle will be won. . . . oh how this play needs such added explanation! The war is on everyone's lips; our nation seethes for and against the Roosevelt pro-British policy. And the Soviet Union and Communism are equally the center of a vast propaganda campaign of lies and distortion. Now, if ever, is the time to tear away the veil. And it is this veil, a fabric of omissions, which hangs between "Watch on the Rhine" and its audience.

If this was an "extremely favorable" review, one can hardly imagine a hatchet job.

But there is more to the story. The *Daily Worker* rushed its review into print a mere three days after the play opened. The Party brass had not by then fully analyzed *Watch's* implications. More significant by far than the *Worker* review was the blast against *Watch* in *New Masses*, the Party theoretical journal, two weeks later, and by a big name—Alvah Bessie. In the 15 April 1941 issue of *New Masses*, Bessie agrees that the performances of the two leads are magnificent, and that "Hellman has attempted a further dramatic evaluation of the central problem of our time—the struggle against the developing forces of reaction" (page 26). But she does not achieve what she has attempted. After the brief praises in Bessie's opening paragraph, we get the full force of the ideological mind-guard. The hero of *Watch*, Bessie says, cannot explain himself to his relatives; the plot of the play forbids this. And from this flawed plot "there grows and spreads a network of fallacy both dramatic and political. . . . it is no longer possible to be anti-Nazi and nothing more. It is necessary today to define 'antifascism,' to delimit its meaning, to rescue the phrase from the warmongers and fascists themselves. This Miss Hellman fails to do."

After making an extensive case for the proletariat—and against Roosevelt, Churchill, and the National Association of Manufacturers—Bessie gets to the interesting part. Communist polemics are not always dreary. To nonbelievers, they can sometimes be deliciously hypocritical. The penultimate paragraph of Bessie's tirade against *Watch* shows a Party propagandist straining to justify support of Hitler *and* opposition to fascism at the same time:

> Hence the issue is—to put it bluntly—bilked; and with all due respect to differences of opinion, there is reason to believe that Miss Hellman alone, with her reputation and her skill, could have successfully and brilliantly stated and elaborated that issue. . . . What she has

written is an anti-Nazi play that, at this particular point in our developing struggle, can be and has already been misused by those who would like to whip us or cajole us into imperialist war under the banner of fighting fascism in Germany. . . . But by not clarifying the issues of anti-Nazism versus true international anti-fascism, *Watch on the Rhine* lends itself to distortion by the enemies of the people, those fascists who are disguised as anti-fascist.

Had someone at the FBI taken the time to read *Watch*, they would have seen that the hero, Kurt, has none of the characteristics of a Communist. As Bernard F. Dick puts it in *Hellman in Hollywood*, "It might be instructive to compare Kurt with a true stage Communist, Quillery in Robert E. Sherwood's *Idiot's Delight* (1936), who calls everyone 'comrade' and extols revolution. Kurt never speaks of the class struggle; he fights against fascism, not for the destruction of the bourgeoisie. He is not a radical, not a Communist, not a Socialist, but a resistance fighter who seems left-wing because the enemy is so totally right-wing."[5] There is in *Watch* no Communist slant whatsoever.

The Communist press did not, during the period of the Hitler-Stalin pact, approve the play. When Hitler attacked the Soviet Union in June 1941, however, the Party line reversed itself overnight. What the Party then needed was precisely anti-Hitler sentiment, and *Watch* provided it in spades. Whatever ideological faults *Watch* suffered from, the Party was in June happy to overlook. So Lillian was back in Communist good graces. But *Lillian did not follow the Party line; the Party line followed her.*

Lillian's next play, *The Searching Wind*, completed in 1944, has been described in chapter 1. It also is antifascist, with no trace of pro-Communism. And this time the FBI got it right: in a report of July 1944, E. E. Conroy in the New York office noted that the *Daily Worker* had reviewed *Wind* on 17 April and did not like it.[6] This lonely bit of exoneration is included in her file.

There was a third Hellman production that caught the attention of the FBI: the movie *North Star*. Like *Watch*, it is mentioned several times in her file, always as a pro-Communist film. An FBI report from Los Angeles on 22 August 1944 quotes at length from a column, by Neil Rau in Hearst's *Los Angeles Examiner*, titled "North Star Insidious Propaganda": "Written by LILLIAN HELLMAN, whose interest in Sovietism is well known, it should get more friends among unthinking sophomoric minds than the late Emma Goldman tried to snare before her deportation. It isn't that 'NORTH STAR' comes out boldly labeled as Soviet propaganda. It is too insidious for that.

The danger is that someone may take the picture's musical comedy version of life in the Nazi invasion as the real thing."[7]

As usual, the Hearst/FBI account is misleading. The story of the conception and production of *North Star* is long and convoluted. The White House, wanting to improve the reputation of its new Soviet allies in 1942, was probably involved. The significant part of the story, however, is that Lewis Milestone took over from Lillian's friend William Wyler (who joined the army) as director of *North Star*; Milestone suggested fifty pages worth of revisions in Lillian's script; she got out of the project in a huff, bought out the rest of her contract from Goldwyn, and in effect washed her hands of *North Star*.[8] She did not repudiate it, but she cannot be held responsible for its smarmy presentation of rural Soviet life. *North Star* was probably the best of the various propaganda films made in Hollywood to boost the stock of our Russian allies in the early years of the war; writing the original script did not make Lillian Hellman a Communist in any way.

Watch on the Rhine, *The Searching Wind*, and *North Star* are the Hellman writings that drew FBI comment in the period before her confrontation with the inquisitors. As for *The Searching Wind*, the FBI admits that the Party did not like it. On the other two, the FBI misrepresents the facts. Lillian Hellman was a prestigious writer whose support the Party always sought, but to assert that she fulfilled any serious promotional function for the Party in her writings is laughable. The Communists thought most of her plays bourgeois irrelevancies.

Is there anything to the doctrine of guilt by association? Probably just a little. People tend to make friends with like-minded persons. Eisenhower and Reagan identified with, and made their friends among, the businessmen and millionaires with whom they staffed their cabinets. Truman's cronies were of a quite different type: old Missouri friends and buddies from World War I. Kennedy brought into the White House the artists and intellectuals who made of it a Camelot. These associations are not without meaning. Church groups, lodges, farmers, veterans, bowling enthusiasts— all tend to congregate with their own kind.

But when it comes to ideology, it is far from clear that anyone who associates with Communists is thereby contaminated. Armand Hammer is no less a capitalist for his extensive dealings with the Russians. Several dozen questionable associates are charged against Lillian by the State Department hearing boards; does this mean that she sought their company *because* they were, or might have been, Communists?

Lillian was friendly with Paul Robeson and Dorothy Parker. Did this make her a Communist? She knew many Hollywood fellow travelers, as would anyone who worked in Hollywood. Did this make her a fellow traveler? She had met Steve Nelson once in Spain; here was indeed a Party member, and at times an agent of the Soviet Union. Steve Nelson is one of the few names of contaminating associates found in her FBI file, and the reference is an interesting one. The Los Angeles FBI report of August 1944 says:

> [name denied] reported that STEVE NELSON, secretary of the Alameda County Communist Party, 1723 Webster Street, Oakland, California, and a member of the State Buro and of the National Committee of the Communist Party, addressed a letter to LILLIAN HELLMAN, care of Warner Brothers Studio, Hollywood, California, dated October 1, 1943, in which he complimented her on her story which was made into a motion picture entitled "WATCH ON THE RHINE." In part, the letter stated:
>
> "I have been out in California now for about four years, and have more or less permanently located in Oakland, carrying on the usual kind of work that I was doing even before I went to Spain. . . . I am taking it for granted that you remember me, but perhaps you have forgotten. Anyway, we met in Valencia in 1937 with DOROTHY PARKER, ALLEN CAMPBELL, LASSER, and LOUIS FISHER."
>
> The letter was returned on October 8, 1943, with the notation "Not at Warner Brothers."[9]

From this, we know two things: (1) The FBI had a mail cover on Steve Nelson, and (2) Lillian and Nelson were close friends indeed.

What is one to make of this? When Steve Nelson's name is thrown at John Melby during his hearings, how can he respond, other than claiming that *he* never met Steve Nelson?

An earlier FBI report also deals with Lillian's personal associations: "[Name denied] indicated that LILLIAN HELLMAN was one of the financial backers of PM which reportedly had a number of Communist party fellow travellers and sympathizers as employees. It also appeared that LILLIAN HELLMAN was a close associate of RALPH INGERSOLL, publisher of PM, and it was reported that she was one of the Communists he had hired for Time Magazine when he was publisher of Time Incorporated."[10] Right church, wrong pew. Lillian was a friend of Ingersoll and did invest in *PM*. Ingersoll did hire Communists, and he was formerly with

Time. But Ingersoll never hired her at *Time*, she never worked for *Time*, and Henry Luce's *Time* was a flagship of the anti-Communist cause.

There is one farcical aspect in the handling of the matter of guilt by individual association in the Hellman case: neither the FBI nor the hearing boards zero in on Lillian's association with Hammett, which was long and influential, and to which most of her friends attribute much of her passion for left-wing causes. Hammett was undoubtedly a Party member.

The bottom line on matters of guilt by association, however, has to be the question: What does the total spectrum of this person's associations imply? Here the FBI file is totally deficient, the hearing boards marginally less so. Of course Lillian had left-wing friends; but were these her only associations? Or the most important ones? The FBI, in the entire 280-page file it released on Lillian, records no interview whatsoever, nor any mention of her friendships with Averell and Kathleen Harriman, Robert and Adele Lovett, Louis Kronenberger, Arthur Cowan, John Hersey, Marshall Field, Ernest Hemingway, Mrs. Christian Herter, Ruth Gordon, Eustace Seligman, Sidney and Laura Perelman, Gerald and Sarah Murphy, or the many other prominent and largely conservative people she knew.

The *whole* of the evidence shows that Lillian's friends ranged across the ideological spectrum, and that no inference about her ideology can be made from her individual associations.

Until about 1950, Lillian was a notorious joiner of organizations. If there was an antifascist, civil liberties, civil rights, or antiwar solicitation, Lillian would sign up. The question is: did she join organizations because she believed in the causes they were furthering, or because she was a Communist? Here we need to look at what she *did* believe.

Lillian was a Roosevelt fan, always. She told John Phillips and Anne Hollander in the 1960s, "Roosevelt gave you a feeling that you had something to do with your government, something to do with better conditions for yourself and other people."[11] She never retreated from this position. She called herself a liberal and often incorporated in that label strong doses of a rather fuzzy socialism. But she did *not* incorporate anything that resembled the national socialist program of Adolf Hitler. It was her antifascism that drove her so long as there was a vestige of pro-Hitler (or Mussolini, or Franco) sentiment anywhere.

Lillian came about her antifascism legitimately, by visiting Germany in 1929 and seeing the anti-Semitism pervading that society. Her Spanish experience in 1937 strengthened this conviction.

Shooting wars and the bitter invective of the Cold War have so dominated the United States since 1945 that the very real dangers of fascism to
Western freedoms in Hitlerite days have often been forgotten. Lillian did
not forget. One can fault her—as she faults herself—for taking "too long to
see what was going on in the Soviet Union." This does not make her a
Communist. To the extent that Communist Russia was for most of the
Hitler period the chief force opposed to fascism, her support of Russia was
understandable.

After World War II, with its terrible devastation, Lillian read with horror
her friend John Hersey's *Hiroshima*. The nuclear age led her to another
enduring belief: there must be no more war. As John Melby explained in his
interrogatory:

> A second contributory factor [to her attitude toward Russians] was I
> am sure her intense emotional reaction to what the war had done to
> the Russian people. She had known intellectually of the human and
> material devastation; then she herself saw something of the magnitude
> and detail of the price tens of millions of people were paying. Being as
> she appeared a thoroughly decent person, with strong and warm
> sentiments, and a real feel for people as individuals, she reacted
> openly and violently to their sufferings as human personalities. She
> would say she could not conceive that people who could endure that
> much could be wrong. From her comments she became, I think,
> somewhat obsessed with the idea that the worst possible eventuality
> would be another war.[12]

It was this commitment to peace that drew her to the Independent
Citizens Committee of the Arts, Sciences, and Professions (ICCASP), the
Wallace campaign, and the Waldorf conference. All three were supported
by Communists and infiltrated by Communists. Lillian knew this; she
protested Communist involvement in the Wallace campaign. But the cause
of peace was important enough to her that she would not shy away from
these organizations because of the Communists.

By far the most significant left-wing organizations to which Lillian belonged were those supporting the Spanish Republic, the Friends of the
Abraham Lincoln Brigade, and the cause of Spanish expatriates. All these
were honeycombed with Communists. (Chapter 1 explores the provenance
of these groups extensively.) Despite the attitudes of J. Edgar Hoover, Ruth
Shipley, and Ronald Reagan (who in the 1980s was still talking about the
Lincolns' having fought on the wrong side), it is clear that many non-

Communists were involved. The final clearing of Veterans of the Abraham Lincoln Brigade, by a unanimous opinion of judges Frank A. Kaufman, David L. Bazelon, and John A. Danaher of the U.S. Court of Appeals in October 1972 is definitive.[13] One *cannot* assume that any supporter of the Lincolns was a Communist.

The other organizational complex that dominates Lillian's FBI file, and that influenced those who thought her a Party member, was composed of the ICCASP; its successor the National Council of the Arts, Sciences, and Professions (NCASP); the Progressive party of Henry Wallace; and the 1949 Waldorf Peace Conference. In all these activities Lillian was associating with Communists.

Enough has been said about these groups in chapters 8 through 10 that no extensive description is necessary here. What is necessary is an assessment of the sincerity of Lillian's commitment to peace. Was it a product of Communist influence, or was it self-generated and genuine? I cannot conceive of disagreement over this. Lillian saw the effects of war in Spain, in the Soviet Union, and in London. Everything she wrote or said about war cries out with heartfelt anguish. And these firsthand experiences were all before the appearance of nuclear weapons; her horror upon reading John Hersey's *Hiroshima* has already been mentioned.

One can argue that Lillian overestimated the Soviet commitment to peace and misjudged the extent to which Soviet domination of Eastern Europe was defensive rather than expansionist; this does not impugn the sincerity of *her* commitment to peace. Her statement to the Waldorf conference is definitive of her position and bears repeating: "It no longer matters whose fault it was. It matters that this game be stopped. Only four years ago millions upon millions of people died, yet today men talk of death and war as they talk of going to dinner."

Participation in the ICCASP and the Wallace movement did not qualify or stigmatize this commitment to peace. Eisenhower was not disloyal because he opposed the arms race. Kennedy was not subversive because of his propeace American University speech. Nixon was not a Communist because he promoted détente. There *is* a cogent argument that the Truman administration policies Lillian and her friends condemned were unwise and threatened to cause future conflict with the Soviet Union (though Garry Wills perhaps overstates these arguments in his introduction to *Scoundrel Time*).[14] The cause of peace was legitimate in the 1940s.

Attacks on the ICCASP, the Progressive party, and the Waldorf conference had a reprise in the 1980s. Peace Links, the nuclear freeze groups,

Physicians for Social Responsibility, and similar organizations sustained attacks from Senator Jeremiah Denton, Republican of Alabama, from President Reagan, and from a host of other anti-Soviet hardliners in 1982. Denton attacked Peace Links and its founder, Betty Bumpers (wife of Senator Dale Bumpers of Arkansas) on the Senate floor in October 1982, claiming that they were "guided" by other groups controlled by Communists.[15] On 11 November 1982, Ronald Reagan charged that "foreign agents were sent to help instigate" the nuclear freeze movement, which had been surprisingly successful in the midterm elections. Reagan's office later claimed that articles in *Reader's Digest*, *Commentary*, and *The American Spectator* proved his charges.[16] This is not the place to review the imbecility of such claims. It is enough to note that in the last years of his presidency, Reagan himself sought to de-escalate the arms race and promote the cause of peace.

Lillian appeared at the Waldorf banquet table with Dmitry Shostakovich in 1949. This was no more sinister than Reagan's meeting with emissaries of the "evil empire" thirty-nine years later.

Lillian was branded with a more rhetorically potent label than "Communist"; she was also called "Stalinist." The writers who charge her with Stalinism base their claim largely on her signature to the 1938 statement in *New Masses*, "The Moscow Trials: A Statement by American Progressives." This is discussed in chapter 1. She was misled in signing the statement and regretted doing it, though she was far too prickly to make abject apology.

Lillian's personal code, as Rollyson notes in the first chapter of his book about her, was that "one lived with one's mistakes, as Karen puts it in *The Children's Hour*, and no amount of expiation cancelled one's past transgressions." And for Lillian, private acknowledgment of error was much easier than public retraction. Rollyson's analysis in chapter 22 is perceptive:

> Lillian once confessed to Catherine Kober that she and her generation had been naive about Stalin. Bobbie Weinstein recalls she and Lillian expected the Soviet Union to eradicate evils like anti-Semitism. In their enthusiastic endorsement of the new world they thought he was creating in the Soviet Union they had not considered seriously the implications of events like the Moscow trials. The whole discussion took perhaps forty seconds, and Lillian was not the least bit defensive about her past. She was simply explaining where she had gone wrong. In private, especially in conversation with a younger person, she had no trouble specifying her political errors. In public, and with enemies,

however, she was a different person. Admitting that her pro-Soviet politics had been wrong would have aided McCarthy and Cold War campaigns against radicals.[17]

Nonetheless, she did admit error, in the commentaries inserted when *Three* was published in 1979: "I was, indeed, late to believe the political-intellectual persecutions under Stalin. When I first visited Russia in 1937, I knew nothing about the purges until I got home and read about them in the newspapers. . . . I bought a history of the Moscow trials and Hammett and I read aloud from it, saying things like 'lawyers are lawyers wherever their training,' and about Vishinsky, the prosecuting attorney, 'what a tricky old bastard,' 'the disgusting cheap-jack,' 'so socialism picked up all the bad junk, after all.'"[18]

As for the supreme leader, to whose service the witch-hunters thought her to be committed, she says she "never thought about Stalin at all."[19] In 1944, when she saw the horrors that the Nazi invasion brought to the Russian people, her earlier sympathy for the Soviet Union was increased. This did not mean approval of Stalin. Opposition to fascism, and to war, dominated her politics for the rest of her life.

The FBI, and her enemies, made much of Lillian's dispute with Tallulah Bankhead. Whether or not Lillian visited Finland in 1937, and saw the raw fascism she described, she was wrong to attack Tallulah for wanting to do a benefit performance of *The Little Foxes* for Finnish relief. American liberals, including Tallulah, were all but unanimous in support of Finland during the Soviet invasion. Perhaps these liberals were overly impressed by the Finnish record in paying World War I debts to the United States. Perhaps they were innocent of the geostrategic interests the USSR had in Finland. Finland then, under Marshall Mannerheim, was indeed becoming a pro-Hitler fascist state. However on balance Lillian must be judged wrong here.

The FBI, in its first report on Lillian in June 1941, was remarkably mild: "It is to be noted that the position taken by Miss Hellman in refusing to aid in a benefit for Finland is identically the same position which was assumed by the Communist Party during the Russo-Finnish episode."[20] Nothing further. Which leaves us back where we started. Lillian's attitude toward Finland suited the Communist party; there is no evidence that she held that attitude because of Communist pressure or indoctrination.

Then, in 1944, Lillian visited Moscow as a guest of the Soviet government. This was instigated by the White House, and Hoover knew it. But the documents cited in chapter 1 leave no doubt that Hoover saw this as a subversive mission. Melby's hearing boards took a similarly jaundiced view.

It is hard, given the present favorable attitude toward such exchanges of visitors, to understand how her wartime mission could have been seen in such a suspicious light. Surely Seattle FBI inspections of her luggage and wallet should have put to rest any suspicions that she was carrying clandestine messages to the Russians. But they did not.

Any fair-minded evaluation of Lillian's travels would reveal beyond a doubt that any friendliness toward Stalin and the Soviet regime that she might have shown during the 1944 trip was more than canceled out by her 1948 visit to Tito.

After the Soviet-Yugoslav split, all Communists who still felt that the leadership of Stalin was necessary for the movement or that there could be only one true route to Communism (the Soviet route) were apoplectic about Tito. His heresy was in no way to be tolerated. Polemics between the two countries offered a preview of those between China and the Soviet Union after their parting of the ways in the late 1950s. The American Communist party was fully committed to the Soviet side and against Tito. But in October 1948, Lillian went to Belgrade to see one of her plays in production and to visit the arch-heretic himself; later she wrote articles sympathetic to the Yugoslavs. As she puts it in an appendix to *Unfinished Woman*, "I had seen the Russian bullyboy side and I sympathized with the Yugoslavs."[21] The series of articles she published at the time supports her 1979 claim.

How more anti-Stalin could she be? Even the FBI is unable to make much of her Yugoslav trip, despite the fact that Hoover, in true paranoid style, suspected that the Soviet-Yugoslav break was not significant—a Communist was a Communist no matter where. In the FBI report of SAC Edward Scheidt in New York on 27 April 1949, two lines are devoted to her trip. The first line is deleted for "national security" reasons. The second says merely "that Lillian Hellman had returned to New York City on October 28, 1948, from Yugoslavia."[22] Whatever whim is involved in the deletion of the first line, it cannot decrease the significance of her trip to Belgrade as an insult to Stalin and to the American Communist party.

But what of her HUAC performance in 1952? To the FBI, anyone who took the Fifth Amendment before a congressional committee was a Communist. To John Melby's hearing boards, Lillian had simply admitted that she had been a Communist until 1950. As shown in chapter 13, neither position will bear scrutiny.

There is nothing else of consequence in Lillian's FBI file, except the Eisler, Budenz, and Martin Berkeley incidents, discussed below. There is, in short, nothing in her associations and activities to brand her as anything other than an early fellow traveler, who alighted from the carriage at least by 1950, and who was in no way acting under Communist orders before that.

As to the Stalinist label, since she was pro-Communist but not a Trotsky-ite during the 1930s, it might have been appropriate then. In the 1980s, it is ludicrous. What could it mean now? She has fully repudiated the purges and Stalin, their instigator, as well as Vishinsky, their prosecutor. There is no possible meaning of the term that could now be applied to her. In this era, Stalinism is simply a swear word applied by fanatical anti-Communists to people whom they dislike.

However deeply felt Lillian's opposition to fascism and war, a more significant determinant of her activities was her personality. She was, on *all* the evidence, a rebel. It is difficult to disagree with her self-diagnosis in *An Unfinished Woman*: "It saddens me now to admit that my political convic-tions were never very radical, in the true, best, serious sense. Rebels seldom make good revolutionaries, perhaps because organized action, even union with other people, is not possible for them."[23]

Can one imagine the disruption within the councils of the Communist party were it to try to ride herd on the tongue and the pen of this cantan-kerous, abrasive, independent-minded woman? Her part in the Wallace campaign was hardly conducive to internal harmony; for an authoritarian, monolithic structure like the Communist party, her presence would have been impossible.

There can be no doubt that the Communist party was monolithic and authoritarian. Joseph R. Starobin in *American Communism in Crisis, 1943–1957* notes of the Party that "the basic premises had been established by a world movement whose wisdom and unity could not be questioned. . . . It held the 'franchise,' the Holy Grail."[24] Benjamin Gitlow in *The Whole of Their Lives* says, "Converts had to prostrate themselves before the supreme revolutionary authority of the communist organization."[25]

Can one imagine Lillian worshiping at a "Holy Grail"? Or prostrating herself before "the supreme revolutionary authority"? We know she wrote with no attention whatever to the Party line. One can imagine Clifford Odets, or Howard Fast, or some other Party flack yielding grudgingly to this kind of ideological correction; never Lillian. Communist writers were for-ever apologizing for doctrinal errors. Albert Maltz wrote an article in the 12 February 1946 issue of *New Masses* claiming that writers should not com-promise their integrity by attention to the Party line. When several more orthodox Party theorists attacked him, he ignominiously recanted.[26] *Watch,*

Searching Wind, and many of Lillian's journalistic writings drew similar Party criticism; she never changed or recanted one line because of it.

Lillian even had trouble with the theater because she insisted that writers were autonomous, and she resisted changes in her scripts suggested by directors and actors. She directed several of her own plays to assure the purity of her script. Harold Clurman, in an introduction to a book about Lillian, says "Miss Hellman has no talent for collaboration. She is a strong individual and a staunch individualist."[27] This is a description of someone who *could not* have been a Party member or a Soviet agent, and whose fellow traveling days had to come to an end.

Lillian's discussion of her relations with Hammett is significant. She never played down his probable Party membership, never pretended he was anything but committed. As she says in *An Unfinished Woman*, she discovered that "a woman who was never to be committed was facing a man who already was. For Hammett, as he was to prove years later, Socialist belief had become a way of life and, although he was highly critical of many Marxist doctrines and their past and present practitioners, he shrugged them off."[28] What Hammett could accept, Lillian would have choked on. Earl Browder and V. J. Jerome, she reports, invited her to formally join the Party. How lucky for their peace of mind that she did not.

Feisty, she was, in a way that no Communist ever could be. John Hersey, who knew her as well as any, said in a tribute to Lillian before the American Academy of Arts and Letters:

> Her notorious so-called Stalinism was, I believe, seven parts loyalty to Dashiell Hammett and three parts a fierce idealism mixed with a measure of perversity. She was far more interested in personality, in character, than in theory. The anger did go deep, and it expressed itself in protest against injustice, greed, hypocrisy, cruelty, and everything shabby and second-rate and dangerous in those who might have power over her—and, incidentally, over the rest of us. The sandpaper in her psyche—her touchiness, her hatred of being physically pushed even by accident, her irrational anger whenever she felt she had been dealt with unjustly—all contributed to her being radically political while knowing that there was no political party that could contain her rebelliousness.[29]

Lillian's last brush with Soviet officialdom illustrates the feistiness that would have driven her out of any authoritarian party she might have joined by inadvertence. In *Three* she records:

I returned to Moscow in 1966, for the first time after the war. My oldest and best friends were now among the leading dissidents. They would guarantee my sympathy, and even more important, my practical help for their colleagues. In 1967, at an invitation whose motive still remains unclear, I returned as a guest of the Writers Union. The union's officials and I were on immediate bad terms and so I was shocked when, without asking me, and because someone else had cancelled out, I was suddenly announced as a delegate to the Writers Congress. I fought that designation until I received assurances that I could make any speech I wanted to make.

I sat waiting all afternoon in the great hall, speech in hand, refusing to allow anybody to read it. Then it became clear that I was not going to make the speech at all unless somebody—and to this day I do not know who—saw it before I would be allowed on the platform. I handed over the speech, my turn was skipped, an hour passed, I left the hall, went back to the Hotel, telephoned the *New York Times*, gave them the speech, packed my bags and took a morning plane to Paris. My speech was published here and in Europe.

None of this disproves my critics or confirms them, either. In truth, I was nobody's girl.[30]

Despite her ferocious independence, and despite the fact that her associations and activities do not brand her as a Party member, there remains the secret testimony in her FBI file.

The FBI enjoyed great prestige and approval with the American public until Congress put teeth into the Freedom of Information Act in 1974. Scholars and journalists were then able to obtain files which, even though sanitized, traced a history of FBI wiretaps, illegal break-ins, hidden microphones, and infiltration of groups that Hoover did not like. But even more important than the discoveries of FBI illegalities were the discoveries (1) that the Bureau's fact-finding ability in general was woefully inadequate, and (2) that far from being a mere investigative agency, the Bureau was the nerve center of the inquisition from 1946 on. J. Edgar Hoover hated Communists, fellow travelers, left-wingers, liberals, and New Dealers; and he worked with HUAC, McCarthy, McCarran, and sympathetic journalists to inflame American opinion about domestic subversion. He also wrote books (such as *Masters of Deceit*) and dozens of articles, heavily influencing the "patriotic" activities of the American Legion and the American Bar Association.[31]

One would not expect that the FBI file on a heretic like Lillian Hellman would be accurate and fair; close inspection shows much of it to be not credible. Four aspects of her file need to be considered: the FBI's selection of witnesses to interrogate; the malicious gossip and rumor included in the file; the unreliability of the professional ex-Communist witness who gave the most damning testimony against her; and the biased evaluations made by the FBI.

When the FBI is requested to do a full field investigation of applicants for federal employment, its agents look for arrest records in police files (including their own criminal division), check with other goverment agencies, and interview people who have known the applicant—such as teachers, ministers, employers, neighbors, landlords, and sometimes relatives. Unless some negative data emerge early in this search, the FBI gets a reasonable cross-section of opinion about the candidate.

When one informer hints that the candidate is "known to associate with Communists," however, or other derogatory findings turn up, the whole conduct of FBI inquiry changes. FBI agents then concentrate on interviewing only those whose opinion of the candidate is likely to be negative, and they ask leading questions designed to elicit a picture of the candidate as subversive. The most thorough analysis of any FBI file on a candidate for a federal job is that of Penn Kimball, who in 1945 applied for the United States Foreign Service. His story, *The File*, shows a thirty-year effort by the FBI and other government agencies to do a job on him. He got neither the appointment in the Foreign Service nor an appointment as a federal communications commissioner in 1963, when he was a respected professor of journalism at Columbia University and Chairman Newton Minow of the Federal Communications Commission requested him; neither did he get a Fulbright grant to study in England in 1974. The development of Kimball's file shows that early in the government investigation, some unknown informant said that Kimball was insufficiently anti-Communist; he had also been seen drinking beer with alleged Communists. This set the tone of the rest of the investigation; the whole file is a tragedy of errors and distortions.

FBI procedures for investigating persons who are not applicants for federal jobs but who acquire reputations as leftists are biased from the start. Lillian Hellman is a classic case. When she signed the "Statement of American Progressives" in support of the Moscow purge trials on 3 May 1938, and when she spoke to the Friends of the Abraham Lincoln Brigade dinner at the Commodore on 18 October 1938, she became an FBI "case": File No. 100-28760, classified as "Internal Security—C." The "C" stands for Communist. She was a heretic.

Lillian's file as released by the FBI is sanitized in such a fashion that one cannot know the names of most of the individuals interviewed with the intent of obtaining derogatory information about her. One does know that all the sources contacted by the FBI were hostile toward her. There is not a single recorded interview of one of her friends. One would not expect the FBI to interview Dash Hammett, Dorothy Parker, Herman Shumlin, or other prominent left-wingers who were themselves suspect to the FBI. But the Harrimans, Lovetts, Herters, Kronenbergers, and her other prominent and ultra-respectable friends would have been interviewed *had the FBI been interested in a balanced picture* of her activities and associates. It was instead interested only in derogatory information.

The FBI surely knew, for instance, that Henry Wallace's wife Ilo was a true conservative who despised the Communists working in Henry's campaign. Why did they not interview Ilo? Curtis MacDougall reports that Ilo, fed up with left-wingers who were hanging around, remarked that she was "going to escape the reds on [her] farm by going away for a weekend with conservative Lillian Hellman."[32] Lillian did take Ilo to the Vineyard. Ilo was certainly the type of person the FBI should have contacted.

Should have, but did not. Hoover's instructions to the New York office on 20 October 1943, read as follows:

> It is desired that a comprehensive report [on Hellman] be submitted in the near future reflecting fully her birth, citizenship, background and Communist activities and connections.
>
> You are reminded that this subject has a national reputation through her writings in which she has opposed Nazism and Fascism. Under no circumstances should it be known that this Bureau is conducting an investigation of her. Accordingly, should any investigation be undertaken by your office it should be handled in a most discreet manner and under no circumstances should it be assigned to the local police or some other agency.[33]

Translation: get the goods on this woman, but don't get caught doing it.

Of course they could not interview Ilo Wallace. The Bureau only wanted testimony *confirming* Lillian's "Communist activities and connections," and they wanted to keep the investigation quiet. Ilo might have talked about it.

Apart from FBI exclusion of probable friendly witnesses in cases where subjects have already been labeled "subversive," there is a basic incompetence and mindlessness about FBI investigations. FBI acceptance of testimony from cooperative witnesses is appallingly uncritical. Even before the revelations of the 1970s, some students of FBI files knew them to contain a lot of trash.

Alan Barth's March 1954 *Harper's Magazine* article, "How Good Is An FBI Report?" concludes that Hoover's belief that the FBI should "'relay all information and facts we secure' has led to the relaying of 'information' culled sometimes from knaves and nitwits, sometimes from bigots, sometimes from persons whose own devotion to the United States ought to be suspect, sometimes from men or women with axes to grind or hatchets to bury in the skulls of employees whom they disliked."[34]

At the time that Barth wrote, there was already in the public record a glaring example of this "vacuum cleaner" approach to gathering hostile information. The 1953 controversy over Charles Bohlen's appointment as ambassador to the Soviet Union was finally settled when Senator Guy Gillette of Iowa told the Senate that the derogatory information in Bohlen's file came from

> a person who said he possessed a sixth sense in addition to the five senses all of us possess. He said that due to his possessing this sixth sense he could look at a man and determine whether or not there was something immoral about him, or something pertaining to moral turpitude in the man's make-up, or some tendency on his part to take action that would not be accepted in good society as moral action. This man said that he looked at Mr. Bohlen and, with this sixth sense of his, he determined that Mr. Bohlen was a man who did have in the back of his mind such a tendency toward immorality as to make him unfit.[35]

This preposterous statement was in Chip Bohlen's FBI file.

The experience of attorney Joe Volpe in his work for the AEC has already been cited: cranks and crackpots whose charges appeared in FBI files told the AEC contradictory stories when cross-examined under oath. The Bureau, on the other hand, was willing to accept any smear, any gossip, so long as it made a heretic look bad.

By 1977, Amitai Etzioni, Professor at George Washington University, could title an article in the *Washington Post* (11 September) about his FBI file "What Our FBI Files Tell About the FBI." He concluded that "the investigation tells more about the FBI and other intelligence agencies than it does about me. What it shows, judging by extensive if incomplete files obtained under the Freedom of Information Act, is the remarkable sloppiness of the agencies, an amateurism in gathering and weighing information that one would not accept from a college freshman."

Five years later Penn Kimball echoed Etzioni's evaluation:

> The quality of their reporting is so shoddy as to make one fear for the safety of the nation. Their reports consist almost exclusively of hearsay gathered from informants whose identity the government continues to refuse to disclose to me, even though many of them must be dead by now. Some of the scuttlebutt goes back 50 years, to anonymous sources in my old hometown in Connecticut. I was an Eagle Scout there, sang in the church choir and left in my teens to go away to prep school at Lawrenceville. No matter. Some of the FBI stuff assembled from local crackpots is really very funny—except that it hurts to laugh when I read my file now knowing that I am still on the books in Washington as a possible political traitor to my country.[36]

Kimball's entire account should be read as a prolegomenon to evaluating Hellman's file.

An equally significant evaluation of the quality of FBI files comes from the very conservative Warren Olney III, chosen by Herbert Brownell to head the Criminal Division of the Department of Justice in Eisenhower's administration. Olney was a California blueblood; his grandfather was mayor of Oakland, his father an associate justice of the California Supreme Court. Olney was what we now call a strict "law and order man," with a record as a tough prosecutor when he served in the California attorney general's office.

Before Olney was confirmed to serve in the United States attorney general's office, he was called in by Senator William Langer of North Dakota, a member of the Judiciary Committee. As Olney tells it in his oral history for Bancroft Library:

> [Langer] took me into his office and he asked me if I had once been a member of the Institute of Pacific Relations. I said "No, I never was a member of that." I wasn't even too sure what it was. "Well," he said, "I've got some FBI reports here that indicate that you were a member of that thing." And I said, "Well, I never was, Senator, and I don't know what it was. I have a recollection that during my father's lifetime, which would be prior to 1939 . . . the institute was founded by Bishop Parsons and a number of others out here who were friends of my father's and whom he respected. I think that my father may have been a member of it at that time. But that's all I know about it." . . . "Well,"

he said, "look at these reports." And he showed me the FBI reports on me. If the Bureau had ever found out that he had let me read their reports about me, they would never have given him any more reports. They are never supposed to show reports to the subject. But he showed them to me. They were the funniest things that I have ever read. They had gotten terribly confused between my father, my grandfather, and me because of the identity of names, and then my mother, who sometimes signed her name Mrs. Warren Olney, Jr. They had gotten some kind of mailing list or something of that sort which indicated that copies of the institute's publications, for a time at least, had gone to 2737 Belrose Avenue, which was my mother and father's address here in Berkeley. . . . They had some reference to my father having been mayor of Oakland, which, of course, he never was; it was my grandfather. There were some things like that that indicated they didn't know very much about our family.[37]

Senator Langer decided that "this was a lot of nonsense" and Olney was confirmed. Had Langer not taken an interest in his case, he, like Kimball, might have been permanently stigmatized.

Lillian Hellman's FBI file is equally ludicrous. The FBI willingness to listen to any *adverse* gossip about an alleged subversive produced, in Lillian's case, the incendiary testimony about the dinner party for Gerhart Eisler (see chapter 10). Since the FBI is still protecting the informant who made this claim, it is impossible to come fully to grips with its provenance and credibility. Lillian denied firmly ever having met Eisler—much less holding a dinner party for him at the time he boarded the *Batory*. Her secretary had no record of such a dinner. None of Lillian's friends who are still living are aware of her having had any contact with Gerhart or being close friends with his wife, Hilde.

The 5 July 1949 FBI report from New York that contains the Eisler dinner party story has a second paragraph which does not bolster the informant's status as a source of information about Lillian. It reads: "[Deleted] Miss HELLMAN has made reservations to fly to Europe in the near future, but [deleted] did not know the nature of the trip or the exact date of the subject's departure."[38] It sounds, perhaps, like servant's gossip, several stages removed. It is unfortunate that Howard Donovan and his crew chose not to confront Lillian with the Eisler charge, and give her a chance to explain why it was false.

Hilde Eisler was deported on 22 June 1949, shortly after Gerhart fled. She joined her husband in East Berlin and began a career in journalism that culminated in the 1970s with her editorship of *Das Magazin*. Gerhart died on 21 March 1968; Hilde is still living in East Berlin. I wrote her in June 1985, inquiring if she and Lillian had been close friends and if Lillian had given a dinner for Gerhart. She answered on 9 August:

> I thank you for your letter of June 19th at the same time I must apologize for answering only today since I was for a longer period absent from Berlin.
>
> Now what your questions Lillian Hellman concerning; I can assure you that Miss Hellman never gave a dinner party for my husband Gerhart Eisler, nor did we even know her personally, to my regret, I must say. It is utterly ridiculous to claim that we were "close friends." These are not the only lies of the FBI informant, I suppose.

The Eisler dinner party story is not self-evidently fraudulent or pathological, as was the testimony of the "sixth sense" witness against Bohlen. But there is no reason whatsoever to believe it.

There is other similar trash in Lillian's file, much of it mindless, none of it quite so specific and damning as hosting a Cominform agent. The New York office sent a five-page report of an informant interview to FBI headquarters on 16 November 1949. The name of the informant was still concealed in 1985, to protect national security. This informant produced such vital information as "she is very friendly with PAUL ROBESON, the Negro singer, and his wife. . . . the subject was very friendly with KENNETH DURANT and his wife. . . . DURANT was the secretary of the Russian envoy's office in the United States. . . . DURANT had been suffering from a stomach ailment and had moved in April, 1944, to a farm at Jamaica, Vermont."[39] Three and a half pages of this report are blacked out, and perhaps there was significant and relevant information in the pages denied; but it does not seem likely. Gossip, quotations from newspaper articles, and endless trivia constitute the bulk of Lillian's file.

Another charge that surfaced in John's hearings came to the FBI in August 1938, from an informant (name denied) who said that "Lillian Hellman attended the 10th National Convention of the Communist Party which took place in New York City during June, 1938."[40] Lillian told John this was not true. As with other FBI ingestions from the gossip mills, this one is not particularly well informed. The Tenth Communist Convention was not held in June 1938; it took place during the last five days of May, and by evening of the thirty-first, the convention was over. There were 22 thousand people at the opening rally of this convention; it is hard to prove that Lillian was not among them. She was not among the official delegates.

The extensive coverage of the *Daily Worker* mentions everybody of prominence who was there, and Lillian is not mentioned. Louis Budenz covered the convention for the *Midwest Daily Record*, which he then edited. His report to the FBI on this convention did get the dates right, but he is hazy on who was there. He also fails to mention the famous playwright.[41]

One fact-gathering procedure the FBI excels at. Their agents are bulldogs at digging out vital statistics. Lillian several times changed her mind about how old she was, and *Who's Who in America* write-ups for different years list different dates for her birth. The FBI would have none of this. A New York report of 14 October 1946 states: "The New Orleans Field Division caused the records of the New Orleans Board of Health and Bureau of Vital Statistics to be checked in respect to the birth of LILLIAN HELLMAN. In volume 130, Page 632, in the records of the Bureau of Vital Statistics, it was set out that LILLIAN FLORENCE HELLMAN was born June 20, 1905, at New Orleans, Louisiana. Her parents were listed as father, MAX B. HELL-MAN, and mother, JULIA A. NEWHOUSE."[42] So it was settled. The Bureau *knew* how old she was.

To be fair, the Bureau must get credit for correcting some of the false reports entering its files. As noted earlier, the report sent to Senator Pat McCarran on 4 December 1952 omitted incorrect charges that Lillian had financed White House pickets during the Communist "peace" offensive of 1941, and that the Communist party leaders who went into hiding in 1951 were secluded at Lillian's Pleasantville farm. Lacking access to all the FBI files on Hellman, we can never know how many false reports went uncorrected.

While much of an FBI file is contaminated by indiscriminate acceptance of "information" from "knaves, nitwits and bigots," perhaps an even more serious liability of files on heretics was the government's dependence, in midcentury, on professional ex-Communist witnesses. Lillian was no exception.

Far and away the most damning accusation against her was that she organized Communist front groups *on orders of the Party*. And when this damning charge came, not from some run-of-the-mill snitch, but from the most prestigious informant in the land, it was altogether lethal. Look, for a moment, at the stature of Louis Francis Budenz.

He was, first of all, in that category of informants most highly prized in the years of the inquisition: an ex-Communist. He was not some ivory-tower idealist with loose connections to the Party; he had been there, worked his way up to managing editor of the *Daily Worker*, seen Commu-

nist machinations from the inside. He had the authority of one who had felt
the lash, hence could describe the pain.

Joseph Alsop explained perhaps better than anyone why Budenz at-
tained this stature:

> When Budenz speaks, moreover, he commands belief, for the reason
> he himself has given. "I think the most truthful people in the world,"
> he has said, "are the ex-Communists, on the whole, and for this
> simple reason: They have learned how utterly incorrect is the morality
> of deceiving for a cause. I want to assure you . . . they certainly have a
> resurrection within themselves, on the whole." On the basis of this
> now widely held theory, valid proofs are no longer demanded by press
> or Congress, as they were when Whittaker Chambers denounced
> Alger Hiss. Instead, the accuser speaks: the next morning's headlines
> announce the accusation; and the accused is marked thereafter as a
> traitor to his country. By these means, while himself remaining a
> curiously shadowy figure, Louis Budenz has played the decisive part
> in convincing numbers of our people that treachery teems in all
> departments of our national life.[43]

Another respected commentator, Richard Rovere, supported this judgment: "No man, for example, has had any greater influence on the public
view of the Communist problem than Louis F. Budenz. On the basis of his
reputation as the government's leading witness in Smith Act cases and
before Congressional committees, he has established an almost universal
acceptance of himself as a high authority and of his books, articles, lectures and television discourses as bearing some imagined seal of official
approval."[44]

Budenz came with a powerful imprimatur: that of the Catholic church.
He began life as a devout Catholic and participated in labor and left-wing
activities until 1935 when he deserted the Church for the Communist
party. He became disillusioned with Communism and rejoined the Church
in 1945 under the tutelage of Monsignor Fulton Sheen. Budenz's first book,
This Is My Story, chronicles this passage in great detail. During his first year
as an anti-Communist, he taught at Notre Dame; from 1946 until his
retirement in 1956 he taught at Fordham. The Catholic orientation of his
activities during these later years was total. Budenz was the prodigal son
returning, living testimony to the pull of the true faith. As Senator Dennis
Chavez of New Mexico noted in his famous speech on Budenz of 12 May
1950, "Budenz has been speaking with special emphasis as a Catholic,
investing his appearances and utterances with an added sanctity by virtue

of the fact that he recently went through the forms of conversion to catholicism."[45] Budenz published regularly in Catholic periodicals and was in great demand as a speaker for Catholic organizations.

Another major source of Budenz's prestige was mentioned by Rovere: Budenz had for a time the full backing of the Department of Justice. He was a major witness in the Foley Square trial of the top Communist party leaders and gave extensive testimony at other trials, at Subversive Activities Control Board proceedings, and at deportation proceedings. Juries believed him. During Truman's administration and the first year of Eisenhower's, Budenz's services were much in demand.

Finally, Budenz had the total support of McCarthy, McCarran, and the Senate China bloc; of the American Legion; and of the Hearst, McCormick, and Scripps-Howard newspapers. It was a powerful coalition. Had Volpe known, in 1953, that the source of the most damning item in Lillian Hellman's FBI file was Budenz, he might not have been so anxious to attempt her rehabilitation.

There were, however, even at that time, challenges to Budenz's credibility. Had Volpe been able to confront the Budenz charges directly, he *might* have been able to shake the board's beliefs somewhat.

Senator Chavez, Budenz's coreligionist, told the Senate: "As a private citizen and as a public witness, this man has impeached and exposed himself as a devious, conspiratorial, warped personality who uses words and information as instruments of propaganda, and not for their intrinsic truth. Budenz is constitutionally unable to give a straight answer, justifying his foul means by the perverted ends he seeks. I do not think he knows truth from falsehood any more."[46] Here indeed was a powerful indictment.

But Chavez did not go into the specifics of Budenz's fabrications; that was left to journalists. Joseph Alsop was the most intense and well informed of them. Alsop had served in China during World War II as an aide to General Claire Chennault. Alsop emerged as a vigorous supporter of Chiang Kai-shek and an opponent of the China hands who thought that Chiang was doomed. There was no taint of softness on Communism attached to Joe Alsop; he was politically invulnerable. He was also a man of integrity. Budenz, in his first books, and in his early testimony, leveled no charges of disloyalty against such China experts as John Carter Vincent and Owen Lattimore; only *after* McCarthy had brought these men into prominence did Budenz claim that they had been Communists. At this, Alsop exploded; he proceeded to take up the cudgels against Budenz.

In October 1951, Alsop spent a full day, at his own insistence, testifying to McCarran's Senate Internal Security Subcommittee. He charged that

Budenz had lied about an event in China that he, Alsop, had witnessed. This event was a conference between Vice-President Henry Wallace, Vincent, and himself about replacing the pro-Communist General Joseph Stilwell. Alsop put his charges forcefully at the beginning of McCarran's hearing:

> On the basis of this testimony of Mr. Budenz, I have written to your committee's chairman that Mr. Budenz was guilty of three untruths.
>
> The first and basic untruth was Mr. Budenz's assertion that the Wallace mission to China carried out a Communist objective. In fact, it did the precise contrary.
>
> The second untruth was that Mr. Vincent guided Mr. Wallace toward a Communist objective. In fact, he did the precise contrary.
>
> The third untruth was that Mr. Vincent was a party member at that time.
>
> The weight of contrary evidence is such as to make this undoubtedly unsupported allegation inherently incredible.[47]

There followed a day's wrangling, with the committee and its counsel, Jay Sourwine, defending Budenz at every turn. At its conclusion, Budenz's credibility lay in shreds. Sourwine tried his best to blunt Alsop's charges:

> Sourwine: Mr. Alsop, do you see any difference between testifying that you do not believe a man and testifying that he is a liar?
>
> Alsop: Yes, I see a considerable difference, Mr. Sourwine.
>
> Sourwine: With regard to Mr. Budenz, have you been attempting to testify that you did not believe him, or to testify that he is a liar?
>
> Alsop: I am attempting to testify that he is guilty of untruth, the language I wrote to the committee, and in the letter I wrote to the chairman I called him a liar. I think he was.
>
> Sourwine: Not because you disbelieve him but on the basis of facts you brought to the committee?
>
> Alsop: The overwhelming evidence before the committee indicates he lied on this occasion.[48]

With that judgment, any reader of the transcript today would be forced to agree. Alsop made the same case, for popular consumption, in an *Atlantic Monthly* article of April 1952.[49]

Since 1953, ex-Communist witnesses have been subjected to considerable examination. One of the best-known studies is by Herbert L. Packer of Stanford Law School, who analyzed the more than 200 thousand pages of testimony given by the four most vocal ex-Communists (Chambers, Budenz, Elizabeth Bentley, and John Lautner). Packer was not enthusiastic about the credibility of any of them, but he made distinctions:

> It has been something of a commonplace to assert that informers' testimony is highly suspect in general and that this is especially true of the testimony of ex-Communists. . . . First, there is the general issue of motive for falsification. It seems generally true that former Communists experience a strong reaction against their old allegiance, and, in many cases, manifest an intense desire to do everything they can to abjure one set of absolutes in favor of another, that what formerly was the purest white becomes for them the deepest black, and that this tendency renders their account of the past suspect. . . . This tendency is most noticeable in Budenz's case, but it afflicts the others as well.[50]

Packer, unfortunately, confines his analysis of Budenz's credibility to testimony before official bodies. Had he analyzed Budenz's extensive writings and had the FBI files on Budenz been available to Packer, his conclusions on Budenz would have been much firmer.

Budenz got into the informing game at the request of the FBI; it interviewed him in 1945 shortly after he started teaching at Notre Dame. Between then and the start of Joe McCarthy's crusade in February 1950, Budenz says that he spent three thousand hours talking to FBI agents. Bureau documents affirm this claim.

By the end of this period, Budenz had largely exhausted his recollections about his Party comrades. Furthermore, the tedium of talking to FBI agents in a solitary room, and of expatiating Party doctrine in a court setting, had begun to bore him. When McCarthy's comet flashed across the sky, Budenz sensed a whole new enterprise for peddling his Communist lore; *he could be a public witness-at-large.* The klieg lights, the TV cameras, the excitement of joining the McCarthy crusade—all this was enticing.

Budenz let it be known at the start of his witnessing that his testimony was always reluctant, always in response to a subpoena, and therefore by inference trustworthy. There was some truth to the reluctance claim; he dreaded any appearance where he would be cross-examined by hostile counsel. When he began giving the FBI "information" about the concealed Communists he knew, he made them promise it would not get to any congressional committee counsel who would cross-examine him on it.[51] And in that sense, Budenz did respond only to subpoena. But basically, his much-touted reluctance was a charade.

In the FBI files, there are many copies of the transcript of a telephone call between J. B. Matthews, an ex-Communist associate of McCarthy, and Budenz. This transcript completely discredits Budenz's claim of reluctance.

Matthews wanted Budenz to testify against Lattimore before the Tydings committee. Budenz was at first hesitant: "It would be hearsay identification." But he would do it, if he were subpoenaed. Then there is a change in tone. Budenz revealed: "I know 400 concealed Communists, J. B., that I cannot mention. . . . Because if I did, why there would be such a furor that I would be discredited. . . . That's why I am taking the thing seriatim, so to speak." But Budenz was "eager to expose" Lattimore and his friends in the Institute of Pacific Relations: "The only thing is, I want to do it in such a way that I don't appear to be too partisan."[52]

This conversation exposes not only Budenz's hypocrisy about being a reluctant witness, but also his uneasiness about the hearsay nature of what he was about to dump into the pubic domain, seriatim. Of course he had to be careful; all he could say about these four hundred "concealed Communists" was that someone had told him they were serving the Party.

The FBI immediately sensed the significance of Budenz's crusade, hence the many copies of this telephone transcript in their files. One even went to the attorney general. Elaborate plans were made to handle this cornucopia of subversion. The New York FBI office, which handled Budenz, established a special category for the new project, the Budenz 400 File, and worked up a mimeographed cover letter giving Budenz's background and the way in which the information was recorded. Space was left in the heading of this cover letter to type in the name of the person accused, and a space was left in the second paragraph to type in the date Budenz gave the information. This cover letter was then attached to a separate sheet setting forth Budenz's charges and put in the file of the person accused. It was mass-production informing.

The cover letter for this project was two and a half pages single-spaced. When Lillian Hellman's file was released to me in 1985, half of the first page, and all of the second page, were blacked out by the FBI under the "national security" exemption to the Freedom of Information Act. This boggles the imagination. What could the FBI have written about Budenz, this long-dead ex-Communist, that would affect the national security thirty-five years later?

The first part of the document released by the FBI reads as follows:

Office Memorandum   UNITED STATES GOVERNMENT
To: Director, FBI   Date: July 27, 1950
From: SAC [Special Agent in Charge] New York
Subject: LILLIAN FLORENCE HELLMAN (LOUIS BUDENZ 400)
SECURITY MATTER—C [for Communist]
(Bufile 100-28760)

LOUIS F. BUDENZ, formerly managing editor of the "Daily Worker" and a Communist functionary until he broke with the Party in October, 1945 has been interviewed during the past few months concerning the concealed Communists whom he knew. The person named above as the subject of this case, was one of those individuals whom BUDENZ described as a concealed Communist. BUDENZ describes a concealed Communist as one who does not hold himself out as a Communist and who would deny membership in the Party.

BUDENZ advised SA [deleted] on June 23, 1950 of all he knew concerning the subject, that he felt was pertinent, and he dictated this information to a stenographer of this office, who was present during the interview.

[There follows the page and a half of material blacked out for "national security" reasons.]

Attached is a blind memorandum dictated by LOUIS F. BUDENZ and containing all the pertinent information concerning the subject which BUDENZ could presently recollect.

The original of each memo has been reviewed by Mr. BUDENZ and he has made any necessary corrections and he has signed the original. The signed original of each memo is being retained in the confidential informant file of LOUIS F. BUDENZ, [phrase deleted].

Not until the final page does the substance of the memorandum appear:

LILLIAN FLORENCE HELLMAN
Author of a number of plays, among them being "The Little Foxes" and "The Children's Hour."

Shortly after my entry into the Communist Party—about 1937—I was advised that Miss HELLMAN was a member of the Communist Party. This arose because of conferences with [deleted] on the West Coast centering around Hollywood's aid to BRIDGES and other such activities.

Later on, repeatedly all through the years, up to 1945, I was officially advised of Miss HELLMAN's continued strong support of the

Communist Party. This advice was given me [deleted] in line with their instructions to me as managing editor of the Daily Worker.

I have also heard in the Politburo definite directions given to Miss HELLMAN in regard to participation in the initiation of several fronts. She has been one of those most frequently serving on Communist fronts.[53]

And that is all Budenz, in July 1950, could "remember" about Lillian Hellman. This was the text that was before the Donovan and Pinkerton boards during Melby's loyalty-security hearings. Budenz did have the titles of two of her plays right, but he could not remember the name of even one of the fronts she was supposed to have organized at Party behest.

When one compares this secret testimony with Budenz's public statements about Lillian Hellman, Budenz's fear of libel suits becomes clear. *He never said publicly what he told the FBI clandestinely*—namely, that she had organized Communist fronts at the "definite directions" of the Party.

Budenz's first book, *This Is My Story*, was published in 1947. It is primarily autobiographical and contains no systematic effort to finger the dangerous traitors in our midst. His second book, published in 1950 (and hence written mostly in 1949) is quite different. The title is *Men Without Faces: The Communist Conspiracy in the U.S.A.*. Here he does name names, approximately 210 of them—Americans who had served the Party as members, fellow travelers, or dupes. Lillian is not among them. How this list compares with his list of four hundred secret members, or with the one thousand names of Communist servants he told Senate committees he was required to keep in his head so that he could write accurately about them in the *Daily Worker*, we may never know.

We do know that the original copy of *Men Without Faces* failed to mention the traitor whom Budenz soon was to call the leader of Communist plans to bring down Chiang Kai-shek—Owen Lattimore. The proofs of Budenz's book had to be revised so that Budenz could slip Lattimore in, early in 1950; but even then, all he could say about Lattimore was that Lattimore had accompanied Wallace on his 1944 trip to China.[54] There is nothing derogatory. Indeed, all the evidence indicates that Budenz knew absolutely nothing about Lattimore until McCarthy had blazed the name across newspaper headlines. In 1947, when Budenz was specifically questioned by a Department of State investigator about Lattimore's loyalty, Budenz knew nothing.[55] In 1948, when the FBI grilled him specifically about alleged Communist influence in the Institute of Pacific Relations, and about the

Amerasia case, he could not connect Lattimore with either.[56] In 1949, when *Colliers* forced Budenz to reconsider some innuendo in the draft of an article he had written for that magazine, he specifically told the *Colliers* editor that Lattimore had not acted as a Communist agent in any way.[57] All his accusations about Lattimore Budenz generated when it became politically profitable for Joe McCarthy in 1950.

Budenz hadn't heard of John Carter Vincent when he wrote *Men Without Faces*, either. By the time he testified for McCarran in 1951, he remembered that Vincent was also a member of the Communist party assigned to guide Vice-President Wallace along the Party line. Budenz's recollections were always changing; before one committee, he said that Thomas I. Emerson was a "dupe of the Communists"; he later called Emerson a full-fledged Communist, a quite different category. About John Stewart Service, he was equally inconsistent: at first, he knew nothing about Service's connections with the Party; later, Service had been very close to the Party. Budenz was generally bolder before McCarran and similarly friendly chairmen; in the case of Hellman, he was bolder to the FBI, but carefully hedged his claims in print. *Men Without Faces* merely notes that Lillian "joined hands" with seven other people in the Theatre Arts Committee, reputedly a Communist front; it makes no mention of her having organized it on Party orders. Four years later, when he published *The Techniques of Communism* in 1954, Budenz was a bit bolder. Lillian was now a "reliable Communist fronter" who was part of the nucleus forming the Independent Citizens Committee of the Arts, Sciences, and Professions. And, in 1954, he calls her a "pro-Soviet writer" whose works are favored in school libraries.[58] Pale stuff, compared with what he told the FBI. Libel proof.

The enormity of Budenz's accusations could be fully revealed only by a complete release of the Louis Budenz 400 file by the FBI. But one can estimate the scope of his charges by culling his books and committee testimony. He lied about novelist Kay Boyle, claiming that she had attended Communist party meetings with him in New York. He lied about Henry Steele Commager, calling him an "active agent of the conspiracy." He falsely accused John King Fairbank of being a "courier for Elizabeth Bentley." He slandered Dean Acheson as the "head of the pro-Soviet bloc in the State Department." He falsely accused Edgar Snow, who was a friend of Mao and the Chinese Communists, of being a *Soviet* espionage agent. Representative Adolph Sabath of Illinois was "a friend and champion of Communist causes"—a palpable untruth. Before a congressional committee, where he had immunity from libel suits, Budenz called Nobel laureate Linus Pauling a concealed Communist. Pauling issued a public statement calling Budenz a liar and asking him to repeat his statement outside of Congress so Pauling could sue him for libel. Budenz did not respond.[59]

As Budenz's charges came tumbling out of his fertile imagination, even the FBI came to doubt them. This doubt is clearest in the instance of his charges against Owen Lattimore. All the Lattimore case officers, and their superiors in the espionage division of the FBI, came to distrust Budenz. On 23 December 1952, Stewart Alsop wrote a column defending Lattimore and John Carter Vincent from what he believed to be Budenz's perjured testimony. Alsop reviewed the long years of FBI informing during which Budenz had no memory of either man and questioned the credibility of Budenz's suddenly acquiring extensive knowledge of their Communist activity in 1950 and 1951. Hoover noticed the article, clipped it, and sent it to his assistant Clyde Tolson with the inquiry: "Is Alsop's statement re Budenz mention of Lattimore and Vincent and FBI correct?" This inquiry went down the hierarchy until it reached the crews handling the Vincent and Lattimore investigations. Back up the hierarchy came the answer: "This is to advise you that Alsop's statements in this regard are correct."[60]

The FBI file on Budenz is equally studded with suspicion of his credibility. At the very beginning of his cooperation with the Bureau, he aroused suspicion by requesting that he be interviewed by a Catholic. (He was.)[61] After two agents interviewed him for five days in December 1945, using a list of seven hundred questions prepared by FBI headquarters, the agents concluded that Budenz, "although a member of the [Communist Party] National Committee, is not as well informed as most members of this committee. Subject stated he was an American communist first and foremost and practically all the other National Committee members were trained in Russia and consequently did not see fit at all times to take subject into their confidence."[62] All of Budenz's subsequent career as an informer can be seen as an attempt to exaggerate what he "knew" so as to overcome this original negative evaluation.

In October 1946, the New York FBI office, then in charge of Budenz, specifically notified headquarters that Budenz was sounding off in public and that they did not accept any responsibility for what he said.[63] In April 1948, after a *New York Sun* story headlined "Budenz Bares Communist Plot to Infiltrate National Guard" appeared, the Bureau was caught off balance; he had never told them this. They sent agents back to him to get his proof. Assistant Director D. M. Ladd then reported to Hoover that it was a fraud, and that "it should be borne in mind that Budenz apparently is inclined to make sensational charges which the press interprets as startling new information, when, in fact, the information is old and not completely substantiated by actual facts."[64]

It was like this for the rest of Budenz's informing career. He was always getting off the reservation, responding to the stimulus of the klieg lights and the expectant audiences, saying things that the Bureau had not heard and on probing found not to be true.

In 1955, it all came to an end. J. Edgar Hoover, confronted with several scandals in the ex-Communist witness program, recommended to Attorney General Herbert Brownell that all of the Justice Department's security informants be fired. Brownell largely accepted this; in April he summarily dismissed those then on the payroll of the Immigration and Naturalization Service, thus ending their government service. Budenz was replaced as a witness in Smith Act trials by the more reliable John Lautner.[65] Louis Budenz, the most garrulous and most pathological of the ex-Communist informers, was shunted aside. But it had been a great ride while it lasted, and Budenz, by carefully tailoring his claims to the forum in which he made them, stayed out of trouble. Other professional ex-Communists were not so fortunate; at least five of them were eventually convicted of perjury.

One may reject the conclusion reached by students of Communist defectors that they desert one fanaticism for another. One may reject the Chavez claim that, after so many years of lying as a Communist, Budenz no longer knew truth from falsehood. One may deny the significance of Budenz's sudden and strategic recollections of Lattimore and Vincent as Party members when he had steadfastly refused to accuse them of this earlier. One may assume that his hearsay testimony was superior to hearsay generally. Even if all these matters are settled in Budenz's favor, about one major fact there can be no cavil: FBI files show in wearying detail that Budenz lied about Lattimore. There is no reason to believe that his accusations against Lillian Hellman were any more valid. Lillian did not organize anything on orders from the Party, and by the time Budenz lied about her, she was no longer even a joiner of left-wing causes.

A second ex-Communist who gave witness against Lillian was Martin Berkeley. His claim before HUAC that Lillian attended a Communist party organization meeting at his house in 1937 made it into Lillian's FBI file but did not figure in John's hearings. Because Berkeley's conduct was so erratic as to offend the HUAC staff, and because he spewed out such a long list of alleged Party members, many of whom denied that they were, his credibility was not high. The FBI did not seek to add Berkeley to its roster of professional ex-Communist witnesses. Victor Navasky's evaluation of Berkeley, noted in chapter 12, is definitive; Berkeley's testimony was riddled with misidentifications.[66] And in Berkeley's article on Hollywood Communists, "Reds In Your Living Room," published by *American Mercury* in August 1953, there was no mention of Hellman. In this forum he would have been subject to suit for libel.

There was a third ex-Communist who testified about Lillian: Raisa Orlova, who had been Lillian's interpreter during her 1944 visit to Russia. Orlova had enough contact with the West to know that Soviet claims of superiority to the democracies were questionable. She eventually married the prominent Soviet dissident Lev Kopelev and defected with him; in 1980 they settled in Cologne. Orlova published her memoirs in 1983; she includes a lengthy description of her assignment as Lillian's guide. In 1944, Orlova had defended the Soviet system, refusing to accede to Lillian's criticisms of it. The most pungent example Orlova gives of Lillian's skepticism is typical: "I even found confirmation of the fact that she was not 'one of us.' She once said, 'I'll start listening to the victories of socialism after you've built the kind of toilets that don't make you want to retch at all the airports from Vladivostok to Moscow.' I gave her a very sharp and dumb reply about our people who had been killed, about the blood that had been spilled, and about the fact that we were protecting them, the Americans. And besides, was it possible to evaluate socialism by such lowly criteria!"[67] For Lillian, it was. Ideology was not for her. She knew that the Soviet system had failed in the most important respect, the welfare of the individual.

Orlova later was hauled in by the NKVD (the predecessor of the KGB) and interrogated by "three people in a row" because she had accepted presents from Lillian.[68] This was the beginning of Orlova's disenchantment. Orlova did not, like Budenz, Chambers, Bentley, and other ex-Communists, turn into a professional witness; her testimony is therefore all the more credible.

Perhaps J. Edgar Hoover's major delusion during his long career was his belief that the United States faced a serious danger from domestic Communism in the 1950s. By contrast with that fundamental misperception, Hoover's claim that the Bureau was a neutral, objective collection agency that did not evaluate its gleanings is of minor significance. Yet this latter delusion masks gross injustice.[69] The Bureau did evaluate evidence in its possession, with the constant bias that *there could be no possible legitimate convergence of aims between a loyal citizen and the Communist party*. This bias permeates Lillian's file.

The Bureau's inclusion of Lillian on several of Hoover's lists obviously required evaluation of her file. The FBI Security Index, meant to contain the names of those who should be incarcerated or watched carefully in the event of hostilities with the Soviet Union, was a much-debated FBI invention. There were several discussions at the FBI about whether Lillian should be on it. Part of the time she was listed as a "key figure" in the New York Communist party, part of the time she was not. In October 1943, Lillian was a "key figure" according to the New York FBI office.[70] In March 1944, she was put on the Security Index on the recommendation of the New York office.[71] In March 1947, that office recommended that she be dropped as a "key figure" but retained on the Security Index.[72] In August 1955, she was taken off the Security Index and placed on the Reserve Index.[73] Each of these changes in her status required a major evaluation.

In fact, headquarters instructions to FBI field offices for selection of candidates for various lists spell out criteria for evaluation. By 1960, the FBI began to suspect that Lillian was not even sufficiently subversive to be included on the Reserve Index. On 18 October 1960, Supervisor 424 (probably in the headquarters office) wrote the special agent in charge in New York about Lillian. This was a form letter, with Lillian's name written in at the top. The letter required New York to verify her residence and employment, review recent entries in her file, submit a report on any new information about her, decide whether new investigation was required, and then decide whether she belonged in "Section A":

Included in Section A will be those individuals falling within the following categories:
1. Professors, teachers and educators.
2. Labor union organizers or leaders.
3. Writers, lecturers, newsmen, entertainers and others in the mass media field.
4. Lawyers, doctors and scientists.
5. Other potentially influential persons on a local or national level.
6. Individuals who could potentially furnish material financial aid.

There follow more specific criteria, such as "Leadership or substantial activities in a major subversive front group over three years ago, together with some indication of sympathy or association with such an organization or a subversive front organization subsequent to the reported membership and no reliable evidence of defection. . . . Membership in a subversive front organization within the past three years and no reliable evidence of defection."

Lillian did not meet these criteria. Supervisor 424 took her off the

Reserve Index, with this evaluation: "A complete review of the subject's file reflects no information which would warrant the belief that the subject may be engaged in espionage or illegal underground activities."[74]

When Hoover sent the unsolicited letter to Assistant Secretary of State Berle in 1944, apparently in an effort to block Lillian's trip to Moscow, Hoover was evaluating her file. Hoover's subsequent orders to Los Angeles, Seattle, and Anchorage for thorough surveillance of her activities, and his order to six possible ports of re-entry to search and interrogate her upon her return, show that the Bureau had performed the most significant of evaluations: it had labeled her as a possible spy. This was not based on any "just the facts" collection of hard intelligence: it was inferential, circumstantial, and subjective.

Hoover's letter to the Bureau of Prisons when Hammett requested that Lillian be allowed to write him in 1951 represented an evaluation of the one hundred or more specific claims about her in the FBI files. The dozen items Hoover listed in this letter represented those the Bureau evaluated as true and significant.[75] The same held for the blind memorandum Hoover sent Senator McCarran in December 1952.[76]

The very decision to include a charge against Hellman, or to exclude it, in any one of the several summary reports prepared by the FBI involved evaluation. The whole process of file building is evaluative. The credibility of each contributor to the file is evaluated: Louis Budenz, in 1950, was evaluated as of "known reliability." The source of the report that Lillian had been hiding the Communist fugitives at her farm in 1951 was originally classed as "very reliable"; the Bureau later downgraded this informant. The unknown informant who said that Lillian had attended the Tenth National Convention of the Communist party was also evaluated as a "reliable source." Strangely, the Bureau does not classify the Eisler dinner party informant at all; this item is noted simply as "reported." But its continued inclusion in summary reports indicates that it was regarded as more likely to be true than the items deleted from the Bureau report to Senator McCarran.

Thus the whole Hellman file represents an evaluation. From 1941 until 1955, when she was taken off the Security Index, the Bureau evaluated her as an internal security risk. Hoover's "just the facts—no evaluation" posture was fraudulent, and the evaluations were in line with Hoover's bias.

Lillian was never a major controversialist in the ideological wars either of Hollywood or of New York. She signed petitions, worked on committees, and made speeches in support of favorite causes. Her prominence in the turmoil of intellectual argument over Communism came about because of such incidents as her refusal to allow Tallulah Bankhead and *The Little Foxes* cast to give a benefit for Finnish war relief, her participation in the Waldorf Peace Conference, and her highly publicized appearance before HUAC. These events, rather than any systematic exposition of her beliefs, thrust her into the ideological wars.

Perhaps, had she not embarked on a second career as memoirist, and had she not published *Scoundrel Time* in 1976, her earlier notoriety would by now have been quite forgotten. *Scoundrel Time* opened old wounds. William F. Buckley, Jr., Nathan Glazer, Sidney Hook, Alfred Kazin, and Hilton Kramer launched bitter attacks on Lillian. William Phillips, editor of *Partisan Review*, was moderate in his criticism but nonetheless took her to task for misrepresenting his magazine's position on McCarthy.

Most of these attacks were knee-jerk affirmations of the early Cold War positions of their authors. Buckley correctly challenged some of her statements about Whittaker Chambers, but the rest of his article is mere diatribe.[77] Glazer noted her misrepresentation of the *Partisan Review* and *Commentary* positions, but was less than accurate about the strong anti–New Deal sentiment activating the witch-hunt.[78] Kazin was simply splenetic.[79] Kramer's article was restrained but amazingly naive about World War II politics; he dragged up the old Yalta controversy, talking about Roosevelt's "concessions" to Stalin as if FDR had in fact given something to Stalin that Stalin's military did not command by force of arms.[80] Roosevelt did err in dealing with Stalin, but the error was in not candidly assessing Russia's post-war intentions and responding to them earlier. On this Vojtech Mastny (*Russia's Road to the Cold War*) is quite correct; Yalta was not the significant event.[81]

But the most invidious assault on Lillian Hellman came from the pen of Sidney Hook. "The Scoundrel in the Looking Glass," a chapter in his book *Philosophy and Public Policy*, published in 1980, states in exaggerated form every possible attack on Hellman. Hook says, "Miss Hellman may or may not have been a member of the Communist party but until Stalin died she was not only a convinced Communist but a Stalinist; and for all her posturing about not really knowing what 'dictatorship' means she may still be a Communist. . . . Of the Communists she writes with sadness and pity; of the liberal anti-Communists she writes with virulent hatred."[82] The first of these sentences is false; the second so misleading as to be laughable. Of Dash Hammett, who was a Communist, she writes with love and affection. Of Joe Rauh, who was anti-Communist, she writes with respect and affection. Of the Hollywood ex-Communists she writes with virulent hatred, and was she not justified in doing so? But of which Stalinists does she write (in 1976, for instance) with sadness and pity? Hook, in his old age, has gone soft on the inquisitors. He accepts as gospel truth the sworn testimony of the likes of Louis Budenz, assumes McCarran accurately indicted the China Foreign Service officers, and rates the Senate Internal Security Sub-committee hearings as "meticulously conducted." None of this is justifiable.

Lillian has not had a fair hearing from these "liberal" anti-Communists, nor from conservatives like Buckley. This is not to say that *Scoundrel Time* is good history. Lillian did not understand the important forces behind the witch-hunt. She saw Joe McCarthy as a sort of super-Torquemada: for instance she says that Melby "went down the drain for no reason except the brutal cowardice of his colleagues under the hammering of Joe McCarthy." The historical fact is that McCarthy never heard of Melby, and John's board members were not subject to any significant indirect McCarthy pressure. Nor were they cowards. They were the first generation of national-security-state bureaucrats.

Had Lillian chosen to write a balanced history, rather than a personal-ized memoir, and done the kind of research in the 1950s that she did for her plays, she would have discovered that while demagogue McCarthy whipped up great public enthusiasm for his crusade, the power behind the scenes was Pat McCarran. Stanley Kutler is right when he says, in *The American Inquisition*, "McCarran's contributions to the perversion of law, politics, and ideology in the period dwarf those of McCarthy. 'McCar-ranism,' not 'McCarthyism,' would be a more apt description for the times."[83] McCarthy was a clown; Pat McCarran and his Senate Internal Security Subcommittee cohorts—James O. Eastland, Homer Ferguson, William Jenner, and Willis Smith—were not clowns. They were powers in the Senate establishment.

Even Lillian's treatment of the morality of informing is simplistic, as Victor Navasky's *Naming Names* makes clear. The witch-hunt as Lillian saw it was a morality play—but it was much more than that.[84] She does not acknowledge the agony of the informers.

One other index of Lillian's status should be noted. There are dozens of books about the American Communist party, some of which include exten-sive lists of Party members. The books about American Communists in which one would most expect to find her listed, were she of that persua-sion, do not mention her. J. Edgar Hoover, in his 1958 *Masters of Deceit*, lists dozens of American Communists, but not Lillian Hellman. In his *A Study of Communism*, published in 1962, her name is again missing. HUAC, that indefatigable searcher-out of Communists, published *Organized Com-*

munism in the United States in 1953, the year after hearing Lillian's testimony, and the book was revised in 1958. It lists 190 individuals as Communists, of whom all but about 15 percent are American; Lillian Hellman is not among them. No scholarly work on American Communism considers her one of the species.

In the final judgment, one is forced to conclude that Ruth Shipley, hardnosed anti-Communist that she was, using the FBI files as she did, solicitous as she was of the good name of the United States abroad to the nth degree, was right: Lillian Hellman was not a Communist in any significant sense, certainly not in the 1950s. It is simple nonsense to call her this; sheer polemics to call her a Stalinist; and plain insanity to believe, as J. Edgar Hoover did at one time, that she was in any way disloyal to the United States of America.

Selected FBI Documents

Appendix 2
Selected FBI Documents

FEDERAL BUREAU OF INVESTIGATION

Form No. 1 THIS CASE ORIGINATED AT **NEW YORK**		CONFIDENTIAL	FILE NO. 100-22366

REPORT MADE AT	DATE WHEN MADE	PERIOD FOR WHICH MADE	REPORT MADE BY
LOS ANGELES	11/21/44	10/7-10/44	GIF

TITLE	CHARACTER OF CASE
LILLIAN HELLMAN, alias Mrs. Arthur Kober	INTERNAL SECURITY (R)

SYNOPSIS OF FACTS:

Subject arrived in Los Angeles October 4, 1944 and departed October 10th by train for San Francisco en route to Seattle to obtain transportation by plane to USSR. While in Los Angeles subject resided at home of her former husband, ARTHUR KOBER, Bel Air, and engaged in numerous conferences with HAL WALLIS, motion picture producer, in regard to her play "The Searching Wind". advised the object of subject's trip to USSR is to confer with motion picture people and as a representative of the Hollywood Guilds and Councils relative to the exchange of motion picture talents between the USSR and the USA. While in Los Angeles subject was in contact on at least three occasions with VLADIMIR POESNER, movie script writer. Subject advised POESNER she expected to remain in USSR for two or three months and hoped to return to the USA via France.

- RUC -

REFERENCE: Report of Special Agent ██████████
Los Angeles, August 22, 1944.
New York teletype to Washington Field, October 2, 1944.
Bureau teletype to Los Angeles and Seattle, October 6, 1944.
Teletype to Bureau, Seattle and New York, October 7, 1944.
Teletype to Bureau, San Francisco and Seattle, October 10, 1944.

DETAILS:

The subject of this investigation is considered a key figure in the New York Field Division.

APPROVED AND FORWARDED		DO NOT WRITE IN THESE SPACES	

COPIES OF THIS REPORT
5 Bureau
2 New York
3 Los Angeles

RECORDED & INDEXED

LA 100-22366   CONFIDENTIAL

The referenced teletype of October 2, 1944 advised that subject had departed from New York City October 2, 1944 for Los Angeles en route to the USSR via Fairbanks, Alaska.

61

62,67D   it was learned on October 7, 1944 that subject was residing at the home of ARTHUR KOBER, 850 Stone Canyon Road, Bel Air, California, telephone CRestview 1-4898.

67D

)67D   subject stated that she was in Los Angeles to talk to HAL WALLIS, a producer, concerning her play "The Searching Wind" for which she intends to write a script upon her return from Russia to New York City. She stated that she was working while in Los Angeles. She continued that she would leave Los Angeles on Tuesday, October 10, 1944 and would proceed from Seattle to Fairbanks, Alaska. She stated that the invitation to visit Russia had pleased her very much and that she intended to stay two or three months. Subject also stated that she hoped to return via France.

67D

The referenced teletype of October 7th to the Bureau, Seattle and New York summarized the above information.

- 2 -   'CONFIDENTIAL'

LA 100-22366

CONFIDENTIAL

62
67DC

On October 10, 194~ ~~~~~ advised Special Agent ~~~~~ that LILLIAN HELLMAN had
been in Los Angeles for about a week conferring with HAL WALLIS on her
play "The Searching Wind", and was scheduled to leave that day for Russia.
This informant stated that the object of subject's trip to the USSR was to
confer with motion picture people there as a representative of the Hollywood Guilds and Councils relative to the exchange of motion picture talent
between Russia and the United States. A Hollywood motion picture magazine
entitled "Variety" carried an article in its issue of October 11, 1944, as
follows:

"Lillian Hellman off on trip to Russia - - Lillian Hellman left
for New York yesterday en route to Moscow on invitation of the
Soviet Government. While in Russia Miss Hellman contemplates
writing new play with the same characters she used in 'The Little
Foxes'. Upon her return next spring she will complete one-picture
deal she has with Hal Wallis to adapt her legit play 'The Searching
Wind'."

62,67C,D

On October 10, 1944 ~~~~~ advised Special Agent ~~~~~
~~~~~ that subject was departing on the Southern Pacific "Lark"
for San Francisco that evening, and would leave San Francisco the following afternoon for Seattle on the "Cascade".

62,67D

~~~~~ advised the writer on October 10, 1944 that a
reservation for the subject in Bedroom M, Car 72 of the "Lark" leaving
Los Angeles at 9 P. M. on October 10th had been obtained by SID STREET
of the Paramount Studios in Hollywood. The referenced teletype of October
10, 1944 advised of the subject's departure from Los Angeles.

67C

On the evening of October 10, 1944 Special Agents ~~~~~
~~~~~ observed subject arriving at the Glendale station
in a 1937 Cadillac sedan bearing California license 57-V-356 registered to
CYRUS DAGGETT, 725 South Westlake Avenue. This automobile was driven by
a liveried chauffeur and subject was accompanied by a man and woman. The
man was described as 40, 5'10", 180 pounds, black receding hair, dark eyes,
glasses. The woman was described as 30, 5'5", 120 pounds, dark brown hair,
dark eyes, attractive face. Subject was described as wearing a dark brown
sheared beaver coat, a dark blue chalk striped suit and brown pumps. The
chauffeur was observed to be carrying a leopard skin fur coat for subject
and a number of books, the top one of which was observed to have the inscription "Russia - - - ". The man and woman both kissed the subject good-
bye. The man was believed to be ARTHUR KOBER, subject's former husband.

- REFERRED UPON COMPLETION TO THE OFFICE OF ORIGIN -

- 3 - CONFIDENTIAL

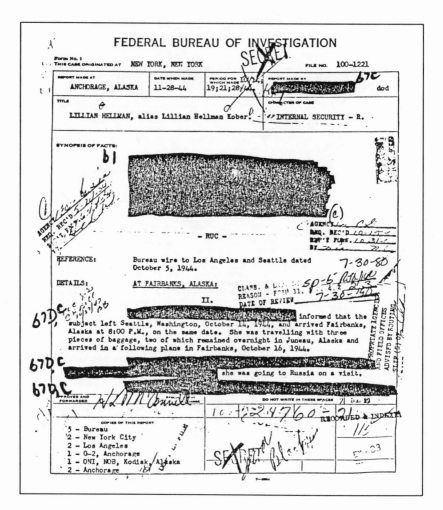

FEDERAL BUREAU OF INVESTIGATION

Form No. 1
THIS CASE ORIGINATED AT NEW YORK, NEW YORK   **FILE NO.** 100-1221

REPORT MADE AT	DATE WHEN MADE	PERIOD FOR WHICH MADE	REPORT MADE BY
ANCHORAGE, ALASKA	11-28-44	19;21;28/	dod

TITLE
LILLIAN HELLMAN, alias Lillian Hellman Kober.   **CHARACTER OF CASE** INTERNAL SECURITY - R.

SYNOPSIS OF FACTS:

— RUC —

REFERENCE: Bureau wire to Los Angeles and Seattle dated
October 5, 1944.

DETAILS: AT FAIRBANKS, ALASKA:
II.
informed that the
subject left Seattle, Washington, October 14, 1944, and arrived Fairbanks,
Alaska at 8:00 P.M., on the same date. She was travelling with three
pieces of baggage, two of which remained overnight in Juneau, Alaska and
arrived in a following plane in Fairbanks, October 16, 1944.

she was going to Russia on a visit.

APPROVED AND FORWARDED

COPIES OF THIS REPORT
5 — Bureau
2 — New York City
2 — Los Angeles
1 — G-2, Anchorage
1 — ONI, NOB, Kodiak, Alaska
2 — Anchorage

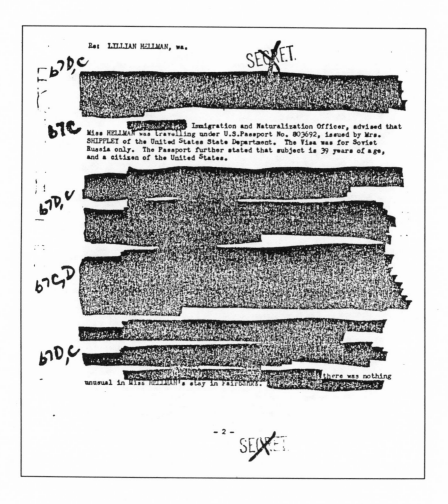

Re: LILLIAN HELLMAN, wa.

SECRET.

Immigration and Naturalization Officer, advised that Miss HELLMAN was travelling under U.S.Passport No. 803692, issued by Mrs. SHIPPLEY of the United States State Department. The Visa was for Soviet Russia only. The Passport further stated that subject is 39 years of age, and a citizen of the United States.

unusual in Miss HELLMAN's stay in Fairbanks. [ ] there was nothing

- 2 -

SECRET

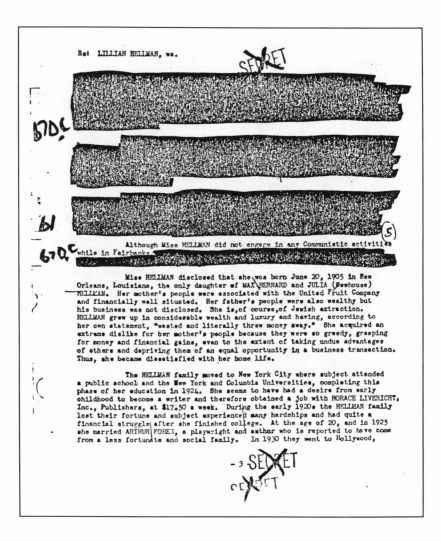

Re: LILLIAN HELLMAN, ws.

SECRET

b7D,C

b7D,C

b7 Q,C

(S)

Although Miss HELLMAN did not engage in any Communistic activities while in Fairbanks.

Miss HELLMAN disclosed that she was born June 20, 1905 in New Orleans, Louisiana, the only daughter of MAX BERNARD and JULIA (Newhouse) HELLMAN. Her mother's people were associated with the United Fruit Company and financially well situated. Her father's people were also wealthy but his business was not disclosed. She is, of course, of Jewish extraction. HELLMAN grew up in considerable wealth and luxury and having, according to her own statement, "wasted and literally threw money away." She acquired an extreme dislike for her mother's people because they were so greedy, grasping for money and financial gains, even to the extent of taking undue advantages of others and depriving them of an equal opportunity in a business transaction. Thus, she became dissatisfied with her home life.

The HELLMAN family moved to New York City where subject attended a public school and the New York and Columbia Universities, completing this phase of her education in 1924. She seems to have had a desire from early childhood to become a writer and therefore obtained a job with HORACE LIVERICHT, Inc., Publishers, at $17.50 a week. During the early 1920s the HELLMAN family lost their fortune and subject experienced many hardships and had quite a financial struggle after she finished college. At the age of 20, and in 1925 she married ARTHUR KOBER, a playwright and author who is reported to have come from a less fortunate and social family. In 1930 they went to Hollywood,

-3- SECRET

SECRET

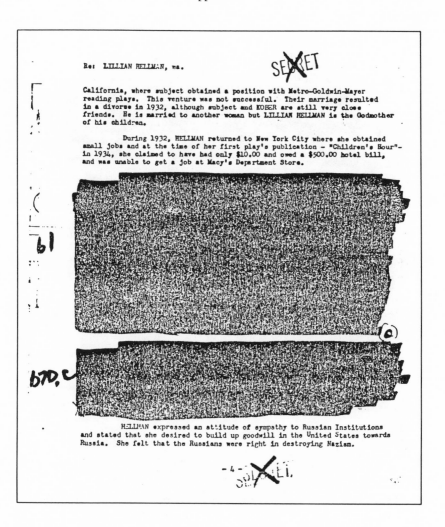

Re: LILLIAN HELLMAN, was.   SECRET

California, where subject obtained a position with Metro-Goldwin-Mayer
reading plays. This venture was not successful. Their marriage resulted
in a divorce in 1932, although subject and KOBER are still very close
friends. He is married to another woman but LILLIAN HELLMAN is the Godmother
of his children.

    During 1932, HELLMAN returned to New York City where she obtained
small jobs and at the time of her first play's publication - "Children's Hour"-
in 1934, she claimed to have had only $10.00 and owed a $500.00 hotel bill,
and was unable to get a job at Macy's Department Store.

HELLMAN expressed an attitude of sympathy to Russian Institutions
and stated that she desired to build up goodwill in the United States towards
Russia. She felt that the Russians were right in destroying Nazism.

                         - 4 -

Re: LILLIAN HELLMAN, wa.

SECRET

61

(S)

Miss HELLMAN stated that her play, "Watch on the Rhine", was inspired from her observations in Germany and Spain and the story and background of an individual in the German underground movement at the time she visited Germany. The play is not a biography of the man whose name was not disclosed, in the underground movement but he furnished her the background information and reviewed the play before it was produced.

Miss HELLMAN got considerable publicity in the Fairbanks Daily News Miner on October 19, 1944. Among other things mentioned, she gave the Fairbanks National War Fund a check for $50.00 as a gesture of appreciation for "Alaskan Hospitality". This donation was an additional offering to her former contribution in New York.

Confidential Informant ▓▓▓ advised that subject departed Ladd Field, Alaska, on October 19, 1944, by Russian plane enroute to Moscow, Russia.

b7D

- REFERRED UPON COMPLETION TO THE OFFICE OF ORIGIN -

100-28760-21

-5- SECRET

FEDERAL BUREAU OF INVESTIGATION

Form No. 1
THIS CASE ORIGINATED AT   NEW YORK

NY FILE NO. 100-25858 MLV

REPORT MADE AT	DATE WHEN MADE	PERIOD FOR WHICH MADE	REPORT MADE BY
NEW YORK	7/5/49	6/16,21/49	▮▮▮▮▮▮▮▮▮

TITLE	CHARACTER OF CASE
LILLIAN FLORENCE HELLMAN, was.	SECURITY MATTER - C

SYNOPSIS OF FACTS:

Informant advises that subject held dinner party in honor of GERHART EISLER prior to his departure from the United States. Informant further advised that subject contemplates visit to Europe in near future.

- P -

ALL INFORMATION CONTAINED HEREIN IS UNCLASSIFIED
DATE 7-30-80 BY sp-57270

REFERENCE: Bureau file 100-28760.
Report of SA ▮▮▮▮▮▮▮▮▮ New York, 4/27/49.

DETAILS:

▮▮▮▮▮▮▮▮▮▮▮▮▮▮▮▮▮▮▮▮▮▮
▮▮▮▮▮▮ LILLIAN FLORENCE HELLMAN had given a dinner party in honor of GERHART EISLER just prior to his departure from the United States. ▮▮▮▮▮▮▮▮▮ there were about eighteen to twenty persons in attendance at this party, ▮▮▮▮▮▮▮▮▮▮ Miss HELLMAN said that she and Mrs. EISLER were very close friends.

▮▮▮▮▮▮▮▮▮▮▮▮▮▮▮▮▮▮ Miss HELLMAN has made reservations to fly to Europe in the near future, but ▮▮▮▮▮▮▮▮▮ did not know the nature of this trip or the exact date of the subject's departure.

COPIES DESTROYED 7-21-68 R147

* P E N D I N G -

AGENCY
REQ. REC'D
REF'T FORW.
BY

APPROVED AND FORWARDED: *Edward Schutt*   DO NOT WRITE IN THESE SPACES

COPIES OF THIS REPORT

5 - Bureau
2 - Washington Field
3 - New York

100-28760- INDEXED - 130

RECORDED - 130

EX-121

U. S. GOVERNMENT PRINTING OFFICE 7—6054

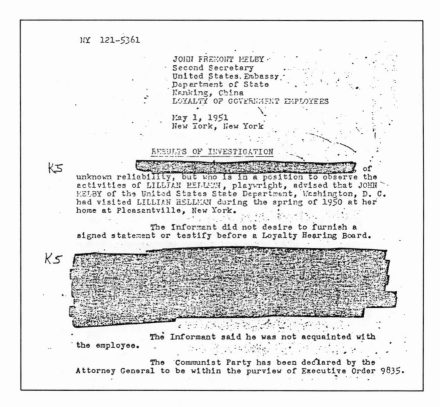

NY 121-5361

JOHN FREMONT MELBY
Second Secretary
United States Embassy
Department of State
Nanking, China
LOYALTY OF GOVERNMENT EMPLOYEES

May 1, 1951
New York, New York

RESULTS OF INVESTIGATION

K5 ▓▓▓▓▓▓▓▓▓▓▓▓▓▓▓▓▓▓▓▓▓▓▓▓▓▓▓, of
unknown reliability, but who is in a position to observe the
activities of LILLIAN HELLMAN, playwright, advised that JOHN
MELBY of the United States State Department, Washington, D. C.
had visited LILLIAN HELLMAN during the spring of 1950 at her
home at Pleasantville, New York.

　　　　The Informant did not desire to furnish a
signed statement or testify before a Loyalty Hearing Board.

K5 ▓▓▓▓▓▓▓▓▓▓▓▓▓▓▓▓▓▓▓▓▓▓▓▓▓▓▓▓▓▓▓▓▓▓▓
▓▓▓▓▓▓▓▓▓▓▓▓▓▓▓▓▓▓▓▓▓▓▓▓▓▓▓▓▓▓▓▓▓▓▓▓
▓▓▓▓▓▓▓▓▓▓▓▓▓▓▓▓▓▓▓▓▓▓▓▓▓▓▓▓▓▓▓▓▓▓▓▓

　　　　The Informant said he was not acquainted with
the employee.

　　　　The Communist Party has been declared by the
Attorney General to be within the purview of Executive Order 9835.

Oct 12, 45

486

100-63
JSG:rol

Office Memorandum · UNITED STATES GOVERNMENT

TO   :   THE DIRECTOR   DATE: October 12, 1945

FROM   :   D. M. Ladd

SUBJECT: LOUIS FRANCIS BUDENZ
            INTERNAL SECURITY - C
            REGISTRATION ACT

Mr. Tolson
Mr. E. A. Tamm
Mr. Clegg
Mr. Coffey
Mr. Glavin
Mr. Ladd
Mr. Nichols
Mr. Rosen
Mr. Tracy
Mr. Carson
Mr. Egan
Mr. Hendon
Mr. Pennington
Mr. Quinn Tamm
Tele. Room
Mr. Nease
Miss Beahm
Miss Gandy

          Your attention is called to the various newspaper articles of
October 11, 1945, reporting that the captioned individual, former editor
of the "Daily Worker" and a Key Figure in the Communist Party, has resigned his position and embraced Catholicism through the influence of the
Right Reverend Monsignor Fulton J. Sheen of Catholic University, Washington,
D. C. It is stated that Budenz will accept a position as professor of Economics
at Notre Dame University. A copy of the article appearing in the "Times Herald"
is attached. You will recall that you were previously advised that Budenz con-
templated taking the above step.

          As you know, in addition to being listed as a Key Figure, Budenz
has also been under investigation for violation of the Foreign Agents Registration Act since he has for a number of months been acting as correspondent for
the London "Daily Worker." He was requested to register by the War Division on
the basis that the "Daily Worker" is controlled by a foreign political party
(The Communist Party of Great Britain) but refused, denying that this control
existed. The Bureau, therefore, made inquiry through London sources for information which would prove direction by the Communist Party of the London "Daily
Worker." The desired data have just been received and are being transmitted
to the War Division of the Department for a decision as to prosecution of Budenz.

          In the event that prosecution is not instituted because of Budenz'
changed status, consideration will be given to making a recommendation that he
be interviewed for any information which he may be willing to give concerning
the Communist political set-up in this country.

ALL INFORMATION CONTAINED
HEREIN IS UNCLASSIFIED
DATE 6-9-86 BY 304

Attachment

RECORDED
&
INDEXED   100-63-122

32 OCT 18 1945

53 NOV 5 1945

Office *Memorandum* · UNITED STATES GOVERNMENT

TO   :   THE DIRECTOR   DATE: May 1, 1950

FROM :   MR. LADD

SUBJECT: LOUIS BUDENZ
           INFORMATION CONCERNING

Mr. John Steelman, the Assistant to the President, mentioned to
Mr. Roach this morning while discussing other matters that he was becoming
highly suspicious of the activities of Louis Budenz. He stated that the
activities of Budenz had also aroused the suspicions of other persons, whom
he indicated were attached to Catholic University here in Washington. His
contact at Catholic University apparently gave Steelman the impression that
they had a "hot potato" on their hands and did not know how to get rid of
him. The undercurrent of feeling seems to be, according to Mr. Steelman, that
they are skeptical of Budenz's so-called return to Catholicism. They view him
as still a "good Communist". Mr. Steelman commented that some Church leaders,
(names not mentioned) have told him that Budenz's testimony before the Tydings
Committee certainly did not help the prestige of the Catholic Church, and although
he, Steelman, has no information to disprove or prove that Budenz is still a
Communist, he stated that he certainly had his suspicions. He commented,
"I hope J. Edgar is keeping an eye on him".

Mr. Steelman stated that he intended to mention this matter to you
when he saw you recently at the swearing-in ceremonies of Stuart Symington,
but the occasion did not arise. He asked Mr. Roach to pass his comments on
to you.

ALL INFORMATION CONTAINED
HEREIN IS UNCLASSIFIED
DATE _____ BY _____

RECORDED - 34

100-63-32

MAY 11 1950
34

MAY 29 1950

488

FEDERAL BUREAU OF INVESTIGATION
U. S. DEPARTMENT OF JUSTICE
COMMUNICATIONS SECTION

OCT 9 1950

TELETYPE

WASH 28 NEW YORK 6 FROM LOS ANGELES   9   6-27

DIRECTOR AND SAC   U R G E N T

LOUIS F. BUDENZ, SOURCE OF INFO. C.B. DE MILLE TELEPHONICALLY ADVISED
THIS DATE THAT BUDENZ, WHILE VISITING IN DE MILLE-S OFFICE, HAD BEEN
REQUESTED BY DE MILLE TO FURNISH A COMPLETE LIST OF CP MEMBERS FUNCT-
IONING IN THE HOLLYWOOD MOTION PICTURE INDUSTRY. BUDENZ INDICATED TO
DE MILLE THAT INFO CONCERNING HIS KNOWLEDGE OF COMMUNISTS IN HOLLY-
WOOD HAS BEEN MADE AVAILABLE TO BUREAU NY OFFICE. BUDENZ
ADVISED DE MILLE THAT IT WOULD BE NECESSARY FOR HIM TO CONFER WITH
NY BUREAU REPRESENTATIVES ON THE MATTER BEFORE MAKING ANY INFO OF THIS
NATURE AVAILABLE TO DE MILLE. DE MILLE, WHO HAS BEEN EXCEEDINGLY
COOPERATIVE WITH THE BUREAU, HAS MADE ASSURANCES THAT ANY INFO AFFORDE
HIM BY BUDENZ WILL BE TREATED AS HIGHLY CONFIDENTIAL. BUDENZ RETURN-
ING TO NYC VIA AIR LINE TONIGHT AND WILL UNDOUBTEDLY CONTACT NY OFFICE
OCTOBER TEN NEXT. BUREAU IS REQUESTED TO ADVISE NY CONCERNING THE
RESPONSE TO BE AFFORDED BUDENZ RE DE MILLE-S REQUEST FOR INFO.

ALL INFORMATION CONTAINED
HEREIN IS UNCLASSIFIED
DATE ____ BY ____

HOOD

END AND ACK PLS
44 RECORDED - 58
XLA R 28 WA C
AND RELAY PLS
4- R
LA R RELAY TO NYC

7.

???

Abbreviations in Notes

AEC   U.S. Atomic Energy Commission
FBI   Federal Bureau of Investigation
FBI/LH   FBI Headquarters file no. 100-28670, Lillian Hellman, Internal
           Security—R (Russia)
FBINY/LH   FBI New York Office file no. 100-25858, Lillian Hellman
FBI/OL   FBI Headquarters file no. 100-24682, Owen Lattimore, Espionage—R
MEM   Melby-Erskine mission

Chapter One

1. All references to Hellman's memoirs (*Unfinished Woman, Pentimento, Scoundrel Time*) are to the collected edition titled *Three*. On the trip to Moscow, see pp. 139–79.

2. Hellman's passport file is obtainable from the Information and Privacy Staff, Passport Office, U.S. Department of State. Subsequent references to this file will be cited as Hellman Passport File.

3. Descriptions of Hellman's life in this chapter come primarily from Rollyson, *Lillian Hellman*; Wright, *Lillian Hellman*; Johnson, *Dashiell Hammett*; Moody, *Lillian Hellman*; and Dick, *Hellman in Hollywood*.

4. See the description of Hammett's influence in Rollyson, *Lillian Hellman*, chap. 3 and throughout.

5. For an account of her affair with Ingersoll, see Hoopes, *Ralph Ingersoll*, pp. 126–35, 187–88.

6. Ibid., pp. 134–35.

7. Rollyson, *Lillian Hellman*, pp. 95–98.

8. Hoopes, *Ralph Ingersoll*, p. 401

9. Available in *Six Plays by Lillian Hellman*. Manfred Triesch, in *The Lillian Hellman Collection*, p. 19, notes that "*Days to Come* . . . has a key position in LH's entire literary output. In her representation of a strike in a brush factory near Cleveland, Ohio, the author enlisted methods of characterization, ideas, and even structural means which were clearly derived from Marxian thought, then so popular among American dramatists. She did not accept a Marxian conclusion, however, so that *Days to Come* symbolizes the young author's search for a method of thinking and writing and her final decision against the ready-made solutions which were believed to lie in Communism."

10. Statistics on Axis contributions to the Spanish Civil War come from Thomas, *The Spanish Civil War*, p. 985.

11. Guttmann, *The Wound in the Heart*, p. v.

12. Hellman, *Three*, p. 76.

13. Eby, *Between the Bullet and the Lie*, p. 98.

14. On Spellman, see Cooney, *The American Pope*, pp. 170–72.

15. I am indebted to Professor Robert Colodny, a member of the Abraham Lincoln Battalion, for much profitable discussion of the Spanish Civil War. See Colodny, *The Struggle for Madrid*; Eby, *Between the Bullet and the Lie*; Rosenstone, *Crusade of the Left*; and Landis, *The Abraham Lincoln Brigade*. Thomas, *The Spanish Civil War*, remains the best overall account of that conflict.

16. FBI Headquarters file no. 100-28760, Lillian Hellman, Internal Security—R (for Russia), serial 1. Subsequent references to this file will be cited as FBI/LH, plus the serial number.

17. FBI/LH, 4.

18. Ronald Reagan shares this view. On 25 October 1984, he told Scripps-Howard editors that the Lincolns "were, in the opinions of most Americans, fighting on the wrong side." This remark attracted little attention until Reagan visited Spain in 1985 (*New York Times*, 10 May 1985, p. A11). Ronald Radosh has recently entered the lists of those who denigrate the integrity of the Lincolns; see "'But Today the Struggle.'" I do not find this effort successful. See the critique by Morton, "Pathetic Fallacies," and Knox, "The Spanish Tragedy."

19. *New York Times*, 5 May 1937.

20. Rosenstone, *Crusade of the Left*, p. 339.

21. Eby, *Between the Bullet and the Lie*, p. 316.

22. *Washington Post*, 25 October 1972.

23. Hellman, *Three*, p. 76.

24. Rollyson, *Lillian Hellman*, chap. 5.

25. Ibid., chap. 30.

26. Gellhorn, "On Apocryphism," and McCracken, "'Julia' & Other Fictions."

27. Hellman, *Three*, p. 132.

28. U.S. Department of State, Loyalty-Security Board, In The Matter of John Fremont Melby, Hearing 1, 26 June 1952, pp. B32–34. Subsequent citations to these hearings will be cited as Melby hearings, the number of the hearing, date, page.

29. See Duranty, "The Moscow Trials," pp. 60–65.

30. American reactions to the purge trials are described in Warren, *Liberals and Communism*, pp. 163–92. A later, massive history of the trials is Conquest, *The Great Terror*.

31. Hellman, *Three*, p. 472.

32. Hoopes, *Ralph Ingersoll*, pp. 188–89, 225.

33. FBI/LH, 57.

34. Hoopes, *Ralph Ingersoll*, p. 372.

35. Rollyson, *Lillian Hellman*, pp. 146–55.

36. FBI/LH, 57.

37. Ralph Warner, "Watch on the Rhine Poignant Drama," *Daily Worker*, 4 April 1941; Alvah Bessie, "Watch on the Rhine," *New Masses*, 15 April 1941; Ralph Warner, "The New Lillian Hellman Play," *Daily Worker*, 17 April 1944.

38. FBI New York Office file no. 100-25858, Lillian Hellman, serial 6. Subsequent references to this file will be cited as FBINY/LH, plus the serial number.

39. Hellman, *Three*, pp. 134–39.

40. Ibid., p. 139.

41. See Hellman, *The North Star*.

42. See reviews by Ralph Warner in *Daily Worker*, 17 April 1944, and *The Worker*, 28 April 1944.

43. Burton Rascoe, "Has Miss Hellman Disappointed 'The Party'?" *New York World-Telegram*, 23 April 1944; "Hellman's New Play," *Washington Times-Herald*, 21 April 1944.

44. Watson interview with author, 8 October 1984.

45. Melby interview with author.

46. Burns, *Roosevelt*, pp. 372–73.

47. Melby interview with author.

48. Hellman Passport File.

49. FBI/LH, 4.

50. Ibid., 6, 7, 8.

51. Ibid., 9.

52. Ibid., 11.

53. Ibid., 20.

54. Ibid., 19.

55. Ibid., 21.

56. Ibid., 22.

57. Ibid., 23.

58. Hellman, *Three*, pp. 143–44.

Chapter Two

1. Melby's official biographical details are taken from his State Department personnel file, Central Decimal Files, Record Group 59, Melby, John F., 123 file, National Archives. Subsequent references to this file will be cited as Melby 123 file, plus date of document.

2. Melby 123 file, 13 March 1938.

3. Ibid., 16 February 1938.

4. Ibid., Daniels, 27 September 1938; Treasury, 16 July 1938.

5. Ibid., 13 March 1938.

6. Ibid., 31 July 1941.

7. Ibid., 2 December 1942.

8. Kennan, *Memoirs*, pp. 189–90.

9. Melby 123 file, 1 August 1944.

10. Ibid., 1 August 1945.

Chapter Three

1. Hellman, *Three*, pp. 194–95.

2. Ibid., p. 163.

3. Diary in Robert Meikeljohn's possession, used with permission.

4. Hellman, "I Meet the Front-Line Russians," and *Three*, pp. 164–77.

5. Orlova, *Memoirs*, p. 117.

6. Ibid.
7. Melby hearings, 1, 26 June 1952, pp. A14–15.

Chapter Four

1. FBI/LH, 30.
2. Ibid., 29.
3. Ibid., 31.
4. Ibid., 34.
5. "Russia Acclaimed by Miss Hellman," *New York Times*, 2 March 1945.
6. FBINY/LH, 70.
7. Westbrook Pegler, "Fair Enough," *Washington Times-Herald*, 24 April 1945.

Chapter Five

1. There is a vast literature on the *Amerasia* case. The best summary account is Latham, *The Communist Controversy in Washington*, pp. 203–16.
2. Buhite, *Hurley and American Foreign Policy*, p. 273.

Chapter Six

1. See Flynn, *You're the Boss*, pp. 185–206.
2. Hellman, *Three*, p. 296.

Chapter Seven

1. See Newman, "Lethal Rhetoric."
2. Quoted in Varg, *Missionaries, Chinese, and Diplomats*, p. 3.
3. Stuart, *Fifty Years in China*, p. 242.
4. On Hurley, see Buhite, *Hurley and American Foreign Policy*.
5. Introduction to Hammett, *The Big Knockover*, p. x.
6. "First U.S.–Soviet Cultural Parley Here Opens Nov. 18," *Daily Worker*, 13 November 1945.
7. Ceplair and Englund, *The Inquisition in Hollywood*, pp. 225–31.
8. Maltz, "What Shall We Ask of Writers?"
9. FBI/LH, 44.
10. Ibid.
11. "PAC Joins Forces With Two Groups," *New York Times*, 12 May 1946.
12. Johnson, *Dashiell Hammett*, p. 211.
13. FBI/LH, 53.
14. A good account of the Wallace firing is in Walton, *Henry Wallace, Harry Truman*, pp. 33–117.
15. FBI/LH, 44.

16. Goodman, *The Committee*, p. 184.

17. See additional discussion of Budenz in Appendix 1.

18. Cited in Caute, *The Great Fear*, p. 26.

19. MacDougall, *Gideon's Army*, p. 109.

20. Ibid., p. 117.

Chapter Eight

1. MacDougall, *Gideon's Army*, p. 151.

2. Ibid., pp. 130, 150.

3. "Wallace Sees U.N. As Sole Peace Hope," *New York Times*, 1 April 1947.

4. FBINY/LH, 94.

5. MacDougall, *Gideon's Army*, pp. 133–38.

6. Ibid., p. 140.

7. "Hellman Returns from Paris," *New York Times*, 26 August 1947.

8. Hellman Passport File.

9. FBINY/LH, 44; David Sentner, "Soviet Joins UNESCO Theatre Parley to Use It as Propaganda Outlet," *New York Journal-American*, 3 August 1947.

10. U.S. Department of State, *Foreign Relations of the United States*, 1947, 7:678–82.

11. Kennan, "The Sources of Soviet Conduct," p. 582.

12. "Two Sessions Here Score Film Inquiry," *New York Times*, 26 October 1947.

13. FBI/LH, 53.

14. "Wallace Attacks Forrestal, Lovett," *New York Times*, 2 October 1947.

15. Hellman, "The Judas Goats."

16. Wright, *Lillian Hellman*, p. 214.

17. MacDougall, *Gideon's Army*, p. 243.

Chapter Nine

1. Hellman, *Three*, p. 685.

2. Clayton Knowles, "PCA Votes 74-Point Platform Embracing Wallace Policies," *New York Times*, 19 January 1948.

3. MacDougall, *Gideon's Army*, p. 597.

4. Melby hearings, 1, 26 June 1952, p. B6.

5. Melby 123 file, 30 March 1948.

6. Wright, *Lillian Hellman*, p. 219.

7. MacDougall, *Gideon's Army*, p. 597.

8. Ibid., p. 372.

9. Ibid., p. 597.

10. FBI/LH, 53.

11. MacDougall, *Gideon's Army*, is the only comprehensive source on this convention. See pp. 484–542. The Anne O'Hare McCormack statement is on p. 488.

12. Hellman, *Three*, p. 687.

13. Ibid., pp. 688–89.

14. Hellman Passport File.

15. This account of her trip comes from the *New York Star*, 4, 5, 7, 8, 9, and 10 November 1948.

16. Wright, *Lillian Hellman*, p. 223.

17. *New York Star*, 8 November 1948.

18. Melby, *Mandate of Heaven*, p. 354.

19. Johnson, *Dashiell Hammett*, p. 222.

20. Johnson, "Obsessed," p. 80.

Chapter Ten

1. Melby 123 file, 18 January 1949.

2. For the Vincent story, see May, *China Scapegoat*.

3. FBI/LH, 53.

4. The *New York Times* had stories on the Waldorf conference every day between 21 and 31 March 1949. The newsmagazines also covered it extensively. The *New Yorker* carried a satirical piece by A. J. Liebling on 9 April 1949.

5. "Peace: Everybody Wars Over It," *Newsweek*, 4 April 1949, p. 21.

6. Hellman as quoted in Belfrage, *The American Inquisition*, p. 98.

7. Kempton, "Witnesses," p. 23.

8. For this account of the Eisler escape, I depend on *Facts on File*, 1949, pp. 125, 133, 157, 165, 173, 181; and on stories in *Time*, 23 May 1949, p. 20, and 6 June 1949, p. 27.

9. *Time*, 23 May 1949, p. 20.

10. *Facts on File*, 1949, p. 181.

11. FBI/LH, 47.

12. See Newman, "The Self-Inflicted Wound."

13. Acheson, *Present at the Creation*, p. 397.

14. Novak, *Choosing Our King*, p. 83.

15. FBI/LH, 53.

16. Rollyson, *Lillian Hellman*, chap. 15.

Chapter Eleven

1. Hellman, *Three*, p. 652.

2. See Wells, "Sounding the Tocsin."

3. Hellman, *Three*, p. 676.

4. On Acheson's "defense perimeter" speech, see Etzold, *Aspects of Sino-American Relations*, pp. 108–20, and McLellan, *Dean Acheson*, chap. 12.

5. On the Hiss case, Weinstein, *Perjury*, is the most complete account. But see also Navasky, "Allen Weinstein's 'Perjury.'"

6. Hellman, *Three*, pp. 605, 649–50.

7. Like Hiss, the Rosenberg case is also still controversial. See Radosh and Milton, *The Rosenberg File*, and Schneir and Schneir, *Invitation to an Inquest*.

8. Reeves, *Joe McCarthy*, pp. 255–314; Oshinsky, *A Conspiracy So Immense*, chap. 10; Kutler, *The American Inquisition*, chap. 7.

9. FBI/LH, 51.

10. Hellman, *Three*, p. 621.

11. See Whiting, *China Crosses the Yalu*.

12. *Time*, 11 December 1950, p. 17.

13. *Newsweek*, 11 December 1950, p. 28.

14. *New York Times*, 19 December 1950.

15. The only significant account of McCarran's influence on foreign policy and internal security is Pittman, *McCarran and the Politics of Containment*.

16. See Harper, *The Politics of Loyalty*, chap. 7, for the Internal Security Act of 1950.

17. See n. 2 above.

18. U.S. Department of State, *Foreign Relations of the United States*, 1950, vol. 6, contains twenty-five documents about MEM.

19. Ibid., pp. 164–73.

20. Ibid., p. 839.

21. Ibid., pp. 167, 170.

22. Ibid., p. 157.

23. Ibid., p. 171.

24. Melby 123 file, 8 March 1952.

25. Melby hearings, 6, 5 February 1953, p. B13.

26. Hellman, *Three*, p. 501.

27. Markowitz, *Rise and Fall*, p. 310.

Chapter Twelve

1. The best account of the Remington case to date is Cook, *Maverick*, chap. 2. Gary May is working on a comprehensive study.

2. *New York Times*, 10 February 1951.

3. See Spanier, *The Truman-MacArthur Controversy*.

4. Ibid., pp. 215–20.

5. Ibid., chaps. 12, 13.

6. U.S. Congress, Senate, Committee on the Judiciary, *Institute of Pacific Relations*. For a balanced critique of these hearings, see Thomas, *The Institute of Pacific Relations*, chap. 4.

7. U.S. Department of State, *Foreign Relations of the United States*, 1951, 6:1498–1502.

8. Melby 123 file, 31 July 1951.

9. "Lillian Hellman's 'Autumn Garden': A Retreat from the World of Reality," *Daily Worker*, 15 March 1951.

10. FBI/LH, 57.

11. Field, *From Right to Left*, chap. 21.

12. Johnson, *Hammett*, chap. 18.

13. Ibid., p. 247.

14. Hellman Passport File.

15. Melby hearings, 6, 5 February 1953, p. A34.

16. Hellman Passport File.

17. Navasky, *Naming Names*, p. 75.

18. Lardner interview with the author, 4 April 1987.

19. Navasky, *Naming Names*, p. 85.

20. Ibid., p. 257.

21. Matusow, *False Witness*.

22. Kimball, *The File*, p. 94.

23. Melby hearings, 6, 5 February 1953, p. A43.

24. Newman, "Clandestine Chinese Nationalist Efforts," pp. 221–22.

Chapter Thirteen

1. William S. White, "M'Carthy Censure Move Fading in the Senate," *New York Times*, 27 January 1952.

2. "Top Loyalty Board Criticized Review," *New York Times*, 6 January 1952.

3. "Public Hearing Set for Vincent Jan. 30," *New York Times*, 26 January 1952.

4. William S. White, "President Assails Senator McCarthy as Pathological," *New York Times*, 1 February 1952.

5. Ibid.

6. "Reds Offered as Aides," *New York Times*, 16 February 1952.

7. Walter S. Waggoner, "State Department Clears Vincent, Returns Him as Envoy to Tangier," *New York Times*, 20 February 1952.

8. Hellman, *Three*, pp. 617–24.

9. Ibid., pp. 665–66.

10. William S. White, "Mrs. Keeney Faces a Contempt Action," *New York Times*, 26 February 1952.

11. Melby 123 file, 8 March 1952.

12. Walter H. Waggoner, "Loyalty-Security Set-Up Is Again under Scrutiny," *New York Times*, 9 March 1952.

13. Hellman, *Three*, pp. 653–55.

14. Quoted in Bentley, *Thirty Years of Treason*, p. 482.

15. Ibid., pp. 482–84.

16. Melby's file does not have the usual classification. Individual reports of agent investigations are entered under the heading "John Fremont Melby, Loyalty of Government Employees" and identified by the name of the agent reporting, the place at which the report was made, and the date. The Norwood report was made 25 April 1952, but the place is blacked out.

17. Bentley, *Thirty Years of Treason*, pp. 495–98.

18. These regulations are set forth in Melby hearings, 1, 26 June 1952, pp. A3–4.

19. Hellman, *Three*, pp. 660–65.

20. Ibid., pp. 628–32.

21. Rauh to Hellman, 30 April 1952, Rauh Papers.

22. Untitled and undated three-page document, one of several drafts prepared by Hellman or Rauh to be given to the press, Rauh Papers. Neither this document, nor any other evidence, indicates that Lillian was issued a Party membership card or paid dues. She likely contributed something to the host or hostess of her "study group." She may have been naive in telling John Melby and Joe Rauh that participating in the study group was equivalent to joining the Party.

23. Rauh to Hellman, 30 April 1952, Rauh Papers.

24. Rauh interview with the author, 20 November 1984.

25. Hellman, *Three*, pp. 658–60.

26. Rauh to Hellman, 11 May 1952, Rauh Papers.

27. O'Reilly, "The FBI and the Origins of McCarthyism," pp. 391–93.

28. See, for instance, Michael Kinsley, "Fifth Amendment Patriots," *Washington Post*, 18 December 1986.

29. Kempton, "Witnesses: Scoundrel Time," p. 25.

30. For the complete hearing see U.S. Congress, House, Committee on Un-American Activities, *Communist Infiltration of the Hollywood Motion Picture Industry*. A shortened version is in Bentley, *Thirty Years of Treason*, pp. 531–41.

31. Melby hearings, 1, 26 June 1952, pp. B59–60. Bentley, *Thirty Years of Treason*, pp. 531–33, has the clearest discussion of Hellman's use of the Fifth.

32. Charles Krauthammer, "Scandal Time," *Washington Post*, 19 December 1986, p. A21. See also the defense of the late CIA Director William Casey in George Carver, Jr., "Successful Legacy of CIA's Casey Cannot Be Doubted," *Washington Post*, 5 January 1987, where Hellman is again the paradigm case of use of the Fifth Amendment.

Chapter Fourteen

1. Melby hearings, 1, 26 June 1952, pp. A1–4.

2. Ibid., pp. A81–82.

3. Ibid., pp. A86–87.

4. Ibid., pp. A90–91.

5. Ibid., pp. C19–21.

6. Ibid., pp. C23–24.

7. Ibid., pp. C25–26.

8. Ibid., p. C27.

9. Ibid., pp. B1–2.

10. Ibid., p. B6.

11. Ibid., pp. B4–5.

12. Ibid., p. B9.

13. Ibid., pp. B14–17.

14. Ibid., pp. B25–27.

15. Ibid., pp. B33–39.

16. Ibid., p. B53.

17. Ibid., p. B54.

18. Ibid., pp. B56–59.

19. Ibid., p. B62.

20. Ibid., p. B64.

21. Ibid., p. B67.

22. Ibid., pp. B75–76.

23. Ibid., p. C3.

Chapter Fifteen

1. All references, including quotations, in the first part of this chapter are to Melby hearings, 2, 30 June 1952.
2. This and subsequent mentions of meetings between Rauh, Hellman, and/or Melby, and his attorney are from Melby hearings, 6, 5 February 1953, pp. A63–73.
3. Ibid., p. A66.
4. Melby hearings, 3, 15 August 1952, p. A3.
5. Ibid., pp. A6–8.
6. Ibid., pp. A13–14.
7. Ibid., pp. A18–19.
8. Ibid., pp. A20–21.
9. Ibid., pp. A31–33.
10. Ibid., p. A40–42.
11. Ibid., pp. B5–6.
12. Ibid., pp. B10–11.
13. Ibid., p. B12.
14. Ibid., p. B21.
15. Ibid., pp. B31–32.

Chapter Sixteen

1. Hellman, *Three*, p. 652.
2. Reeves, *Joe McCarthy*, pp. 437–40.
3. Ibid., pp. 444–46.
4. Melby hearings, 6, 5 February 1953, p. A70.
5. Melby hearings, 4, 31 October 1952, pp. A4–5.
6. Ibid., pp. A11–19.
7. Volpe's role in the AEC is mentioned frequently in U.S. Atomic Energy Commission, *J. Robert Oppenheimer*.
8. Moody, *Lillian Hellman*, p. 238.
9. Melby hearings, 6, 5 February 1953, p. A69.
10. Melby hearings, 5, 23 January 1953, p. B27.

Chapter Seventeen

1. U.S. Atomic Energy Commission, *J. Robert Oppenheimer*, p. vii.
2. Mosely, *Dulles*, p. 310.
3. U.S. Department of State, *Foreign Relations of the United States, 1952–1954*, 1:1428–33.
4. Ibid., p. 1403.
5. Ibid., pp. 1403–6.
6. U.S. Department of State, Loyalty-Security Board, In The Matter of Joseph Maria Franckenstein, 21 and 22 October 1952. Transcript in the Boyle Papers. See also the account of this case in Spanier, *Kay Boyle*, pp. 176–79.

7. The Sipes-Lay document, dated 24 September 1954, is also in the Boyle Papers.

8. "'Subversive' File Names 2,000,000; Young Says U.S. Lists Have Unassessed Data —Kay Boyle Denies Red Links," *New York Times*, 29 November 1955; "Echoes From The Past," *New York Times*, 24 April 1957.

9. Melby hearings, 5, 23 January 1953, pp. A39–B6.

10. Ibid., pp. A14–15, A18–19, B7–9.

11. Ibid., pp. B15–20, B28–31.

Chapter Eighteen

1. Melby hearings, 6, 5 February 1953, pp. A1–2.

2. Ibid., pp. B6–7.

3. Hellman, *Three*, pp. 646–47.

4. Hellman Passport File.

5. Melby hearings, 6, 5 February 1953, p. B9.

6. Ibid., pp. B10–30.

7. Ibid., pp. B31–35.

8. Ibid., pp. B38–39.

9. Ibid., pp. B44–46.

10. Rauh interview with the author, 20 November 1984.

Chapter Nineteen

1. Hellman Passport File.

2. The best summary of Shipley's operation is in Kutler, *The American Inquisition*, pp. 89–95. See also Caute, *The Great Fear*, pp. 245–51.

3. Kutler, *The American Inquisition*, pp. 89–91.

4. U.S. Congress, *Congressional Record*, 6 June 1952, pp. 6690–95.

5. Erskine, "You Don't Go If She Says No."

6. Kutler, *The American Inquisition*, p. 93.

7. Caute, *The Great Fear*, pp. 246–47.

8. See discussions of Dulles in chaps. 17 and 19.

9. Hellman Passport File.

10. Melby hearings, 7, 13 March 1953, p. A1.

11. Ibid., pp. C6–9.

12. Ibid., pp. C19–21.

13. Ibid., p. C41.

14. See the account of this hearing in Johnson, *Dashiell Hammett*, chap. 20.

15. Brown, *Loyalty and Security*, p. 429.

16. Telephone Calls Series, Dulles Papers.

17. Dulles, *John Foster Dulles*, p. 89.

18. Transcript of interview with John W. Hanes, Jr., Hanes Oral History, pp. 110–11.

19. James Reston, "Rights of a U.S. Jobholder," *New York Times*, 25 November 1953.

20. Name Series, Box 32, "Stevenson, Adlai," Whitman Diary Series.

21. Reeves, *Joe McCarthy*, p. 597.

22. Ambrose, *Ike's Spies*, p. 175.

23. Rauh interview with the author, 20 November 1984; Volpe interview with the author, 4 April 1985.

24. Cited in Kemper, *Decade of Fear*, p. 81.

25. Ibid., pp. 81–82.

26. U.S. Congress, Senate, Committee on Post Office and Civil Service, *Federal Employees Security Program*, pp. 400–402, 407–8, 682–83, 726–32.

27. See the account in Brown, *Loyalty and Security*, pp. 57–60.

28. Ibid., p. 182.

29. McGuire's report as Melby remembers it.

Chapter Twenty

1. Hellman, *Three*, pp. 711–14. Carl Rollyson filed a Freedom of Information request with CIA and got copies of nine letters from and to Lillian which the Agency had intercepted between 1960 and 1980. This is a tiny fraction of the total they must have intercepted.

2. Hellman Passport File.

3. "M'Carthy Calls 23 for Book Inquiry," *New York Times*, 28 June 1953.

4. Rauh to Hellman, 6 August 1953, Rauh Papers.

5. Hellman, *Three*, pp. 704–5.

6. Telephone interview with O'Sullivan, 24 September 1985.

7. Kimball Johnson to Pierce J. Gerety, 11 August 1958, Melby Papers.

8. Harriman to Melby, 6 February 1951. Both Rusk and Harriman letters are in Melby Papers.

9. Rusk interview with the author, 29 September 1984.

10. All correspondence about Melby's efforts to return to government employment is in Melby Papers.

11. Moyers letter to author, 28 February 1985.

12. Correspondence in Melby Papers.

13. Hellman, *Three*, pp. 180–201.

14. Rollyson, *Lillian Hellman*, chap. 25.

15. Telephone interview with Schell, 25 August 1985.

16. Telephone interview with Peck, 25 August 1985.

17. FBI/LH, 72.

18. Karl E. Meyer, "Clark Scores FBI over 'Ideology,' Lack of Diversity," *Washington Post*, 18 November 1970.

19. See Watters and Gillers, *Investigating the FBI*.

20. Ibid., p. 415.

21. FBI/LH, 19 November 1970, no serial number.

22. Johnson, "Obsessed," p. 80.

23. Rollyson, *Lillian Hellman*, p. 518.

24. Letter in Melby Papers.

25. Gammon interview with the author, 19 November 1984.

26. Letter in Melby Papers.

Appendix 1: Was Lillian Hellman a Communist?

1. Caute, *The Fellow-Travellers*, p. 1.
2. Ibid., p. 4.
3. Ibid., p. 7.
4. FBI/LH, 1.
5. Dick, *Hellman in Hollywood*, p. 85.
6. FBI/LH, 9.
7. FBI/LH, 12.
8. Dick, *Hellman in Hollywood*, p. 100.
9. FBI/LH, 12.
10. FBI/LH, 6.
11. Phillips and Hollander, "The Art of the Theater I," p. 61.
12. Melby hearings, 1, pp. A13–14.
13. Lawrence Meyer, "Lincoln Brigade Is Finally Cleared," *Washington Post*, 25 October 1972.
14. The original publication of *Scoundrel Time* by Little, Brown in 1976 carried a polemical introduction by Garry Wills. This introduction does not appear in *Three*.
15. Donnie Radcliffe, "The New 'Links' for Peace," *Washington Post*, 7 October 1982.
16. Leslie Maitland, "Sources Are Cited for Charge of Soviet Tie to Arms Freeze," *New York Times*, 13 November 1982.
17. Rollyson, *Lillian Hellman*, chap. 22.
18. Hellman, *Three*, p. 205.
19. Ibid., p. 203.
20. FBI/LH, 1. For Lillian's description of the fight with Tallulah, see *Three*, pp. 485–86.
21. Hellman, *Three*, p. 206.
22. FBI/LH, 44.
23. Hellman, *Three*, p. 132.
24. Starobin, *American Communism in Crisis*, pp. 20–21.
25. Gitlow, *The Whole of Their Lives*, p. 4.
26. See the description of this incident in Navasky, *Naming Names*, pp. 287–302.
27. Clurman introduction to Moody, *Lillian Hellman*, p. xiv.
28. Hellman, *Three*, p. 133.
29. Hersey, "Tribute to Lillian Hellman."
30. Hellman, *Three*, pp. 206–7.
31. See especially O'Reilly, *Hoover and the Un-Americans*.
32. MacDougall to author, 1 May 1985.
33. FBI/LH, 5.
34. Barth, "How Good Is an FBI Report?" pp. 26–27.
35. Ibid., pp. 27–28.
36. Kimball, *The File*, p. 9.
37. Olney Oral History, pp. 331–32.
38. FBI/LH, 47.
39. FBI/LH, 49.
40. FBI/LH, 3.

41. *Daily Worker* coverage is in issues of 25 May through 31 May 1938. Budenz's report is in New York FBI Office file no. 66-6709, Communist Party, U.S.A., serial 1143.

42. FBI/LH, 39.

43. Alsop, "The Strange Case of Louis Budenz," p. 29.

44. Rovere, "The Kept Witnesses," p. 34.

45. U.S. Congress, *Congressional Record*, 81st Cong., 2d sess., 12 May 1950, p. 6969.

46. Ibid., p. 6971.

47. U.S. Congress, Senate, Committee on the Judiciary, *Institute of Pacific Relations*, p. 1404.

48. Ibid., pp. 1485–86.

49. Alsop, "The Strange Case of Louis Budenz."

50. Packer, *Ex-Communist Witnesses*, p. 216.

51. FBI Headquarters file no. 100-24628, Owen Lattimore, Espionage—R., serial 1151. Subsequent references given as FBI/OL plus serial number.

52. FBI/OL, 515.

53. FBI/LH, 51.

54. Budenz, *Men Without Faces*, p. 265.

55. FBI/OL, 2327.

56. Ibid., 488.

57. U.S. Congress, Senate, Committee on Foreign Relations, *State Department Employee Loyalty Investigation*, pp. 513–16.

58. Budenz, *The Techniques of Communism*, pp. 34, 228.

59. Pauling to author, 26 August 1985.

60. FBI/OL, 4023.

61. FBI Headquarters file no. 100-63, Louis Francis Budenz, Internal Security, serial 138.

62. Ibid., 141.

63. FBI New York Office file no. 62-8988, Louis Francis Budenz, Internal Security—C, serial 3.

64. FBI Headquarters file no. 11-63, Louis Francis Budenz, serial 281.

65. See Packer, *Ex-Communist Witnesses*, p. 12; and Caute, *The Great Fear*, pp. 132–38.

66. Navasky, *Naming Names*, pp. 75, 85, 148–50, 305, 317.

67. Orlova, *Memoirs*, pp. 117–18.

68. Ibid., p. 127.

69. See Donner, *The Age of Surveillance*, pp. 175–76.

70. FBI/LH, 5.

71. FBI/LH, 8.

72. FBI/LH, 40.

73. FBI/LH, 59.

74. FBINY/LH, 202.

75. FBI/LH, no serial number, dated 13 October 1951.

76. FBI/LH, 57.

77. Buckley, *A Hymnal*, pp. 139–52.

78. Glazer, "An Answer to Lillian Hellman."

79. Kazin, "The Legend of Lillian Hellman."

80. Kramer, "The Blacklist and the Cold War."

81. Mastny, *Russia's Road to the Cold War*, especially chap. 7.

82. Hook, *Philosophy and Public Policy*, p. 232.

83. Kutler, *The American Inquisition*, p. 184.

84. The phrase is Rollyson's. See his *Lillian Hellman*, p. 481.

❧ *b i b l i o g r a p h y* ❧

Manuscript Sources

Abilene, Kansas
Dwight D. Eisenhower Library
 John Foster Dulles Papers.
 Ann Whitman Diary Series.
Berkeley, California
Bancroft Library, University of California
 Warren Olney III Oral History.
Carbondale, Illinois
Morris Library, Southern Illinois
  University
 Kay Boyle Papers.
Independence, Missouri
Harry S. Truman Library
 John Fremont Melby Papers.
New York, New York
FBI Office
 Louis Budenz File.
 Lillian Hellman File.
Princeton, New Jersey

Seeley G. Mudd Manuscript Library
 John W. Hanes, Jr., Oral History.
Washington, D.C.
FBI Headquarters
 Louis Budenz File.
 Lillian Hellman File.
 Owen Lattimore File.
 John Fremont Melby File.
Library of Congress
 Joseph Rauh Papers.
National Archives
 U.S. Department of State, Central
  Decimal Files, Record Group 59,
  Melby, John F., 123 File.
U.S. Department of State
 Information and Privacy Staff. Lillian
  Hellman Passport File.
 Loyalty-Security Board. In the Matter
  of John Fremont Melby.

United States Government Publications

U.S. Congress. *Congressional Record*. 1950–52.
———. House. Committee on Un-American Activities. *Communist Infiltration of the Hollywood Motion Picture Industry*, pt. 8. 82d Cong., 2d sess., 1952. Hearing of 21 May, pp. 3541–49.
———. House. Committee on Un-American Activities. *Organized Communism in the United States*. 85th Cong., 2d sess., 1958.
———. Senate. Committee on Foreign Relations. *State Department Employee Loyalty Investigation*. 81st Cong., 2d sess., 1950.
———. Senate. Committee on the Judiciary, Internal Security Subcommittee. *Institute of Pacific Relations*. 82d Cong., 2d sess., 1952. Rep. 2050.
———. Senate. Committee on Post Office and Civil Service. *Hearings on the Administration of the Federal Employees Security Program*. 84th Cong., 1st sess., 1956.
U.S. Department of State. *Foreign Relations of the United States*, 1947. Vol. 7, The Far East, China. 1972.

———. *Foreign Relations of the United States,* 1950. Vol. 6, East Asia and the Pacific. 1977.

———. *Foreign Relations of the United States,* 1951. Vol. 6, Asia and the Pacific, pt. 2. 1977.

———. *Foreign Relations of the United States, 1952–1954.* Vol. 1, General: Economic and Political Matters, pt. 2. 1983.

Books and Articles

Acheson, Dean G. *Present at the Creation.* New York: New American Library/Signet, 1969.

Alsop, Joseph. "The Strange Case of Louis Budenz." *Atlantic* 189 (April 1952): 29–33.

Ambrose, Stephen E. *Ike's Spies.* Garden City, N.Y.: Doubleday, 1981.

Barth, Alan. "How Good Is an FBI Report?" *Harper's* 208 (March 1954): 25–31.

Belfrage, Cedric. *The American Inquisition, 1945–1960.* Indianapolis: Bobbs-Merrill, 1973.

Bentley, Eric. *Thirty Years of Treason: Excerpts from Hearings before the House Committee on Un-American Activities, 1938–1968.* New York: Viking, 1971.

Brown, Ralph S., Jr. *Loyalty and Security.* New Haven: Yale University Press, 1958.

Bryer, Jackson R., ed. *Conversations with Lillian Hellman.* Jackson: University Press of Mississippi, 1986.

Buckley, William F., Jr. *A Hymnal: The Controversial Arts.* New York: Putnam's, 1978.

Budenz, Louis F. *Men Without Faces: The Communist Conspiracy in the U.S.A.* New York: Harper & Brothers, 1950.

———. *The Techniques of Communism.* Chicago: Henry Regnery, 1954.

———. *This Is My Story.* Chicago: Whittlesey House/McGraw-Hill, 1947.

Buhite, Russell D. *Patrick J. Hurley and American Foreign Policy.* Ithaca: Cornell University Press, 1973.

Burns, James MacGregor. *Roosevelt: Soldier of Freedom.* New York: Harcourt Brace Jovanovich, 1970.

Caute, David. *The Fellow-Travellers.* New York: Macmillan, 1973.

———. *The Great Fear.* New York: Simon and Schuster, 1978.

Ceplair, Larry, and Stephen Englund. *The Inquisition in Hollywood.* Garden City, N.Y.: Anchor/Doubleday, 1980.

Colodny, Robert. *The Struggle for Madrid.* New York: Paine-Whitman, 1958.

Conquest, Robert. *The Great Terror: Stalin's Purge of the Thirties.* New York: Macmillan, 1968.

Cook, Fred J. *Maverick.* New York: Putnam's, 1984.

Cooney, John. *The American Pope: The Life and Times of Francis Cardinal Spellman.* New York: Dell, 1984.

Dick, Bernard F. *Hellman in Hollywood.* Rutherford, N.J.: Fairleigh Dickinson University Press, 1982.

Donner, Frank J. *The Age of Surveillance.* New York: Random House, 1981.

Dulles, Eleanor Lansing. *John Foster Dulles: The Last Year.* New York: Harcourt, Brace & World, 1963.

Duranty, Walter. "The Moscow Trials." In *They Were There*, edited by Curt Riess, pp. 60–65. Freeport, N.Y.: Books for Libraries Press, 1944.

Eby, Cecil. *Between the Bullet and the Lie*. New York: Holt, Rinehart and Winston, 1969.

Erskine, Helen W. "You Don't Go If She Says No," *Collier's* 132 (11 July 1953): 62–65.

Etzold, Thomas H., ed. *Aspects of Sino-American Relations Since 1784*. New York: New Viewpoints, 1978.

Field, Frederick Vanderbilt. *From Right to Left*. Westport, Conn.: Lawrence Hill, 1983.

Flynn, Edward J. *You're the Boss*. New York: Viking, 1947.

Garrow, David J. *The FBI and Martin Luther King, Jr*. New York: Norton, 1981.

Gellhorn, Martha. "On Apocryphism." *Paris Review* 79 (Spring 1981): 280–301.

Gitlow, Benjamin. *The Whole of Their Lives*. New York: Scribner's, 1948.

Glazer, Nathan. "An Answer to Lillian Hellman." *Commentary* 61 (June 1976): 36–39.

Goodman, Walter. *The Committee*. Baltimore: Penguin Books, 1969.

Guttmann, Allen. *The Wound in the Heart*. New York: Free Press, 1962.

Hammett, Dashiell. *The Big Knockover*. New York: Random House, 1966.

Harper, Alan D. *The Politics of Loyalty*. Westport, Conn.: Greenwood, 1969.

Hellman, Lillian. "I Meet the Front-Line Russians." *Collier's* 115 (31 March 1945): 11, 68, 70.

———. "The Judas Goats." *The Screenwriter* 3 (December 1947): 7.

———. *The North Star*. New York: Viking, 1943.

———. *The Searching Wind*. New York: Viking, 1944.

———. *Six Plays by Lillian Hellman*. New York: Vintage, 1979.

———. *Three*. Boston: Little, Brown, 1979. Includes the texts of *An Unfinished Woman*, *Pentimento*, and *Scoundrel Time*, with "new commentaries by the author."

Hersey, John. *Hiroshima*. New York: Penguin Books, 1946.

———. "Tribute to Lillian Hellman." *Proceedings of the American Academy and Institute of Arts and Letters*. Second series, no. 35. New York, 1984.

Hook, Sidney. *Philosophy and Public Policy*. Carbondale: Southern Illinois University Press, 1980.

Hoopes, Roy. *Ralph Ingersoll*. New York: Vintage, 1979.

Hoover, J. Edgar. *Masters of Deceit*. New York: Henry Holt, 1959.

———. *A Study of Communism*. New York: Holt, Rinehart and Winston, 1962.

Johnson, Diane. *Dashiell Hammett: A Life*. New York: Random House, 1983.

———. "Obsessed." *Vanity Fair* 48 (May 1985): 79–81, 116–19.

Kazin, Alfred. "The Legend of Lillian Hellman." *Esquire* 48 (August 1977): 28–30, 34.

Kemper, Donald. *Decade of Fear*. Columbia: University of Missouri Press, 1965.

Kempton, Murray. "Witnesses: Scoundrel Time." *The New York Review of Books* 23 (10 June 1976): 22–25.

Kennan, George F. *Memoirs: 1925–1950*. Boston: Little, Brown, 1967.

——— [X, pseud.]. "The Sources of Soviet Conduct." *Foreign Affairs* 25 (July 1947): 566–82.

Kimball, Penn. *The File*. New York: Avon Books, 1985.

Knox, Bernard. "The Spanish Tragedy." *The New York Review of Books* 34 (26 March 1987): 21–28.

Kramer, Hilton. "The Blacklist and the Cold War." *New York Times*, 3 October 1976.

Kutler, Stanley I. *The American Inquisition*. New York: Hill and Wang, 1982.

Landis, Arthur H. *The Abraham Lincoln Brigade*. New York: Citadel Press, 1968.

Latham, Earl. *The Communist Controversy in Washington*. New York: Atheneum, 1969.

McCracken, Samuel. "'Julia' & Other Fictions by Lillian Hellman." *Commentary* 77 (June 1984): 35–43.

MacDougall, Curtis D. *Gideon's Army*. 3 vols. consecutively paginated. New York: Marzani & Munsell, 1965.

McLellan, David S. *Dean Acheson: The State Department Years*. New York: Dodd, Mead, 1976.

Maltz, Albert. "What Shall We Ask of Writers?" *New Masses*, 12 February 1946, 19–20.

Markowitz, Norman D. *The Rise and Fall of the People's Century*. New York: Free Press, 1973.

Mastny, Vojtech. *Russia's Road to the Cold War*. New York: Columbia University Press, 1979.

Matusow, Harvey. *False Witness*. New York: Cameron & Kahn, 1955.

May, Gary. *China Scapegoat: The Diplomatic Ordeal of John Carter Vincent*. Washington: New Republic Books, 1979.

Melby, John F. *Mandate of Heaven*. Garden City, N.Y.: Anchor/Doubleday, 1971.

Moody, Richard. *Lillian Hellman, Playwright*. New York: Pegasus/Bobbs-Merrill, 1972.

Morton, Brian. "Pathetic Fallacies." *The Nation* 243 (29 November 1986): 614–17.

Mosely, Leonard. *Dulles: A Biography of Eleanor, Allen, and John Foster Dulles and Their Family Network*. New York: Dial Press/James Wade, 1978.

Navasky, Victor. "Allen Weinstein's 'Perjury': The Case Not Proved against Alger Hiss." *The Nation* 226 (8 April 1978): 393–401.

———. *Naming Names*. New York: Penguin Books, 1981.

Newman, Robert P. "Clandestine Chinese Nationalist Efforts to Punish Their American Detractors." *Diplomatic History* 7 (Summer 1983): 205–22.

———. "Lethal Rhetoric: The Selling of the China Myths." *Quarterly Journal of Speech* 61 (April 1975): 113–28.

———. "The Self-Inflicted Wound: The China White Paper of 1949." *Prologue: Journal of the National Archives* 19 (Fall 1982): 141–56.

Novak, Michael. *Choosing Our King*. New York: Macmillan, 1974.

O'Reilly, Kenneth. "The FBI and the Origins of McCarthyism." *The Historian* 95 (May 1983): 372–93.

———. *Hoover and the Un-Americans*. Philadelphia: Temple University Press, 1983.

Orlova, Raisa. *Memoirs*. New York: Random House, 1983.

Oshinsky, David M. *A Conspiracy So Immense*. New York: Free Press, 1983.

Packer, Herbert L. *Ex-Communist Witnesses*. Stanford: Stanford University Press, 1962.

Phillips, John, and Anne Hollander. "The Art of the Theater I: Lillian Hellman—An Interview." In *Conversations with Lillian Hellman*, edited by Jackson R. Bryer, pp. 53–72. Jackson: University Press of Mississippi, 1986.

Pittman, Von V., Jr. "Senator Patrick A. McCarran and the Politics of Containment." Ph.D. diss., University of Georgia, 1979.

Radosh, Ronald. "'But Today the Struggle': Spain and the Intellectuals." *The New Criterion* (October 1986): 5–15.

Radosh, Ronald, and Joyce Milton. *The Rosenberg File*. New York: Vintage, 1984.

Reeves, Thomas C. *The Life and Times of Joe McCarthy*. New York: Stein and Day, 1982.

Rollyson, Carl E. *Lillian Hellman: Her Legend and Her Legacy*. New York: St. Martin's, 1988.

Rosenstone, Robert A. *Crusade of the Left: The Lincoln Battalion in the Spanish Civil War*. New York: Pegasus, 1969.

Rovere, Richard. "The Kept Witnesses." *Harper's Magazine* 210 (May 1955): 25–34.

Schneir, Walter, and Miriam Schneir. *Invitation to an Inquest*. New York: Pantheon Books, 1983.

Spanier, John W. *The Truman-MacArthur Controversy and the Korean War*. New York: Norton, 1965.

Spanier, Sandra Whipple. *Kay Boyle*. Carbondale: Southern Illinois University Press, 1986.

Starobin, Joseph R. *American Communism in Crisis, 1943–1957*. Berkeley: University of California Press, 1972.

Stuart, John Leighton. *Fifty Years in China*. New York: Random House, 1954.

Thomas, Hugh. *The Spanish Civil War*. New York: Harper & Row, 1977.

Thomas, John N. *The Institute of Pacific Relations*. Seattle: University of Washington Press, 1974.

Triesch, Manfred. *The Lillian Hellman Collection at the University of Texas*. Austin: University of Texas Press, 1966.

U.S. Atomic Energy Commission. *In the Matter of J. Robert Oppenheimer*. Cambridge: MIT Press, 1970.

Varg, Paul. *Missionaries, Chinese, and Diplomats*. New York: Octagon Books, 1977.

Walton, Richard J. *Henry Wallace, Harry Truman, and the Cold War*. New York: Viking, 1976.

Warren, Frank A., III. *Liberals and Communism*. Bloomington: Indiana University Press, 1966.

Watters, Pat, and Stephen Gillers. *Investigating the FBI*. New York: Ballantine Books, 1973.

Weinstein, Allen. *Perjury: The Hiss-Chambers Case*. New York: Knopf, 1978.

Wells, Samuel F., Jr. "Sounding the Tocsin." *International Security* 4 (1979): 116–58.

Whiting, Allen S. *China Crosses the Yalu*. New York: Macmillan, 1960.

Wright, William. *Lillian Hellman: The Image, The Woman*. New York: Simon and Schuster, 1986.